D1604364

Hacker's Guide™ to Visual FoxPro© 7.0

By Tamar E. Granor, Ted Roche, Doug Hennig and Della Martin

With Steven M. Black

Hentzenwerke Publishing

Published by:
Hentzenwerke Publishing
980 East Circle Drive
Whitefish Bay WI 53217 USA

Hentzenwerke Publishing books are available through booksellers and directly from the
publisher. Contact Hentzenwerke Publishing at:
414.332.9876
414.332.9463 (fax)
www.hentzenwerke.com
books@hentzenwerke.com

Hacker's Guide to Visual FoxPro 7.0
> By Tamar E. Granor, Ted Roche, Doug Hennig and Della Martin
> With Steven M. Black
> Copy Editor: Jeana Randell
> Cover Art: Robert Griffith

ISBN: 1-930919-22-0

Manufactured in the United States of America.

Dedicated to fostering the international communication of ideas,
in the hopes of making the world a better place—
now and for future generations.

Our Contract with You, the Reader

In which we, the folks who make up Hentzenwerke Publishing, describe what you, the reader, can expect from this book and from us.

Hi there!

I've been writing professionally (in other words, eventually getting a paycheck for my scribbles) since 1974, and writing about software development since 1992. As an author, I've worked with a half-dozen different publishers and corresponded with thousands of readers over the years. As a software developer and all-around geek, I've also acquired a library of more than 100 computer and software-related books.

Thus, when I donned the publisher's cap four years ago to produce the *1997 Developer's Guide,* I had some pretty good ideas of what I liked (and didn't like) from publishers, what readers liked and didn't like, and what I, as a reader, liked and didn't like.

2002 marks our fifth season. (For those of you who are keeping track, congratulations. I can't count that high anymore.) John Wooden, the famed UCLA basketball coach, had posited that teams aren't consistent; they're always getting better—or worse. We'd like to get better…

One of my goals for this season is to build a closer relationship with you, the reader. In order for us to do this, you've got to know what you should expect from us.

- You have the right to expect that your order will be processed quickly and correctly, and that your book will be delivered to you in new condition.

- You have the right to expect that the content of your book is technically accurate and up-to-date, that the explanations are clear, and that the layout is easy to read and follow without a lot of fluff or nonsense.

- You have the right to expect access to source code, errata, FAQs and other information that's relevant to the book via our Web site.

- You have the right to expect an electronic version of your printed book to be available via our Web site.

- You have the right to expect that, if you report errors to us, your report will be responded to promptly, and that the appropriate notice will be included in the errata and/or FAQs for the book.

Naturally, there are some limits that we bump up against. There are humans involved, and they make mistakes. A book of 500 pages contains, on average, 150,000 words and several megabytes of source code. It's not possible to edit and re-edit multiple times to catch every last misspelling and typo, nor is it possible to test the source code on every permutation of development environment and operating system—and still price the book affordably.

Once printed, bindings break, ink gets smeared, signatures get missed during binding. On the delivery side, Web sites go down, packages get lost in the mail.

Nonetheless, we'll make our best effort to correct these problems—once you let us know about them.

In return, when you have a question or run into a problem, we ask that you first consult the errata and/or FAQs for your book on our Web site. If you don't find the answer there, please e-mail us at books@hentzenwerke.com with as much information and detail as possible, including 1) the steps to reproduce the problem, 2) what happened, and 3) what you expected to happen, together with 4) any other relevant information.

I'd like to stress that we need you to communicate questions and problems clearly. For example…

- "Your downloads don't work" isn't enough information for us to help you. "I get a 404 error when I click on the **Download Source Code** link on www.hentzenwerke.com/book/downloads.html" is something we can help you with.

- "The code in Chapter 10 caused an error" again isn't enough information. "I performed the following steps to run the source code program DisplayTest.PRG in Chapter 10, and I received an error that said 'Variable m.liCounter not found'" is something we can help you with.

We'll do our best to get back to you within a couple of days, either with an answer or at least an acknowledgment that we've received your inquiry and that we're working on it.

On behalf of the authors, technical editors, copy editors, layout artists, graphical artists, indexers, and all the other folks who have worked to put this book in your hands, I'd like to thank you for purchasing this book, and I hope that it will prove to be a valuable addition to your technical library. Please let us know what you think about this book— we're looking forward to hearing from you.

As Groucho Marx once observed, "Outside of a dog, a book is a man's best friend. Inside of a dog, it's too dark to read."

Whil Hentzen
Hentzenwerke Publishing
March 2002

Table of Contents

The body
Of
Benjamin Franklin
Printer
(Like the cover of an old book
Its contents torn out
And stripped of its lettering and gilding)
Lies here, food for worms.
But the work shall not be lost
For it will (as he believed) appear once more
In a new and more elegant edition
Revised and corrected
by
The Author.

Benjamin Franklin, *Epitaph on Himself*, 1728

Acknowledgments for the Third Edition

This makes the seventh book for which at least one of us is listed as a principal author. So, over the years, we've thanked a lot of people for helping us do it right. Nonetheless, there are some whose contributions to this volume are significant enough to warrant special mention.

As usual, we'll start out with those who contributed to the earlier editions of the *Hacker's Guide*. You'll find their names in the Acknowledgments for those editions.

Also, despite the fact that we've done it before, we have to thank our publisher and good friend, Whil Hentzen. He continues to provide a channel for quality Visual FoxPro books, and recognizes that authors and editors who really know a product are a key resource.

We were fortunate enough to convince Jeana Randell to serve as our copy editor once again. Her ability to make us look better without removing the Hacker's attitude is nothing short of miraculous.

Once again, quite a few people sent us corrections or updates to earlier editions, or suggestions for improvements. (Yes, we know we messed up the parameters to MessageBox().) We've incorporated a great deal of their feedback into this edition. Our thanks to the following: Bill Anderson, Sergey Berezniker, Art Bergquist, Thomas Bishop, Chaim Caron, Pierre Chaillet, Robin Connelly, Dan Covill, Sue Cunningham, Malcolm Donald, Jim Duffy, Hank Fay, Garrett Fitzgerald, Dan Freeman, Stanley Gainsforth, Carl Karsten, Mike Lewis, Tim McConechy, Paul McGucken, Paul McNett, Barbara Peisch, Viv Phillips, Paul Rosier, Rip Ryness, Steve Sawyer, Robert Stone, Cindy Winegarden and Mike Woram. Please forgive us if you sent us feedback and we haven't listed you here—we still value your contribution.

As usual, the Fox team at Microsoft contributed to this book in many ways, most importantly, of course, by making VFP 7 such a great product. A few members of the team helped out in specific ways, so special thanks to Randy Brown, Gene Goldhammer, Brad Peterson, Jim Saunders and Mike Stewart.

Kevin McNeish and Alex Weider worked with Tamar and Doug on *What's New in Visual FoxPro 7.0* (also available from Hentzenwerke Publishing), and helped them to understand a number of VFP 7's new features.

Visual FoxPro's beta testers are the best. (That's not just our opinion, by the way. Microsoft thinks so, too.) We all learned a lot from our fellow testers, and appreciate the free-flowing discussions that both shape the product and make sense of the new features. Similarly, among us, we frequent a number of the online discussion groups for VFP, and thank everyone who participates for the in-depth discussions on every facet of FoxPro, thereby helping spread FoxPro information and knowledge.

Finally, thanks to Tamar's son, Nathaniel Granor, who used his own brand of hacker's skills to provide the cover for the preview of the HTML Help version of the book.

Of course, we do have lives outside of FoxPro and all need to thank some people on those fronts.

As always, my family has stepped out of the way to enable me to nurture my writing habit. Loving thanks to Marshal, Solomon and Nathaniel.

Tamar

Thanks to my co-authors for pitching in and doing a terrific job on this edition. Thanks once again to family and friends, near and far, for their support. In particular, thanks to Steve, Mom and Dad, Laura, Whil and Tamar.

Ted

Once again, my wife Peggy and son Nicholas had to put up with my spending evenings and weekends slaving over a hot computer. They are the loves of my life and I feel incredibly blessed.

Doug

Thanks to my wonderful husband, Mike, who provided me with love and support while I spent days, nights and weekends writing. Mike also was a terrific source of expert information about operating system concepts, performance analysis and hardware. My children, Kelsey and Kerry, have been wonderfully patient through this whole process. And many thanks to my parents for instilling in me a desire to learn and share my knowledge, and for all their encouragement in my endeavors.

della

Acknowledgments for the Second Edition

As with the original Hacker's Guide, lots of people have made this book better. We'll start right off the bat by thanking all the people we thanked the first time around. (See the Acknowledgments for the First Edition for their names.) It was a lot easier (though not as much as we'd hoped) to write this book when we started with 800 solid pages.

Our technical editor for this edition, Doug Hennig, improved the book in many ways. He caught us when we were sloppy or lazy, shared his extensive knowledge with us, and even fixed many of our grammatical mistakes (though we're still not sure we agree with him about when you need "that" and when you don't). Jeana Randell, our copy editor, was all that we could ask and more. She managed to improve our writing without changing the meaning, and was flexible about style issues without letting us run wild.

Steven Black again contributed his expertise, updating his original masterful work on the Builders and Wizards, and letting his zest for the Class Browser and Component Gallery produce an in-depth guide to these complex tools.

A number of people let us know about mistakes and misprints in both the original Hacker's Guide and early versions of this one. Thanks to Steven Black, Dan Freeman, Chaim Caron, Doug Hennig, Paul Maskens, Hale Pringle, Andrew Ross MacNeill, Tom Piper, Hans Remiens, Brad Schulz, Edwin Weston and Gene Wirchenko. If we left your name out of this list, it doesn't mean that your contribution didn't count, only that you've caught us in another mistake.

Similarly, a lot of people pointed out VFP problems with words like "you might want to include this in the Hacker's Guide." We can't possibly list all of those people here, but your contributions are appreciated and they all make this a better book.

A few people offered us so much wisdom that we must include their names (or they'll come after us). Thanks, in no particular order, to Christof Lange, Mac Rubel, Drew Speedie (technical editor for the first edition), Jim Booth, Gary DeWitt, Steve Dingle, Dan Freeman, and everyone else who taught us something, made a point clear, or asked a hard question that made us rethink an issue.

Thanks to the contributors of material for the disk: Sue Cunningham, the Wyoming Silver Fox, Toni Feltman, Jim Hollingsworth, Ryan Katri, Ken Levy, Andrew Ross MacNeill, Guy Pardoe, the late Tom Rettig and Randy Wallin.

The folks at Microsoft have been remarkably helpful and kind to a couple of people who make a habit of pointing out what's wrong with their product. Special thanks to Susan Graham (now formerly of Microsoft), Calvin Hsia, Robert Green, Randy

Brown, John Rivard, Allison Koeneke, and the hard-working beta team: Phil Stitt, Jim Saunders, Hong-Chee Tan, Steve Pepitone, Dave Kappl and Steve Klem for putting up with our incessant questions, and the whole VFP team (including some people who don't actually work for Microsoft) for giving us this great toy to pound on. Similarly, the DevCon '98 speakers helped to plug a few holes in our knowledge and give us some ideas about what you could do with this version of VFP.

Thanks, too, to the other teams at Microsoft responsible for the tools we used to build this book. The Word team produced Service Release 2 just in time to fix some of the most horrific bugs with generating HTML from Word. Despite our many grumblings about its shortcomings, Word is one of the world's most powerful word processors, and its capability to do Automation made assembly of the book and the HTML Help file a far easier process. Thanks, too, to Word MVP's and/or CSP's Cindy Meister, Colleen Macri, George Mair and Chris Woodman, for their help in figuring out how to get Word to do what we wanted rather than what *it* wanted.

Many people encouraged the creation of some sort of hypertext documentation. HTML Help came along just at just the right time to be used for this version of the book. The HTML Help team has done an incredible job with a product whose specs won't sit still, treating us to versions 1.0, 1.1, 1.1a and 1.1b in less than a year. Thanks to Dan Freeman and Steven Black for their insistence on its value, Stephen Le Hunte for his incredible HTML Reference Library, and to the wonderful folks on the WINHLP-L mailing list for explaining it all, especially Help MVPs Cheryl Lockett Zubak and Dana Cline, and list contributor Patrick Sheahan for his hack to make the Fonts button appear.

As always, the VFP beta testers taught us a lot, showed us all kinds of strange behaviors, and made the whole process a lot more fun. Thanks, too, to all of the readers of our first version, for the encouraging words and support.

We're not sure what to say to our good friend, Whil Hentzen, who's been crazy enough to take on publishing books as a sideline to his software development business. Guess "thanks for everything, Whil" will have to do. Special thanks, also, to Whil's wife, Linda, who holds it all together and fits right in with the crowd.

Finally, once again, we have to thank the two people who got us into this in the first place, Woody Leonhard and Arnold Bilansky. Perhaps thanks are also due to an anonymous cab driver in Toronto who let us do all the talking the day we met so we could discover we were friends.

On a personal level, life doesn't stop while you spend nearly a year writing a book and we each owe a lot to the people around us.

Once again, my family has had too little of me for too long. I owe my husband, Marshal, and sons, Solomon and Nathaniel, more than I can possibly explain for their love, patience (especially while I talked about things they knew nothing about), and help.

As before, my extended family and good friends have been supportive and helpful throughout, as have the people at *Advisor*.

Tamar

Through the year of turning this crazy idea into the book before you, life went on. Thanks to Ellen, my dear wife, for putting up with it all. You are my strength and my inspiration. Thanks, Steve, for entertaining yourself for nearly a year. Thanks and farewell to my best beta tester, Chloe. Thanks to my coworkers at Blackstone for their suggestions, support and encouragement.

Ted

Acknowledgments for the First Edition

As with any work of this sort, a lot of people have contributed to this book in many different ways. We'll take the chance of thanking them by name, knowing we're bound to leave someone out. Whoever you are, we really do appreciate whatever you did.

Two people have made this a substantially better book. Drew Speedie, our technical editor, kept us honest, pushed us harder, and offered many gentle suggestions based on his own hard-won expertise. Steve Black may know more about Visual FoxPro's Builders and Wizards than anyone alive except their designers (maybe even more than them, too). Thanks to him, the chapter on that subject is a true hacker's delight.

Many other folks turned the light on for us or made us look harder at something or just plain told us what we needed to know. Thanks to: the Toms—Rombouts and Rettig—for filling the holes in the history of Xbase; Dan Pollak, beta tester extraordinaire and true Hacker, who figured out a bunch of stuff we missed; Mac Rubel, off whom many thoughts and ideas were bounced, especially in the area of error handling; Doug Hennig, for helping Ted through the database container; Harve Strouse, who helped Tamar finally to understand Present Value and Future Value (at least long enough to write about them); Tom Meeks, who made sense of DrawMode and its friends; Nancy Jacobsen, who educated us about colors and made us think hard about what a user interface should be; Ken Levy and Paul Bienick for their help in getting us to understand the Browser and OLE Automation; Andy Neil, the master of multi-user; Brad Schulz, PrintMaster, for his help on printing issues; Tamar's father (the retired Math teacher), who helped her make sense of MOD()'s weird behavior with negative numbers; the Visual FoxPro Beta tester community, who pushed and prodded and poked and showed us all kinds of ways VFP could be used and abused. Thanks to all of the DevCon '95 speakers, each of whom brought their own talents and perspectives to bear on this wonderful product, and produced wonderfully lucid sessions with a product still not done.

We have (at least until this book comes out) many friends at Microsoft. Our respect for the group that built Visual FoxPro is tremendous—this is an awesome product—and we thank them all. Special thanks to a few people who helped us in various ways: Susan Graham, Erik Svenson, Gene Goldhammer, Randy Brown and Calvin Hsia.

A few people kindly helped us to fill the disk. Thanks to: Sue Cunningham, Walt Kennamer, Roy L. Gerber, Andy Griebel, James Hollingsworth, Ken Levy, Andrew Ross MacNeill, Tom Rettig, Randy Wallin and Ryan Katri, Rick Strahl, and our friends at Flash, Micromega and Neon.

Our thanks to all the FoxFolk who allowed us to include their records in our sample data.

Dealing with Addison-Wesley has been nothing like the stories we hear about publishers. Our editor, Kathleen Tibbetts, has been helpful and pleasant throughout. Working with Woody Leonhard was a special bonus. Thanks, too, to Arnold Bilansky, who first suggested we take on this book together.

On to more personal thanks.

Solomon and Nathaniel have had nearly a year of "Mom'll take care of it after the book." Hey, guys, it's after the book—I'll take care of it now. My husband, Marshal, has gone way above and beyond the call of duty in taking on extra responsibilities and letting me work on "the book, the book, the book." He also has an amazing knack to know when I need to hear "of course, you can do that" and when I need the challenge of "gee, I don't know if you can do that." I couldn't have done this without him.

My extended family (Ezekiels, Granors and Fishbeins) have all contributed in tangible and intangible ways. Special thanks to my parents who never once said to me (at least not about work), "Girls can't do that."

So many of my friends have helped out by driving carpool, watching my kids, letting me moan, and more than I can't begin to name names. You know who you are and I really do appreciate it. I owe you all a lot.

Editing a monthly magazine while writing a book while beta-testing a massive product definitely falls into the major league stress category. Everyone at *Advisor* has been understanding and helpful.

Tamar

This book was only possible through the love and support of my family. My wife Ellen has tolerated more long hours and stress than any spouse should have to put up with. She is the wind beneath my wings. Thanks to son Steve, for letting Dad finish "The Book." Thanks, too, to my extended family for their support, especially my dad, who knew I could write long before I did.

Ted

About the Authors

Tamar E. Granor, Ph.D., has developed and enhanced numerous FoxPro and Visual FoxPro applications for businesses and other organizations. She currently focuses on working with other developers through consulting, mentoring and subcontracting. Tamar served as Editor of *FoxPro Advisor* magazine from 1994 to 2000, where she is currently Technical Editor and co-author of the magazine's popular *Advisor Answers* column.

Tamar is co-author of *What's New in Visual FoxPro 7.0*, *Microsoft Office Automation with Visual FoxPro*, and the *Hacker's Guide to Visual FoxPro 6.0*, winner of the Visual FoxPro Developer's Choice award. She is the Technical Editor of *Visual FoxPro Certification Exams Study Guide*. All of these books are available from Hentzenwerke Publishing (www.hentzenwerke.com).

Tamar is a Microsoft Certified Professional and a Microsoft Support Most Valuable Professional. Tamar speaks frequently about Visual FoxPro at conferences and user groups in Europe and North America. She served as Technical Content Manager for the 1997–1999 Visual FoxPro DevCons and was part of the coordination team for the Visual FoxPro Excellence Awards. You can reach Tamar at tamar@thegranors.com.

Ted Roche develops stand-alone, client-server and Web applications using Microsoft Visual FoxPro, Microsoft SourceSafe, SQL Server, and other best-of-breed tools. He is a consultant with Ted Roche & Associates, LLC, http://www.tedroche.com, based in New Hampshire. Ted is author of *Essential SourceSafe* (Hentzenwerke Publishing), co-author of the award-winning *Hacker's Guide to Visual FoxPro* series, and a contributor to five other FoxPro books. In addition to numerous magazine articles, he has spoken at conferences worldwide. Ted is a Microsoft Certified Solution Developer, Microsoft Certified System Engineer, and Microsoft Support Most Valuable Professional.

Doug Hennig is a partner with Stonefield Systems Group Inc. He is the author of the award-winning Stonefield Database Toolkit, co-author of *What's New in Visual FoxPro 7* from Hentzenwerke Publishing, and author of *The Visual FoxPro Data Dictionary* in Pinnacle Publishing's Pros Talk Visual FoxPro series. He writes the monthly "Reusable Tools" column in *FoxTalk*. Doug has spoken at every Microsoft FoxPro Developers Conference (DevCon) since 1997 and at user groups and developer conferences all over North America. He is a Microsoft Most Valuable Professional (MVP) and Certified Professional (MCP). Doug's Web site is www.stonefield.com; you can reach him at dhennig@stonefield.com

Della Martin has worked on some of the most unusual FoxPro and Visual FoxPro applications. She got her start writing a recruiting database for Duke Basketball while attending Duke University. She has a degree with a double major in Design and History.

Continuing in the line of non-traditional database applications, Della worked for Woolpert, an architectural and engineering firm, where she specialized in GIS work for such diverse applications as water distribution systems, military master planning, oil well evacuation plans, and facility management programs. She moved on to the University of Tennessee to work on a military logistics application, JFAST, perhaps the most well known VFP application in the world. At nearly every DevCon since 1994, attendees have seen this cutting-edge application, which includes sophisticated briefing and analysis tools developed by Della using Automation with many Microsoft products.

Della now works for TakeNote Technologies, a Developer's Choice training and consulting firm, as a developer and instructor. Della has written for *FoxPro Advisor* and *FoxTalk* magazine, and served as a judge for the 1998 and 1999 Visual FoxPro Excellence Awards. She speaks at various conferences, including the Great Lakes Great Developers Workshop, VFP DevConnections, and the Essential Fox conference. *The Hacker's Guide to Visual FoxPro* is her second book; she co-authored *Microsoft Office Automation with Visual FoxPro*, with Tamar Granor. Della lives in Cary, North Carolina, with her husband and two children. You can reach Della at dmartin@takenote.com or dmartin2@nc.rr.com.

How to Download the Files

Hentzenwerke Publishing generally provides two sets of files to accompany its books. The first is the source code referenced throughout the text. Note that some books do not have source code; in those cases, a placeholder file is provided in lieu of the source code in order to alert you of the fact. The second is the e-book version (or versions) of the book. Depending on the book, we provide e-books in either the compiled HTML Help (CHM) format, Adobe Acrobat (PDF) format, or both. Here's how to get them.

Both the source code and e-book file(s) are available for download from the Hentzenwerke Web site. In order to obtain them, follow these instructions:

1. Point your Web browser to http://www.hentzenwerke.com.

2. Look for the link that says "Download."

3. A page describing the download process will appear. This page has two sections:

   • **Section 1:** If you were issued a username/password directly from Hentzenwerke Publishing, you can enter them into this page.

   • **Section 2:** If you did not receive a username/password from Hentzenwerke Publishing, don't worry! Just enter your e-mail alias and look for the question about your book. Note that you'll need your physical book when you answer the question.

4. A page that lists the hyperlinks for the appropriate downloads will appear.

Note that the e-book file(s) are covered by the same copyright laws as the printed book. Reproduction and/or distribution of these files is against the law.

If you have questions or problems, the fastest way to get a response is to e-mail us at books@hentzenwerke.com.

Foreword to the Second Edition

I was thrilled that Tamar and Ted decided to update their *Hacker's Guide* for Visual FoxPro 6.0. The easily understandable style of the *Guide* will help Fox developers come up to speed quickly on the wonderful new features in VFP 6. I continue to enjoy the way they examine each and every feature, even the potential "gotchas."

An innovation of the 6.0 *Guide* is the HTML Help version that comes on CD. You'll have all the fabulous content of the *Hacker's Guide* in the easily searchable Table of Contents and Index of HTML Help. I appreciate the fact that I can still sit in my comfortable easy chair and read straight through the book, and yet I have the *Guide's* valuable information at my fingertips when I'm using VFP at my desk.

Tamar and Ted, thanks again for sharing your knowledge with the Fox community.

Susan Graham
Former Visual FoxPro Program Manager
Microsoft Developer Division

Foreword to the First Edition

When I first learned that Tamar and Ted were planning to "take the plunge" and write a Visual FoxPro book, I couldn't have been more pleased. Tamar's ability to explain complex concepts is well known, as is Ted's depth of knowledge about many aspects of the product.

In *The Hacker's Guide to Visual FoxPro for Windows* Tamar and Ted make the learning curve much flatter for novice users of Visual FoxPro, as well as for those who are already fairly comfortable with the product. They discuss concepts new to the Xbase developer (such as Object Oriented Programming), as well as old concepts with new guise (no more READs!). They also present a great deal of information in their reference component, which is the heart of the book. However, my favorite section is "Franz and Other Lists—a collection of lists containing information one can never seem to find in the Help file (it's usually there, but it can be hard to find). And don't miss the section on Frequently Asked Questions.

As in the articles they've written and in the talks they've given, Tamar and Ted provide technical information, strategies and source code on a Companion Disk. They provide clear and concise explanations of complex subjects such as SQL, the new event model and parameterized views. I especially appreciate the real-life examples of why to use a feature in a particular way. It truly aids in understanding.

Even though the content of this book is basically technical, the style of this *Hacker's Guide* is informal, quite amusing, and is a particularly easy read. How many of you get the reference in the title *Controls and KAOS?*

It has been my pleasure to work with Tamar and Ted on the many FoxPro beta cycles I've managed over the past few years. (Nobody has read our help file and docs as thoroughly as Tamar has!) Their insights and opinions have helped us improve each of our products, and this perspective is demonstrated to great advantage in the *Hacker's Guide.* This book will be a valuable resource to Visual FoxPro users.

Susan Graham
Visual FoxPro Program Manager
Microsoft Developer Division

Who Needs This Book?

We love Visual FoxPro. We'd rather use it to develop applications than any other product we've ever worked with.

But (isn't there always a "but"?) Visual FoxPro isn't perfect. Some parts of the language don't work as they should. Others do what they're supposed to, but we can't imagine why anyone thinks you'd want to do that. And some pieces do exactly what they're supposed to and it's a good thing to do, but it's hard as heck to understand. We should add that the Visual FoxPro documentation is good—in fact, it gets better with each new version—but there are still too many places where it's incorrect, incomplete, or sometimes a bit incomprehensible.

Enter this book. This is the book for the times when you've done just as the manual shows, but it still doesn't work and you're running out of hair to pull out. It's for those days when you think you've found a command that does what you need, but you can't make any sense of what Help has to say about it. We'll tell you how it really works or why you shouldn't do it the way the manual shows—or tell you that it doesn't work at all, and show you how to do it another way.

What This Book is Not

This is an "intermediate-level" book. This book is not a replacement for the online Help or the Language Reference manual. It's a supplement. If something works the way it's documented, we won't repeat all the gory details. Instead, we summarize that and add anything the manual doesn't tell you.

On the other hand, if a command or function or property or event or method doesn't work as documented or if the documentation doesn't make sense, we dig down and explain it in detail. And, of course, in those cases, we still tell you the stuff the manual doesn't say.

This book is not the way to begin learning Visual FoxPro. Other books out there, including Whil Hentzen's book in this series, *The Fundamentals*, are designed to teach you Visual FoxPro. If you're new to Visual FoxPro, get one of those books and work your way through it. Then get this book to help you move on.

This book is not a guide to the Visual FoxPro IDE. While we do talk about the tools and even provide some tips and tricks on that front, this book really focuses on the programming language itself.

This book is not an advanced application framework. There are several good commercial frameworks available that will provide you with all the code you need to start plugging your information into their systems and getting working apps out the other end. In fact, Visual FoxPro (beginning with version 6) even comes with a decent framework you can use right away. We like and work with several of the frameworks, and we do not intend to duplicate their work here. Instead, we try to provide an advanced reference when you need to step outside the framework's box, or need to troubleshoot something the framework isn't doing right. You may also use this book to develop your own framework, but that exercise, as our professors loved to say, is left to the student.

We assume you're already familiar with the basics of Visual FoxPro, that you know how to use the Power Tools, and that you've spent some time with the product. Although we cover some introductory material, it's not at the level you'd want if you're a beginner.

So Who Does Need This Book?

Immodestly, we say anyone who's serious about working in Visual FoxPro needs this book at his or her side. Once you've gotten past the "Help, I don't know where to begin" stage and spent some time working with Visual FoxPro, you're ready. As soon as you've spent a long day and a sleepless night fighting one of the less-than-intuitive behaviors or trying to make something work that just plain doesn't, you're probably well past ready.

In putting together this book, we've learned a tremendous amount about what's going on under the hood. Despite having learned most of it the hard way, we all use the book (in particular, the HTML Help version) every working day. We're looking forward to having this new edition on our desktops to replace the VFP 6 version. If a file could be dog-eared, that one would be.

Hacking the *Hacker's Guide*

In any book of this size, there are bound to be mistakes, omissions or places we just missed the mark. If you think you've caught us on one of these, drop us an e-mail (via books@hentzenwerke.com) and we'll check it out for the next edition. Check the Hentzenwerke Web site regularly for updates and corrections. To make that easier for you, in the HTML Help version you'll find a button at the end of every topic that'll navigate right to updates for that topic, if there are any.

While we do love tracking down FoxPro problems, we're all too busy to do it on a one-to-one basis except for our clients and closest friends. So, if you need help with a particularly complex problem or general advice about how to proceed, please take advantage of one or more of the wonderful online resources for VFP. There's a list of them in "Back o' da Book." (Of course, if that doesn't help, we're always interested in new consulting opportunities.)

For what appears truth to the one may appear to be error to the other.

Mahatma Gandhi, 1922

Tamar E. Granor
Elkins Park, Pennsylvania

Ted Roche
Contoocook, New Hampshire

Doug Hennig
Regina, Saskatchewan, Canada

Della Martin
Cary, North Carolina

How to Use This Book

Insert flap (A) in slot (B). Turn crank (C) so that teeth (D) engage with flap (A).

Every Instruction Manual You've Ever Used

"So how do you use a book like this? We don't imagine that many of you will sit down and read it cover to cover. Of course, if you're the type who reads language reference manuals sequentially, be our guest."

We wrote those words in the first edition of this book. Since then, we've learned that a lot of you *are* the type who read language manuals in order. A surprising number of people have told us that they read the original *Hacker's Guide* from front to back before turning it into a reference book. We're flattered and astonished (especially by the one reader who told us he reads the book cover to cover once a year).

Nonetheless, we still think that most of you have a few other things to do with your time, so this edition is still organized so that you don't have to read it all before you can put it to work. In fact, with this edition, we've made it a lot harder to read the book sequentially—more on that below.

The book is divided into five sections. The first, "Wow, What a Concept!" is an overview of Visual FoxPro, organized by the various components of the language: Xbase traditions and assumptions, SQL, OOP, data structures, Web support, and more. We recommend you read it, even if you've been working with FoxPro since FoxBase days. We hope you'll find a few little nuggets tucked away in there.

The second section, "Ship of Tools," looks at Visual FoxPro's Power Tools, including some of our favorite tips and tricks for working with the tools, with more in-depth coverage of debugging and source control.

Section 3, "Franz and other Lists," is a somewhat random assortment of lists—from hardware suggestions, to things that sure feel like bugs when you run into them, to optimization tips. A lot of what was in this section in the first edition migrated into other parts of the book in later editions. In particular, many of the "It's a Feature, Not a Bug" items have been moved into the appropriate entries in the reference section to make them easier to find.

After you finish with all those appetizers, Section 4 is the main course. It's a complete reference to Visual FoxPro's commands, functions, properties, events and methods. We've even thrown in a few operators like "%" and "&".

This is the part of the book we really don't expect you to sit down and read sequentially. In the VFP 6 edition of the book, Section 4 occupied more than 750 8½" x 11" pages, but it rapidly became clear that few readers actually looked at those pages. Instead, virtually everyone who bought the book went ahead and used the HTML Help version to read the reference section. So, this time around, we've chosen to save trees (as well as the backs of the poor lackeys at Hentzenwerke Publishing who have to move these books around). For VFP 7, Section 4 appears only in the electronic version of the book.

Finally, Section 5 is for those daring souls who want to take the product a little further. It covers the various Active technologies as they relate to VFP (some are like siblings, while others are more like that annoying second cousin you wish would go away); two incredibly deep tools, the Class Browser and Component Gallery; VFP's Builder and Wizard technologies; and VFP's incredibly flexible version of IntelliSense.

Hey, CHM. Can you give me some Help here?

After the original *Hacker's Guide* came out, lots of people asked us whether we could make it available in some online format (ranging from Windows Help to PDF to HTML to who knows what). They wanted access to the contents no matter where they were, without having to carry the book along. While we sympathized (especially when we were on the road ourselves), we just didn't have the resources to do the job.

When we prepared the VFP 6 edition, we planned a digital version from the beginning. Anyone buying the book was also entitled to a complete copy of the book in HTML Help format. At that time, HTML Help was just appearing and you needed it for VFP 6's Help file, so we figured it was a safe bet that all our readers would have it. That seems to have been a good choice.

This time around, we're going one step farther and, as we said above, putting the reference section only in the electronic version. We suspect most readers will notice, only because the printed book no longer makes a good monitor stand.

For the curious, let us add that we created both the book and the Help file using Automation from VFP (where we track the progress of the book) to Word. In addition, we used VFP to do extensive post-processing on the generated HTML, parsing it and applying textmerge with VFP's lightning-fast string manipulation features.

Feel free to copy the Help file onto your hard drive (even more than one, if you have multiple machines yourself), but please do us the courtesy of not sharing it with everyone you know. (You will find appropriate copyright notices in there.) We've put a tremendous amount of time into this book, and illegal copies deprive us of the income to pay for that time.

I Think, Therefore Icon

We have pretty mixed emotions about icons—they're great as a supplement to text, but not as a replacement. (After all, humans didn't spend centuries going from written text to pictographs; it was the other way around.) The icons in this book flag those portions of the text you'll want to pay particular attention to if you're having problems, trying to understand why Microsoft makes it work this way, or just skimming for cool features of Visual FoxPro. Here are the icons we use in the book and their meanings. You'll find the icons that appear only in the HTML Help file in "How to Use This Help File."

This ugly creature identifies bugs, both the ones that Microsoft recognizes and the ones we think are bugs, even though Microsoft says they're just fine. Although many of the bugs we identified in earlier versions have been fixed, there are still plenty of these to go around.

This critter indicates bugs from earlier versions that are now fixed. We debated removing the bug notices entirely, but decided that, since many of us have to work with multiple versions of VFP, in most cases leaving the description in the book and marking it as fixed would be a better choice.

This doodad is supposed to say "design" to you. We use it whenever something is less than intuitive but not wrong, just hard to understand. We also use it sometimes when we think the design stinks.

This one probably speaks for itself. It's for stuff we think is incredibly cool ("cool", we think, should be the official adjective of Visual FoxPro). These things are jaw-droppers—enjoy them.

Code-dependent

When Ted and Tamar started writing the first edition of this book, they noticed that each of them had somewhat different coding conventions. Nothing major, but some real differences, especially in capitalization. Since the styles were pretty readable and since the skill of being able to read code written by different people is an important one, they chose not to change their varied styles. By the time they wrote the VFP 6 edition, their styles had converged somewhat, but there were still differences.

With this edition, we've added two more authors, who each have their own unique coding styles. So you may find what appear to be inconsistencies among the examples. We think each individual example is internally consistent. (We're sure you'll let us know, if not.)

Many of the examples show class definitions in code. Others show code to assign values to various properties in forms. The truth is that we usually don't do it that way—we use the Designers. But code makes better examples. Just about any class you see in code here can be created as a visual class, too.

Who Ever Heard of a Sin Tax?

We're capable of drawing the kind of syntax diagrams contained in the FoxPro manuals. In fact, we learned in school how to draw even more obscure syntax diagrams than that. For this book, though, we wanted to present the syntax of each command in the least threatening way possible. So, we use a simpler notation than the manuals. The flip side is that our notation is a little bit ambiguous.

Here are the rules we're using. FoxPro keywords use either all uppercase or mixed case. For the most part, Xbase-style keywords are in uppercase, while OOP-type keywords are mixed.

Vertical bars ("|") indicate choices—pick one or the other, but not both. Square brackets ("[ ]") indicate options—use it or not, your choice. Those two are the same as in the manuals.

What we didn't do was use angle brackets ("< >") to enclose the things you need to substitute into commands. Most of the time, you can recognize them because they begin with a single lowercase letter to indicate their type ("c" for character, "n" for numeric, and so on). It does get confusing when a command requires something like a filename or table name that isn't any of those types. Names are shown in mixed case (which can be confused with OOP-style keywords).

For the most part, we've tried to use meaningful names in our diagrams so you can see what a command or function is looking for, even without reading further.

A Class Act

In the reference entries on Visual FoxPro's base classes, you'll find charts showing properties, events, and methods for that class. Rather than showing you every single PEM for every single base class, we've chosen to include only those that are special for that class. So, none of the classes list Top or Left in their reference entries—those are pretty much the same across the board. On the other hand, Style means something different to just about every class that has it, so you'll find it listed in several of the base class sections.

For a complete list of the PEMs of any base class, check Help.

Version Mania

Writing about software is like chasing a moving target. This edition of the book was written about the initial release version of Visual FoxPro 7.0. Before we finished it, though, Service Pack 1 was released. It fixed a number of the bugs we'd identified (including some of the worst ones). We've updated the book to mark those bugs as fixed. However, it is possible that SP1 has added new bugs we didn't manage to uncover. We also imagine that there'll be further service packs, and look forward to more of the issues we've raised being addressed.

Up-to-the-Minute Coverage

We made a few mistakes in earlier editions of this book. Not only that, but as noted above, the product changed after we finished the book. Fortunately, Hentzenwerke Publishing believes that the job isn't done just because the book went to press.

As we accumulate additions and corrections, they'll be posted on the Hentzenwerke Web site. To make it even easier for you, we've added a button to each topic in the electronic version of the book that'll take you directly to any available updates for that topic. Let us know how it works out for you.

On your mark! Get set! Go hack!

How to Use the Help File

Help a man against his will and you do the same as murder him.

Horace, *Ars Poetica*

When we decided to offer an electronic version of the VFP 6 edition of this book, HTML Help seemed to be the obvious candidate. Microsoft had decreed it the "help of the future" (at least until the next "help of the future"), and VFP 6's Help used the technology.

For the most part, we haven't regretted our choice, and for this edition, continue to offer an HTML Help version of the *Hacker's Guide*. In fact, with this edition, we're depending even more on the HTML Help version by including the Reference section only in the electronic book, and not in the printed book.

However, one of our biggest gripes about HTML Help is that it doesn't come with "Help on Help." Fortunately, we found a separate help file for HTML Help on Microsoft's Web site and we've included it in the downloads for this book. Of course, it's in HTML Help format, too, so if you don't know how to use HTML Help, it may not be much help. All things considered, this section is devoted to teaching you how to use the *Hacker's Guide* help file effectively. It covers both things specific to this help file and a number of the tricks we've learned to make working with HTML Help easier. Do check Microsoft's help file, too, for additional tidbits.

All the things we said in "How to Use this Book" apply to the help file as well, though we suspect that most of you (except those who bought only the electronic version of this book) won't choose the help file as the right way to read the front and back of the book. It's the Reference section that really is effective this way (and, of course, that's one of the reasons for the change in this version).

Getting There

The first challenge you may run into with HTML Help is getting it to run. HTML Help depends on many of the same DLLs as Microsoft's Internet Explorer (IE). In fact, IE is really just a simple shell around the DLLs that render HTML, interpret scripts, provide navigation, and the rest of the features we take for granted on the Web. For this reason, the easiest way to be sure your computer has the correct files to run HTML Help is to install Internet Explorer. Some folks go ballistic upon hearing this, but please understand—IE does not *have* to have an icon on the desktop, it does not *have* to be the default browser, and it does *not* take up significantly more space than is required to install all the gew-gaws needed for HTML Help. Even if you are convinced that IE is just another step in Microsoft's plan for world domination, installing it is the easiest way to read HTML Help files.

We encourage you to get the latest version of IE to be sure you have the most recent fixes for bugs and security problems. In addition, you might want to consider installing HTML Help Workshop and HTML Help Runtime Update (HHUpd.EXE) also available on Microsoft's Web site. (We don't give links here, because we're sure they'll change within a month or two. But the main search page at Microsoft should be able to turn them up.) Both of these files install updated OCX and DLL files that may make reading the help file a more positive experience.

What's In There?

A structure becomes architectural, and not sculptural, when its elements no longer have their justification in nature.

Guillaume Apollinaire, *The Cubist Painters*

Like so many applications these days, HTML Help has two panes. The left pane controls what you see in the right pane. The left pane has three pages (tabs): Contents, Index and Search. The right pane contains one chunk of the book at a time—a chapter from the front or back of the book or a listing from the Reference section.

The pages in the left pane have two things in common. First, each provides a way of getting to the entry you want. Second, each includes a way of re-synching the list if you jump around using links.

In the Reference section, the items in the See Also listing are links, as are some other items, like the lists of properties, events and methods in the entries for the base classes. Just click on them to go to the named item.

If you'd like to make more room for the content, you can adjust the ratio between the two panes by dragging the bar between them left or right. You can also get rid of the left pane by clicking the Hide button. Non-intuitively and inexplicably (and totally the opposite of what Internet Explorer does), clicking Hide shrinks HTML Help to the size of the right pane. You can then stretch it out (or maximize it) to make the right pane (guess it's not really the "right pane" at that moment) bigger. Use the Show button to make the left pane reappear.

As in a browser, the Back and Forward buttons take you back or forward one action. (Interestingly, it appears that scrolling sometimes counts as an action, so you may find yourself at the bottom of the page rather than the top. We kind of think this is a good thing.) Pressing Backspace is the same as clicking the Back button. Use Shift+Backspace (really!) as a keyboard replacement for the Forward button.

HTML Help demonstrates the confusion at Microsoft these days when it comes to interface design. The top of the HTML Help form contains no true menu (text prompts dropping down lists of options). Neither is what's there truly a toolbar, as it cannot be undocked. Worst of all, just to prove they know how to mangle a metaphor but good, the Options button on the thing-that's-not-a-toolbar does call a drop-down menu.

I'd Be Content to Do That

Strong and content I travel the open road.

Walt Whitman, *Song of the Open Road*

The Contents page shows you the table of contents for the book. It looks an awful lot like the one in the printed version, except that it's set up in a drilldown format. If you want to go through the book sequentially, this is the page for you.

In the listing for the Reference section, every command, function, class, property, event, method and system variable is included (along with some of the more unusual operators). We didn't write a separate Reference entry for each item, though—they're logically grouped. Choosing an item from the Contents list takes you right to the appropriate Reference section.

We've also added to the Contents list some keywords that aren't commands, just to make them easier to find. So you can go to ENDCASE and click, and it'll bring up the entry for DO CASE, for example.

When you click a link in the right pane, the Contents list keeps up with you. It always highlights the item you're now looking at.

Index, Outdex

And for the citation of so many authors, 'tis the easiest thing in nature. Find out one of these books with an alphabetical index, and without any farther ceremony, remove it verbatim into your own . . .

Miguel de Cervantes, *Prologue to Don Quixote*

The Index page is the same as the Reference portion of the Contents list, except for two things. First, it provides a text box to let you type in what you're looking for. Second, when you click on a link in the right pane, the Index doesn't follow along. So you can come back to where you were in the Index after wandering down a path of links.

 The Search text box offers incremental search—that is, you start typing and it jumps to the first item that matches what you've typed so far. Unfortunately, there seem to be some bugs in the search algorithm—it has trouble with similar items in different cases. For example, if you type "deleted", the highlight lands on the Deleted property, shown in the Index as "Deleted". However, if you add a left parenthesis (so your search string is now "Deleted("), the highlight does *not* move to "DELETED()", as it should. More interestingly, if you type "DELETED" in the first place, you land on "DELETED()," missing "Deleted" entirely.

Clicking the Display button on the Index page takes you back (in the right pane) to the currently highlighted item in the Index. Clicking Locate on the toolbar/menu brings up the Contents list with the item that's currently displayed in the right pane highlighted in the Contents list.

The Search is On

The philosophic spirit of inquiry may be traced to brute curiosity, and that to the habit of examining all things in search of food.

W. Winwood Reade, *The Martyrdom of Man*

The Search page lets you look for things in ways we didn't consider. Type in any string, press Enter (or choose the List Topics button) and a list of items containing your string appears. Then choose the one you want to see.

As with the Index page, the Search page doesn't keep up with you as you follow links. Instead, it patiently sits there displaying the matches from the last search. As on the Index page, choosing the Display button returns you to the highlighted item in the list. The Locate button also behaves as it does on the Index page, taking you to the Contents page with the current item highlighted.

A couple of pointers when using the Search tab. The search engine is not the brightest star in the heavens, and many common VFP phrases stump its somewhat limited intellect. First, it ignores non-alphabetic characters, so searching for #DEFINE finds DEFINE MENU and DEFINE WINDOW, as well as #DEFINE. Second, we suspect the help authors had some special intentions for parentheses, as we have never been able to include them without getting "Help cannot search for that phrase." This is maddening when searching for something like USER(), because every use of "user" comes up if you do not include the parentheses. (As an aside, because "similar word" searching is turned on, a search for "user" also turns up matches to "using," "used" and even "us." (We understand the first two; we can't imagine why "us" is considered a "similar word" to "user.")

Enclose phrases in quotation marks to locate topics that contain that exact phrase. Note that this technique does not work with single words to prevent similar word matching.

You can use the Boolean operators AND, OR and NOT as well as the NEAR operator to limit your search. Use "ugly" AND "interface" to locate that one section, "ugly" NOT "interface" for the others, "Julian" OR "Gregorian" for calendar discussions.

The Key to the Future

> Woe unto you, lawyers! for ye have taken away the key of knowledge

> *The Bible*

Most of us are touch typists and, as a result, like to keep our hands on the keyboard (not to mention avoiding the physical wear and tear of moving the arm back and forth between keyboard and mouse). It turns out you can do pretty much everything in HTML Help with the keyboard, but it ain't easy to figure it out. Some of the keyboard shortcuts are pretty obscure, and, to make matters worse, the relevant topic in the Help for HTML Help is called "Use accessibility shortcut keys." Sounds like something that's only for those with physical disabilities, doesn't it? How about calling it "Keyboard shortcuts"?

The one that took us the longest to find (in fact, we didn't find it until we got the help file) is moving focus from the left to the right pane. We tried everything we could think of (tabs, Shift+tabs, arrows, Shift+arrows, you name it), even asking other people, and came up empty. It turns out the magic key is F6. Now that's intuitive, isn't it?

Once you get to the right pane, you can use the keyboard to navigate within the entry and to follow a link. Once you follow a link, for some reason it takes two tabs to land on the first link in the new section. Same thing when you back up. We're not sure where focus is when you get there or after that first tab. (This seems to be an HTML Help "feature," since we see it in every HTML Help file we try.)

To go back from right to left, you can use F6 again. In addition, all three pages of the left pane have hot keys, as does the Options drop-down menu.

Not only are many of the keystrokes unintuitive, some of them don't work as documented and others don't seem to be documented at all. For instance, Alt+LeftArrow and Alt+RightArrow seem to navigate back and forth in the history list, but this behavior is undocumented. To open and close folders, use the numeric keypad's + and – when the appropriate item is highlighted. Also undocumented is that Shift+LeftArrow and Shift+RightArrow move you up and down a level in the Contents hierarchy. It's worth spending some time trying various keystrokes to see what they do. You can't damage anything by doing so, so why not check it out?

Icon Take Much More

HTML Help offers the capability to set the icon of each topic to have its own individual bitmap. We decided not to go hog-wild, and just kept to a few different ones. The book icon is for the front of the book. Each major section appears as a folder. The individual sections appear as a text icon. Every language item or chapter that's new or changed in VFP 6 Service Pack 3 or VFP 7 is marked in the Contents listing with a red star.

Just the Way You Want It

Custom, then, is the great guide of human life.

David Hume, *An Enquiry Concerning Human Understanding*

We had many difficult design decisions to make in creating the help file. If for some reason you cannot abide our choices in fonts, font sizes or colors, all is not lost. First, if your problem is just the font size, use the Font button to cycle among five different choices. We hope one of them will suit you. The Font button is a hack—obviously, the code is somewhere within the HTML Help engine, but there is no way to add it to your help file using the HTML Help Workshop interface. The good news is that we got it to work; the bad news is that we haven't figured out if it has a keyboard shortcut.

If the fonts and colors we've chosen really drive you nuts, you can change it, but it's not easy. We used a cascading style sheet (CSS), which is compiled into the Help file. You can decompile the file, edit the CSS, then recompile it. Alternatively, if you want to change *all* Internet content (not just HTML Help, but all pages viewed in a browser), you can use the Internet Options item under the Options button and click the Accessibility and Fonts buttons to have things your way.

You can also filter what's available on the Contents page. Right-click anywhere within the Contents page and choose Customize from the context menu. When you choose it, a Customize dialog appears with a wizard that lets you limit the items shown to those introduced in particular versions of FoxPro. So, if you want to know what's new in VFP 7, choose the Custom option button on the first page, and then uncheck everything except Visual FoxPro 7.0 on the second. When you finish the wizard, Contents shows you only the items that were introduced in VFP 7. (We've chosen to leave all of the front and back of the book chapters available, no matter which subset you're in.) To restore the list to include all items, either choose the All option button or check every version.

LoOKs LIke a RaNSom NoTE

At first glance, the alphabetical listings of language elements on the Contents and Index pages look like someone forgot to proofread it. Some items are all caps, some are mixed case, some have parentheses, others don't, and sometimes the same item appears more than once.

Relax—there *is* method to our madness. Due to its long evolution and liberal borrowing from other languages (see "It's Always Been That Way" for details), VFP has not only an assortment of traditions in terms of capitalization, but also quite a few keywords that have multiple meanings. We've done our best to sort things out so you can find what you need.

Here are our rules (which we tried to follow universally). Xbase and SQL commands, functions and keywords are listed in ALL CAPS. Properties, events, methods and other OOP keywords use Mixed Case. Functions are shown with trailing parentheses. Events and methods are not.

So, for example, NewObject is a method, while NewObject() is a function. Similarly, Alias refers to the property, and ALIAS() is the function. DEBUG is a command and Debug is a property.

For the most part, this system provides us with a unique string for each language item. But once in a while, it breaks down. For example, there's a Run event and a Run method. In those cases, we've included the additional phrasing needed to clarify things.

What all this means, in practice, is that after you've typed enough to get to the right word, sometimes you'll have to press an extra down arrow or two to get to the item you want.

Keep it Handy

> More helpful than all wisdom is one draught of
> simple human pity that will not forsake us.
>
> George Eliot, *The Mill on the Floss*, 1860

When we were working on the VFP 6 version of the book, it didn't take us long to figure out that keeping a shortcut to HackFox.CHM on the desktop means that it's only a double-click away.

Other people prefer to access the file from within VFP. You can replace the VFP help file with this one by issuing SET HELP TO HackFox.CHM, including the appropriate path, of course. (For some reason, doing it this way turns off the F1 shortcut, but typing Help or choosing Help from the menu works.)

If you'd like to keep Microsoft's help file available, but also put the *Hacker's Guide* on the menu, try code like this:

```
DEFINE BAR 10 OF _msystem KEY Alt+F1 PROMPT "Hacker's Guide"
ON SELECTION BAR 10 OF _msystem RUN /n hh.exe hackfox.chm
```

Of course, you'll need to add the appropriate path to the file.

We also find that we live on the Index page most of the time, so that we can quickly find the section we want. The combination of the shortcut and the index is way faster than pulling the book off the shelf and finding the right page. We hope you find it as useful as we have.

Section 1: Wow, What a Concept!

Ignorance is preferable to error; and he is less remote from the truth who believes nothing, than he who believes what is wrong.

Thomas Jefferson, *Notes on the State of Virginia*, 1781-1785

Section 1 introduces the major themes of Visual FoxPro, starting with its history and covering the fundamentals of each of its major sub-languages. Think of it as the "If it's Tuesday, this must be Belgium" Tour of Visual FoxPro.

"It's Always Been That Way"

The past is but the beginning of a beginning, and all that is and has been is but the twilight of the dawn.

H. G. Wells, *The Discovery of the Future*, 1901

"In the beginning"—isn't that how histories normally begin? But what is the beginning of Visual FoxPro? It has bits and pieces from so many different languages and technologies that there's no one beginning. Visual FoxPro is a true hybrid.

One bit of lineage is clearer than the rest, though, and that is FoxPro's Xbase heritage. For that, there's at least a partial beginning. "In the beginning, there was the dot."

In this beginning, it was 1975 and a programmer named Wayne Ratliff was working at the Jet Propulsion Laboratory (JPL) in Pasadena, California. He wanted to participate in the football pool, but felt he needed to really work over the statistics to have a fair shot at winning. Naturally, he wanted to use a computer to help him. Somehow, he got sidetracked into exploring programming languages. Along the way, he was introduced to microcomputers and to an internal language at JPL called JPLDIS.

In 1978, Ratliff started writing his microcomputer version of JPLDIS (developed by Jeb Long and others). Along the way, he omitted some commands, added some and modified others. The language was called Vulcan, as a tribute to Star Trek. Ratliff began licensing Vulcan in 1979.

When marketing Vulcan became too much for Ratliff, he made a deal with George Tate and Hal Lashlee to take over the marketing. They brought in an ad man named Hal Pawluk who gave the product a new name, dBASE II, and named the company Ashton-Tate. dBASE II started shipping in 1981. (By the way, note that there never was a dBASE I and, according to several sources, Ashton was George Tate's pet parrot. You can probably win a few bucks on those.)

Eventually, Ratliff and co-worker Jeb Long left JPL to work full-time with a team of programmers on a new version of dBASE (to be called dBASE III). As part of that process, it was ported to the IBM PC. dBASE III was finally released in June 1984.

A Fox in the Hen House

The fox knows many things, but the hedgehog knows one great thing.

Archilochus, Early seventh century B.C.

In the midst of all this, a computer science professor at Bowling Green State University named Dave Fulton got a consulting contract for which dBASE II seemed the appropriate tool. But, when the work was done, the resulting system was too slow. Fulton and his group decided the solution was to write their own, faster version of dBASE II. The product they created was a marketing failure (through no fault of their own), but from the ashes of that product, the run-time libraries were salvaged in hopes that some commercial gain could be made from them.

The result was FoxBase, one of many dBASE clones that hit the market. The difference between FoxBase and the others: It survived and found its own niche.

Once dBASE III appeared, Fulton's group geared up to apply the Fox magic to it. FoxBase+ shipped in July 1986. A little more than a year later, FoxBase+ 2 was released, with dBASE III Plus compatibility. FoxBase+ 2 also included a number of tools to aid in application development. One of them, FoxView, let the developer lay out screens visually, then generate code for that layout. The code was generated by running a script written in another tool called FoxCode, which meant the same layout could result in many different programs.

Suited to Everyone

> Suspicion all our lives shall be stuck full of eyes;
> For treason is but trusted like the fox.
>
> William Shakespeare, *King Henry the Fourth*

Back in Perrysburg, Ohio (home of Fox Software), the development team was hard at work on a Macintosh version of FoxBase+.

In developing the Mac version, many of the programmers took a real liking to the Mac's interface. So, Fulton and the gang decided to bring many of the benefits of the Mac to PC programmers. Work started on FoxPro in the fall of 1988.

Not coincidentally, dBASE IV, the successor to dBASE III Plus, was released in October 1988. The new FoxPro would be dBASE IV-compatible, but for the first time, the decision was made to deviate from total compatibility. Instead, the new FoxPro would be better. Naturally, it would still be faster. It turned out that making FoxPro better than dBASE IV wasn't all that hard—the initial release of dBASE IV was terribly buggy and poorly received. (By this time, Ashton-Tate had a number of problems. George Tate had died in 1984 and the company never really recovered.)

It was also in the fall of 1988 that Ashton-Tate filed a lawsuit against Fox Software for infringing on their copyright of the dBASE language. It took more than two years and Borland's acquisition of Ashton-Tate before this issue was dropped.

FoxPro 1.0 was released in November 1989, still including the FoxView-FoxCode pair for designing input screens. FoxPro remained true to its Xbase roots, but incorporated lots of new commands for using windows and menus. The Mac influence was definitely felt. FoxPro 1.0 also added the first of many sub-languages: the low-level file functions that let you manipulate files as streams of characters. The term "low-level" is something of a misnomer because these really just provide the same file input/output capabilities most programming languages have, but they are lower-level than FoxPro's other input/output facilities.

A Two-Oh Punch

> The delight that consumes the desire,
> The desire that outruns the delight.
>
> Algernon Charles Swinburne, *Dolores*, 1866

Naturally, the new capabilities offered in FoxPro 1.0 weren't enough for the FoxPro community. The FoxPro user interface included all kinds of neat widgets like push buttons, radio buttons, scrollable lists, and so forth. It didn't take long for FoxPro developers to start clamoring for access to these goodies.

FoxPro 2.0 was the response to these demands. It appeared in July 1991, and featured a collection of so-called "Power Tools." Developers were told to use the new Project Manager, Screen Builder, Menu Builder, Report Writer and so forth to design and build applications. For the first time, anything you could do with the Power Tools could be done with code, too. Best of all, the Power Tools stored their data in regular FoxPro tables and, in the case of the Screen Builder and Menu Builder, used regular FoxPro code to convert that metadata into programs. Like the earlier FoxView and FoxCode, this open architecture meant you could roll your own, if you chose, but now you didn't need to learn the arcane syntax of the template language. This was all made possible with the addition of very few commands, comprising a textmerge sub-language.

Another new language was introduced into FoxPro in this version. FoxPro 2.0 featured four SQL commands (CREATE TABLE, CREATE CURSOR, INSERT INTO and SELECT). Up to this point, all new commands had pretty much followed the Xbase style. But this group came from an entirely different background—not quite the other side of the tracks, but a whole different way of thinking about code, a non-procedural way. With the SQL commands, you indicate what you want, but not how to get there; FoxPro figures that out internally. This "set-oriented" view of data opens FoxPro up to opportunities both in larger-scale Xbase applications and in new client-server venues, which would have been difficult, if not impossible, to reach without the SQL syntax.

FoxPro 2.0 also introduced the infamous "foundation READ," which could be used as part of a structure to provide so-called "event-driven" programs. These applications, which are the norm today, allow a user to begin one task, leave it unfinished while moving on to another, then freely switch between the two, or even three, four or 15 tasks. The foundation READ of FoxPro 2.0, while kludgy in the extreme, was the beginning of the path to the rich event model of Visual FoxPro.

Crossroads

FoxPro 2.0 was very well received and won lots of awards. But was that enough for FoxPro users? Of course not! They kept asking for more. One of the big things they asked for was a version of FoxPro on platforms other than DOS. FoxBase+/Mac users felt left out because DOS users had now had two major upgrades and they hadn't. Plus, Windows was looking more and more important.

So, the next task for the Fox group was to cross the road—that is, to make FoxPro cross-platform. Work proceeded simultaneously on the Windows and DOS versions of FoxPro 2.5 through 1991 and 1992. The 1991 Developer's Conference (DevCon) featured demos of both the Windows and Unix versions of FoxPro then in development. At the 1992 DevCon, almost every presenter used the then-in-beta Windows version.

In March 1992, the Fox world shook when it was announced that Microsoft and Fox were to merge. Given their relative sizes and importance, it was clear that "merger" was a euphemism for "acquisition." However, the story was that the development team including Dave Fulton would make the move to Redmond. The merger became final in June and by fall, nearly all of the former Fox employees had trekked cross-country.

FoxPro 2.5 for Windows and for DOS were released in January 1993. They included a "Transporter" for moving applications between the two platforms. The Mac and Unix versions were promised to follow soon. Some folks complained that the Windows version wasn't a true Windows product, but they were answered by those who pointed out that "true Windows products" don't work cross-platform. Other than those needed for cross-platform operation or for new Windows capabilities, FoxPro 2.5 didn't introduce many new commands and functions.

So What's "Soon" Anyway?

> With foxes we must play the fox.
>
> Thomas Fuller

While DOS and Windows developers learned to write cross-platform applications, Mac and Unix developers waited and waited. It wasn't until the spring of 1994 that

FoxPro/Mac made its appearance. FoxPro/Unix never made it in version 2.5. By the time that product was ready in August 1994, the ante had been upped to 2.6 across the board.

Version 2.6 was an interesting project. Its primary reason for existence was to attract dBASE users before dBASE 5 for DOS and dBASE for Windows shipped. A bunch of new commands were added to create 2.6—almost every one of them was labeled "for dBASE compatibility," whether or not it was actually useful. Most didn't even rate their own entry in the help file. And some, despite their downplaying by Microsoft, were truly useful additions to the language.

In the summer of 1994, the family was finally completed with the release of FoxPro 2.6 for Unix. That was the only FoxPro for Unix that ever was.

Third Time's the Charm ... Or is it?

> High thoughts must have high language.
>
> Aristophanes, *Frogs*, 405 B.C.E.

By 1994, the programming world was changing. On the data side, client-server was the next big thing. Programming-wise, it was object orientation. So, of course, Microsoft decided to include both in the next version of FoxPro. They also updated the name to be in line with their other development tools, and FoxPro 3.0 became Visual FoxPro 3.0.

Visual FoxPro still contains all the Xbase commands it ever had (and more), the "low-level file function" sub-language, the textmerge sub-language, and the SQL sub-language with lots of additions. But wait, there's more.

The major new language in Visual FoxPro is that of OOP, Object-Oriented Programming. There's also a sub-language for client-server operation. Altogether, Visual FoxPro 3.0 contained more than 1,000 commands, functions, system variables, properties, events and methods. It was released in June 1995. The initial version of VFP had some serious problems. Because the product was released before Windows 95 and since most of the computing world still worked in 16-bit versions of Windows, this 32-bit application had to cooperate with the Win32S subsystem to run under Windows 3.1 and Windows for Workgroups. A lot of people found that combination less than stable.

In many ways, it makes sense to think of VFP 3.0 as actually being "version 1" of a new product. Major portions of the product were brand-new code, from the object orientation to the new controls like grids. And, as with most version 1's, it didn't take long for updates to come along. The first one, VFP 3.0a, was released only in the Far

East because the enhancements it offered were related to dealing with the languages used in that part of the world. However, in December of 1995, Microsoft released version 3.0b, which fixed a number of bugs in 3.0, as well as added support for double-byte character sets (the kind used for Japanese and Chinese and other languages that use pictographs rather than strings of characters to make words). Visual FoxPro was one of the first Microsoft products to support this level of internationalization (since Unicode hadn't yet been accepted) and that drove a lot of popularity for FoxPro in the foreign markets. While Microsoft doesn't release sales figures, we've found that FoxPro is very popular worldwide.

A Mac version of 3.0 was released in May 1996. Though it was initially popular, its extreme slowness and hardware hunger, together with Microsoft's lukewarm support, made it something of a niche product. Mac enthusiasts kept waiting for an improved version, but it never appeared and we feel confident that there'll never be another Mac version of VFP.

Whatever Happened to Version 4?

> Glorious, stirring sight! The poetry of motion! The *real* way to travel! The *only* way to travel! Here today—in next week tomorrow! Villages skipped, towns and cities jumped—always somebody else's horizons! O bliss! O poop-poop! O my! O my!
>
> Kenneth Grahame, *The Wind in the Willows*, 1908

VFP 3.0b was barely out the door before the development team started getting serious about what we figured would be VFP 4.0. Wrong again. To bring FoxPro into synch with Microsoft's other development products, the version after 3.0b was 5.0.

Where the first version of VFP focused on improving the programming language, most of the focus for this version went into the developer tools. VFP 5 featured a new debugger, color-coded syntax, an improved editor, and integration with source control tools (especially Microsoft's Visual SourceSafe). There were language improvements, too, of course, including offline views and a bunch of new properties. In addition, VFP 5 can be an Automation server as well as a client.

VFP 5.0 was released in August 1996. Like so many versions before it, an update wasn't too long in the making.

Version 5.0a was released in December 1996. It was primarily a bug-fix release. The most notable thing about it was its inclusion in the Visual Studio product. Visual Studio combined Microsoft's developer products (including Visual Basic, Visual C++, Visual InterDev, Visual SourceSafe and, of course, Visual FoxPro, and more) into a single package. In this first version, pretty much the only common thing about the products in the box was that they were in the same box and shared an installation routine. But the history of the Office product line suggested that the products would grow more together as time passed.

After 5.0a, there were two minor revisions to VFP 5, included in Visual Studio Service Packs. The last version was build 415, with a release date of October 21, 1997.

Now We Are Six

But now I am six, I'm as clever as clever,
So I think I'll be six now, for ever and ever.

A.A. Milne

After the quick turn-around between VFP 3 and VFP 5, things settled down a bit. Visual FoxPro 6.0 was released in 1998 as part of Visual Studio 6 as well as an independent product.

The big changes were focused in several areas. The first primarily affected developers—the ability to address projects programmatically. In addition, a lot of work was done to make VFP a stronger player in the component world. Among other things, VFP 6 was better at hosting ActiveX controls than its predecessors and supported OLE drag and drop. There was lots of other new stuff, too—cool new functions, additional properties, and more.

There still wasn't much besides the packaging that made VFP 6 seem a member of Visual Studio. That turned out to be a foreshadowing of things to come.

Visual Studio 6 had five—count 'em, five—service packs. The first two didn't offer much for VFP developers, but Service Pack 3 was a whopper. In addition to a tremendous number of bug fixes (including a whole bunch for the notorious C0000005 error), it included a new Session class to provide private data sessions without the overhead of a form, the ability to created multi-threaded DLL's, and the ability to compile code on the fly.

The last two service packs focused mostly on bug fixes as well, though there were also enhancements aimed at those running VFP through Windows Terminal Server. The final service pack for VFP 6 gives the product a build number of 8961 and a date of August 17, 2000 (unless you check with the VERSION() function, in which case the date is August 18).

Lucky Seven, or On Our Own

Every man is the architect of his own fortune.

Appius Claudius

If VFP 5 seemed to ship practically before VFP 3 was out of the box, and VFP 6 followed at a reasonable interval thereafter, the wait for VFP 7 seemed endless. Development started right away, and the product was demo'd at conferences as early as Summer '99, and finally released to manufacturing on June 26, 2001.

By the time VFP 7.0 was released, a few things had changed. VFP was no longer part of Visual Studio. That was because of the really big change—Microsoft's introduction of the .NET framework and the conversion of Visual Studio into Visual Studio .NET. Because making VFP a full participant in .NET (that is, having it compile to the Common Language Runtime) would have meant removing or disabling many of the features that make FoxPro FoxPro, the Fox team decided to take another route and pulled the product out of Visual Studio, after discussion with the VFP community.

One of the big wins in this change was the ability to control their own shipping schedule. As of this writing, VFP 7 has been on the market for several months and the first Service Pack is just starting to ship, while Visual Studio .NET is still in beta.

VFP 7's enhancements cover a wide range of territory. There's so much that's new that you could write a book about it. (In fact, Doug and Tamar, along with Kevin McNeish, did—check it out at www.hentzenwerke.com.) VFP 7 includes developer productivity enhancements, such as IntelliSense; language enhancements, including major upgrades to the textmerge sub-language; data enhancements, including database events and an OLE DB driver; and COM and Web enhancements, including the ability to create and consume Web Services. There's also the beginning of a new sub-language for working with XML. In addition to all the new stuff, the long wait gave the Fox team time to include many of the smaller items that VFP developers have been demanding for years, such as word-wrap in grid headers, case-insensitive searching in several places, and much, much more.

By now, lots of things work differently in different versions of VFP. Wherever possible, we point that out and let you know where it's working and where it's broken.

So Now What?

Strengthen me by sympathizing with my strength, not my weakness.

A. Bronson Alcott, *Table Talk*, 1877

The proliferation of sub-languages is a key factor in developing in Visual FoxPro. There are almost always several ways to tackle anything you might want to do. We'll point this out over and over again and let you know where we think one approach is better than others.

The remaining chapters in this section introduce each of Visual FoxPro's major sub-languages. Each covers the basic terminology and the fundamental assumptions you need to understand when dealing with that group of commands.

DBF, FPT, CDX, DBC—Hike!

Let's look at the record.

Alfred E. Smith, 1928

The transition from the FoxPro 2.x model of the universe to the Visual FoxPro mindset was pretty revolutionary on a lot of fronts. While we cringe to use the hackneyed and overused term, the introduction of databases in Visual FoxPro was a major paradigm shift and one that took some getting used to. The introduction of the database container, local and remote views, vast improvements in client-server connectivity, and a slew of new data types, commands, and functions was mind-boggling. We'll try to give you an overview of the data changes here, and refer you to areas where you can get more information throughout the book.

If you're coming from an Xbase background, you might think you're encountering some NewSpeak in Visual FoxPro, but it's all for a good cause. Individual DBF files used to be referred to as "databases" but now, a better term, that used by Visual FoxPro, is to call individual DBF files "tables" and the new DBC a "database container" or just "database" for short. While it's frustrating to try to change terminology you've been using for years, we've found it does lead to greater understanding of the new scheme of Visual FoxPro. Not only that, but the new names bring us in line with the rest of the relational database world.

The Database Container

A database container (DBC file) is a Visual FoxPro table that links together the tables, indexes, views and special code associated with your data. When a table is added to a database, many new features become available. You can define code to validate individual fields or entire records before they are saved, each with its own individual error message. A default value and caption can be specified for each field.

Database containers also allow you to specify *persistent relations*, saving hours of tedium in system development. These relations form the basis for enforcement of relational integrity (RI) at the database level, through the use of stored procedures and record-level triggers. In addition to RI enforcement, our own program code can be triggered on the insertion of a new record, the updating of an existing record, or the deletion of a record. Program code can also run at the field level, specifying default values, validation rules and error messages. Individual fields can have default captions and control classes assigned to them.

All of these features are controlled by the database engine itself, with no need for the developer to write supporting code. Even cooler, all of these features are available when directly editing the table, like in a Browse. This offers far greater reliability and integrity for the data we use.

Better Tables

Cool new features were added to the DBF table, too. A table can be "free," not associated with a particular database, or it can be "contained" within a DBC. This "containership" is not the same as, say, Access's monolithic MDB files—no data from the tables is actually stored within the DBC, just links to the tables, views and other elements. This structure is like the Project Manager, which holds references to source documents but not the documents themselves.

Whether free or contained, tables gained new features: several new field types, the capability to store NULL values within fields, and the ability to flag character or binary data in fields not to be translated between different language versions of Visual FoxPro.

The Database Container

Xbase programmers had gotten into a rut. In every application, in every screen, in every routine, they had to code the same functionality. "Customer.DBF is related to Orders.DBF by the Cust_ID field." "Customer mailing address state needs to be validated against the States.DBF table." "Every time a record is added to the AR table, run the routine to post an audit trail record." If the developer forgot one of these rules in just one place in an application, the consistency of the data was in jeopardy and a long, arduous troubleshooting session was sure to result. To compound the error, it was possible that these rules were in place in all programs, but a database change made interactively by a programmer or user could still be responsible for bad data. What a headache!

Visual FoxPro's competition, the Relational DataBase Management Systems (RDBMSs) and Client-Server systems, developed solutions to these problems. RDBMSs made leaps and bounds in functionality, while the basic data model of Xbase hadn't changed since the development of dBASE. With the release of Visual FoxPro, Microsoft determined it was time for an improvement in the basic model. Visual FoxPro introduced some new terminology and some incredible power in the form of the new DBC databases. As we mentioned above, we used to call each individual DBF file a database, but this terminology is not really consistent with most other database management systems. Besides, those folks with their poky-slow RDBMSs would sneer at us: "That's not a real database—where are the persistent relations? Relational Integrity? Security? Triggers? Stored Procedures?"

It's in there.

Visual FoxPro databases contain and support:

- Tables—DBF files specially marked for use only within a database.

- Long, long, long table and field names (128 characters!).

- Field-level validation functions, default values, error message text and comments.

- Record-level validation.

- Separate trigger functions for insert, update and delete.

- Primary and candidate keys.

- Persistent relationships—define a relation once and it is preserved.

- Local views—updateable cursors spanning multiple tables.

- Remote views—easy access to data stored within other DBMSs.

- Stored procedures—common method code accessible from all procedures within the DBC.

- Database events—events that fire when something is done to the structure of the database or to one of its contained members.

Tables added to a DBC can have long names associated with the table itself and its constituent fields. These names are stored in the DBC.

Triggers and stored procedures are Visual FoxPro code fragments that run automatically when their associated event occurs. Field-level procedures fire when a field is modified. Record-level procedures fire when an attempt is made to commit a new record to a file, update an existing record, or delete a record from a table.

Primary and candidate keys both uniquely distinguish a record from all others. Indexes designated as either of these don't accept duplicate values, but instead generate an error message.

Persistent relationships can be defined once within the DBC, and are then available throughout the system. When tables engaged in a persistent relationship are brought into the data environment of a form or report, the relationship is brought with them. While the relationship can be modified in each place it exists, if the most common relationship is defined within the DBC, far less work is needed in each subsidiary form and report to put a system together.

After creating tables and their relationships within the DBC, run the Relational Integrity Builder by issuing the command Modify Database and then choosing Edit Referential Integrity from the Database menu or the context menu. The Relational Integrity Builder appears. When you are done and choose OK, the builder regenerates the RI stored procedures needed to ensure relational integrity in the database.

Views are cursors on warp speed. A view is defined like a SQL SELECT, allowing you to join multiple tables (and use their persistent relations, if set), select the output fields, and order and group records just like a SELECT. But views are really cool because they can be updateable, so changes made to the records in the resulting cursor can be "written through" onto the tables. This has fantastic implications for manipulating and updating data.

Remote views have all the coolness of the local views just mentioned, with a simple but profound variation—the data is not Visual FoxPro data. Using ODBC, the Connection Designer, and the View Designer, Visual FoxPro has become, in one fell swoop, one of the most powerful clients in a client-server relationship. Even cooler, because both local and remote views can be defined, a Visual FoxPro client-server system can be designed, prototyped and tested on local data stores, and converted to remote data storage when ready to go into production. This is a big attraction to developers who want to work on client-server systems on their client site, but don't want or need to set up servers in their own offices. For more information on using client-server architectures, see "Your Server Will Be With You in a Moment."

Had enough views yet? There's one more variation on the theme: offline views. An offline view is defined as any other, but it allows an operator to actually "check out" a set of records, make changes, and then re-synchronize with the original source. This is a cool feature for "road warriors," anyone who needs to disconnect from the main network, go on the road, do some work, and then reconnect and update the main files.

Database events, added in VFP 7, let you control the structure of a database the way rules and triggers let you control the content. Although they're not turned on by default, once you turn them on for a particular DBC, VFP fires events whenever you perform pretty much any action on the database container or the tables, views, relations and connections it contains. For example, when you create a table, the BeforeCreateTable and AfterCreateTable events fire. When you remove a view, the BeforeDropView and AfterDropView events fire. By putting code into the procedures called by these events (named "DBC_" followed by the event name, such as "DBC_BeforeCreateTable"), you can perform additional actions when these events occur. For example, you could update an audit log whenever a table's structure is modified, or update a security log whenever a user opens a view or table. Even better is the ability to disallow the action by returning .F. in the "before" event. This allows you to do things such as preventing unauthorized users from opening the payroll table and seeing who makes how much money (or worse, changing salaries) or from making changes to stored procedures. See "Mr. Database Event, You're Fired!" later in this section for some ideas of things you can do with database events.

Stored procedures allow programming code for the triggers, rules and database events, as well as any other associated code, to be stored within the DBC. For example, the Referential Integrity Builder's code for performing cascaded updates or deletes is placed in the stored procedures area. This is also where you can place code that otherwise might be a "calculated field," an item wisely not supported within the data model, or a UDF. For example, the routine to format a postal code based on the country is a routine you might include within your main DBC to produce the effect of a calculated field on your customer table. Rather than requesting Customer.PostalCode, you could specify CustPostCode(Customer.PostalCode) and get the built-in code to do the work. This has advantages over a stand-alone UDF because it's always available when the data is. The downside is that this code is only available for the current SET DATABASE database, so stored procedures are not a replacement for stand-alone or procedure libraries. They are, however, still a great place to store database-specific code.

One issue to be aware of with stored procedures is that, while VFP does a great job of locating them, it doesn't make the database containing the procedure the current one. (For example, if the DefaultValue property of a field in a table belonging to a database that isn't the current one calls a stored procedure in that database, VFP will run the proper stored procedure, even if a procedure with the same name exists in the current database.) That is, DBC() returns the name of the current database, which isn't necessarily the one the procedure is in. This may have implications for your code. For example, say a stored procedure called from the DefaultValue property for a primary key field in a table opens the NEXTID table, which contains the next available primary key to use. If that table doesn't exist in the currently selected database, the USE command will fail. The solution is to either specifically SET DATABASE to the desired database in the stored procedure (be sure to SET DATABASE back to the previously selected one at the end of the procedure) or to include the database name in the USE command (USE MYDATABASE!NEXTID).

Compatibility—The Good, the Bad and the Ugly

Consistency is the last refuge of the unimaginative.

Oscar Wilde

The best—and the worst—feature of Xbase is the cross-compatibility (sometimes) of the basic file structures. It's great news if you're trying to tie together an analysis piece in a spreadsheet with a data-entry product written in a front-end language and output via a third-party reporting tool, but it's hell when you're trying to hide the payroll figures.

Cross-compatibility has allowed the development of "clone" products, which perform many of the functions of the original, but either extend the functionality or improve the performance. (Fox was originally an example of both—see "It's Always Been That Way"). In addition, this compatibility allowed the development of a third-party marketplace where add-on products—database repair tools, viewers and translators—could flourish.

The flip side of compatibility is that, like the cop when someone else is speeding, it's never there when you need it. DBFs created by one product (such as FoxPro 2.x) might not be readable in another (FoxBASE+) because of enhancements to the language, and backward (but not forward) compatibility. VFP 7 continues this trend: If you turn on database events for a database, that database and its tables are no longer accessible in earlier versions of VFP or in the VFP ODBC driver (they are accessible with the VFP OLE DB provider, however). Fortunately, you can turn database events back off again, making them accessible once more, so it's not a drastic one-time-only thing.

We will not repeat the file extensions table, found under "File Extensions and File Types" in Help. However, we do recommend you use the Help and a good introductory FoxPro book to review the formats of PJX/PJT projects, SCX/SCT screens, FRX/FRT reports, and LBX/LBT labels.

There are a few file extensions and structures you might not see described elsewhere, but you should be aware of them. If you are called upon to examine (or exhume) applications written in another Xbase language, you might see and need to examine these files:

Extension	Purpose
BAK	Backup files—sometimes DBFs, sometimes something else.
DBT	dBASE III (and later) memo files.
NDX, IDX	Clipper or FoxBASE/FoxPro stand-alone indexes, compact or non-compact.
MDX	dBASE IV compound indexes.
NTX, NDX	Clipper and dBASE indexes, respectively.

A Rose by Any Other Name

You might think a DBF is a DBF, but alas, this is not so. Tables created with older products, such as FoxBASE and dBASE III, have the DBF extension, but may not be fully compatible with Visual FoxPro. Visual FoxPro DBFs cannot be read with these products, either. The first clue you may get is an error when attempting to USE a table. FoxPro determines this by reading the first byte in the DBF file (see the SYS(2029) function). If the byte is wrong, the dreaded "Not a table" message appears.

Visual FoxPro continues the tradition of backward-compatibility, since it can read DBF files created with earlier products. However, in order to facilitate linking with DBC database containers, Visual FoxPro 3.0 introduced changes to the DBF header structure that make Visual FoxPro DBFs unreadable with earlier products. If you need to "regress" a Visual FoxPro table to an earlier format, you can use the TYPE FOX2X keywords with the COPY TO command.

Header Structure, bytes 0 – 31	
Location	**Meaning**
0	DBF Type, reported by SYS(2029).
1, 2, 3	Date last updated as YY, MM, DD. See LUPDATE(). Yes, astute reader, this is a Y2K problem, but was resolved in VFP 6.
4, 5, 6, 7	Number of records, returned by RECCOUNT().

Header Structure, bytes 0 – 31	
8, 9	Location of first data record, also HEADER().
10, 11	Record length, returned by RECSIZE().
12 – 27	Unused.
28	Bit 0: Is there a structural CDX? Bit 1: Is there an associated memo file? Bit 2: Is this file used as a DBC?
29	Code page signature. See CPZero.PRG for translation of these values to code page values.
30, 31	Unused.

Field Records: one for each field in the table, each 32 bytes long	
Offset	**Meaning**
0 – 10	Field name, padded with CHR(0).
11	Field type, same values as TYPE().
12, 13, 14, 15	Starting location of field within record.
16	Length of the field (binary), like FSIZE().
17	Decimal length, if applicable.
18	Field-level flags: Bit 0: Is this a "system" (hidden) field? Bit 1: Is this field nullable? Bit 2: Is this field NOCPTRANS?
19 – 31	Unused.

End of table header	
CHR(13)	Terminating character to indicate end of field information.
263 bytes	"Backlink" containing the path and file name of the database container that owns this table. CHR(0) if a free table.

The tables above show the internal structure of a Visual FoxPro table. Several VFP traits are of key interest. Byte 0, the so-called "signature byte," is always 48 (hexadecimal 0x30) for Visual FoxPro tables. Byte 28 was used in earlier FoxPro versions to designate that a CDX file was used by storing a CHR(01) in that location. This has been expanded in VFP to include whether a memo file is used for memo or general field information and also whether the table is a database container. This is accomplished by adding 2 for memo fields and 4 for DBCs. A similar pattern of "bit flags" occurs for each field record stored in the header. Byte 18 of each field record contains three bit flags: Bit 0 indicates whether the field is displayed or is a hidden ("system") field; bit 1 flags whether the field can store null values; and bit 2 determines whether the field is translated to the current code page or treated as binary data.

Nulls

What is man in nature? Nothing in relation to the infinite, everything in relation to nothing, a mean between nothing and everything.

Blaise Pascal, *Pensées*, 1670

How many answers can there be to a simple question? How about three? "Yes," "No," and "I Don't Know." For years, Xbase had no good way to store the "I Don't Know" answer for many fields. Logical fields were restricted to .T. and .F. A character field left empty was indistinguishable from one for which the value was unknown. Numeric values were treated as zeroes if they were not filled in.

So what, you ask? Who needs them? Consider this case: You ask 10 septuagenarians their age. Eight answer: 72, 78, 73, 76, 70, 79, 72, 74. Two refuse to answer. You plug your eight answers into a field named AGE and issue the command CALCULATE AVG(AGE) for the 10 people. What's your answer? 59.4. Now, who's going to believe that? If, instead, you REPLACE AGE WITH .NULL. for the two people who refused to answer, your average is a far more believable 74.25. Nulls are very useful in many statistical calculations.

Nulls can be used in any field designated as nullable. Fields can be made nullable by checking the box at the right edge of the field description within the Table Designer, or by using the NULL keyword in CREATE TABLE or ALTER TABLE. Fields in remote views from server systems can be defined as nullable by their DBMS server, and this carries over into the view.

Understanding how nulls work within calculations is important. If any of the fields or memory variables within your system is allowed to take on the null value, you must anticipate how this value can affect your calculations, functions and processing. The ISNULL() function can be used to test for the presence of a null value, and the NVL() function can substitute another value (such as zero or a blank) for a value found to be .NULL. Why can't we just test a variable to see if it is equal to .NULL.? This gets back to the concept at the beginning of this section: .NULL. means "I don't know." What's the value of a mathematical expression involving .NULL.? I don't know—.NULL. One half of .NULL.? I don't know—.NULL. Is .NULL. equal to .NULL.? I don't know—.NULL. The first three characters of .NULL.? I don't know—.NULL.

Null values "propagate" through functions—if any value is not known, the result can't be known. We can't test an unknown value against another value (even another unknown) and know if they're equal. Hence the need for an ISNULL() function.

Because null values can propagate through the calculations of a system, we discourage their indiscriminate use. Carefully bracket your use of them to test and properly handle the null values. When a null value is appropriate for the data design, nothing else will do. We applaud the fact that Visual FoxPro has been endowed with this cool feature.

An interesting feature is how nulls are actually stored within a table. Since many of the field types can hold any value from 0x00 to 0xFF in each byte, it is impossible to store null values within the current disk space allocated for each field. Instead, Microsoft created a new field, called _NullFlags. _NullFlags is a "system" field (bit 0 of byte 18 in the field record portion of the file header is set to 1). This field contains a bitmap, one bit for each nullable field in the table, in the physical order of the fields in the table. If a field is to be null, the associated bit is set on (to 1). This seems awfully kludgy to us, but it does work, and reliably: Physically rearranging the order of fields in the table, or programmatically using only some fields with SET FIELDS TO doesn't seem to trip it up. There doesn't seem to be any way within the language to access _NullFlags directly (our hacker instincts made us try), which is probably all for the best. However, having hidden, system fields in a table, which don't show up in a DISPLAY STRUCTURE, and which can trip up your space calculations (see the reference sections on AFIELDS() and RECSIZE()) is not what we consider a great leap forward. In this era of "what do you know and when did you know it," a little more in the way of full disclosure should be expected.

Take a Memo, Miss Jones

Memo and general fields store their data in a separate file, the FPT. It makes sense, since memo field data can be of varied lengths, from an empty note to a monstrous embedded WinWord dissertation. Storing this data in a separate, non-fixed-length format should minimize the use of disk space. However, poor tuning or cleanup practices can lead to severe memo field bloat. Here are two tips to minimize the "out of disk space" blues.

Each time data is written to a memo field, new blocks are added to the end of the FPT, data is added to them, and then the pointer contained within the memo header is updated to point at the new data. The old data remains within the file, and the space it occupied is not reclaimed. Over a period of time, memo fields can grow beyond control without containing that much information. This is the dreaded "memo field bloat." The ADDITIVE clause of the REPLACE command does not alleviate this, it just makes it easier to tack one more sentence onto the end of a long memo—internally, the same process occurs.

In development, you can reclaim the space with the PACK MEMO command. This packs the file in place, replacing the memo field with a far more compact one. However, as we discuss in "Commands to Use Only Interactively," the PACK command leaves the developer in the dark if something goes wrong in mid-flight. See that section for suggested work-arounds.

VFP provides the SET BLOCKSIZE command to allow you to tune and optimize your use of memo fields. BLOCKSIZE accepts a numeric argument: Passing it 1 through 32 creates blocks of 512 bytes times that number; a number greater than 32 creates blocks of that number of bytes. A newer option, SET BLOCKSIZE TO 0, stores the memo blocks as individual bytes, rather than as blocks. It seems to us that this method wastes the least "slack space" at the end of each memo, but might in some circumstances lead to greater overhead in processing and reading millions of teeny little blocks. We're not sure where the breakpoint is between the speed of I/O and the speed of the processor overhead, and like many other benchmark items, we encourage you to try it in your environment with your machines and data, to see what works out best for you.

dBASE III had a somewhat different method of storing the memo fields (general fields did not exist) in the DBT file. FoxPro can read and write DBT files, but should you choose to COPY a table containing a DBT memo, the new file will have an FPT memo field instead.

But We Speak Icelandic Here

Nothing could be worse than porting an application to a new platform, tweaking all the forms and programs to handle the new (or missing) features, and then discovering the data is unreadable. But this was exactly what happened to many FoxPro developers as they brought their information from DOS to Windows in the 2.5 release. What happened?

What happened was code pages. A code page is the translation table that the computer uses to translate each of the characters stored on disk—8 little bits, storing one of 256 different patterns—into the single character we're used to seeing on the screen. While some of these codes are pretty standardized, people who speak any one of the thousands of languages other than English use a different code page to represent their characters. Code pages can be loaded and manipulated in DOS using the NLSFUNC, CHCP and MODE commands. A typical U.S. code page is 437 for DOS and 1252 for Windows.

In most database applications, code page translation would be a one-step, pain-in-the-neck translation from the "old" way to the "new" way, but FoxPro supports access from multiple code pages simultaneously. Remarkably, it accomplishes this feat, pretty much transparently, through the use of a code page byte, stored within DBF headers and also stored as part of compiled code.

That sounds like the happy end to the story, right? We should all ride off into the sunset now. Well, it's not always that simple, pardner.

What happens if you're storing data in a field in some sort of a packed or encrypted format, where you use all 256-byte combinations, and you need to share that data with someone whose code page differs from yours? Well, without any other actions, the other user will read your data and see different numbers, translated courtesy of the Visual FoxPro engine, automatically and transparently. It's not a bug, it's a feature.

Luckily, there's a solution to this one. As part of defining a table at creation (see CREATE TABLE) or while maintaining a table (see ALTER TABLE), a field can be flagged as NOCPTRANS, which tells the FoxPro engine "Hands off! Don't mess with this one."

Note that the NOCPTRANS flag stored within the table itself is automatically set for Double, Integer, Datetime and Currency fields, even though it can't (and shouldn't!) be set ON or OFF programmatically for these field types. That's because the values in these fields are stored in a binary/packed format, and translation would lead to some awfully funny numbers.

Date Math

Date math is really cool. Amaze your friends, astound your competition and baffle the crowd with your ability to glibly say, "Of course, everyone knows there have been over 280,000 days since the signing of the Magna Carta, and in that time, blah blah blah..." while simply calculating:

```
? date() - {^1297-03-28}
```

A note about the curly braces above. One of the more common questions we hear is about these funny looking things, and why expressions such as:

```
{06/ + ALLTRIM(STR(RAND ()*30)) + /90}
```

return empty dates. The key to understanding these braces is to understand that they are delimiters, wrapping around a set of characters and giving FoxPro an idea of what's contained inside, but they are not functions with the power to evaluate their contents. Just as double and single quotes delimit a character expression, curly braces designate a date or datetime expression. Use a conversion function, such as CTOD() or DATE(), to evaluate a character function and return a date.

The second strange thing most veteran Xbase developers will notice is the prefixed caret and the strange ordering of YYYY-MM-DD. This is the strict date format, stealthily introduced into the product in Visual FoxPro 5.0. In VFP 6, the SET STRICTDATE command provides us with some ability to audit existing code and detect potential Year 2000 compatibility problems. See "Strictly Speaking..." below for more details.

There are practical uses for this neat technology, too. Calculating 30-60-90-day aging on an account is a piece of cake. A number of days can be added or subtracted from a date, or one date can be subtracted from another to return the difference in days. The various parts of the date can be returned using the DAY(), MONTH() and YEAR() functions for numeric calculation or CMONTH() and CDOW() functions for character display. Dates can be converted to character format (DTOC()) or from character to date (CTOD()) relatively easily.

In Visual FoxPro, dates are stored within tables as eight characters of the format YYYYMMDD. Obviously, this practically limits dates to the range of Year Zero to 9999, but that should be long enough for most of the business processes we hope to model in VFP.

A few cautions are in order. In the "good old days," we often extracted portions of a date using substring functions, modified it, and plunked it back into the value, as in the following:

```
* BAD CODE *
* Calculate the last day of the month for a supplied date dDate
nMonth=VAL(LEFT(DTOC(dDate),2)) + 1  && increment the month
nYear = VAL(RIGHT(DTOC(dDate),2))    && extract the year
if nMonth = 13
  nMonth = 1
  nYear = nYear + 1
endif
* Now create a new date, the first of next month,
* and decrement it one day
* to get the last date of the current month
return CTOD(STR(nMonth,2)+"/01/"+STR(nYear,2)) -1
```

Pretty clever, huh? This worked great for many small U.S.-centric companies in the 1980s, but with the internationalization of trade, this code is far too bigoted to make it in the 21st century. The assumptions (and we all know what an assumption does, right?) that the first two characters of a date are the month, the last are the year and the middle is the day, all separated by slashes, are Stone Age logic. Check out the SET DATE command—you can bet that your branch offices in Toronto and London have. Make no assumptions about the internal position of digits within a date. Let's try this again. Trapped in a dBase III world, we could just rewrite the function, preserving the state of SET DATE, SET MARK and SET CENTURY, changing them as needed, dissecting and reassembling a date, and then resetting the SET variables again, but there's a far more graceful way, using newer FoxPro functions:

```
* Dlast() - Return the last day of the month from supplied dDate
dNewDate = GOMONTH(dDate,1) && Add a month to the date
dNewDate = dNewDate - DAY(dNewDate) && Subtract number of days in month
return dNewDate
```

On the Other Hand...

You can do some really dumb things with date calculations. The date and datetime field types are really meant for storing contemporary dates and times, and are inappropriate for storing date/time fields in historical, archeological, astronomical or geological time spans. It's overly precise to try to store the start of the Jurassic era in a date field, and in fact, it's impossible to store dates Before the Common Era (BCE) or BC. Since no one really seems to know what time it is, even dates as recent as four centuries ago make the precision of the date math functions questionable.

For example, GOMONTH() won't go back farther than the year 1753, the year after England took on the "Gregorian shift" of the calendar, jumping 11 days overnight and adding the bizarre leap-year rules of "every four, except in years ending in 00's, except those divisible by 400." Okay, got it? Sheesh. Star-dates had better be easier than this. So GOMONTH() works for Mozart, but falls apart for Bach.

It's not just GOMONTH(), either. Adding and subtracting enough days yields wild results too. For example: {^1999-7-5} − 730246 yields "03/00/0000". Yes, DAY()

verifies this date is Day Zero, and YEAR() says Year Zero. Hmmph. Stick with the recent past, present and future, and you should be okay.

It's About Time, It's About Dates...

My object all sublime
I shall achieve in time—
To make the punishment fit the crime.

Sir W. S.Gilbert, *The Mikado*, 1885

A new field type, datetime, was introduced in VFP 3. While primarily intended as a compatibility feature for ease of use with similar fields in tables in a client-server environment, datetimes offer the intrepid FoxPro programmer some neat opportunities.

Datetime is stored as an eight-byte field. Supposedly the first four bytes store the date and the last four store the time. We haven't hacked this one apart, but we'd love to hear from the hackers who have.

Like currency fields stored without a unit of measure, we suggest there may be problems of determining just when this time occurred—there is no "time zone" designation. Is this GMT, Eastern Daylight Savings Time, or Bering? If you anticipate dealing with a database with multiple time zones, we suggest you consider a region-to-GMT offset table and store all times as absolute GMT datetimes for ease of calculation.

Datetimes, like dates, can be specified explicitly by using curly braces. As we explain above, delimiters don't work as conversion functions, evaluating the expression given to them, but rather just indicate constants. Nonetheless, Visual FoxPro is pretty clever, accepting any of the standard date delimiters (slash, dot or hyphen) and either 12- or 24-hour formatted time, regardless of the settings of SET MARK TO or SET HOURS. The order of the month, day and year, however, must be the same as that set by SET DATE. The only exception to that is the use of the strict date form described above. In that case, the order of the date or datetime is always in the form:

{^YYYY-MM-DD[,][HH[:MM[:SS]][A|P]]}

That syntax diagram also is a little misleading. It appears that you could supply only an hours component and the datetime would resolve. But, in fact, you get an error message. If you include only the hours component, you must either include the comma separating the date from the time, or follow the hours with a colon to have VFP interpret your datetime constant without error. And a bit of trivia: The smallest expression to generate an empty datetime is {/:}.

Strictly Speaking...

Mere facts and names and dates communicate more than we suspect.

Henry David Thoreau, *Journals*

Visual FoxPro 5 introduced the idea of "strict" date entry with the cleverly named StrictDateEntry property. The property allows "loose" data entry where we depend upon the machine to interpret the varieties of hyphens, dashes and slashes we throw at it. At the same time, the Fox team added a curveball: a new format for loose StrictDateEntry that allows the data-entry operator to override the preformatted date sequence by preceding the date with a caret. Following the caret, the date is always interpreted in a consistent manner: year, month, day, and, in the case of datetime values, hour, minute and second.

This innovation in VFP 5 laid the groundwork for the introduction in VFP 6 of the SET STRICTDATE command. This command, essential for ensuring Year 2000 compliance in code, generates errors at compile time, and optionally at run time, reporting that code contains dates that can be ambiguous. Since the ordering of day, month and year is determined by SET DATE, both in the run-time and development environments, "constants" (as well as expressions using the date conversion functions like CTOD()) can be interpreted in more than one way. The SET STRICTDATE command lets you flag these variable constants unless they, too, now use the strict date format of caret, year, month, day. For conversion from string to date or datetime, the DATE() and DATETIME() functions have been beefed up.

Float, Double, Integer, Numeric and Currency—What's in a Number

There are a number (sorry) of different fields in Fox, all of which seem to store the same or similar data. The reason for this is primarily backward and sideways compatibility with previous Fox and Xbase products. There are some differences, however...

Float

Seems to be same as numeric. Float exists to allow compatibility with other database products that treated numeric and float fields differently. Visual FoxPro treats them no differently internally.

Double

Always stores as length 8, but allows you to change decimal places from zero to 18. A fixed format used primarily for client-server compatibility, it's manipulated internally the same as any other numeric by FoxPro, but stored differently.

Integer

Integer was probably one of the most useful data types introduced in Visual FoxPro 3.0. Stored in only four bytes on disk, the field has a range from –2147483647 to plus 2147483647. If you need to track whole numbers only, this can be a compact and efficient way to do it. We find these fields to be ideal as primary keys, since they're small and form smaller indexes, and also are easy to manipulate and increment. They're also the fastest way to join tables in a SQL SELECT.

Numeric

A numeric field allows up to 20 numeric digits to be entered, but one space is occupied by the decimal point, if used. Microsoft describes accuracy as 16 digits, but 14 seems closer to the truth. Check this out:

```
lnNumeric = 98765432109876543210  && Here's 20 digits
* In VFP 3, you'll see these numbers with no digits
* to the left of the decimal point and with exponents
* of 20. In VFP 5, Microsoft adopted the more common
* syntax of making the mantissa a single digit shown below:
? lnNumeric                    && displays 9.8765432109876E+19
? STR(lnNumeric)               && displays 9.876E+19
? STR(lnNumeric,16)            && displays 9.876543210E+19
? STR(lnNumeric,20)            && displays 9.8765432109876E+19
? STR(lnNumeric,25)            && displays 9.876543210987639000E+19
```

Numeric fields are stored in character format, such as ".98765432109876E+20".

Currency

> Only one fellow in ten thousand understands the currency question, and we meet him every day.

> Kin Hubbard

A currency field is a fixed numeric field, always stored as eight bytes, with four decimal places. These fields are marked by default as NOCPTRANS, since the data is packed. Currency is a funny field type. Just as datetime stores a time without a time zone, currency stores a value without a unit. Also like datetime, this field type was introduced primarily for compatibility with client-server databases. But is this currency in dollars, euros, or yen? An international application needs to know if it's running in Zurich or New Delhi.

Like datetime, currency introduces some new functions and delimiters into the language. NTOM() and MTON() convert numerics to currency and vice versa (think "money" rather than "currency"). The dollar-sign delimiter preceding a numeric literal forces the type to currency.

Math involving currency and other numerics introduces a new kink. What's the result of multiplying two currency values—a numeric or a currency value? What about trigonometry on these values? We could engage in quite a diatribe on the meaning of unitless and "unit-ed" variables being processed together, but it doesn't really matter—Microsoft has a method to its madness, and while it might be different from what we would've come up with, it works under most circumstances: Basic four-function math (addition, subtraction, multiplication and division) involving currency gives results in currency. Exponentiation and trigonometry yield numerics.

Logical

"Contrariwise," continued Tweedledee, "if it was so, it might be; and if it were so, it would be; but as it isn't, it ain't. That's logic."

Lewis Carroll, *Through the Looking-Glass*, 1872

Not too much has changed with the logical field type since the FoxPro 2.x days. With the introduction of NULLs, described above, a logical field can contain a third value, .NULL., as well as the standard values of .T. and .F. (Okay, it's true they could contain a fourth state of BLANK, but we strongly argue against ever using it.) Logical fields take up one byte in a table, even though they really only need a single bit. With the data compression Microsoft implemented in double, datetime, currency and integer fields, as well as shrinking the size of the memo and general fields from 10 bytes to four, we're surprised they didn't try to implement some sort of byte-and-offset addressing for storing multiple logical fields in a single byte as well.

Hip Hip Array!

Arrays are not truly a different type of variable, but they are a method of aggregating several values, of the same or different types, into one place. Arrays make it easier to handle things like disk directories (ADIR()), field descriptions (AFIELDS()), and object properties, events and methods (AMEMBERS()). Arrays can be used to hold data on its way to and from tables—SCATTER, GATHER and INSERT all support array clauses. Understanding how to manipulate these arrays, especially how they are referenced by different functions, is an important aspect of Visual FoxPro programming.

Arrays come in two flavors—one-dimensional and two-dimensional—distinguished by the number of subscripts supplied with them. However, internally, both array types are stored the same way, and functions that work with one type work with the other as well. This can lead to some confusion. Suppose you create an array:

```
LOCAL ARRAY aRay[2,5]
```

We would view this array as a table of two rows and five columns, and on the whole, Visual FoxPro would be willing to go along with us on this. But if we try to locate a value that we know is in the third element of the second row by using the ASCAN() function:

```
aRay[2,3] = "My value"
? ASCAN(aRAY,"My value")
```

Visual FoxPro returns 6! Well, what would you expect? 2? 3? Since Visual FoxPro is limited to returning a single value from a function, it returns the ordinal number of the element in the array. We can use the function ASUBSCRIPT() to get the appropriate row and column values:

```
? ASUBSCRIPT(aRay,ASCAN(aRay,"My value"),1)   && returns 2
? ASUBSCRIPT(aRay,ASCAN(aRay,"My value"),2)   && returns 3
```

(Actually, starting in version 7, ASCAN() can optionally return the row where it found the value. See the Reference section for details.)

Even more interesting, we can just use the single digit returned. The fact is that FoxPro is willing to use any combination of rows and columns we supply to reference an element, as long as we do not exceed the defined number of rows:

```
? aRay[6]     && Displays "My value"
? aRay[1,6]   && Also displays "My value"
? aRay[2,3]   && "My value" again
? aRay[6,1]   && Whoa! Errors with "Subscript is outside defined range"
```

You can determine the number of rows and columns of an array by using the ALEN() function.

You can change the dimensions of an array on the fly by issuing another DIMENSION, LOCAL ARRAY or PUBLIC statement, depending on the scope of your variable. Redimensioning does not erase the values of the array, but it can rearrange them in some pretty funny ways. The values originally assigned to the array in ordinal form are reassigned to the new array with the same ordinal values. This can result in some pretty useless-looking arrays, with values slipping diagonally across the columns. Instead, try out our aColCopy() function (under ACOPY() in the Reference section) for a better way to do this.

Many functions also redimension arrays automatically to fit the contents of the function. As a general rule, functions redimension arrays to fit only those values the function returns. Typically, the array is created or redimensioned only if the function has something to put in it. We note in the Reference section where functions don't follow these thumbrules.

The array manipulations you'll often want to do are inserting and deleting rows from the array, and you'll probably suspect that AINS() and ADEL() are the functions to do this. Foolish mortal. AINS() does, in fact, create a row of new values (all initialized to .F.), but it does this by pushing the following rows down, until the last falls off the array into the bit bucket. ADEL() reverses the process, causing rows of elements to move up over the deleted one, and leaving an empty row at the bottom. In both cases, a call to DIMENSION or its equivalent before or after the function, respectively, will complete what you need to do. Again, more information on this, and the far less simple column operations, is available in the Reference section, under the associated functions, as well as in the overview "Array Manipulation."

Passing an Array

An array can only be passed to another routine using explicit referencing. That means the array name must be preceded with the symbol "@" when passed as a parameter. Forgetting to append this symbol causes only the first element of the array to be passed; this is one of our favorite programming omissions that drive us mad trying to troubleshoot.

An array passed by reference, as we explain in "Xbase Xplained," really has only one occurrence in memory, and all changes performed by called routines have their effect on this one array. Caution is called for.

Returning an Array

VFP 7 added the ability to return an array from a function by again using the "@" symbol and the array name in the RETURN statement. However, there are some gotchas with this technique; see RETURN in the Reference section for details.

International Settings: Using the Control Panel

Henry IV's feet and armpits enjoyed an international reputation.

Aldous Huxley

There's a wonderful though little-used resource for international settings—dates, times, currency, etc.—available through the Windows Control Panel, in the Regional Settings applet. These dialogs are available to your users, and you don't have to maintain the code! What you do have to do is check to see if your users have modified them. Check out the Registry under HKEY_CURRENT_USER\Control Panel\International and modify the behavior of your application appropriately. See SET SYSFORMATS for more information on using the user's Windows settings.

General Fields: Object Linking and Embedding

I drink to the general joy of the whole table.

William Shakespeare, *Macbeth*

General fields are Visual FoxPro's implementation of the technology formerly known as "Object Linking and Embedding," then "OLE," and then "Active" something or other. While the marketeers don't seem to be happy with any name they've thought of so far, the idea of this portion of the implementation remains the same: Provide a portal between FoxPro and some other application (the "OLE Server") and store the information about that link and the data shared here.

OLE, er, Active, er, this stuff is no cakewalk. For many of the gory details, see the section "Active Something" as well as the individual reference sections for APPEND GENERAL, MODIFY GENERAL, OLEControl and OLEBoundControl.

A couple of cautions here. General fields contain several pieces of information: All contain "display data," and have either a path to data (for linked data) or the embedded data itself. The "display" or "presentation" data is a raw BMP that Visual FoxPro uses to show that the field is occupied. In Word 2.0, this was the big blue W logo. Word 6.0 allowed you to store a representation of the first page of a document. MS Graph showed—surprise!—the graph. But some OLE severs can be a problem. Graphics servers, which store pictures, are usually forced to provide Visual FoxPro with a BMP for presentation data, even if their graphic is in another format (like the far more compact JPG format). This BMP can be HUGE; a large image rendered in 24-bitplanes (roughly a bazillion colors) can take megabytes of space. This space is used even if the data is only *linked* to the field! Anticipate a large amount of storage space if you choose to link very large or very high-resolution documents. Consider other techniques (such as just storing the path and file names in a character field, and using a cursor to hold one image at a time) if disk space is a concern.

One last note about general fields. A general field is nothing more than a special form of the memo field that contains binary data, including a "wrapper" around the data that tells FoxPro who to call to manipulate this data—the OLE server. When data is called up and changed and saved back to the memo field, new blocks of the memo field are allocated for the new data, and the old blocks are internally marked as not used. These old blocks are never reused. What happens over a period of time is that the memo file will grow and grow and grow. To alleviate this problem, you can consider using the PACK MEMO command to shrink the file (but only after reading the cautions in "Commands Never to Use") or use the equivalent COPY/SELECT, RENAME, DELETE routine to refresh the file.

Mr. Database Event, You're Fired!

Database events fire whether you do something visually or programmatically, in a run-time or development environment, through VFP code or through ADO. So, they're sort of like triggers, except they fire in response to things you do to a database or its members rather than the contents of a table. Think of them as "Events for the Data Definition Language" instead of "Events for the Data Manipulation Language." See "Database Events" and related topics in the Reference section for complete details on the events that are available and how each works.

Let's explore some ideas for where you might use database events. There are two different kinds of things you can use them for: development tools and run-time behavior.

Development Tools

Database events can be used in a number of tools that can make development easier and more productive. Examples include enforcing standards, handling renamed objects, and team development.

Your organization might have standards for naming tables, views and fields (for example, perhaps all tables in the Accounts Receivable database should start with "AR", the first character of all field names must represent the data type or be a four-letter abbreviation for the table, and so on). You may also require the Comment property of every table, view and field to be filled in. Rather than writing an auditing tool you have to remember to run, you could create database events that automatically warn if the standard isn't followed. The following events are all candidates for this: AfterAddTable, AfterCreateTable, AfterModifyTable, BeforeRenameTable, AfterCreateView, AfterModifyView, BeforeRenameView, AfterCreateConnection, AfterModifyConnection, and BeforeRenameConnection.

While changing the name of a table is easy, it isn't so easy to track down every place the former name is used. Stored procedures, forms, reports and PRG files can all reference the former table name. You can put code in AfterRenameTable (as well as AfterRenameView and AfterRenameConnection) to open a project, go through all files in the project, look for the former name (the cPreviousName parameter passed to the event contains this), and either replace it with the new name (contained in the cNewName parameter) or at least print the locations or add them to the Task List so a developer can make the changes manually. Because a database might be used by more than one project, you might have to provide a way to track which projects to process.

Handling renamed fields and indexes is trickier; because AfterModifyTable and AfterModifyView don't tell you what changes were made, you have to store the previous structure somewhere (such as in a cursor in BeforeModify events or in metadata), and then in the AfterModify events try to figure out what happened. It's not easy; a renamed field looks no different than if you were to delete one field and add another.

When anything in the database changes (such as tables or views being added, removed or altered), database event code could automatically send an email to every member of the development team informing them of the changes. You could also log who changed something and when, and even prompt the user to enter a short comment about the change.

Besides these serious uses, imagine the fun you can have with your fellow developers when you put code in various "before" events that returns .F. to prevent them from doing something or makes fun of them in some way (think of the French knight mocking King Arthur in "Monty Python and the Holy Grail"; sound files are available for download from various Web sites). Sit back and watch them try to alter the structure of a table, remove a table, and so on. For even more fun, make the events time-specific, such as only between 3 p.m. and 4 p.m. on Thursdays. April 1 is a particularly good day to wreak havoc!

Run-time Behavior

Database events can also be used in a run-time environment to provide functionality VFP developers have requested for years. Some uses include table and database security and hacker prevention.

Returning .F. from BeforeOpenTable prevents a table or view from being opened. Obviously, you don't want to do this for every table and view under all conditions (otherwise, the database would be rendered useless), but opening tables based on user security may make sense for some applications. Here's an example:

```
PROCEDURE DBC_BeforeOpenTable(cTableName)
IF UPPER(cTableName) = "PAYROLL"
    RETURN gcUserName == "ADMIN"
ELSE
    RETURN .T.
ENDIF
```

This code assumes that a global variable named gcUserName contains the name of the logged-in user, and prevents anyone but ADMIN from opening the PAYROLL table.

As with table security, an entire database can be secured by conditionally returning .F. from the OpenData event.

Sometimes, we need to prevent someone from altering the structure of a table or view. We're not so worried about malicious hackers as those users who embody the expression "a little knowledge is a dangerous thing." Such users could be using a development copy of VFP or ADO via Access or Excel. To prevent this, return .F. in the BeforeModifyTable and BeforeModifyView events.

To prevent someone from changing or disabling the events for the DBC (which would allow them to get around everything that database events are providing for you), return .F. in the BeforeModifyProc and BeforeAppendProc events, and in BeforeDBSetProp if the property being changed is "DBCEvents" or "DBCEventFileName." This approach isn't foolproof, since someone with a development copy of VFP can USE the DBC (that is, open it as a table, which is what it really is), modify the code in the Code memo of the StoredProceduresSource record, and then close and COMPILE DATABASE. To prevent this, use a separate PRG file for the database event code, and build that PRG into the application's EXE so it can't be viewed or altered. The downside is that now the DBC can be opened only when the EXE is running, preventing its access from ADO. In some situations, that may not be a bad thing, though.

To prevent someone from seeing the code in the stored procedures (for example, because it contains proprietary information), return .F. in the BeforeModifyProc and BeforeCopyProc events.

Conclusion

File storage within Visual FoxPro is similar to earlier versions of FoxPro, but with some powerful enhancements provided by the Database Container. New fields and field capabilities have been added. VFP 7 still retains the trademark backward compatibility, allowing it to read all dBase III and Fox tables. Some compatibility with older versions has been lost, but we feel the benefits of the new features far outweigh the limitations, and that workarounds are available for most of the incompatibilities.

Xbase Xplained

> To him who looks upon the world rationally, the world in its turn presents a rational aspect. The relation is mutual.
>
> Georg Wilhelm Friedrich Hegel, *Philosophy of History*, 1832

FoxPro's oldest heritage is its Xbase heritage. As we said in "It's Always Been That Way," Xbase has a long and varied history. This section explains the basic language concepts that derive from that history.

dBase was originally conceived primarily as an interactive language. Because of this, many of the older commands' default behaviors focus on interactive results, with optional clauses available to use the command programmatically.

Do You Work Here?

The nature of a relational database like FoxPro is that you need to work with many tables at once. You couldn't get much work done if you had access to only one table at a time. Xbase handles this by providing multiple work areas, each capable of handling one table and its related indexes.

The available number of work areas has been one of the carrots manufacturers have used in the Xbase competition. In ancient Xbase history, there were two work areas. By dBase III Plus and FoxBase+, 10 work areas were provided and each table could be opened with up to seven index files. In FoxPro 2.5, the number of available work areas went up to 225. Since you'd run out of file handles long before you could open 225 different tables, you'd think that would be sufficient for anyone's needs, even if some tables are open several times. But Visual FoxPro raised the stakes again, providing 32,767 work areas. Yes, 32K work areas! (In fact, there are 32,767 work areas per data session. More on data sessions later.) While this seems extravagant (in fact, ridiculous) at first glance, it leaves room for a lot of things going on behind the scenes that weren't there before. Visual FoxPro's buffering and multiple data sessions require a lot more work areas than ever before. Remember that each file still needs one or more file handles (See "Hardware and Software Recommendations"), so while you can open the same tables many times, you still can't open 400 tables at once—not that you'd ever want to.

It's also interesting that Visual FoxPro's databases, a much newer concept than tables, don't require work areas. We guess Microsoft found a better way to handle this internally. There's no documented limit on how many databases you can open simultaneously, but databases require file handles (three, actually—one each for DBC, DCT and DCX) so there is presumably some limit, even in the most recent versions of Windows.

Work areas are numbered from 1 to 32767 and can be referenced by number, as in:

```
SELECT 27
```

Doing so is usually a bad idea, except when hacking from the Command Window. Similarly, it is poor form to refer to the first 10 work areas by the letters A–J, a historical vestige of the days when there were only 10 work areas.

Once a table is open in a work area, you should refer to that work area by the table's alias, like this:

```
SELECT Customer
```

Before that, it doesn't matter which work area you use. You can get to the lowest available work area by issuing:

```
SELECT 0
```

or to the highest available work area (why? we dunno, but you can) with:

```
SELECT SELECT(1)
```

To open a table in the lowest available work area, there are two choices. As above, you can use SELECT 0:

```
SELECT 0
USE MyTable
```

or you can incorporate the 0 in the USE command:

```
USE MyTable IN 0
```

There is one subtle (and undocumented) difference between those two sequences. The first leaves you in the work area containing the newly opened MyTable. The second leaves you in whatever work area you were in before. It opens the table, then returns to the current work area. We can't tell you how many times we've fallen into this trap.

As the previous paragraph implies, you're "in" one work area at a time. That is, one work area is always current. You can refer to fields of the table open in that work area without aliasing them. Also, many commands are scoped to the current work area.

To make a different work area current, you SELECT it, preferably by using the alias of the table open in that work area:

```
SELECT MyOtherTable
```

To close the table open in a work area, issue USE with no alias:

```
USE   && Closes the table in the current work area
```

Or specify an alias to close that one:

```
USE IN MyTable   && Closes the table opened with alias "MyTable"
```

This last example shows it's actually less and less necessary to switch to a particular work area. In recent versions, virtually all of the Xbase commands have an IN clause that lets you specify to which work area a command applies. Rather than saving the current work area, selecting another, doing whatever you need to do, and then returning to the original work area, you can just do the task IN the relevant work area.

So What's Your Point?

Xbase (unlike SQL) is a record-based language. Just as Xbase always believes one work area is the "current" area, one record in each table is also "current." So, in each open table, Xbase maintains a record pointer. The record pointer always points to a single record. Many commands operate on the record pointed to.

Lots of Xbase commands move the record pointer. Some are specifically designed to move the pointer, while others do it more or less as a side effect. The second type is discussed in the next section, "Scope, FOR, WHILE (and Santa) Clauses."

Commands designed to move the record pointer can be further divided into two groups: those that move it based on position and those that move it based on content. GO and SKIP fall into the position category, while LOCATE, CONTINUE and SEEK are in the content category.

Both GO and SKIP are affected by an active index order. If you've SET ORDER TO something other than 0, GO TOP and GO BOTTOM move to the top and bottom of the current order, respectively. (However, they can do so pretty slowly. See "Faster Than a Speeding Bullet" in "Franz and Other Lists" for hints on doing this better.)

Only GO <n> is absolute. It moves to the record whose record number is <n>, regardless of any order. This, of course, makes GO <n> nearly useless. Its only real utility is in returning the record pointer to a previous position after a command has moved it. For example:

```
nHoldRec=RECNO()
COUNT FOR category="Oddities"
GO nHoldRec
```

Unfortunately, even that simple piece of code won't always work. If the record pointer is at EOF() before the COUNT, the GO fails. Instead, you have to do it like this:

```
nHoldRec=IIF(EOF(),0,RECNO())
COUNT FOR category="Oddities"
IF nHoldRec=0
   GO BOTTOM
   SKIP
ELSE
   GO nHoldRec
ENDIF
```

Except in the situation above, stay away from referring to records by their record numbers. Record numbers are a volatile thing. If you delete some records and pack the table, the record numbers change. The real point is that you don't need record numbers. FoxPro has plenty of other tools you can use to find a particular record.

Scope, FOR, WHILE (and Santa) Clauses

Xbase commands operate on groups of records—a group may be as small as one record or as large as an entire table. There are three ways to specify which records are affected by an Xbase command. They are Scope, the FOR clause and the WHILE clause. All three reflect the record order-based nature of Xbase processing.

Almost all the record processing commands that originated in Xbase accept all three clauses. The group includes DELETE, RECALL, REPLACE, LIST, DISPLAY, AVERAGE, COUNT, SUM, CALCULATE, LABEL FORM, REPORT FORM, SCAN and LOCATE, as well as some others.

The next few sections describe each of the record-selection mechanisms. Then, "Combining the Clauses" talks about their interactions.

A Grand Scope

The designers of Xbase provided several ways of choosing a group of records based on their position in the table: choosing all the records in a table, choosing a single record, choosing several records in sequence, and choosing all the records from the present location to the end of the table. They grouped these four choices together and called them "scope." You specify them by including the appropriate clause, respectively: ALL, RECORD <n>, NEXT <n>, or REST. Note that <n> differs in each context: It means a record number for RECORD, but means "how many" for NEXT. Also, be aware that NEXT and REST are interpreted according to the current index order. Commands that accept a scope clause use a default scope if no scope term is included. Those commands that have the potential to be destructive default to NEXT 1. Commands that can't do any damage to the database's records generally default to ALL. For example, DELETE and REPLACE have a default scope of NEXT 1, while LIST and REPORT default to ALL.

You'll find that you use ALL and NEXT quite a bit, while RECORD and REST seem somewhat antiquated in a set-based world. In fact, there are some good times to use REST, but we haven't used RECORD in years.

FOR Better or FOR Worse

The FOR clause allows a command to process records based on content, regardless of the position of the record in the table.

Prior to FoxPro 2.0, this made a FOR clause something to be avoided at all costs. With Rushmore optimization, FOR clauses can be very fast. (That's "FOR better.") However, if a FOR expression can't be optimized, it can ruin performance. (That's "FOR worse.")

FOR accepts a logical expression and processes all records for which that expression is true. This makes it just the thing for getting a list of all customers in the U.K.:

```
BROWSE FOR Country = "U.K."
```

or for replacing all instances of a misspelled string with the correctly spelled version:

```
REPLACE LastName WITH "Quayle" FOR LastName="Quail" AND NOT IsBird
```

Note that giving REPLACE a FOR (or WHILE) clause changes its default scope to ALL.

Any command including a FOR clause may be optimizable. See "Faster Than a Speeding Bullet" for hints on how to optimize these commands.

WHILE Away the Hours

WHILE is used when records are already ordered the way you want. It processes records starting with the current record and continues until it encounters a record that doesn't meet the condition.

WHILE is handy for things like totaling all the detail records of an invoice:

```
SELECT Detail
SET ORDER TO InvId
SEEK Invoice.InvId
SUM DetAmt WHILE InvId=Invoice.InvId TO InvTotal
```

or changing the area code for all the people with a particular phone exchange:

```
SELECT People
* Tag Phone is on the actual phone number field;
* area code is a separate field.
SET ORDER TO Phone
SEEK "555"
REPLACE AreaCode WITH "610" WHILE Phone="555"
```

Our first version of the "SEEK, then REPLACE WHILE" example ran into a nasty, subtle problem in working with ordered data. We planned to show changing the ZIP code field for everyone in a particular ZIP code (something that actually happened to Tamar a few years ago). The code looks like this:

```
SET ORDER TO Zip
SEEK "19117"
REPLACE Zip WITH "19027" WHILE Zip="19117"
```

But, using this approach, you can't do that. With order set to ZIP code, once you change the ZIP code field for a record, it moves to its new position. In the example, as soon as one record gets the new ZIP code, it moves to join the other "19027"s. Unless you're particularly lucky, when the record pointer moves forward, it's no longer on a "19117" record and the REPLACE ends. You can run into the same problem when you SCAN with order set.

To do the ZIP code replacement, you need to use REPLACE FOR instead:

```
REPLACE Zip WITH "19027" FOR Zip="19117"
```

When you use WHILE, you need to position the record pointer at the beginning of the group of records you want to process. When you finish, the record pointer is on the first record that doesn't match the criteria.

Combining the Clauses

Scope, FOR and WHILE can be combined in a single command. The interactions are logical, but not necessarily intuitive.

First, realize that FOR has an implied (or default) scope of ALL. Any command containing FOR without a scope clause or a WHILE clause checks all records. This means it's not necessary to use the ALL keyword here:

```
REPLACE ALL vegetable WITH "Lettuce" FOR vegetable = "Broccoli"
```

If no other scope is included, and there's no WHILE clause, the record pointer is left at EOF() after a FOR clause.

WHILE has an implied scope of REST, but it may stop short of the end of the file if the WHILE condition is no longer met.

So, what happens when you combine these babies? Adding scope to either FOR or WHILE means that it behaves as it usually does, but processes records only in the specific scope. So:

```
BROWSE NEXT 20 FOR State = "Confusion"
```

displays all of the next 20 records that meet the FOR criteria, but shows matches only from among those 20, even if fewer than 20 are included.

Combining FOR and WHILE seems contradictory, but actually it's not. The key to understanding such a command is knowing that the WHILE is in charge with the FOR just helping out. In other words, we process records until we find one that fails the WHILE test, but we process only those that pass the FOR test. For example:

```
SELECT Employee
SET ORDER TO GroupId
SEEK "     2"
LIST First_Name, Last_Name WHILE GroupId = SPACE(5)+"2" ;
   FOR NOT EMPTY(Photo)
```

lists only those employees in Group 2 for whom we have a photo on file.

As we mentioned above, a few commands accept only FOR and not WHILE. LOCATE accepts both a FOR and a WHILE clause, but the FOR clause is required in that case. That is, to find Group 2 employees with photos, you can:

```
LOCATE FOR NOT EMPTY(Photo) WHILE GroupId = SPACE(5)+"2"
```

but you can't use WHILE to look for all the Group 2 people, like this:

```
LOCATE WHILE GroupId = SPACE(5)+"2"
```

This behavior makes some sense. Using just WHILE with LOCATE isn't very useful. You might as well use SKIP and test the condition. WHILE requires the records to be in order anyway, so LOCATE WHILE is overkill. However, we might want to search only in a specific group of records for the first record that meets a condition. LOCATE FOR with a WHILE clause does that for us.

Shall I Compare Thee to a Summer Day?

One of the most confusing aspects of Xbase is the way string comparison works. The Xbase way is to compare strings only to the end of the right-hand string. If they match up to that point, they're considered equal.

Given Xbase's interactive history, it's not really bad behavior. When you're searching for a particular record or want to find all the records that match a given string, it's kind of nice to not have to type out the whole string to match. But in programs, this behavior can be a disaster.

The SET EXACT command controls string comparisons for Xbase commands. For more than you ever wanted to know about this subject, check out SET EXACT in the Reference section.

Operator, Operator, Give Me Number Nine

> "Reeling and Writhing, of course, to begin with," the Mock Turtle replied, "and the different branches of Arithmetic—Ambition, Distraction, Uglification, and Derision."
>
> Lewis Carroll, *Alice's Adventures in Wonderland*, 1865

Remember seventh grade (or maybe it was sixth or eighth) when you learned a mnemonic that went something like "Please Excuse My Dear Aunt Sally?" Right about now, you're probably scratching your head and saying, "Oh, sure, those are the Great Lakes, right?," or "Yeah, that sounds familiar, but what's it about?" unless, like us, you remember this kind of stuff forever, and you're sitting there saying "Sure, parentheses, exponents, multiplication, division, addition, subtraction." You got it: The mnemonic provides the order of precedence of numeric operators. That is, when you see:

```
3 + 7 * 4
```

you know that it's 31, not 40, because multiplication comes before addition (except in the dictionary). On the other hand:

```
(3 + 7) * 4
```

is 40 because parentheses come before any other operators. When there are multiple operators at the same level, they're evaluated from left to right.

In Xbase, there are a bunch of other operators besides arithmetic operators. Comparison operators (=, <>, <, >, <=, >=, and $) are used to compare values (big surprise). Logical operators (AND, OR, NOT) are used to combine logical expressions (often comparisons).

Some of the operators used for arithmetic can also be applied to other data types (all of them for double, integer and currency, + and - for characters, - for dates and datetimes). There's also one additional arithmetic operator (%, which is the same as MOD()) that applies to numeric, float, double, integer and currency values.

The arithmetic precedence rules have been extended to cover the full set of operators. Arithmetic operators used on other types have the same precedence as when they're used with numbers. The % has the same precedence as multiplication and division.

The complete precedence rules for FoxPro are somewhat different from those in some other programming languages. In particular, logical operators come below arithmetic and comparison operators:

- Parentheses

- Exponentiation

- Multiplication/Division/Modulo

- Addition/Subtraction

- Comparison

- NOT

- AND

- OR

Maybe the FoxPro version of the old mnemonic should be "Please Excuse Miss Daisy Mae And Sally Combing Nits All October"? Maybe not.

Just Some Routine Inquiries, Ma'am

A subroutine (or sub-program, as some folks call them) is a program that is called from another program, performs a task, and then returns to the calling program, which picks up where it left off. We like to think of the original routine as getting moved to the back burner until the subroutine finishes executing; then it comes back to the front burner again.

Like many programming languages, FoxPro has two kinds of subroutines: procedures and functions. The big difference in using them is that a function returns a value while a procedure doesn't, so a function call can appear as part of an expression while a procedure call cannot.

By the way, many people refer to functions and even procedures as UDFs for "user-defined functions." This is to distinguish them from FoxPro's built-in functions. Historically, there have been some places where a built-in function could be used, but a UDF could not, though we can't think of any in Visual FoxPro.

In many programming languages, there's a distinction drawn between procedures and functions: A subroutine is one or the other. Not so in FoxPro. Here, any subroutine can be either a procedure or a function. In fact, it's not the name you give the subroutine when you define it (either PROCEDURE MyRoutine or FUNCTION MyRoutine) that determines whether it's a procedure or function; it's the way you call it. That is, the same subroutine can be called as a function sometimes and as a procedure at others. Like this:

```
DO MyRoutine with Param1, Param2
```

or

```
? MyRoutine(Param1, Param2)
```

Why does this matter? Two reasons. One we already mentioned: Functions return a value. When you call a function as a procedure, the return value is thrown away. (When you call a procedure as a function, and there's no return value, the function returns .T.)

Throughout Xbase history, when you called a routine as a function (with the parentheses at the end), you had to do something with the result. You couldn't write:

```
MyRoutine()
```

Instead, you needed to assign the result to a variable, use it in an expression, display it, or throw it out. Here are examples of each:

```
MyResult = MyRoutine()    && value assigned to MyResult
IF MyRoutine() > 7 ...    && value tested
? MyRoutine()             && value displayed
= MyRoutine()             && value thrown out
```

The equal notation in the last example says to run the function and throw away the return value. The only reason to do it that way is if you're running the function for what it does and not for what it returns—that is, for its side effects. (More on side effects later.)

Starting in VFP 5, you can cut to the chase and just call the function without doing anything with the result.

Pass the Parameters, Please

The other important distinction between procedures and functions has to do with parameter passing. Parameters are the way that one routine communicates with another. Think of the name of a subroutine as an instruction to do something, and the parameters as the items the instruction applies to. Let's look at a built-in function as an example:

```
UPPER(LastName)
```

says "Apply the UPPER function to the LastName field and return the result." Since UPPER() converts whatever you give it to uppercase, you get back something like this:

```
"GATES"
```

Sometimes the routine needs several pieces of information to carry out its task. For example, the built-in function SUBSTR() returns part of a character string you pass it (that is, a substring). It accepts two or three parameters: the string to work on, the place the substring starts, and, if you want, the length of the substring. Here's an example:

```
SUBSTR("The quick Visual FoxPro jumped over the slower dogs", ;
       11, 13)
```

returns:

```
Visual FoxPro
```

A subroutine must indicate what parameters it expects to receive. There are three ways to do so: by using the PARAMETERS statement, by using the LPARAMETERS statement, and by listing them in parentheses in the routine's header line (PROCEDURE or FUNCTION declaration). The PARAMETERS statement creates the parameters as private variables, while the other two methods create them as local variables. (See "Scope It Out!" below for the distinction between private and local variables.)

There are two ways of passing parameters: by value and by reference. The passing method indicates whether the subroutine can affect the original item passed to the routine.

If you want to be technical about it, the parameters specified in the subroutine are called "formal parameters," while the items you pass are called "actual parameters." The method of passing parameters determines whether the actual parameters change when the formal parameters are changed.

Got it? Neither did we, nor did our students the first few times. So let's not be technical about it. Think of it this way, instead: When you pass by value, the items you pass are copied to the parameters listed in the subroutine. Any changes to the parameters don't affect the items in the call. When you pass by reference, FoxPro makes an internal connection between the parameters and the items you pass, so changes to the parameters ripple back to the items you passed.

In fact, it turns out that the names of the two methods are pretty informative. When you pass by value, the value of the item is passed, not the item itself. When you pass by reference, FoxPro creates a reference to the original item. Better now?

Now here's the sneaky part. Ordinarily, you don't explicitly specify the parameter-passing method—it's implied by the subroutine call. Functions pass parameters by value; procedures pass by reference. Remembering that it's the call that determines whether it's a procedure or a function, that's a major implication. The same routine may behave very differently, depending how you call it.

Here's a very simple example. We usually check parameters at the beginning of a routine to make sure they're the right type and have realistic values. Suppose the beginning of a subroutine looks like this:

```
PROCEDURE ProcessDate
PARAMETER dInput

IF TYPE('dInput')<>"D"
   dInput=DATE()
ENDIF
* Now do whatever
```

Now look at these two calls to the routine:

```
MyDate = "Sandy"
? ProcessDate( MyDate )
```

or

```
MyDate = "Sandy"
DO ProcessDate WITH MyDate
```

In the first case, the variable MyDate isn't affected by the error checking in the routine. In the second case, MyDate gets changed to today's date (and isn't Sandy's mother surprised?).

Normally, this isn't a problem because most routines are called either as procedures or as functions, not both. So let's move on to another issue.

There's a principle of structured programming that says functions shouldn't have "side effects." This means that functions should accept some parameters, do some processing and return a value—without changing anything in the environment. (It reminds us of the scouting maxim for visiting the wilderness: "Take only pictures, leave only footprints.")

This is why parameters are passed to functions by value. (There is one case, discussed below, where it's essential to pass by reference.) Anyway, suppose you don't have any principles and you want to pass a parameter to a function by reference. Can you do it?

Of course you can—this is FoxPro, after all. In fact, there are two ways to do it. One is global while the other is local. The global approach uses a SET command—SET UDFPARMS. You can SET UDFPARMS TO VALUE (the default) or TO REFERENCE. When you do so, all subsequent function calls use the specified method.

The local approach is to prefix the actual parameter (the item you're passing) with the "@" symbol. For example:

```
=MyFunction(@MyVariable)
```

calls MyFunction, passing MyVariable by reference.

On the whole, we prefer local approaches to local problems. Remember that environmental slogan, "Think Globally, Act Locally"? The same thing applies here. Consider the overall effects of your actions, but take the actions over the smallest possible scope. The problem with SET UDFPARMS is that it can have unexpected effects. Suppose you change it to REFERENCE and call a function. Suppose that function in turn calls another function, which expects its parameters to be passed by value. The inner function may change one of its parameters (not expecting that to affect anything outside the function), which in turn changes the results of the function you called. What a mess.

What about the one case where you have to pass by reference? When you specify an array in a function call (with UDFPARMS set to VALUE), only the first element of the array is passed. Makes it a little hard to, say, total the array elements. To pass an entire array to a function, you must pass by reference. So, a call to our fictional array-totaling function would look like:

```
nTotal=SumArray(@aMyArray)
```

What about the flip side—suppose you want to pass by value to a procedure. Surprisingly, there's only one local way to do it—no equivalent of SET UDFPARMS in sight. All it takes is to turn the actual parameter into an expression. This is best demonstrated by the fact that you can pass constants to a procedure. For example, the following is a valid procedure call:

```
DO MyProcedure WITH 14, 29, 93, "Hike"
```

as long as MyProcedure expects four parameters.

But how do you turn a variable into an expression? Simple: Put parentheses around it and it becomes something that FoxPro evaluates before passing. Voila—passing by value. Here's an example:

```
DO MyOtherProcedure WITH (MyVariable), (MyOtherVariable)
```

We've noticed in the last few years that more and more programmers (ourselves included) have a tendency to use only functions and not procedures. This is partly a consequence of object-oriented programming (methods, after all, feel an awful lot like functions). We're not sure yet whether this is a good thing or a bad thing. Since many of the routines we write actually do something other than returning a value, calling them as functions certainly does violate the old rule about side effects. If nothing else, be sure to document the effects your code has on the environment.

Two's Company ... Three's Even Better

FoxPro has allowed you to pass fewer parameters than a routine expects for quite a long time. The actual parameters are matched to the formal parameters (those declared with a PARAMETERS or LPARAMETERS statement) one by one, and the extra formal parameters at the end get initialized to .F. The PARAMETERS() function (and the superior PCOUNT()) tells you how many parameters were actually passed, so you can give the rest useful defaults.

In Visual FoxPro things are even better, though more confusing, too. You can choose to omit actual parameters even if they're not at the end of the list. Just put in a comma placeholder and the corresponding formal parameter gets initialized to .F.

While we welcome this change because it means parameters can be grouped logically instead of based on the likelihood of needing them, it also introduces new complexity. It used to be simple. Check PARAMETERS() and you knew that everything after that had defaulted to .F. Now, that's not enough. You have to check each parameter to make sure it's got a value of the right type. Of course, that's a good idea in any case, since you can also pass the wrong type anyway.

Mom Was Right

The mess you can cause with SET UDFPARMS leads to an observation about subroutines in general. They should make no assumptions about the environment in which they're called and should clean up after themselves. This means a routine shouldn't expect a certain variable to exist or that any SET commands (like SET EXACT or SET DELETED) will have particular values. If it changes any of those, it should set them back to their original values before exiting. Routines following these rules will be welcome in any programming neighborhood.

Can You Offer a Subroutine a Good Home?

There are at least three places you can store subroutines in FoxPro. Each routine can be stored in its own PRG file (for performance implications, see "Faster Than a Speeding Bullet"), a routine can be stored with the program that uses it, or you can group a bunch of routines together into a "procedure file" (which can contain functions as well as procedures).

Prior to FoxPro 2.0, separate PRG files were too much trouble to manage. You had to remember where possibly hundreds of little programs could be found. So, most people stored subroutines used by only one program with that program, and stored more widely used subroutines in a procedure file. But there were problems with that approach, since only one procedure file could be used at a time, and there was no way to save the name of the current procedure file before switching to another.

The Project Manager changed all that. It remembered where you left a function so you didn't have to. Suddenly, keeping every routine in a separate PRG file became feasible. Several well-respected FoxPro developers suggested directory structures to aid in this endeavor. Others offered programs to automate the process of breaking a procedure file into its component parts.

With Visual FoxPro, the waters have been muddied. The SET PROCEDURE command now supports an ADDITIVE clause, so multiple procedure files can be set. On the other hand, the Project Manager is still happy to do the work for you. Finally, object orientation means that code is stored with data for anything defined as an object, and the database allows some code to be stored there as well.

Our preference is still for stand-alone PRG files for code that isn't object method code.

Scope it Out!

> Desiring this man's art, and that man's scope,
> With what I most enjoy contented least;
> Yet in these thoughts myself almost despising,
> Haply I think on thee.
>
> William Shakespeare, *Sonnet 29, l. 7*

By now, it should be no surprise that the word "scope" has two distinct meanings in FoxPro. One is discussed above in "Scope, FOR, WHILE (and Santa) Clauses." The other (which has nothing to do with the first) applies to visibility of variables.

Variables in FoxPro have three possible scopes: public, private and local. They vary as to which routines (other than the one in which the variable was created) can see and change the variable.

Doing It in Public

Public variables are exhibitionists. They're visible in every routine in an application except any that have an identically named private or local variable. Anybody can use their value; anybody can change it.

Any variable you create in the Command Window is public. Otherwise, to create public variables, you need to use the PUBLIC keyword. In older versions of FoxPro, PUBLIC was picky—if the variable existed when you tried to make it public, you got an error message. Although VFP no longer complains about this, most FoxPro programmers make it a habit to write it this way:

```
RELEASE PublicVar
PUBLIC PublicVar
```

The RELEASE doesn't do any harm if the variable doesn't exist already, but protects you if it does. Variables created this way start out life as logical with a value of .F.

Public variables stick around until you explicitly release them. It's not good enough to say RELEASE ALL, either. You've got to list them out, one by one, in order to release them (unless you do it in the Command Window, where RELEASE ALL does release all public variables—go figure). That's as good a reason as any to stay away from public variables.

Actually, you should keep public variables to a minimum. As with SET commands, they're often a global solution to a local problem. Frequently, creating a private variable at the appropriate level in your program will give you the same results.

There is one "gotcha" involving public variables. If you pass a public variable by reference (see "Pass the Parameters, Please"), that variable is hidden within the called routine. This means a reference to the variable within the called routine gives an error message. This is just another reason to avoid public variables as much as possible.

It's a Private Affair

The term "private variable" is really a misnomer. These variables aren't private. (In fact, local variables behave as the word "private" implies; see below.) Private variables are visible in the routine that creates them and in all routines lower in the calling chain, unless those routines have their own private or local variable of the same name.

Let us run that by you again. When you declare a private variable, it hides any variables of the same name that were created higher in the calling chain, but can be seen by routines lower in the calling chain.

Hmm, how about an example? Suppose you have a routine MyRoutine that creates a variable called MyVar, then calls a subroutine called MySub. MySub can see MyVar and act on it. However, if MySub declares its own private version of MyVar, MyRoutine's MyVar is hidden and MySub acts only on its own version of MyVar. Here's some code to demonstrate the point:

```
* MyRoutine.PRG

MyVar1 = 7
MyVar2 = 10

? "In MyRoutine before calling MySub", MyVar1, MyVar2

* Note that MyVar1 and MyVar2 are NOT passed as parameters
DO MySub

? "In MyRoutine after calling MySub", MyVar1, MyVar2

RETURN

PROCEDURE MySub

PRIVATE MyVar2
MyVar2 = 2

? "In MySub before doubling", MyVar1, MyVar2

MyVar1 = 2 * MyVar1
MyVar2 = 2 * MyVar2

? "In MySub after doubling", MyVar1, MyVar2
RETURN
```

If you run this program, you'll see that MyVar1 ends up with a value of 14, but MyVar2 (in MyRoutine) remains 10. So, using private variables, you can hide information from a higher-level routine, but not from a lower level.

If you don't specify otherwise, variables are created private. Private variables are released when you return from the routine that created them. You can explicitly release them sooner with the RELEASE command.

You can explicitly make a variable private by declaring it with the PRIVATE keyword. You must do this if a variable of the same name exists at a higher level in the calling chain.

Unlike PUBLIC and LOCAL, though, declaring a variable PRIVATE doesn't create the variable—it just means that if you create that variable, it will be private. This makes some sense when you notice that PRIVATE can take a skeleton and make all variables matching that skeleton private—the others take only a specified list of variables. The skeleton allows you to do things like this:

```
PRIVATE ALL LIKE j*
```

which means any variable you create beginning with J is private.

Local Initiative

Prior to Visual FoxPro, public and private were the only choices for variables. Visual FoxPro adds local variables, which makes writing black-box code much easier.

Local variables can be seen only in the routine that creates them. No other routine can access or change them. This makes them perfect for all those bookkeeping tasks you need in a routine, like loop counters, holding part of a string, and so forth.

Here's an example to demonstrate why local variables are much easier to work with than private variables. Suppose you have a routine that sums a specified subset of an array. That is, you pass the array, a starting element and the number of elements to sum, and the function returns the sum of those elements. Here's the function:

```
* ArraySum.PRG
* Return the sum of a specified group of elements
* of an array.

LPARAMETERS aInput, nStart, nNum
    * aInput = Array to Sum
    * nStart = Element to start
    * nNum = Number of elements to sum

LOCAL nCnt,nSum
    * nCnt = Loop Counter
    * nSum = running total

* Do some error checking.
* Complete checking would also make sure
* each array element summed is numeric.

IF TYPE("nStart") <> "N" OR nStart < 1
   nStart = 1
ENDIF

IF TYPE("nNum") <> "N" OR nStart + nNum - 1 > ALEN(aInput)
   nNum = ALEN(aInput) - nStart + 1
ENDIF

nSum = 0

FOR nCnt = nStart TO nStart + nNum - 1
   nSum = nSum + aInput[nCnt]
ENDFOR

RETURN nSum
```

If you have a numeric array called MyArray and want to total the third through eighth elements, you'd issue this call:

```
? ArraySum(@MyArray,3,6)
```

Now suppose you need a function that totals each row of a two-dimensional array. You could write all the summing code again or you could take advantage of the code you've already written. The following function calls on ArraySum to total each row and just stores the result. It takes advantage of the fact that FoxPro represents all arrays internally as one-dimensional. (See "Hip, Hip, Array" in "DBF, FPT, CDX, DBC—Hike!" for more on that subject.) For good measure, the function returns the number of rows.

```
* SumRows.PRG
* Sum each row of an array, returning the results
* in a one-column array.

LPARAMETERS aInput, aOutput
    * aInput = Array with rows to be summed
    * aOutput = One-dimensional array of sums

LOCAL nCnt, nRowCnt, nColCnt
    * nCnt = loop counter
    * nRowCnt = number of rows in input
    * nColCnt = number of columns in input

nRowCnt = ALEN(aInput, 1)
nColCnt = ALEN(aInput, 2)

* Dimension aOutput appropriately
DIMENSION aOutput(nRowCnt)

FOR nCnt = 1 TO nRowCnt
    aOutput[nCnt] = ArraySum(@aInput, nColCnt * (nCnt - 1) + 1,
nColCnt)
ENDFOR

RETURN nRowCnt
```

If you have a two-dimensional array called My2DArray, you'd get the row totals like this:

```
DIMENSION MyTotals[1]
= SumRows(@My2DArray, @MyTotals)
```

The key point here is that, in writing SumRows, we didn't have to worry about what variables ArraySum used. Since SumRows makes all its variables local, no routine that it calls can damage its environment. Think of local variables as "a piece of the rock" for your routines.

You create local variables with the LOCAL keyword. Local variables are released when you complete the routine in which they were created. You can create local arrays, as well as scalars, using LOCAL. Newly created local variables have logical type and a value of .F.

You may have noticed the LPARAMETERS declaration in those two functions. LPARAMETERS is also an addition in Visual FoxPro. It creates formal parameters as local variables, protecting them in the same way that LOCAL protects variables.

We recommend all procedures and functions use local variables and local parameters for all internal tasks. Use private variables only when you explicitly want lower-level routines to have access to those variables—for example, when SCATTERing fields for a form (something you don't really need to do in VFP).

SQL—The Original

> You taught me language; and my profit on 't
> Is, I know how to curse: the red plague rid you,
> For learning me your language!
>
> William Shakespeare, *The Tempest*, 1611–1612

SQL, which stands for Structured Query Language, is a set-based language. Unlike Xbase, which cares about individual records, SQL is interested mostly in groups of records. (The Xbase concept most similar to SQL's point of view is the FOR clause.) The name "SQL" is read by some folks as a series of letters ("ess queue ell") and by others as "sequel"—we use either one, depending on the phase of the moon, though we lean more toward the latter these days.

The biggest difference between SQL and Xbase is that Xbase is procedural while SQL is not. In Xbase, you have to tell the computer exactly what to do to get from point A to point B—without step-by-step instructions, Xbase has no clue. SQL, on the other hand, lets you tell it what you want and it figures out how to give it to you. This is most apparent with SELECT-SQL, which lets you indicate what records should be placed in a result set without having to navigate the tables containing them.

In database theory, languages for manipulating databases are divided into two sets: the Data Definition Language (DDL) and the Data Manipulation Language (DML). Despite its name, SQL (like Xbase) incorporates both. The entire SQL language (defined by an ANSI standard) is quite large; FoxPro has supported a subset for many years now, with that subset growing in almost every version. (Supporting only a subset is not a unique FoxPro weakness. In fact, few vendors support the entire standard at any level, and most have proprietary, incompatible extensions as well.)

SQL first poked its way into FoxPro 2.0 with two DDL commands (CREATE TABLE and CREATE CURSOR) and two DML commands (SELECT and INSERT). Naturally, this wasn't enough for FoxPro users and they immediately started clamoring for more. Visual FoxPro finally added to the set, with the addition of both DDL and DML commands.

The most recently added data-definition command (new in VFP 3) is ALTER TABLE, an extremely powerful command that lets you add and remove fields and indexes, set various properties of fields, and create persistent relations among tables. All this in one command—no wonder its syntax diagram occupies nearly a full page.

CREATE TABLE has been significantly enhanced in Visual FoxPro, too. Its syntax diagram is also pretty hefty.

VFP 3.0 also introduced two new SQL data manipulation commands: DELETE and UPDATE. DELETE is fairly similar to the Xbase version of DELETE, though it has a few wrinkles of its own. (See its entry in the "Visual FoxPro Reference" for the nasty details.) UPDATE is a lot like Xbase's REPLACE, though again there are some differences, primarily in syntax. What makes these two commands such welcome additions is that you can use exactly the same commands on FoxPro data and on data originating from other sources. Besides, all those folks who've been writing SQL code in other languages really want to do it their way.

VFP 5 didn't add any new SQL commands to the language, but it seriously enhanced our old favorite, SELECT. Queries offer the chance to lay out joins explicitly and to use the various flavors of outer joins. VFP 5 also gave us the ability to limit SELECT's result set by number or percent of matching records, though this isn't quite as powerful as it sounds. VFP 7 added to SELECT again, finally giving us the ability to make the cursors it creates read-write (see below for an explanation of "cursors").

So Which One Do I Use?

In theory, you could do all your data definition and manipulation using only FoxPro's SQL commands. Or you could ignore the SQL commands and use only the traditional Xbase commands. We know people who prefer either approach, including some who'll zealously campaign for their chosen method.

We don't recommend either, though, for two reasons. Some things are easier to do in Xbase while others are easier in SQL. (And some work best with a marriage of the two.) If you're using one approach and your code starts to seem convoluted, step back and see if you can use the other. For example, if a process takes five successive complex queries, stop and think about whether you can do it by setting relations instead.

The second reason we can't arbitrarily recommend one approach over the other is speed: Some things are faster in Xbase; others are faster in SQL. There's really no way to tell which approach is faster without testing. Any time you can think of both procedural and SQL solutions, you should probably test both solutions to see which runs faster. Sometimes, the results will surprise you.

Is a Cursor Someone Who Uses Bad Words?

In addition to tables, SQL works with data in cursors. The term "cursor" is shorthand for "CURrent Set Of Records."

In FoxPro, a cursor is similar to a table, though it has some differences. The most important difference is that cursors are temporary. When you close them, they disappear into thin air, never to be seen again—at least not until you create them again from scratch.

There are three ways to actively create cursors in Visual FoxPro. As you'd expect, the CREATE CURSOR command creates cursors. You list the fields you want and their characteristics, and FoxPro does the rest, thoughtfully leaving the new cursor open in the current work area.

SELECT-SQL also can create cursors to hold query results. Cursors created this way are read-only, unless you explicitly make them read-write. (The simple approach to making cursors read-write was added in VFP 7; in older versions, there is a trick for this. USE the cursor AGAIN in another work area.)

The VFP-only method for creating cursors is to open a view. By definition, all SQL views use cursors. When you issue USE <viewname>, the underlying query is executed and the results put in a cursor. Views may be updateable, depending on how they're defined.

In addition to these three types of cursors, there's also a tendency in VFP to refer to any open table, cursor, or view as a cursor—hence, functions like CursorSetProp().

Work Areas? What Work Areas?

> Oh, why don't you work
> Like other men do?
>
> Anonymous, *Hallelujah, I'm a Bum*, c. 1907

Unlike Xbase, SQL has no concept of a current work area. Each SQL command, instead, indicates what table it's working on. Tables are opened automatically if they're not already open and, when appropriate, they're secretly reopened.

Even though they don't officially recognize work areas, several of the SQL commands do change the current work area. Both CREATE commands (CREATE CURSOR and

CREATE TABLE) leave you in the previously empty work area containing the newly created object. If you send query results to a cursor or table, SELECT makes the work area containing the results current.

INSERT INTO, DELETE and UPDATE don't change work areas, but they do open the table if it's not already open.

Who Needs Consistency Anyway?

> Consistency is contrary to nature, contrary to life.
> The only completely consistent people are the dead.
>
> Aldous Huxley

The seven SQL commands available in Visual FoxPro have no fewer than three different ways of referring to the table (or tables) they operate on.

SELECT and DELETE use a FROM clause to list tables. INSERT uses INTO. The others don't have a special keyword—the table name simply follows the command itself (as in CREATE TABLE Inconsistent ...). We can't blame Microsoft (or even Fox) for this one, though, because the commands do conform in this respect to the ANSI standard for SQL. This is a good place to point out that, like most other SQL database systems, while FoxPro's SQL commands are ANSI-compliant in some respects, they deviate in others. The bottom line is, if you're familiar with ANSI SQL, you'll want to check the FoxPro manuals or Help before you start coding.

WHERE, Oh WHERE, Can My Data Be?

Three of the four DML commands in FoxPro's version of SQL use a WHERE clause to determine which records are affected. WHERE is essentially identical to the Xbase FOR clause, with minor variations in string comparisons (see SET ANSI and SET EXACT) and operator syntax. In DELETE and UPDATE, WHERE filters the table. In SELECT, WHERE both filters the data and can specify join conditions used to combine records from multiple tables (but see "Won't You JOIN me?" below).

The WHERE clause can contain any valid logical condition. To optimize these commands, make sure tags exist for each expression involving a field that appears in the WHERE clause.

Won't You JOIN Me?

Unlike VFP's other SQL commands, SELECT can involve multiple tables directly. (Other commands may include multiple tables through sub-queries, but not in the listing of tables.) When there is more than one table, you need to indicate how to match up records from the different tables. In VFP 3 and earlier versions of FoxPro, you did this in the WHERE clause along with your filter conditions. Beginning in VFP 5, you can also use the ANSI JOIN syntax to specify how to combine tables.

The advantage of the newer syntax is that it lets you specify outer joins (where unmatched records in one or more tables are included in the result) as well as the inner joins that WHERE lets you include. For details on the JOIN syntax, see the entry for SELECT-SQL in the "Visual FoxPro Reference."

No Room at the Top

Set thine house in order.

The Second Book of Kings, 20:1

Because SQL is set-based, certain concepts fundamental to Xbase don't have exact analogues in SQL. SQL usually doesn't care where a record is in the table; there's no such thing as a SQL record number. When you manipulate records with SQL commands, you mostly do it based on the records' contents, not their positions. SQL has no NEXT or REST clauses.

Similarly, FoxPro's version of SQL doesn't know from first and last (or, as we call them in Xbase, TOP and BOTTOM). Before VFP 5, there was no way to say "the first 10" or "the most recent 25." VFP 5 added TOP n and TOP n PERCENT syntax to SELECT, but its utility is quite limited—the clause applies to the overall query results, not to each group within the result. When you need "the first 10" or whatever in each group of records, you have to use a hybrid approach that combines SQL with Xbase's record number to produce the desired results. It requires a multi-step process and you still need enough space to select all the matching records first. (Tamar has published the solution to this one elsewhere, most recently in the November '99 issue of *FoxPro Advisor*.)

Fix 'Er Up

Debugging SQL commands tends to be a little trickier than debugging Xbase or OOP language. That's because a single SQL statement may be a whole page of code. Finding a syntax error in a 30-line query is like the proverbial search for a needle in a haystack.

So what do you do? The first step is to check for the obvious, especially if you've just been editing. Make sure every line but the last ends with a semicolon, make sure there are commas between all the fields in the field list (and not after the last field), check for typos, and so forth. If all that fails to turn up the problem, start taking the command apart: Remove and comment out (you'll have to use some cut-and-paste here since VFP can't handle commented lines in the middle of a command) whole clauses or parts of clauses until you figure out what the offender is. Another good approach is to avoid the problem in the first place by building up your SQL statements, especially queries, a little at a time. Then, when an error occurs, you'll know it's related to the last thing you added.

The other issue you can run into is performance—commands, especially queries, that don't run fast enough. Check out "Faster Than a Speeding Bullet" for overall performance tips, and look at SYS(3054) in the Reference section for a way to find out exactly what's bogging your query down.

OOP is Not an Accident!

> The poetical language of an age should be the current language heightened, to any degree heightened and unlike itself, but not … an obsolete one.

Gerard Manley Hopkins, 1879

We've heard about Object-Oriented Programming (OOP) for more than 20 years. At first, it was just theory. Then, we started hearing about this language called SmallTalk. In the last few years, OOP's been everywhere, and the claims of who has it and how it revolutionizes programming have grown louder and louder.

So what is OOP? Why is it important? And has it really changed the way we program?

Object-Oriented Programming is a different way of looking at programming than the procedural approach found in traditional programming languages. (It's different than the "give me what I want—I don't care how" approach of SQL, too.) Conventional programming languages look at the world in terms of actions—first you figure out what to do, then you figure out what to act on. OOP looks at the world in terms of objects—first you figure out what objects you want, then you figure out what actions the objects should take.

OOP is not a replacement for everything you have learned about making a computer work up to this point. We know naysayers who claim you need to throw out everything you've done before and start from scratch. That's just not true. OOP is a better, more realistic way of looking at the processes and entities and their interactions, modeling them, describing them, abstracting them and enhancing them, but it does not change the requirements of our systems to perform the functions they do. It just looks at packaging them differently. Consider the FoxPro 2.x way of maximizing a window: ZOOM WINDOW MyWindow MAX. You start out by indicating the action you want to take (ZOOM WINDOW), then indicate what object to apply the action to (MyWindow).

The OOP equivalent is MyWindow.WindowState = 2. You start out by indicating that you want to deal with MyWindow, then you narrow it down to MyWindow's WindowState. Finally, you indicate what you're doing—setting that state to 2 (which is maximized).

This may seem like only a minor syntactic difference, but in fact, we're really turning the whole process on its head. The hidden difference here is the change from passive elements to active elements. In procedural code, windows, controls, and so on are all passive things that we act on with commands. In OOP, windows, controls, and so on are active objects that know how to do things—we simply tell them what we want them to do. (See "The Message is the Medium" below for more on this.)

It's worth noting that this difference is also the major one between the DOS and GUI worlds. In DOS, you use a Command-Object syntax: What shall I do? and, by the way, who should I do it to? In graphical environments like Windows and Mac, you choose a thing and then decide what to do to it. It's not a surprise, then, that the big move to object orientation has come with the move to GUIs—it's much easier to program when your language works like your environment.

The Object of My Affections

> Nothing can have value without being an object of utility.

> Karl Marx, *Capital*

Not surprisingly, the basic unit in OOP is an object. An object is an entity that has some characteristics and knows how to do some things. For example, a form is an object. So is a check box or a grid.

The formal name for the object's characteristics is *properties*. The official name for the things it knows how to do is *methods*. (There are some special methods called *events* that react to user and system actions—see "A Gala Event" for more on this.)

Object orientation is really packaging. We put the properties together with the methods so the object is self-contained. To use the object, you don't need to depend on anything outside the object itself. This essential feature of object orientation is called *encapsulation*—that's one of several rather intimidating words you'll find floating around the OOP world.

Encapsulation is really pretty simple. Instead of putting data in one place and code that operates on it in another (the traditional procedural division), you package them together, so when you have one, you also have the other. If you've ever worked with abstract data types, you're familiar with this concept. If not, we suspect it'll grow on you pretty quickly.

Don't confuse the data that's encapsulated in objects with your database data. Although there's talk about object-oriented database management systems, we're not dealing with those here. The properties of an object are its data; the methods are the code. Perhaps *information* would be a better term here: Encapsulation is the feature where an object possesses the *information* about itself and the method code to act upon that information.

A Class Act

To be an Englishman is to belong to the most exclusive class there is.

Ogden Nash

Where do objects come from? Well, there's the Mama object and the Papa object and they get together with the birds and the bees and nature takes its course. Oops, wrong kind of object.

So where do objects come from? We don't just pull them out of thin air. Instead, we base each object on a class. The class forms a blueprint or template for the object, and we can create as many objects as we'd like, based on a single class. (More on where these class things come from below.)

The class definition determines what properties and methods an object has. Every object based on a particular class has the same set of properties and methods. What distinguishes one object from another is the values of those properties. (For example, one check box might have its caption to the left while another has the caption to the right. All that's been changed is the value of the Alignment property.)

Visual FoxPro provides two ways of defining classes: in code and through the Visual Class Designer. (Actually, there's a third way—using the Form Designer—but that's really a variation on using the Class Designer.) In either case, though, you do the same kinds of things: Specify the properties and methods of the class, and indicate initial values for the properties.

The act of creating an object based on a class is called *instantiation*; the object created is called an *instance* of the class.

That's Quite an Inheritance

I would rather make my name than inherit it.

William Makepeace Thackeray

Suppose you have a class that's almost what you want for some purpose, but not quite. The procedural thing to do is to copy the class and make the changes you need.

But then you're stuck with two different classes to maintain. What if you find a bug in the original? You have to remember to change not just the original, but also the copy you modified. And what if you then need another class a little different than either the original or the modified version? You copy and change it again. Now you've got three things to maintain. And it keeps getting worse and worse.

One of the most powerful features of object orientation is the ability to create subclasses of existing classes. The subclass inherits the properties and methods of the original, but allows you to make changes. Most important of all, changes to the original class are inherited by the subclass.

Inheritance is the second of three characteristics a language must have to be considered object-oriented. (It's also the one missing from Visual Basic versions prior to VB.NET—VB is considered to be object-based, not object-oriented.)

So where do all these classes come from anyway? No, not Mama and Papa classes—you've been dozing through our explanation. All classes, ultimately, are descendants of one of the base classes built into the language. In the case of Visual FoxPro, we've been supplied with a rich set of base classes from which all of our classes are built. More on these a little later.

Our favorite example of inheritance is pretty simple. Say you work for LargeCo, a large corporation, and there's a corporate standard for input forms. The standard includes the corporate logo as wallpaper. Then, LargeCo is gobbled up by EvenLarger Corporation, which declares that all forms must have its corporate logo as wallpaper.

In FoxPro 2.x, you might have handled the original requirement by saving a screen containing just the logo and copying it as the basis for all your new screens. Works great until EvenLarger comes along—then, you have to go back to every screen you've created and change the wallpaper.

Okay, how does this work in Visual FoxPro? You start off by subclassing VFP's base form class. In your subclass, you set up the wallpaper with LargeCo's corporate logo. Now, whenever you need a new form, you subclass it from your corporate form and start building. Doesn't seem so different from what you did in FoxPro 2.x.

But here's the payoff. Along comes EvenLarger—what do you have to do? You go back to your original subclass (the one based on VFP's form class). You change the wallpaper to the new corporate logo and voila! All your other forms inherit the change. That's right—with inheritance, you make the change once!

So are you sold yet? We are.

Inheritance is actually even more powerful. Not only does a subclass inherit the properties and methods of the class it's based on, it also inherits the code in the methods. You can override that code by specifying different code for the same method of the subclass. If you don't override, it's as if you'd put the inherited code right in the subclass' method. (See "Hierarchies and Lower-archies" below for how to have the best of both worlds.)

Polymorphism is Mighty Morphism

There's one more key feature of object orientation, and its name is even more obscure than encapsulation or inheritance. This one is *polymorphism*. Actually, though, this one's pretty simple. It means that different objects can have methods with the same name. The methods don't have to behave the same way (though it's a good idea for them to do similar things).

In other words, you no longer have to struggle to come up with unique names for minor variations on a theme. Every object can have a Print method—no more PrintInv, PrintCust, PrintThis, PrintThat. Just issue SomeObject.Print and that object gets printed.

The Message is the Medium

Okay, we've defined all the buzzwords and talked about objects and classes, but how does all this fit together? The key is in *message passing*. No, not the like the kind that got you in trouble with your second-grade teacher. Well, maybe like that, actually.

The basic idea in OOP is that objects know how to take care of themselves. They contain all their data and a set of actions to perform on that data. But sometimes, they need something from another object to get the job done or they have information that another object needs. So they send a message to the other object, asking that object to do something, asking for information from that object, or telling the other object something important. These correspond roughly to invoking a method of another object, checking a property value from another object, and changing a property value in another object.

You can access a property of any object by giving the object's name, then a period ("."), then the property name. For example, the Picture property (which provides the wallpaper) of a form called MyForm is referenced with:

```
MyForm.Picture
```

To change a property, simply assign it a new value. To give MyForm the Fox bitmap for wallpaper, you'd write something like:

```
MyForm.Picture = "F:\VFP\Fox.BMP"
```

To store the current value of MyForm's picture property in a memory variable, perhaps so it could be changed and later restored, you'd write something like:

```
cCurPict = MyForm.Picture
```

You reference methods similarly. Use the object name, a period, and the method name. If the method accepts parameters, enclose them in parentheses. Parentheses are optional if you're not passing parameters, but we recommend always using them when calling methods. To call MyForm's Refresh method, for example, you can write:

```
MyForm.Refresh
```

or

```
MyForm.Refresh()
```

We like the second form better because it makes it clear that Refresh is a method.

The Protection Racket

> Woman must not depend upon the protection of man, but must be taught to protect herself.
>
> Susan B. Anthony

Some objects have properties or methods that can be dangerous in the wrong hands. The way you prevent these dangers is by marking those properties and methods as "protected." Protected properties and methods can be accessed only by methods of the same object.

If other objects need access to the value of a protected property, you can provide a method (not protected) whose sole function is to return that value.

For example, the code in the Developer Downloads for this book (available at www.hentzenwerke.com) contains a class designed to keep track of connections to remote servers. That class uses an array to contain the connection information and has a property indicating how many connections it's currently tracking. Letting the outside world touch that counter property would be suicidal for this class. Instead, that property is protected and there's a Count method that returns the current connection count.

Some OOP theorists believe that all access to properties should come through methods, that no object should be able to directly read or change the properties of another. Visual FoxPro does not follow that philosophy by default, but you can design your classes to do so, if you wish. (See "Assign of the Times" below for another approach to this problem.)

Crouching Tiger, Hidden Property

> Society is a masked ball, where every one hides his real character, and reveals it by hiding.

> Ralph Waldo Emerson, *The Conduct of Life*, 1860

In VFP 5 and later, you can go even farther to protect properties and methods from outside abuse by marking them as "hidden." Protected properties and methods can be seen in subclasses of the original class; hidden properties and methods cannot. They can be seen only in objects of the class that creates them.

The hidden characteristic seems particularly useful when you're building classes to be distributed without source. You can keep some properties and methods from even being visible in subclasses and use them for internal bookkeeping. Unfortunately, VFP keeps this approach from being as useful as it should because hidden methods can't even be accessed indirectly through calls up the class hierarchy. (See "Climbing Trees" below for an explanation of such calls.)

Assign of the Times

> Remember that you are an actor in a drama, of such a part as it may please the master to assign you, for a long time or for a little as he may choose.

> Epictetus, *Encheiridion, no. 17.*

We said above that some people think one object should never directly change the properties of another. The reason is that the object being changed doesn't know it's being changed. VFP 6 gives your objects the opportunity to know when they're being changed and even when they're being used (a feature we might have found handy at some time in our lives).

Each property can have two events associated with it automatically: an Access method and an Assign method. When a property has an Access method (the method name is propertyname_Access), that method is called whenever someone reads the value of the property. An Assign method (named propertyname_Assign) is called whenever someone changes the value of the property. You can put code in these methods to prevent the access or assign, to log it, or to do anything else you want.

In addition to Access and Assign methods for properties, you can also create a method for all objects called This_Access. If it exists, this method is fired when any member of the object is accessed. This_Access accepts the member object reference as the parameter, so you know what was accessed. It must return an object reference, too (or you'll see error 9, "Data type mismatch"). It doesn't replace a property's Access method, because you can't control the values that are returned to the property, but you can take action based on what was accessed. This_Access fires before the property's Access method.

Hierarchies and Lower-archies

In a hierarchy, every employee tends to rise to his level of incompetence.

Laurence J. Peter, *The Peter Principle*, 1969

One of the most confusing aspects of object-oriented programming is that there are two different hierarchies at work. We mentioned above that you can create subclasses based on existing classes. In fact, you can do this over and over again, building a tree (the computer science kind of tree, not the nature kind of tree) of classes of as many levels as you'd like.

At the top of this tree, known as the class hierarchy, are Visual FoxPro's base classes—more on those a little further along. The next level contains subclasses derived directly from base classes. At the next level are subclasses derived from the subclasses one level up. And so on and so forth.

The reasonably standard OOP term for the class one level up the hierarchy is *superclass*. For reasons we can't comprehend, Visual FoxPro instead calls the class one level up the hierarchy the *parentclass*. Reminds us of the old joke, "How many Microsofties does it take to change a light bulb?" — "None, they just declare darkness the new standard."

Inheritance applies to the class hierarchy. An object based on a class at the bottom of the tree has properties and methods specified for that class, plus it inherits any properties and methods of its parentclass, and those of the parentclass of its parentclass (you might call it the grandparentclass) and so on, all the way back to the root of the tree.

When a method of an object is called, the class the object is based on is checked. If it has code for that method, the code is executed. If there's no code there, we start climbing the class hierarchy, looking for an ancestor of this class that has code for the specified method. As soon as we find some code for that method, we execute it and stop. But until we find it, we keep climbing the tree until we reach the Visual FoxPro base class the object is ultimately derived from. Even if no code is specified anywhere on the tree, if the base class has some default behavior, like redrawing the object upon invocation of the Refresh method, that behavior occurs. (Actually, that base behavior normally occurs even if there's code somewhere in the hierarchy—see "Ain't Nobody's Default But My Own?" later in this chapter.)

Contain Yourself

Now what about the other hierarchy we mentioned? This comes from the fact that one object can contain another. For example, a form is an object (based on the Visual FoxPro Form base class). A form usually contains all kinds of other objects like text boxes, check boxes, grids, and so forth. Some of the objects in a form can contain other objects. For example, a grid contains columns, which in turn can contain headers and controls.

So the second hierarchy is the containership hierarchy. This is the map of what's inside of what. The most important point about the containership hierarchy is that inheritance has nothing to do with it at all. Objects do not inherit anything from their containers or from the objects they contain.

The second most important thing about the containership hierarchy is that the term "parent" is used here, too. (This is one reason we're frustrated by Microsoft's choice of parentclass over superclass.) The parent of an object is the object that contains it. For example, the parent of a column is the grid containing that column. The parent of a text box might be a form. Don't confuse "parent" with "parentclass"—they really are two different things.

One other terminology note: The objects inside another object are called *members* of the containing object. The term "members" is also used more broadly to refer to the properties and methods of an object, as well as to the objects it contains.

Climbing Trees

At various times, we need to climb each of the hierarchies. Let's start with the class hierarchy. Say you're defining a subclass and, for some method, you want to do everything the parentclass does, but then do a few more things. Your first instinct might be to copy all the code from that method of the parentclass into the corresponding method of the new subclass. Why shouldn't you do this?

What happens if you have to change the parentclass' behavior? If you've done cut-and-paste to the subclass, you're out of luck. The changes aren't inherited.

So what should you do? Call the parentclass' method explicitly from the subclass' method. There are two ways to do this. One way uses a notational trick, since you can normally only call methods of objects, not of classes. A special operator "::" lets you call up the class hierarchy—the notation is:

```
ClassName::Method
```

The second way to call up the class hierarchy is by using the DoDefault() function. This function, which can only be used in method code, calls the same method one level up the hierarchy—it was added in VFP 5.

Both DoDefault() and the "::" operator let you have your cake and eat it, too. A subclass' method can call the same method of its parentclass and then do some more work. Or, if you prefer, it can do the extra stuff first and then call the parentclass' method. Or both: Do something, call the parentclass' method, and then do something else. A common term describing this is *augmenting* the parent's method. If you completely change the method, and don't call the parent method (a clue there's a design problem), this would be termed *overriding* the parent method.

Moving around the container hierarchy is actually a lot more common and uses the dot notation. To send a message from one object to another, you have to be able to find the recipient. You can do that by walking down the container hierarchy until you reach the object you want. For example, to refer to a spinner named spnDays on a page called pagPage1 of a page frame called pgfCalendar of a form called frmWhoKnows, you write:

```
frmWhoKnows.pgfCalendar.pagPage1.spnDays
```

What a mouthful!

You want class definitions to be as reusable as possible. Because you might create many instances of a single class, you don't know when you're writing code what the name of the actual object will be. You also may not know what the parent of an object is. For example, a text box might be contained by a form, a column or a page (of a page frame).

A special operand, This, lets you refer to the current object without knowing its name. The Parent operator lets you move one level up the container hierarchy without knowing what's up there. For example, to find the name of the parent of the current object, you'd write:

```
This.Parent.Name
```

You can use Parent repeatedly to climb multiple levels:

```
This.Parent.Parent.Parent.Left
```

gives you the left edge of the object three levels up in the hierarchy. If This is a check box in a column of a grid on a page of a page frame, that expression would refer to the page's Left property.

Because you don't always know how deep in the hierarchy you'll be, This has two cousins, ThisForm and ThisFormSet, which let you jump quickly to the top of the container hierarchy. Then you can climb back down one level at a time. Say you want to address the button cmdSave that's on the current form. You can reference it with:

```
ThisForm.cmdSave
```

without worrying about where you are now on the form.

Base Clef

All fantasy should have a solid base in reality.

Sir Max Beerbohm, *Zuleika Dobson*, 1911

Visual FoxPro comes with a set of built-in classes known as the base classes. FoxPro's base classes cannot be changed, but most of them can be subclassed. In fact, we recommend that one of the first things you do is subclass all the input controls and build your own forms and form classes from your subclassed controls, rather than from FoxPro's base class controls. We suggest you do this even if you change not one thing about the control because someday, you're going to want to make changes. (Starting with VFP 6, Microsoft has provided a set of "one-off" classes to start from, as part of the FoxPro Foundation Classes (check out the HOME()+"FFC\" directory) so you don't have to do this yourself anymore.) If you've used the base classes in your forms, there'll be a lot of work ahead.

There are several ways to break the Visual FoxPro base classes into groups. The biggest division seems to be between containers and non-containers. Containers can hold other objects while non-containers can't—simple enough. There's also the question of whether a class can be subclassed in the Class Designer. Then, some classes are visible while others aren't. Finally, different classes came into the language at different times. The table below shows all of Visual FoxPro's base classes and classifies them according to all four criteria.

Base Class	Container?	Subclass-able in Class Designer?	Visible?	Version Introduced
ActiveDoc	No	Yes	No	VFP 6
Checkbox	No	Yes	Yes	VFP 3
Column	Yes	No	Yes	VFP 3
ComboBox	No	Yes	Yes	VFP 3

Base Class	Container?	Subclass-able in Class Designer?	Visible?	Version Introduced
CommandButton	No	Yes	Yes	VFP 3
CommandGroup	Yes	Yes	Yes	VFP 3
Container	Yes	Yes	Yes	VFP 3
Control	Yes	Yes	Yes	VFP 3
Cursor	No	No	No	VFP 3
Custom	Yes	Yes	No	VFP 3
DataEnvironment	Yes	No	No	VFP 3
Editbox	No	Yes	Yes	VFP 3
Form	Yes	Yes	Yes	VFP 3
FormSet	Yes	Yes	Yes	VFP 3
Grid	Yes	Yes	Yes	VFP 3
Header	No	No	Yes	VFP 3
Hyperlink	No	Yes	No	VFP 6
Image	No	Yes	Yes	VFP 3
Label	No	Yes	Yes	VFP 3
Line	No	Yes	Yes	VFP 3
ListBox	No	Yes	Yes	VFP 3
OLEBoundControl	No	Yes	Yes	VFP 3
OLEControl	No	Yes	Yes	VFP 3

Base Class	Container?	Subclass-able in Class Designer?	Visible?	Version Introduced
OptionButton	No	No in VFP 3 Yes in VFP 5 and later	Yes	VFP 3
OptionGroup	Yes	Yes	Yes	VFP 3
Page	Yes	No	Yes	VFP 3
Pageframe	Yes	Yes	Yes	VFP 3
ProjectHook	No	Yes	No	VFP 6
Relation	No	No	No	VFP 3
Separator	No	No in VFP 3 Yes in VFP 5 and later	Yes	VFP 3
Session	No	No	No	VFP 6 SP 3
Shape	No	Yes	Yes	VFP 3
Spinner	No	Yes	Yes	VFP 3
Textbox	No	Yes	Yes	VFP 3
Timer	No	Yes	No	VFP 3
ToolBar	Yes	Yes	Yes	VFP 3

The table points out some of the terminology problems in Visual FoxPro. We have a base class named Control. We also refer to the various objects that let users enter data as "controls." And, in fact, something derived from the base class Control might just be a control, but so are a lot of other things. Why couldn't they have picked a different name?

Similarly, there's a base class called Container, but a lot of the other base classes are containers, too. Doesn't English have enough words to go around? Do we have to overload a few of them so badly?

To complicate this particular issue even further, Container and Control are very similar classes. They're both designed to let you create complex controls (the input kind) built out of multiple objects. The difference is that objects based on Control don't allow other objects access to the contained items, while objects based on Container do. In other words, using Control as the basis for an object is kind of like protecting all its member objects.

Not Quite All There

Since in true OOP, every class can be subclassed, we like to think of those base classes that can't be subclassed in the Class Designer as being "half-classed." For the most part, each of these classes is a necessary component of some container class. You can subclass these classes in code, but you still can't incorporate your subclasses in the containers (or subclasses of them) that normally contain the base classes. For example, you can subclass Grid, but your subclass will still be made up of Columns, which will still contain Headers. Similarly, Pageframes always contain Pages; you can't base a Pageframe subclass on a subclass of Page.

Even with CommandButtons and OptionButtons (which you can subclass visually), when you make a CommandGroup or an OptionGroup, it's always built of CommandButtons or OptionButtons—you can't build it out of a subclass.

We can see the reason for this limitation, but we keep hoping it will go away.

Other classes have similar limitations in that they can only be created in code (Session). These are half-classed in their own way, too, in that they don't allow Visual FoxPro programmers the range of tools available within the development environment, or respect the individual programmer's preference for visual or code-based tools.

The details of each of the base classes are discussed in the Reference section, so we won't go into them here.

Ain't Nobody's Default But My Own?

Certain behaviors are built into Visual FoxPro's base classes. For example, when you press a key, that keystroke is placed in the keyboard buffer. When there are tables or views in the data environment, you don't need to write code to open them and set up the specified relations. Generally, these behaviors are tied to certain events. The keystroke entering the keyboard buffer is part of the KeyPress event. Opening tables and setting relations is part of the OpenTables method (which behaves more like an event in many ways).

Even if you override the method code for these events with your own code, these default behaviors occur anyway. And that's a good thing. You wouldn't want to have to code your own version of putting a keystroke in the keyboard buffer or opening the tables in the DE. Nor would you want to have to call up to the base class every time you override a method.

But, once in a while, you want to override the default behavior as well. Perhaps you want to eat the keystroke because you're doing something special with it. Sure enough, there's a way to handle it. To prevent an event from firing its default base class behavior, put the command NoDefault on a line anywhere in the method for that event. Since the base class default behavior always happens last, NoDefault can go anywhere in the method code.

NoDefault and DoDefault() are two more places where the words used for things cause confusion. Given their names, it's not unreasonable to think that they're exact opposites. It's not unreasonable; unfortunately, it's also not true. NoDefault turns off the *built-in* behavior of a method; it has no effect on user code. DoDefault() executes the *user* code for a method one level up the class hierarchy and can cause the built-in behavior to occur earlier than it otherwise would. It's not at all uncommon to have both NoDefault and DoDefault() in the same method code. The most common reason to combine them is to make the built-in behavior happen sooner. For example, we sometimes issue NoDefault followed by DoDefault() at the beginning of the OpenTables method. Then, we can add some code to do things like create indexes for views that were opened.

Taking Some Extension Classes

At the same time as VFP has been OOP-ified, so have a lot of other parts of the programming world. In particular, many of the tools for allowing applications to interact now use object-oriented techniques. This includes ActiveX, COM Automation and various data access technologies, like RDO and ADO.

This means that you'll find yourself writing OOP-y code not just to handle tasks in VFP, but to handle much of the interaction with other applications. For example, Automation with Word or Excel involves creating an Automation object and then setting properties and calling methods. So does using ADO to access non-VFP data.

In addition, a number of objects that are accessible directly from VFP (that is, without having to explicitly create them) are really ActiveX objects. For example, the Project and File objects added in VFP 6 use ActiveX technology. You can't subclass them in VFP, but you talk to them through properties and methods.

Give Me the Whole ScOOP

We've just skimmed the surface on object orientation here. After working with it for several years now, the OOP way of looking at things feels pretty natural to us. So many tasks are performed more simply using OOP.

But using OOP effectively is more than just a code thing. Designing applications to take advantage of OOP requires a new way of looking at them. Each version of VFP since the introduction of OOP has more tools—like the Class Browser, IntelliSense, and the Object Browser—to help implement and use good object-oriented principles, but the tools don't take the place of a good knowledge of how OOP works.

Design Isn't Just for Art Majors

Design is perhaps more important in the OOP world than it is in the structured programming world. (OK, we can argue that design is terribly important regardless of what kind of programming you're doing—but if you're arguing, you probably already know the importance of design. If you're not arguing, you need to know that design is important!) There's so much to say about design issues. How do you know if your object design is right or wrong? Why do you design to interface, not implementation? Why do you design for the general case and code for the exceptions? There's a Hentzenwerke book dedicated to OOP, *Advanced Object Oriented Programming with VFP* by Markus Egger (see www.hentzenwerke.com for more information). Also check the appendices for some references on object-oriented analysis and design.

Controls and KAOS

> Who controls the past controls the future;
> who controls the present controls the past.
>
> George Orwell, *1984*

Controls are the means of interacting with users. Some, like the text box and the command button, are visual elements of the user interface; others, like the timer and the session controls, don't have a visual element, but work behind the scenes to support the user interface. Understanding the intricate ways in which the properties, events and methods are evaluated and executed is essential to grasping how Visual FoxPro works. In this section, we'll discuss what controls are and some of the features common to controls. We'll go on to look briefly at each control (you'll find more in the Reference section), and discuss where it's appropriately used. At the end of the discussion, we'll explain how the built-in characteristics of controls can be extended to create more complex and customized controls, tailored to meet your clients' needs, capable of interacting with your users in ways beyond those anticipated by Visual FoxPro's designers.

What's a Control?

Most controls are objects that are manipulated, like light switches, sliders or radio buttons, and hence can be thought of as computer representations of real-world controls. This metaphor falls a bit short, however, for some controls, such as the timer, which doesn't have a visual representation, is invisible to the end user, and can't be "grasped." For our purposes, we think a sufficient definition is that controls are the objects on forms that perform specific actions when acted upon by an event generated by the user interface, program code or the system.

Controls can be placed on a form in a number of ways. The simplest is to use the Form Controls toolbar. However, some of the other approaches offer more power, including dragging fields from the Data environment or controls from the Component Gallery. Properties, events and methods contain the information that determines what a control looks like, what characteristics it has, and what it should do when acted upon. Hence, the control's appearance and behavior is *encapsulated* within the control—one of the key principles of object-oriented programming. (See "OOP is Not an Accident" for more on the principles of object orientation and how they're implemented in Visual FoxPro.) The properties of forms and controls are changed through the Property Sheet. Their events and methods can be customized using the method code editor.

While there appear to be a dazzling number of properties, events and methods associated with the collection of controls (in fact, there are more than 2,660 combinations of controls with properties, events and methods), many of the properties, events and methods are common to most controls and perform the same function (or a very similar function) for most of them. Hence, they can be understood just as easily with a blanket statement rather than repeating something like "The Top property determines how far from the top of its container the control appears" in each control's reference section. In fact, we don't repeat that information in the Reference section of this book. The tables there list only those PEMs (that's common shorthand for "properties, events and methods") that are of particular interest for that control. The VFP Help does contain complete lists for each control.

Here is a quick synopsis of the most common PEMs.

Common Control Properties

A property is nothing more than a characteristic of an object. Properties describe things like the object's height, width, color, and whether the object should have certain capabilities, such as being enabled or being visible. Properties are manipulated in

Visual FoxPro in pretty much the same manner as memory variables, and can be thought of in many respects as private memory variables scoped to a single control.

There are two common ways to manipulate the properties of a control: at run time using assignment commands and during development using the design mode tools. (In fact, you can manipulate properties programmatically at design time, too. See "Builders and Wizards and Bears, Oh My!" for more on this.) To refer to properties programmatically, use the "dot notation" explained in "OOP is Not an Accident":

```
ThisForm.PageFrame1.Page7.Command1.Caption = "OK"
```

You're probably thinking, "I've got to type all that?" No, not always; rarely, in fact. IntelliSense is there to help out. See "IntelliSense and Sensibility" for more details on how IntelliSense helps make these object references easy to get into your code.

Properties are assigned visually using the Property Sheet. Formally, Microsoft calls this the "Properties Window" but we've gotten used to the "Sheet" terminology, especially since this window is often set to be "always on top" (see the right-click menu for that option)—something that seems more intuitive for a sheet than a window. We've heard it variously called the "Properties Form," "Property List," "Properties Sheet," "Property Sheet" and "PropSheet." We think all are fine, as long as folks know what you're talking about. Let's review some of the more common properties and what they are usually used for:

The **Name** property of a control does what it says: tells you the control's name. You use the name to refer to the control programmatically.

Parent provides an object reference to the object containing the control. For a control sitting right on a form, for example, Parent holds a reference to the form. For a control on a page of a page frame, Parent contains a reference to the page. Parent helps you climb up from the control you're on to the outside world. This is the containership hierarchy, not to be confused with the inheritance hierarchy—see ParentClass, below, for that.

Value holds whatever the control currently contains, generally some variation on the user's input. **ControlSource** lets you bind the control's Value to a field, variable or property—when Value changes, so does the item named in ControlSource.

The control's location and size are specified with the **Top**, **Height**, **Left** and **Width** properties. All of these measurements are expressed in units determined by the object's **ScaleMode**—either pixels or foxels. (Stick with pixels—we haven't come across any good reasons to use foxels.)

Font characteristics are specified with the **FontName**, **FontSize**, **FontBold**, **FontUnderline**, **FontStrikethru** and **FontItalic** properties—almost all controls have these. The **FontCondense**, **FontExtend**, **FontOutline** and **FontShadow** properties are oddballs, included for compatibility with the Macintosh but having no effect on Windows fonts. (By the way, if you want to use the Transparent characteristic of fonts, it's only available using the old FoxBase STYLE "T" clause on those commands that support it.)

The **Comment** and **Tag** properties have no designed use. They're there to provide a place to leave notes or do whatever you want. We haven't seen very many people actually use these properties. On the whole, it seems better to add custom properties as needed. The term Tag, by the way, is a carryover from Visual Basic, and is not at all related to the tags Visual FoxPro uses in its indexes.

The **Enabled** property determines whether an object is capable of reacting to external events like clicking, typing, or tabbing to a control. A disabled control is "grayed-out" and can't be accessed.

Color settings for a control can be specified in a number of ways. The most obvious are the properties **BorderColor**, **ForeColor** and **BackColor**, with their equivalents of **DisabledForeColor** and **DisabledBackColor**, which apply when the object's Enabled property is False. However, in most cases you'll want to use the **ColorSource** property instead, so the control's colors are based on the user's Windows system choices. A number of controls also have other color settings that affect particular aspects of their appearance (such as **ItemForeColor** and **FillColor**).

The **BaseClass**, **Class**, **ParentClass** and **ClassLibrary** properties describe the pedigree and history of a control, and are fixed at the time a control is created. These allow you, at run time or design time, to examine the lineage of a control and act appropriately.

A couple of properties help you hook your controls into your Help system. **HelpContextID** and **WhatsThisHelpID** each contain an identifier for the control that can link to a Help entry.

Every VFP object has the **Application** property. It contains an object reference to the instance of Visual FoxPro in which that object was created. For self-contained applications (the kind that use only VFP), there's not too much use for this property. However, when a VFP application is started by another application, this reference gives you a handle to the VFP engine. (See "It was Automation, You Know" for an explanation of why another application might run a VFP application.)

Common Control Events

Events introduce some difficulties in talking about Visual FoxPro. When we speak of "adding code to the MouseDown event," it is easy for our audience to sense that an event is somehow a different kind of thing from a method. This is a linguistic issue, not a complication of Visual FoxPro. An event is an occurrence that is communicated to your application. This event might be the fact that the mouse is passing over a control, or that a timer's Interval has elapsed. When your application, via the underlying FoxPro engine, receives this message, a method with the same name as the event is run automatically. So when we talk about modifying the MouseDown event, we are really speaking of "the method associated with the MouseDown event." Events happen. There is nothing we can do about them and certainly nothing modifiable about them. We're not going to keep trying to say "The method associated with the MouseDown event," but since we do want to distinguish an automatically run event from a method, like most VFP developers, we shorten it to "the MouseDown event."

Init and **Destroy** events occur when an object is created and destroyed. These two events fire only once in the life of a control. This is a good place to establish settings that the control depends on, and to clean up these settings upon the control's release.

The **Error** event is the place to put a local routine designed to handle errors that the control might generate. This is a great place to put specific code in your custom controls when you anticipate that the user might be able to perform some error-causing action. You can handle it internally and gracefully within the control, making the control a more useful black-box object, and, again, encapsulating the object's behavior. For example, a disk drive combo box, where you select the drive to which you save your file, could be a useful custom class. The picker itself should detect that the disk has not been inserted, and handle the error with a message box rather than passing control to a default error handler. On the whole, we expect little code to end up in this event. Under no circumstances should you consider cutting and pasting the same complex code to handle every conceivable error into all of your top-level subclasses' Error events. Instead, we expect to use Error as part of a larger error-handling scheme. (See Error in the Reference section.)

The **InteractiveChange** and **ProgrammaticChange** events allow you to include code in the control to react to a user's or program's actions immediately, creating a more responsive system.

Other interactions are handled by events such as **MouseDown**, **MouseUp**, **MouseEnter**, **MouseLeave**, **Click**, **RightClick**, **DblClick**, **Drag** and **KeyPress**. (Some more esoteric interactions are handled by events such as **MiddleClick** and **MouseWheel**.) Most of these events are pretty self-explanatory, although the sequence in which they occur might not always be apparent. An easy way to trace the firing sequence of events is to use the Event Tracking option in the Debugger, run the form, try some things and then examine the results. For example, clicking a command button in a command group (one which previously did not have the focus) can fire a blizzard of events. In this example, a check box called Check1 had focus before the click—we've also pulled out the whole series of MouseMove firings that occurred en route to the button, and left only the last one.

```
form1.commandgroup1.MouseEnter(0, 0, 162, 98)
form1.commandgroup1.MouseMove(0, 0, 163, 100)
form1.commandgroup1.MouseLeave(0, 0, 163, 101)
form1.commandgroup1.command1.MouseEnter(0, 0, 163, 101)
form1.commandgroup1.command1.MouseMove(0, 0, 163, 101)
form1.commandgroup1.command1.When()
form1.commandgroup1.When()
form1.check1.LostFocus()
form1.commandgroup1.command1.GotFocus()
form1.commandgroup1.Message()
form1.commandgroup1.command1.MouseDown(1, 0, 165, 108)
form1.commandgroup1.MouseDown(1, 0, 165, 108)
form1.Paint()
form1.commandgroup1.command1.MouseUp(1, 0, 165, 108)
form1.commandgroup1.MouseUp(1, 0, 165, 108)
form1.commandgroup1.InteractiveChange()
form1.commandgroup1.command1.Click()
form1.commandgroup1.command1.Valid()
form1.commandgroup1.Valid()
form1.commandgroup1.command1.When()
form1.commandgroup1.When()
form1.commandgroup1.Message()
form1.commandgroup1.Click()
```

Other common events include **Resize**, which fires when a container's size is changed, and **GotFocus** and **LostFocus**, which fire when a control receives and loses focus.

Beginning with VFP 6, controls have a bunch of events whose names begin with OLE. These events handle actions related to OLE drag and drop. See "OLE Drag and Drop" in the Reference section for an exhaustive look at this feature.

VFP 6 also added a new wrinkle to events with Access and Assign. These events can be attached to any property and fire when the property is either read or changed.

Because the existence of these events is under developer control, they add a new dimension to controls. (See the Reference section for details.)

Common Control Methods

Methods are similar to events, in that they contain a block of code to be executed. The main difference is that events are triggered by something outside the direct control of the developer, but methods are called explicitly. Compared to events and properties, there are not many common methods. That's because methods are really the determining factor in creating a unique control—unique behaviors of an object indicate that it needs to be considered a unique control. This is one of the reasons that Microsoft decided to combine the FoxPro 2.x "Invisible Button" and "Push Button" controls into a single CommandButton in VFP; they are functionally identical, differing only in a few properties. However, ComboBox and ListBox are two separate controls. Although they share a number of methods, there are enough differences between them to justify separate structures.

The **ZOrder** method sends the specified control to the front or back of its group of overlapping controls. ZOrder moves items along the Z-axis, the third dimension we simulate on our monitors. But ZOrder is not just for appearance; it also affects the firing order of some events—see the ZOrder entry in the Reference section for more details on this. Some controls contain their own ordering properties (such as Pageframe's PageOrder)—those properties determine the horizontal (X-axis) or vertical (Y-axis) order of the contents. ZOrder determines the depth (Z-axis) order.

Move allows movement of controls on a form under programmatic control. **Drag** and **OLEDrag** initiate native drag and drop and OLE drag and drop, respectively.

The **Refresh** method redisplays a control, also firing the Refresh method of any contained controls.

SetFocus moves the focus programmatically to the control (similar to the function performed by the _CUROBJ memory variable in FoxPro 2.x).

AddObject, **NewObject** and **RemoveObject** allow the addition or subtraction of controls from container objects. **CloneObject** creates a duplicate of the control inside the same container.

The **SaveAsClass** method is pretty cool. It allows us to save the definition of any control to a class library, both at design time and at run time! This can be really useful in an interactive development session, where you can programmatically alter a live object's properties until you get them just right, and then save your result right from the Command Window, putting the live form into a visual class library.

The **SetAll** method programmatically sets a property of all objects or objects of a particular class within a container. **ResetToDefault**, added in VFP 3.0b, lets you return a property to its default value—very handy, since a control is created faster when properties are set to default than when they're explicitly assigned the default value.

AddProperty, added in VFP 6, lets you add properties to an object at run time. **ReadExpression**, **ReadMethod**, **WriteExpression**, and **WriteMethod** let you examine and change properties and methods programmatically. Except for WriteMethod, they're available at run time, as well as design time.

ShowWhatsThis displays the WhatsThisHelp for the control.

The remainder of methods built into Visual FoxPro are typically contained in only a few objects, and are more appropriately discussed in the Reference section for that object.

Visual FoxPro Controls

Controls can be broken down into groups in a number of ways. We have chosen to focus on them from the end user's point of view—what the end user is going to use each control for. This isn't an exhaustive view of them; it would take another book at least as long as this one to explore all the capabilities of each. We're trying to focus more on the use of each control and to provide some pointers. Further information about specific controls can be found in the Reference section.

Text-based controls: TextBox, EditBox, Label and Spinner

These controls allow you to enter one item of text. A text box is typically restricted to a few words or phrases, occupying a single line of form real estate. An edit box, typically bound to a memo field, allows free-form entry of a variable-length block of text from one word to a large narrative, providing scrollbars as necessary. A label simply displays text, and does not allow a user to change it. Spinners are used for numeric entries and allow both direct text entry and selection by means of up or down arrows.

Choices: CheckBox, ComboBox, ListBox and OptionGroup

These controls allow the user to select the most appropriate answer or answers from a set of choices. Check boxes are used for on/off, true/false-type answers. Option groups also allow only one answer, though typically from a larger number of choices. Combo boxes and list boxes allow the choice of one or more answers from a list. Normally, check boxes and option groups are defined during the design of a form to have a particular shape and prompts. The two kinds of lists, on the other hand, tend to be more flexible, allowing population at run time. The nice thing about the Visual FoxPro object model is that the properties of these objects are available at run time, so the rules above are typical guidelines and not carved in stone.

Check boxes, in the Windows interface, normally are used just as an on/off, true/false switch. Occasionally, though, a check box is used as a button that immediately fires further actions, such as calling up a dialog. (See the Project Class check box on the Projects page of VFP's Options dialog, for example.) Our take is that this use of a check box, even when the prompt ends in an ellipsis, is bad design, since it confuses users. Use buttons when you need them and save check boxes for indicating if something is or it isn't.

Option groups also allow only one choice, and are typically sized and populated with their choices at design time. You can arrange the choices in any visual configuration—you're not limited to rows, columns or even grids of them.

Combo boxes, formerly known as drop-downs or popups, take up little real estate when inactive. List boxes take a larger piece of screen space, but allow the user to see several options at once. Both combo boxes and list boxes can be populated from a number of sources, ranging from a hard-coded list entered at design time to a list programmatically generated at run time from an array, table or query. Both can handle multi-column lists. List boxes have the added advantage of allowing for multiple selection, and for the addition of mover bars to let the user move things around in the list. Combo boxes, on the other hand, can be configured to allow the user to enter data not on the list. Whichever you use, keep in mind that these controls are meant for choosing from small- to medium-sized lists and not for choosing among thousands or tens of thousands of options. Your users will *not* be amused as they scroll through the choices one at a time. (Despite the incremental search available in both controls, some users will scroll through one at a time.) In general, list boxes are suited to somewhat larger sets of choices than combo boxes.

Using combos and lists with a huge number of items has been a perennial source of bugs and performance issues in FoxPro. VFP 3 had problems with multi-selection of more than about 60 items on a list; FoxPro 2.x actually crashes under some conditions with 600 or more items in the list. Not only is this poor interface design for us, but it is also difficult for the Fox team to program in the Windows environment. Avoid very large data sets for these controls if at all possible.

Actions: CommandButton, Timer and Hyperlink

The action controls are used to fire an action immediately upon selection.

Command buttons are variously referred to as "push buttons" or just "buttons." (For whatever reason, option buttons are rarely, if ever, called just "buttons.") Command buttons can show text or a bitmap, or be invisible to create a "hot" region on the form. (Don't confuse the last option with the Visible property—an invisible button is still an active participant in the form, but any control with its Visible property set to False is both invisible and disabled.)

Timer controls might seem like a bit of an odd duck in this category, but timers are unique no matter how you categorize things. They are the only invisible controls that directly cause actions to occur, unlike the more passive Custom class objects. But they do cause actions, which is why we plunked them here. Timers are a welcome addition to our arsenal, allowing us to dynamically take a look at the current state of a form to check status, update displays, and so forth.

Hyperlinks, added in VFP 6, are also unusual. Like timers, they're invisible, but unlike timers, they don't have any special events that fire on their own. What they do have, though, is a couple of methods useful for manipulating a browser. The most important is NavigateTo, which can open a browser looking at a particular Web page or file.

Containers: Grid, Column, PageFrame, Page, CommandGroup, Container, Control and Toolbar

Containers are objects that can contain other controls. A container class is a great place to put a chunk of code that should affect all of the contained objects, like the logic to turn off navigation buttons when at the top or bottom of the data set, or to disable visually contained controls when their container is disabled.

Grids contain columns, which in turn contain other controls. Some of the contained controls are specific to grids, such as Columns and Headers, while the individual cells hold the controls suited to the field, like text boxes, check boxes, combo boxes and the rest. Grids are normally used to display the contents of a table, like the Browse of old. Unlike Browse, grids are incredibly configurable, with the ability to use different controls for different data, change colors and fonts on the fly, and much more. They're also incredibly difficult to get just right for data entry—many of the developers we know would rather climb Mount Everest than configure a grid for entering data. As a display device, though, or a tool to select a particular record, they're hard to beat. A fellow developer was heard to say, after evaluating a number of other ActiveX data grids, that the only thing worse than the VFP Grid was any other choice.

Page frames allow the creation of tabbed or tabless sets of pages. The hottest thing around when VFP 3 first came on the scene, tabbed dialogs have already fallen out of favor to some extent, but they still have their uses. A page frame contains pages, which contain controls.

Command groups contain sets of command buttons. These seemed terribly important when VFP was new, but much less so now. Using individual buttons provides more control and greater flexibility. Bundling command buttons with other controls like check boxes and combos in a container provides nearly all the benefits of command groups, but with added flexibility.

The other three classes in this category, Container, Control and Toolbar, are not exactly controls in their own right, but they are container objects. Controls (isn't this confusing?) and toolbars cannot be directly created from the Form Controls toolbar, unlike the other controls listed in this section, including Containers.

 Yet another mangled piece of overloaded terminology here. The Container class is one of a number of classes, all of which are referred to as "container classes." To confuse matters more, Control is a class, but "controls" refers to a whole set of classes, and "control" is a general-purpose term for any member of that set. We try to distinguish between the individual Container class and the set of container classes, and between the Control class and the controls, with our use of capitalization, but, as in the heading above, we don't always succeed. It looks like we're stuck with these names for the long term, so bear with us.

Containers and Controls seem to be very similar. Each is essentially a box with the standard set of properties and events: border, background and foreground color and style, size and location, mouse events, and so forth. Both can contain other controls. The difference between the two is that a Container object contains other controls whose properties can be manipulated at design time and run time, while a Control hides the individual controls it contains from manipulation. Control allows you to create true "black box" controls whose innards are hidden from manipulation except through your predefined interface, while Container is more of a grouping mechanism.

A Toolbar is a funny thing. Sometimes it behaves like a form. Sometimes it's more like a control or a container (lowercase) control. Unlike the other visual objects, there is no separate Toolbar Designer power tool. You create a toolbar by defining a class for it, either visually or through code, and then add it to a form set or create it in code. A surprising collection of objects can be added to a toolbar. Most common are command buttons, separators, option buttons, combo boxes and check boxes, with both kinds of buttons and check boxes normally using a graphical style. (Check out Word's Formatting toolbar to see all of those control types.) However, the Class Designer allows the addition of pretty much every VFP control except grids to a toolbar. That can lead to some pretty strange looking toolbars. In some versions of VFP, some pretty strange things start to happen, too, when out-of-the-ordinary controls are thrown on a toolbar. See the Reference section for details.

Graphical Elements: Image, Line, Shape and Separator

These graphical items can be used to segregate related areas, draw on the form, display images, or separate related groups of buttons on a toolbar. Unlike the graphical elements in FoxPro 2.x and the Box and Line methods of forms, these are full participants in the form, and can react to clicks and drag-and-drop events. (We are amused that Separators are on the Form Controls toolbar when you can't put them on a form. But the same toolbar is used in the Class Designer; in addition, a toolbar can be added to a formset in the Form Designer, so it does make sense.)

ActiveX: OLEBoundControl and OLEControl

VFP's ActiveX container controls have some very special functionality: They allow Visual FoxPro to open a window into another application, and to control the display and functionality of that application. OLEControls also are used to add third-party ActiveX controls to forms, giving the form capabilities beyond those (or better designed than those) built into VFP.

It's worth noting that Microsoft created a bit of a mess for itself by including the term "OLE" in the names of these classes. Since they did that, "OLE" has been transformed into "ActiveX"—you'll see a reflection of this in the ToolTip and status bar message if you pass the mouse over these items on the Form Controls toolbar.

User Interface Issues with Controls

Much has been written about the importance of good user interface design, and we don't want to beat the issue to death here. (Well, since we're all pretty passionate on this subject, actually we do want to beat it to death, but we won't.) Check out the appendices for some suggested reading on this topic if you haven't dealt with this before. A clean, easily understood and consistent user interface can enhance users' confidence in their abilities with your system, and improve their opinion that they are dealing with a polished and professional application.

The most important user interface principle to bear in mind with controls is consistency throughout an application. If a command button with a printer icon calls up a print dialog on one form, a check box with the same icon in another form should not toggle an option that determines whether the output of an action should be printed. The user is bound to call you, swearing the application isn't working the way it did yesterday. All forms should share similar prompts—when completing a form, the users should not have to vacillate between selecting "Close," "Cancel," "OK" or "Quit" button prompts, if the resulting action on the different forms is the same.

Think about the way your application is to be used. If the predominant use of a form is for high-volume, heads-down data entry, requiring the user to switch from keyboard to mouse to keyboard is murder on efficiency (and the wrists). On the other hand, a form more likely to be used by someone trolling for new relationships between the pieces of information should be tailored to the more creative "What happens if I click here and select this" operation of a click-happy mouse user.

Another consideration is accessibility. All controls in your systems should be accessible by several means. The minimum is to provide keyboard and mouse access. In many cases, you'll also want a shortcut key and perhaps a menu option. This is a convenience for power users, who will discover these shortcuts and use them to run your application faster. But this is more than an issue of sophistication. Many of your users will have a preference for the keyboard over the mouse, or vice versa, and the application should be accessible to them. In addition, users with limited visual or motor skills should be able to operate your application. As more companies become sensitive to this issue of making provisions for their disabled workforce, this issue will become more prominent. Microsoft itself has jumped onto this bandwagon in the last few years and now offers accessibility guidelines for applications, and new accessibility features (including an Accessibility Browser) within Visual FoxPro. See SYS(2800) in the Reference section. The bottom line is that you should plan and design your application from the beginning to accommodate as many interface styles as reasonably practical.

Finally, let the user know what is going on. Nothing raises the stress level of a user more quickly than a system that wanders off and appears to hang when they tell it do go do something. If your application will take a while to complete a step, change the mouse pointer to an hourglass, display a progress thermometer or tell the user that the operation will take some time to complete. Give the user a chance to cancel long operations if she doesn't have the time or resources to complete a step. Let the user be in charge.

User interface design is not a subject that comes naturally to many of us. Study some of your favorite applications to see how they handle your actions. Maybe more important, study some applications you hate, to see what makes them so miserable to use—and be sure not to do those things in your applications. Read some references in the field. Above all, make the user feel comfortable, confident and in control.

Extending the Reach of Controls

The most profound aspect of the many facets of Visual FoxPro is that the developer is not limited to the functionality built into the language, but rather that this functionality is the basis from which the developer can extend the capabilities of Visual FoxPro to the needs of the client. This is true in many different ways, including controls.

Custom controls are useful in a number of circumstances. Because controls in an object-oriented hierarchy inherit behavior and characteristics from their parents, a class hierarchy can make it far easier to distribute changes throughout a system. For example, changing all the command buttons in a system to use FixedSys rather than Arial is just a matter of changing the FontName property in the parent class definition upon which all of your buttons are built. In addition, encapsulating small bits of thoroughly tested code at various stages of the class tree ensures a more robust and bug-free final result. Once you have written solid code for a Next button, preserve that button in a class library and use that class wherever the button is needed. If you find a bug in the behavior, you can fix it in one place. If you need additional functionality in some places, you can subclass and refine the class definition.

Creating a custom control is easy. Build the control you want, using a blank form in the Form Designer. (If you spend a lot of your time developing custom tools, you may find that a custom "workbench" form can speed the process.) Click the control to select it, and then select the "Save As Class" option from the File menu. Select a name and location for the Visual Class Library in which you'd like to store your custom controls, and then save it. If you prefer, you can just start with the Class Designer—it looks a lot like the Form Designer, except that the Run (!) button on the toolbar is disabled.

There are several ways to use your own controls in the Form and Class Designers. First, the View Classes button (the one that looks like books) on the Form Controls toolbar lets you choose among various sets of classes. You can add your own class libraries using the Add option provided by that button. To make a particular library available all the time, register it using the Controls page of the Tools | Options dialog. These visual class libraries are registered and stored in the Windows Registry, under the entry HKEY_CURRENT_USER\ Software\ Microsoft\ VisualFoxPro\ <version number>\Options\VCXList. (Fill in 3.0, 5.0, 6.0, or 7.0 for <version number>.)

We strongly recommend that you never use the base classes that come with Visual FoxPro. Create your own set of custom controls, consisting of all controls available in the default Form Control Toolbar but subclassed one level. Starting with VFP 6, such a set of controls is provided for you in the _base library found in the FFC subdirectory of your VFP home directory. We (and all the experts we know) recommend you do this because the base class controls supplied by Microsoft cannot be customized and cannot have custom properties or methods attached to them, whereas the subclassed group you have created (or the ones in _base) have that ability. (In fact, you'll probably want to subclass further to give you the ability to change things on an application level, as well.)

One of the things we find frustrating about VFP is that you can't make changes across all the controls. If you want to use 24-point Haettenschweiler throughout all your development, you have to change it in each of your "base" classes (the ones we just told you to create). Of course, once you do so, you're done, and when you come to your senses, it's not too hard to change back to something reasonable again. However, we'd like it even more if all the VFP base classes derived from a single class, where this kind of change could be made once. We actually suspect that, internally, this may be true in VFP 6 and later, but we have no external evidence to back it up.

Custom controls can be built from more than one component. The Reference section contains an example (under "Container") for Shapes, where two shapes and a text box are combined to form a thermometer control. These controls can be turned into a custom class as described above—just select all of the controls you want to combine, and then select "Save As Class". Visual FoxPro automatically dumps the selected controls into a Container control as part of saving them into a visual class library. As before, if you know what you want, you can just use the Class Designer in the first place, drop a Container on it, and add what you need. Remember to use your subclasses to create these complex objects—any base class object you used as part of a custom control cannot have additional properties or methods attached to it.

Controls are the only means our users have to communicate with our applications. It's important to provide them with a rich, consistent and helpful set of tools with which to do their jobs. Visual FoxPro's powerful built-in controls, combined with the object-oriented structure that allows us to customize and build upon the capabilities of those controls, provides us with the means of delivering the tools our clients need.

A Gala Event

The great events of life often leave one unmoved...

Oscar Wilde

What is an event? What do we need to do about it? The FoxPro family was a leader in the Xbase world in moving from a procedural application to an event-driven interface, even in DOS. With Visual FoxPro, FoxPro became fully attuned to the rich event model of the underlying Windows interface. Visual FoxPro can create far more responsive applications, and applications that are more consistent with the behaviors of other Windows programs. We'll examine the different events that are possible, under what circumstances they occur, and what code is appropriate for each of them.

What's an Event?

Simply put, events happen. In OOP terms, an event is an occurrence outside your control, about which one of your objects is notified with a message. An event can be system-generated, user-initiated, or caused by another object in the application. When

Windows handles the resizing of a form, it sends a message perceived by the form as a Resize event. When the user clicks on a control, the control receives a Click event. When a Timer control in your application counts down its elapsed time, a Timer event fires.

As we discussed in "Controls and KAOS," there is no difference between the code contained in an event and that in a method. When we talk of modifying "the Mouse event," it's shorthand for "the code contained in the method associated with the Mouse event." We won't apologize for using this shorthand, nor do we expect to stop.

The set of events is fixed. Unlike methods, it isn't possible to design your own custom events. Although you can customize the code that occurs (or specify that nothing occurs) when an event happens, you cannot create additional events. Starting in Visual FoxPro 7.0, the EventHandler() function allows you to bind to events from ActiveX controls and COM objects, so that you can designate Visual FoxPro code to run when these events occur. Internally, Visual FoxPro has provided us with such a rich event model that few events are missing. In fact, with the addition of Access and Assign methods in VFP 6 (see the Reference section), and database events in VFP 7 (again, see the Reference section), the object model only gets richer with each version.

How to Handle Events

In days gone by, it was a major undertaking to get FoxPro to just stop and let the user direct what was to happen next. Xbase was originally designed as a procedural language, where the program demanded input and then performed its process. The emphasis has shifted over the years, with improving user interfaces, toward an event-driven system, where the tables are turned in such a way that it is the user who seems to be controlling events and the computer that responds. The shift in FoxPro to this new way of doing business has been a gradual and not altogether smooth transition.

Several alternative event-handling methods have been proposed over the years, and each has its proponents. Until the release of Visual FoxPro, there were good reasons why each method might have been desirable under some circumstances. A simple looping structure, checking for a keystroke, could be used as a basis for the application. Several means of detecting a keystroke, using WAIT, INKEY(), CHRSAW() or READ, could respond to the event. In FoxPro 2.0, an alternative, named the Foundation Read (and quickly nicknamed "The Mother Of All Reads," or MOAR, for short) became popular. This READ worked without any corresponding GETs, causing the READ VALID code snippet to fire when an event occurred. Several elegant application frameworks were developed based on this parlor trick. But, like the techniques before them, this method could be tricky to implement under some circumstances, and had kinks and limitations. Visual FoxPro solved the need for these artificial constructs by allowing our applications to become part of the native event loop of the FoxPro engine. In essence, we can now tell FoxPro "Just wait until something happens, or until we tell you it's time to quit."

The READ EVENTS command sets the event handler in action after establishing your environment. There was some discussion that a more suitable command would have been "WAIT HERE," but WAIT is already overloaded. Just what should Visual FoxPro do if someone issued WAIT HERE NOWAIT "What now?" TO lcFred AT 10,10? Or perhaps "ENERGIZE!" (but some dumb bunny's already cornered the market on that one) or "MAKE IT SO" (but Paramount might sue)? So, READ EVENTS it is. It doesn't READ anything at all, and EVENTS go right past it without a raised brow, but that's the command to start the ball rolling.

When you're done in Visual FoxPro and ready to close up shop, CLEAR EVENTS is the command to tell READ EVENTS to stop whatever it has been doing. CLEAR is one of the most heavily overloaded commands in the language, releasing everything from class libraries cached in memory to DLL declarations to menu items defined with @ ... PROMPT or even CLEARing the screen. We would have preferred newer, cleaner terminology, like "STOP" or "ALL DONE", but no one asked us.

It's Not My Default!

When an event occurs, you probably want to provide some code for it to run. When the user clicks on a button, or a timer times out, you need to provide code to describe what happens next. That's easy. You can do that. You're a programmer, right? We spend most of the rest of the book telling you how to do that. But what happens when you don't want any code to run, or perhaps want absolutely nothing at all to happen? If the code fragment for the event you're concerned with is left blank, the same event for the control's parent class is searched to find code to run. If there's nothing there, the same event in the parent's parent class is searched, and so on and so forth. Even if there's no code for that event anywhere in the inheritance hierarchy (that's what determines who gets Uncle Scrooge's millions, right?), there's often some default behavior associated with the event. For example, by default, when the user presses a key, the KeyPress event fires—the default behavior is to put the key in the keyboard buffer. To get a control to do nothing, not even the default behavior, you issue the NoDefault command, valid only in methods.

User interface events occur even when NoDefault is issued. For example, when a command button is clicked, the button is visually depressed (guess it needs a good therapist). Check boxes and option buttons display when they have been toggled. If you want no action from one of these controls at all, NoDefault is not for you—use the When event to return .F. for a complete lack of response.

We run into another situation a lot: We need to let the normal action of the class occur, but we just need to do one teensy-weensy thing besides that. Normally, when you put code in an event, the search described above doesn't happen. That is, once you add some code, the parent class isn't checked for code in that event. The parent class' code is said to be *overridden*. (The fortunate exception here is that the built-in behavior of the event always occurs, even if there's code, unless you specifically suppress it with NODEFAULT.) In the bad old days, we'd just cut and paste the code from one class to another, and then modify it, but these are the good new days. The newer (and better) way to do this is to perform what code we need, and then call on the code from the parent class (or its parent or its parent or …). Or, if it's more appropriate in your situation, call the code from the parent class (or its parent or … you get the idea) and then perform your custom code.

There are two ways to call the code from the parent class. In VFP versions 5 and later, use DoDefault(). Put DoDefault() in any method and it calls the same method in the parent class (and yes, you can pass parameters).

In all versions of VFP (though we'd only use this version in VFP 3), you can use the operator :: to call up one level in the class hierarchy. The simple version is just:

```
NameOfTheParentClass::NameOfTheMethod
```

but this locks you into the parent class and method name you are using when you write the code, and isn't portable. If you change the parent class or move the method code to a different method, you may not be invoking the code you meant. If you want code that works anywhere, anytime, use:

```
LOCAL cMethodName
cMethodName = SUBSTR(PROGRAM(),1+RAT(".",PROGRAM()))
= EVALUATE(This.ParentClass+"::" + cMethodName)
```

This calls the method of the parent class from which this class is derived, reinstating the "normal" code hierarchy as if no code were present in the class.

Obviously, either form can be a real time-saving device, since many subclasses differ in just one aspect from the parent, and the parent code can be called before, after, or even in the middle of the custom code written for this subclass. More importantly, though, calling up the hierarchy makes your classes more maintainable. Imagine changing code near the top of the class hierarchy and finding it doesn't affect some of the objects derived from that class! Wouldn't that be frustrating? More importantly, wouldn't that defeat the primary object of object orientation—reduced maintenance? By always calling up the hierarchy, except when you explicitly want to override the normal behavior, you know what to expect when you use a particular subclass.

In some cases, you might want to simply change the time at which the built-in behavior of the VFP base classes occurs (such as putting a character in the keyboard buffer or opening tables). The built-in behaviors normally occur after the custom code in an event, but there are times when you want VFP to do its thing before your code, or in the middle of your code. For those situations, you can combine DoDefault() and NoDefault. Issue DoDefault() at the point at which you want the built-in behavior. Issue NoDefault at any point in the code (or at least, any point that actually gets executed). We like to put the two together to make it clear what's going on, though.

Finally, we should point out that there's nothing magical about either keyword. Like anything else in FoxPro, they take effect only if they get executed. So, you can write code that figures out what's going on and suppresses base behavior or calls up the class hierarchy only when it's appropriate.

"Ready, Aim, Fire"

In order to have your code perform as you expect it to, it's essential that you understand the order and the circumstances in which a particular event's code will be called. For the purposes of this discussion, we break up the VFP classes into four groups: general non-container controls, containers, forms and form sets, and the rest (which includes some classes that don't have anything to do with forms). A fifth group, database events, added in VFP 7, is covered in the Reference section. Most of the event model discussions can be explained by looking at individual controls, but some events only make sense (or only occur) in terms of higher-level objects.

Non-container Controls

Init fires when the object is first created or "instantiated." This method is similar to the "constructor" methods of other object-oriented languages. (It differs from constructors in that it doesn't actually create the object.) If the object should be populated with data at run time, or if its properties should be altered based on the present circumstance in the user's environment (say, her selection of currency values calls for a change to InputMask, or his color set calls for a change to the contrasting colors of a control), Init is the place to do it.

Despite the fact that Init code is the first to run after an object has been created, we have been able to change the properties of an object in the Init of another object that fires before the Init of the targeted object. However, trying the same code in the form's Load event generates the expected "Unknown member" error. We suspect that all of the objects are instantiated first, and then their Inits are run in the same order. We don't recommend depending on this undocumented behavior, though it has remained the same for four versions.

Destroy fires when the object is released in one of three situations: the container is being released (like a form closing), a release method is fired, or all references to the object go out of scope.

An Error event fires when an error occurs in a method of the control (or in a program or ActiveX control method called from a method of the control) and the Error method contains any code (at any level of its class hierarchy). The method can call a global event handler object, or assume the responsibility for dealing with an anticipated error, handling it locally for greater encapsulation of the control's behavior.

Other events fire when the corresponding user actions occur. For example, when the mouse enters the boundaries of the control, the MouseEnter event fires, followed by a series of MouseMove events. The MouseLeave event fires when the mouse moves off the control. MouseEnter and MouseLeave are new in VFP 7.

Similarly, a control's GotFocus event fires when the control receives the focus. LostFocus fires when the control loses focus, and so forth.

Containers

A container behaves much like other controls. It has similar, if not identical, events associated with it. Init occurs when the object is created, Destroy when it is released. Error fires when an error occurs; the user interface events (MouseOver, Drag, Click) fire as they do for the non-containers. The difference between a container and other controls is the sequence of event firings for the container and its contained controls.

Init events start with the innermost controls. This makes sense once you realize that a container cannot perform its actions until its contents exist. (Yeah, we guess you could argue that you can't put the controls anywhere until the container exists, but that's not how it works.) Therefore, objects are created from the inside out. If a text box is placed in the column of a grid and that grid is on the page of a page frame in a form, the sequence of Init firings is: text box, column, grid, page, page frame, and finally form. This is probably counter-intuitive to our mental models of a form; first you get a box, then you fill it with stuff, right? But there is some logic to the idea that first you create the individual controls and then you can run the routines from the container that affects them all.

Destroy events fire in the opposite order, from the outside in, as if the container is imploding. This, too, makes some sense from a programming point of view, since the destruction of the container forces the things inside to go "ka-blooie," too.

Containers and their contained controls also share some user interface events. The amount of sharing and interaction between the two objects depends on how tightly bound the two objects are to each other. For example, when a text box is placed on a page or in a column of a grid, that text box pretty much has free reign over what occurs on its turf. Once the object gains the focus, events are within the domain of that control. Once focus is lost, the container can then fire related events, such as the AfterRowColChange event in a grid.

On the other hand, "dedicated" container controls that hold only one type of control, such as option groups and command groups, tend to be much more involved in interactions with their contents. When the mouse is moved over a command button in a command group, the MouseMove event of the button fires first, followed by the MouseMove event of the button group. See "Controls and KAOS" for the sequence of events when a button in a button group is clicked—the key point is that some events fire at both the button and the group levels.

Forms, FormSets and Toolbars

Forms, formsets and toolbars are just big containers. Like the other controls before them, they have Init, Destroy and Error, as well as Click, DblClick and the other Mouse events. But they also have some additional events and features.

The data environment's OpenTables and CloseTables methods fire automatically (despite the fact that they're methods) if automatic opening of tables has been selected using the cleverly named AutoOpenTables and (you'll never guess) AutoCloseTables properties. In this case, these two methods behave more like events than methods. If manually initiated opening or closing is selected, explicit calls to the OpenTables and CloseTables methods are required to open and close tables. The BeforeOpenTables and AfterCloseTables events fire immediately before and after (respectively) the tables are opened or closed.

We found BeforeOpenTables a hard event to understand at first. BeforeOpenTables fires immediately before the tables are actually opened, but after the OpenTables method has been called and the custom code in it has run. Placing a DEBUGOUT in each of the methods gives the unintuitive sequence OpenTables, then BeforeOpenTables, but in fact, the BeforeOpenTables event is fired because the OpenTables code is preparing to actually open the tables. (You can't use Event Tracking to test this sequence because OpenTables isn't an event.) The key point is that BeforeOpenTables fires *not* before the OpenTables method, but before that method's default behavior of opening tables occurs.

In any event (pun intended), the data environment events are wrapped around the form, so that the form has data available from the time it starts until it finishes.

The Load event fires before all other form events, including the initial data environment events, offering a handy place to take care of form-wide settings. Unload is the last event on the form to fire, although the data environment's Destroy events occur after the form is long gone. Activate and Deactivate fire when the form or toolbar gets the focus (is "activated") or loses the focus. The Paint event fires in toolbars or forms whenever the object needs to be redrawn because of the removal of an overlying object or a change in the size of the object or its contents. The

QueryUnload event, unique to forms, allows the form to sense the reason it's being released and either prevent incorrect actions, or ensure that all processing is complete before the form terminates.

Other Objects

VFP 6 introduced some new objects that don't fit into any of the categories above: ActiveDoc, Hyperlink and ProjectHook. VFP 6 SP3 introduced the Session object. All have Init, Destroy and Error events. Hyperlink and Session have no additional events (and we're sort of inclined to think of them as non-container controls), but the other two classes each have some events that are different from any others in VFP.

Active docs have several events that let them interact with their "host" (that is, the browser in which they're running). The Run event fires when the active doc has been created and is ready to go. It's essentially the "main program" of the active doc. ShowDoc and HideDoc fire when their names say—when the active doc application becomes visible or invisible. CommandTargetQuery and CommandTargetExec fire when the user performs actions in the host, to offer the active doc a chance to respond. Finally, ContainerRelease fires when the host lets go of the active doc.

Project hooks have events that fire when the user (developer, in this case, presumably) acts on the associated project. QueryAddFile, QueryModifyFile, QueryNewFile (added in VFP 7), QueryRemoveFile and QueryRunFile fire when the specified action occurs on a file in the project—issuing NoDefault in one of those methods prevents the action from taking place. BeforeBuild and AfterBuild are also well named because they fire when a build is initiated and completed. You shouldn't need to deal with any of these events at run time, since project hooks are essentially a design-time creation.

The Whole Event

Let's run through the whole event loop now, just to tie it all together. Your user has started your application. You've run the startup routine, perhaps instantiating a number of application-wide objects. These might include an Application object, to contain application-wide preferences, keep track of the current status and get the ball rolling. Other objects your application might use are a Security object, to accept a login and password and to dole out permissions as requested; a Data Manager object, to control the flow of data to and from your various forms; a Form Manager object, to keep track of active forms and handle any interactions among them; and an Error Handler object, to take care of errors not dealt with locally. (In VFP 6 and later, take a look at the classes in the _framewk library found in the Wizards subdirectory to get a sense of how you can distribute responsibilities in an application. Be forewarned: This is complex code, though quite well written. Don't expect to fully understand it on the first pass.)

Once everything is set up the way it should be, your program issues the READ EVENTS command to get the event loop started, and your application sits back and waits for the user to pick something to do. The user chooses a form to work on, and the form begins.

The data environment starts the ball rolling by optionally setting up a private data session for this form, opening the tables, setting up relations, and instantiating cursors. OpenTables (if it has code) and BeforeOpenTables fire first and the tables get opened. The Load event of the form or form set fires next. This is the first form event, and a place to put code that should run before the rest of the form gets to work, such as settings to be used throughout the form. There follows a flurry of Init events—first created are the data environment and its contents (from the inside out), and then controls from the innermost outward, by ZOrder within a container level. This ends finally with the Init of the form, and is followed by the Activate event of the form. Next, the Refresh methods are called (by whom? Refresh is a method, not an event), one for each control and for the form itself, from the outside in. Finally, the control designated to be the first on the form (by TabIndex) fires its When clause, to make any last-minute changes before it accepts the focus. If the When returns .T. (or nothing at all—.T. is assumed), the GotFocus events fire—first the form's, then any container's, and finally the control's. And there we sit, waiting for the next action.

While a control is sitting on a form, snoozing, waiting for something to happen, no events fire, except perhaps the Timer event of a timer control. When the user tabs to a control, or brings his mouse over a control, that's when the fun begins. If the mouse was used to select a control, the MouseMove event can be the first to sense the approach of the user's pointer. (If both container and contained controls have code in their MouseMove events, the container can even prepare the controls for the arrival of the mouse. But watch out—MouseMove fires a lot. Too much code there could slow things down. On a fairly powerful machine, 50,000 repetitions of a totally empty loop were enough to result in some visual oddities.) Along with the MouseMove event, as the mouse moves over the boundaries of the controls, the MouseEnter event fires. Likewise, if you roll off the control, the MouseLeave event fires. MouseEnter and MouseLeave were added in VFP 7.

The When event determines whether the object is allowed to gain focus; if When returns .F., the events stop here for now. Once it's been confirmed that the new object can have the focus, the last object's LostFocus event runs. Next up are the new object's GotFocus and Message events.

What goes on when the user is within the domain of an individual control depends to some extent on what the control is and what it is capable of doing. A simple command button can sense and react to MouseDown, MouseUp, Click and Valid events, all from a single mouse click, but we find we usually put code only in the Click event.

Although it is nice to have the other options there, we suspect that many of the events don't see much use except when designing very specific interfaces per clients' requests. A more complex control, like a combo box or a grid, can have a richer set of interactions with the user. We leave the specifics of each control's behavior to the Reference section, but cover below exactly which controls have which events.

Finally, the user wants to leave our form. We usually provide our users with a Close button for that purpose. But they can also select the Close option from the form's control menu or the close ("X") button on the title bar. In the last two cases, the QueryUnload event occurs, letting us detect the user's desire to quit, so we can ensure the same handling that occurs when he uses the Close button. If QueryUnload lets the form close, the form's Destroy event fires, followed by the Destroy events of the objects on the form. The form's Unload event follows the Destroy events of all contained objects. The data environment then shuts down. If the data environment's AutoCloseTables property is set to true, the tables close and the AfterCloseTables event fires. (If, on the other hand, AutoCloseTables is false, the tables close only if the CloseTables method is called programmatically.) The data environment's Destroy events follow. Like its associated form, the data environment implodes, firing first the data environment's Destroy, and then the Destroy events of any contained relations and cursors.

Event, Event—Who's Got the Event?

So, with 36 different base classes and 72 events to choose from, how's a body to know which classes support which events? Well, we suppose you could just open them up in the Form or Class Designer and check it out, but we've saved you the trouble by putting together this table. The events are listed in descending order based on how many base classes have them.

Event	Object(s)	Meaning
Init	All base classes in VFP 6 and later. In earlier versions, some classes omitted this event.	Fires when the object is created and can accept parameters. If Init returns .F., the object is not created. Contained objects fire before containers, in the order added; see ZOrder in the Reference section.

Event	Object(s)	Meaning
Error	All base classes in VFP 6 and later. In earlier versions, some classes omitted this event.	Fires when an error occurs in the method of an object. Receives the error number, method name and line number. If there's no code here or in its class hierarchy, the error handler established with ON ERROR, or as a last resort, the built-in VFP "Cancel Ignore Suspend" dialog, fires.
Destroy	All base classes in VFP 6 and later. In earlier versions, some classes omitted this event.	Code runs just before an object is released. Containers fire before contents.
DragOver, DragDrop	All base classes except ActiveDoc, Column, Cursor, Custom, DataEnvironment, FormSet, Header, Hyperlink, ProjectHook, Relation, Separator, Session, and Timer	Fire during and on completion, respectively, of a native VFP drag and drop operation. Each receives parameters to accept a reference to the data being dragged and the mouse coordinates.
MouseMove	All base classes except ActiveDoc, Cursor, Custom, DataEnvironment, FormSet, Hyperlink, OLEControl, OLEBoundControl, ProjectHook, Relation, Separator, Session, and Timer	Tracks mouse movement over an object. Receives status of Ctrl, Alt, and Shift keys, as well as left, middle, and right mouse button statuses.

Event	Object(s)	Meaning
MouseWheel	All base classes except ActiveDoc, Cursor, Custom, DataEnvironment, FormSet, Hyperlink, OLEControl, OLEBoundControl, ProjectHook, Relation, Separator, Session, and Timer	Fires on use of the rotating wheel available on some pointing devices. Receives parameters indicating direction of movement, current position, and the status of the Ctrl, Alt, and Shift keys.
MouseEnter, MouseLeave (VFP 7)	All base classes except ActiveDoc, Cursor, Custom, DataEnvironment, FormSet, Hyperlink, OLEControl, OLEBoundControl, ProjectHook, Relation, Separator, Session, and Timer	Fires when the mouse enters or leaves, respectively, the boundaries of the control. Receives status of Ctrl, Alt, and Shift keys, as well as left, middle, and right mouse button statuses.
MouseDown, MouseUp, Click	All base classes except ActiveDoc, Column, Cursor, Custom, DataEnvironment, FormSet, Hyperlink, OLEControl, OLEBoundControl, ProjectHook, Relation, Separator, Session, and Timer	Fire when the user uses the left (primary) mouse button. Typically detected in the order shown.

Event	Object(s)	Meaning
RightClick, MiddleClick	All base classes except ActiveDoc, Column, Cursor, Custom, DataEnvironment, FormSet, Hyperlink, OLEBoundControl, OLEControl, ProjectHook, Relation, Separator, Session, and Timer	Fires when the right or middle mouse button, respectively, is clicked. These are not preceded by MouseDown and MouseUp events.
OLEDragOver, OLEDragDrop	All base classes except ActiveDoc, Column, Cursor, Custom, DataEnvironment, FormSet, Header, Hyperlink, OLEBoundControl, OLEControl, Relation, Separator, Session, and Timer	Fire during and on completion, respectively, of an OLE drag and drop operation. Receive parameters describing the drag action in progress, including a reference to the dragged data object.
OLEGiveFeedback	All base classes except ActiveDoc, Column, Cursor, Custom, DataEnvironment, FormSet, Header, Hyperlink, OLEBoundControl, OLEControl, Relation, Separator, Session, and Timer	Fires for the drag source of an OLE drag and drop each time the OLEDragOver event fires for a drop target. Allows the source to control the potential results of a drop and the icon in use.

Event	Object(s)	Meaning
OLEStartDrag, OLECompleteDrag	All base classes except ActiveDoc, Column, Cursor, Custom, DataEnvironment, FormSet, Header, Hyperlink, OLEBoundControl, OLEControl, ProjectHook, Relation, Separator, Session, and Timer	Fire for the drag source of an OLE drag and drop when the operation starts and when it ends. OLEStartDrag lets the data source indicate valid actions. OLECompleteDrag lets it respond to whatever occurred.
OLESetData	All base classes except ActiveDoc, Column, Cursor, Custom, DataEnvironment, FormSet, Header, Hyperlink, OLEBoundControl, OLEControl, ProjectHook, Relation, Separator, Session, and Timer	Fires for the drag source of an OLE drag and drop when the drop target requests data. Receives a reference to the data object and the format requested by the drop target.
DblClick	All base classes except ActiveDoc, Column, CommandButton, Cursor, Custom, DataEnvironment, FormSet, Hyperlink, OLEControl, OLEBoundControl, ProjectHook, Relation, Separator, Session, and Timer	Fires when the user double-clicks.

Event	Object(s)	Meaning
UIEnable	CheckBox, ComboBox, CommandButton, CommandGroup, Container, Control, EditBox, Grid, Image, Label, Line, ListBox, OLEBoundControl, OLEControl, OptionButton, OptionGroup, PageFrame, Shape, Spinner, TextBox	Fires when control becomes visible or invisible because of activation or deactivation of the page it sits on in a page frame. This method receives a parameter indicating whether the page is being activated (.T.) or deactivated (.F.). We think that separate UIEnable and UIDisable events would be more consistent with the rest of the event model.
GotFocus, LostFocus	CheckBox, ComboBox, CommandButton, Container, Control, EditBox, Form, ListBox, OLEBoundControl, OLEControl, OptionButton, Spinner, TextBox	GotFocus occurs when the control is tabbed to or clicked on. The When event fires before, and determines whether, GotFocus fires. LostFocus fires when another control is clicked on or tabbed to, and that control succeeds in gaining the focus using its When event.

Event	Object(s)	Meaning
When	CheckBox, ComboBox, CommandButton, CommandGroup, EditBox, Grid, ListBox, OptionButton, OptionGroup, Spinner, TextBox	Good old When, a useful carryover from FoxPro 2.x, fires before GotFocus. A control can't have the focus unless When says it's okay. When also fires on each up-arrow and down-arrow keystroke while scrolling through a list box, but does not fire while scrolling in a combo box (use InteractiveChange for that).
Valid	CheckBox, ComboBox, CommandButton, CommandGroup, EditBox, Grid, ListBox, OptionButton, OptionGroup, Spinner, TextBox	Valid usually fires when a change is made. Even if no changes are made, tabbing though a combo box, edit box or text box fires its Valid event. Returning a numeric value from Valid determines the next control to get focus. Zero forces focus to stay on the current control without firing the ErrorMessage event; negative values move back through the tab order; positive values move forward.

Event	Object(s)	Meaning
ErrorMessage, Message	CheckBox, ComboBox, CommandButton, CommandGroup, EditBox, ListBox, OptionButton, OptionGroup, Spinner, TextBox	When Valid returns .F., ErrorMessage fires to display an error message. We hardly ever use this—we handle the problem in the Valid, prompting the user if necessary, and use the return of zero in Valid to handle this. Message is an old-fashioned way of putting text on the status bar—consider StatusBar and StatusBarText instead.
KeyPress	CheckBox, ComboBox, CommandButton, EditBox, Form, ListBox, OptionButton, Spinner, TextBox	Allows processing of input keystroke-by-keystroke, rather than waiting for input to be completed.
Moved, Resize	Column, Container, Control, Form, Grid, OLEBoundControl, OLEControl, PageFrame, Toolbar	Fire when the object has been moved or resized, respectively.
InteractiveChange, ProgrammaticChange	CheckBox, ComboBox, CommandGroup, EditBox, ListBox, OptionGroup, Spinner, TextBox	What UPDATED() always should have been, but at a finer level. Fires each time a change is made to a control's Value, even before focus has shifted from the control. InteractiveChange detects user changes; ProgrammaticChange fires on changes performed in code.

Event	Object(s)	Meaning
Activate, Deactivate	Form, FormSet, Page, ProjectHook (VFP 7), Toolbar	Occur when container gets the focus or the Show method is called, and when it loses the focus or the Hide method is called, respectively. With regard to the ProjectHook, these events occur when the developer activates or deactivates the Project Manager by clicking on or outside the window, or using the ACTIVATE WINDOW <project> command.
RangeHigh, RangeLow	ComboBox, ListBox, Spinner, TextBox	These events have two distinct uses, both of them outdated. For text boxes and spinners, these can be used to prevent out-of-range entries. Don't do it this way—use Valid instead. For combo boxes and list boxes, these are used only in forms converted from FoxPro 2.x to indicate the first element and number of elements settings.
DownClick, UpClick	ComboBox, Spinner	Not to be confused with MouseDown, fires when the down or up arrow of a spinner is pressed or, for combos, when the arrows on the scrollbar are used.

Event	Object(s)	Meaning
Load, Unload	Form, FormSet	Load is the first form event to fire, before Init, Activate and GotFocus. Load fires for the form set before the form. Unload is the last form event to fire, reversing the order: form first and then form set.
Paint	Form, Toolbar	Fires when the item is repainted. CAUTION: Don't Resize or Refresh an object in its Paint event—a "cascading" series can occur!
Scrolled	Form, Grid	Fires when the user uses the scrollbars. Parameter indicates how the scrollbars were used.
BeforeOpenTables, AfterCloseTables	Data Environment	Wrappers around the automatic behavior of the Data Environment. Occur before and after tables are automatically opened and closed, respectively.
BeforeRowColChange, AfterRowColChange	Grid	Fire before the Valid of the row or column of the cell being left, and after the When of the cell being moved to, respectively.
Deleted	Grid	Fires when the user marks or unmarks a row for deletion.
DropDown	ComboBox	Fires when user opens the list part of the combo box.

Event	Object(s)	Meaning
Timer	Timer	Fires when a timer is enabled and its Interval has passed.
BeforeDock, AfterDock, Undock	ToolBar	Microsoft missed a great chance here for a property to tell you which toolbars are attached just below the menu—a WhatsUpDock property. These events probably won't shock you: BeforeDock fires before a toolbar is docked, AfterDock after the fact, and Undock when the toolbar is moved from a docked position.
QueryUnload	Form	Fires when a form is released other than through a call to its Release method or explicit release of the referencing variable. Allows testing of the ReleaseType property to determine how the form is being released and takes appropriate action.
BeforeBuild, AfterBuild	ProjectHook	Fire before and after a project is built, whether through the interface or the Build method.
QueryAddFile, QueryModifyFile, QueryNewFile (VFP 7), QueryRemoveFile, QueryRunFile	ProjectHook	Fire when the specified action is taken on a file in the project. NODEFAULT in the method prevents the indicated action.

Event	Object(s)	Meaning
ShowDoc, HideDoc	ActiveDoc	Fire when the user navigates to or from an active document application, respectively.
Run	ActiveDoc	Fires when an active document application is all set up and ready to go. Use it to start the application doing something useful.
CommandTargetQuery, CommandTargetExec	ActiveDoc	Fire when the user of an active document application in a browser begins or completes an action in the browser that might be handled by the application.
ContainerRelease	ActiveDoc	Fires when the browser holding an active document application lets go of the application. Allows the app to figure out what to do next.
ReadActivate, ReadDeactivate, ReadShow, ReadValid, ReadWhen	Form	Based on the FoxPro 2.x READ model, these work only in the "compatibility" modes. Ignore them unless you're converting older apps.

Add Your Own Events

In addition to the events provided by the designers, versions starting with VFP 6 let us add our own custom events. Sort of. The new Access and Assign methods let us attach code to any property of any object. The Access method for a property fires when the property's value is read; the Assign method fires when a value is stored to the property (whether or not it's actually changed). In addition, the This_Access method fires whenever any property of the object is read or written.

We consider these events even though their names are "Access method" and "Assign method," because they fire on their own under specified circumstances. That makes them events, by us. If we did add these to the table above, they'd have to go at the top, since not only does every object support them, but for the property-specific versions, a given object can have as many Access methods and as many Assign methods as it has properties.

How to Mangle the Event Model

There are a few items, especially those which have been retained in Visual FoxPro "for backward compatibility" that can cause some real difficulties with the new event model. We cover a few of them here for your consideration. We think these are some of the first items you should be looking at revising if you're moving a FoxPro 2.x application to Visual FoxPro.

On Key Label commands

An ON KEY LABEL command defines an action to be performed as soon as the keystroke is received. Unlike keyboard macros and keystrokes processed in input controls, "OKLs," as they are often called, are processed immediately, interrupting the current processing between two lines of code. If these routines do not restore the environment to exactly the condition it was in before the OKL initiated, the results, as Microsoft likes to say, can be unpredictable. Disastrous is more like it. We recommend trying newer alternatives, like the KeyPress event of the affected controls, rather than depending on being able to control all the side effects of this shot-in-the-dark.

ON Commands In General

ON commands are a different kind of event handler. ON KEY reacts to each keystroke, ON ESCAPE to pressing the ESCape key, and ON KEY = only to a specific keystroke (with a READ to be in effect). Give up on these. Use the newer Visual FoxPro events. While there are exceptions—Christof Lange's very clever Y2K solution is one of them—generally speaking, anything done with the old ON model can be done in a more extensible, supportable way with the new event model. ON ERROR and ON SHUTDOWN are the necessary exceptions that prove the rule.

BROWSEs

Integrating BROWSE with READ was the sought-after Holy Grail of FoxPro 2.x. BROWSE, arguably one of the most powerful commands in the language, was a bit testy about sharing the stage with READ. Because BROWSEs did not make it easy to detect when they were activated and deactivated, it was difficult to properly manage them within a READ situation. Although several plausible solutions were advanced, most were very sensitive to changes in the environment and difficult to work with. With the advent of grids in Visual FoxPro, these complexities have been eliminated (and totally new ones introduced), as should BROWSEs from your application code. If you haven't heard enough of this topic, tune in to "Commands Never to Use."

"Your Server Will Be With You in a Moment"

If we do not lay out ourselves in the service of mankind whom should we serve?

Abigail Adams, 1778

Client-Server: definitely one of the buzzwords of the nineties. Or is that two of the buzzwords—we haven't figured out yet whether "client-server" is one word or two. We're not alone in this. A salesman for a major vendor asked to define client-server a few years ago responded, "Client-server? Why, that's whatever it is I'm selling today."

So why all the fuss about client-server? Because most organizations have their data spread out over multiple machines in at least as many formats. Client-server is advertised as the ticket to using all that data without forcing everyone to use the same applications or having to convert everything to a common format.

Of course, now that we're in the zeros (or is that the aughts?), client-server should be passé, right? Well, although it certainly gets less attention than it did when we wrote earlier editions of this book, client-server still has a lot of life left in it.

UDA, ODBC, ADO, OLEDB, DAO, RDO, I Don't Know!

We noticed a trend several years ago while surfing the Microsoft Web site. Where previously there had been little or no talk about database issues, now we were starting to see some action. WebDb, DAO and RDO were the first, then OLE DB, ADO and UDA. Acronymomania! From little attention, Microsoft turned its focus from the Office suite and network wars first to the Internet and then to the enterprise. Like drinking from a firehose, suddenly we were drowning in new terminology, 1.0 products and "preview" betaware. With Visual Studio 6, we started to see the first stable products of this craze. Now, these tools have been used successfully for several years, so we'll take a deeper look at all those acronyms and a few more (like MTS and COM+) a little later, in "n-Tiers of a Clown," below.

Let's get back to client-server. In Microsoft's world, client-server and database connectivity are implemented through ODBC, or "Open DataBase Connectivity." ODBC is to databases what Print Manager is to printers. Just as Print Manager and appropriate drivers let you send all sorts of documents to whatever printers you want,

ODBC, together with a set of drivers, lets you use data from whatever database management system you want in an assortment of applications. Windows comes with a bunch of drivers. You can get other (and perhaps more up-to-date) drivers from the manufacturer of the DBMS you need to talk to.

Visual FoxPro provides two methods of performing client-server: views and SQL Pass-Through. Views are everyman's entree to the client-server world. You can grab server data, manipulate it in FoxPro, and then return it to the server. SQL Pass-Through gives you more control at the cost of more responsibility. You communicate with the server through a special set of functions—you can pass commands directly to the server to be executed. (SQL Pass-Through is an updated version of what the Connectivity Kit provided in FoxPro 2.x.)

So What's a Server, Anyway?

A client is to me a mere unit, a factor in a problem.

Sir Arthur Conan Doyle, Sherlock Holmes in *The Sign of Four*

Let's get some basic terminology down. Start with "client" and "server." The server's the one who has the data you want. It might be a mainframe on the other side of the world, Oracle on your network, or Access on your machine. The server is also called the "back end." Server data is sometimes referred to as "remote" data.

The client is the one who wants the data—in our case, your Visual FoxPro application. The client is sometimes called the "front end." Data that originates in the client is called "native" or "local" data.

ODBC is the translator here. It sits between the client and the server and converts the client's requests into a form the server understands. Then it converts the server's responses back into the client's format.

A key ODBC concept is a "data source" (also known as a DSN)—an application and a database it owns. When you want to get your hands on server data, you tell ODBC what data source to use. For testing purposes, our favorite in years past was Microsoft Access with the ODBC drivers pointing at a doctored-up copy of Access' sample Northwind Traders database. (The doctoring was to remove embedded spaces in the names of the Northwind tables and fields. In defiance of pretty much every other DBMS out there, Access lets you use spaces in names of things. Kind of like Visual FoxPro's long names, which also let you embed spaces in table and view names. In both cases, while Visual FoxPro can handle it, it's generally more trouble than it's worth.) These days, we're more inclined to use SQL Server or MSDE (Microsoft Database Engine, which is essentially a free, albeit limited, edition of SQL Server), pointing to the SQL Server version of the Northwind database.

To create a new ODBC data source, use the Windows ODBC Data Source Administrator, available from the Windows Control Panel (in Windows 2000 and later operating systems, choose "Administrative Tools" within the Control Panel to find the ODBC icon). You can create a user data source (available to the currently logged-in user only), a system data source (available to all users), or a file data source (the information is stored in a file rather than in the Registry with user and system data sources). The exact steps for creating a data source vary, depending on the ODBC driver used, but they generally involve selecting the server (if necessary) and "database" (for example, an actual database in the case of SQL Server, Oracle, or other DBMS, or a directory containing DBF files in the case of VFP free tables or dBase files).

You can define a data source that doesn't point at a particular database, but then you'll get prompted to specify one every time you open that data source.

All of this terminology can be misleading, since for some data sources, such as an Access table on your local machine, the data is neither remote, nor is there truly any process running that you can call a server. Using ODBC to connect to this data source is not truly "client-server" in its pure sense, but, thanks to the abstraction of ODBC, it will appear exactly the same to the consumer of the data, the client. This abstraction of interfaces is key to letting us prototype a client-server application using a "one-tier" ODBC data source.

Data From Afar and From Anear

'Tis distance lends enchantment to the view.

Thomas Campbell, Pleasures of Hope

Views are a very cool idea. They let you take data from a variety of sources and handle it all pretty much the same way. Once you get your hands on the data, you don't have to worry about where it came from.

A view is a subset of the data in a database, organized in a way that makes sense for a particular operation. Often, data in a view is denormalized to make it easier to report on or more logical for the user who's working with it.

Views in FoxPro can be based on remote data, native data or a combination of the two. This makes it possible to process data without regard to the original source of the data. From your application's perspective, the data in the view is just data; it doesn't know or care whether it started out in FoxPro, Access, SQL Server, or Joe's Original Database.

Data in a view can be updated. It's your choice whether the updated data gets passed back to the original data source and, if so, when that happens. By definition, all the fields in a view are updateable locally (in Visual FoxPro). It's your responsibility not to let users make updates that don't get passed to the server. Having their updates thrown away tends to make most users a little grouchy, so ensure that your interface makes it clear when data is updateable and when it is not.

Views are based on queries. A view is defined by specifying a query that collects the data to populate the view. Like so much else in Visual FoxPro, this can be done either by command or using the visual tools (in this case, the View Designer, known for short as the VD—we can't believe they left this name in).

It's much easier to create views with the VD than in code, but you have to accept the serious limitations of working within the VD. In Visual FoxPro 5, in a move to make VFP more ANSI-SQL-compatible by supporting the new JOIN clause, Microsoft broke the View Designer badly. Because of the way join clauses form intermediate results between tables, multiple joins to the same tables (such as a parent with two sibling children) often cannot be expressed properly by the Designer. It complains while saving a view that it will not be editable again, or gripes that columns cannot be found. Fortunately, we have the coded method to fall back on. When you create views in code (using CREATE SQL VIEW), you generally need a long series of calls to DBSETPROP() to establish update criteria. One solution is a hybrid approach. Get as far as you can with the VD, coding your simple views, then use the cool utility GENDBC (which ships with FoxPro) to get the code to create the view. Make further modifications to the code, run it, and you've got your view. Our preferred approach, though, is to use one of the freeware utilities available for this task: eView from Erik Moore or ViewEdit from Steve Sawyer. See the Resources section at the back of the book for information on these tools.

You can also create parameterized views. With these, one or more variables appear in the query's WHERE clause preceded by "?". When you open the view, the value of those variables is substituted into the query. No big deal, right? Except that, if the variable doesn't exist, the user is prompted for a value. Imagine a view that pulls out all customers in a single country. Rather than writing separate versions for each country, or some deviously tricky, macroized routine you'll never figure out how to debug, you use a parameter for the country and the user fills it in at run time. If the query parameter does exist, the user isn't prompted, so if you prefer to create your own dialog for the user, or can derive the parameterized value from the environment, you can create the parameter and refresh the view yourself. We often find ourselves coding this trick in calls to the Refresh() function.

A Forward Pass

For I will pass through the land of Egypt this night …

Exodus

SQL Pass-Through (or SPT) is for those who need to be in control. Instead of simply defining a view once and opening it as needed, with SPT you send the necessary commands to the server each time you want to see some data.

SPT works a lot like FoxPro's low-level file functions. You open a connection, which gives you a handle. After that, you refer to the connection by the handle and call on appropriate functions to communicate with the server. When you're done, you close the connection.

By providing more or less direct access to the server, SPT also lets you handle administrative functions on the server end of things. You can even perform tasks like creating tables on the server. Definitely, this mode is for those who know what they're doing.

This makes SPT sound quite difficult and challenging. Perhaps the best use of SPT is to call stored procedures written on the server, and have them return cursors with the information (even if that cursor is a one-record table containing only one field). The stored procedures are written in the native language of the server; for example, SQL Server uses T-SQL. You can debug the stored procedure in its native environment (which may be more, less, or differently robust than VFP, but it likely checks the syntax properly and accesses the appropriate help files). For small development shops, this may mean that you get to learn all about the server's native language (which isn't a bad idea if you're working with that server), but for larger shops, it may mean that you can ask the DBA (who is hopefully familiar with the language) to write a stored procedure to do what you need. This gives you the best of both worlds: You don't have to debug a complex SQL Server or Oracle statement that lives as a text string in VFP, and you might be able to get someone else to help optimize, write, or maintain the code.

Which commands you can actually pass depends on the server. Different servers have different capabilities. You'll need to learn the capabilities and liabilities of the servers you want to work with.

I've Got Connections

In historic events, the so-called great men are labels giving names to events, and like labels they have but the smallest connection with the event itself.

Leo Tolstoy, *War and Peace*

To access remote data, you need a data source. You also have various options regarding the way Visual FoxPro interacts with that data source. Since you're likely to want to do it the same way over and over again, FoxPro lets you create what it calls a connection.

A connection is simply the name of a data source, along with various properties; the connection is stored and assigned a name. When you create a view or open a communication channel with SPT, one of your options is to use a named connection. Without it, you have to specify the data source and all the appropriate properties. Individual views can have their connection specified in the CREATE VIEW command or within the VD interface (look under Advanced Options on the Query menu pad). Sharing a connection is the preferred option in a production environment, because connections consume valuable resources on the server. In addition, some servers are licensed by connection, rather than by user, and an errant application can consume many more connections than necessary, limiting the number of users.

The Connection Designer lets you specify connections more or less visually. You can create connections in code with (what else?) the CREATE CONNECTION command. Connect and disconnect with (brace yourself) SQLConnect() and SQLDisconnect().

Developers raise a legitimate concern that connection definitions are stored within the DBC and could include user IDs and passwords to access back-end databases. We agree. There are good solutions out there as well. First, don't store the password with the connection. Either ask the operator for it at run time, or store it in an encrypted field. Starting in VFP 7, it's easier to do this with remote views because the USE command has a CONNSTRING clause that overrides the connection information the view was defined with. This allows you to specify things like the user name and password at run time rather than design time.

Buzzwords? You Want Buzzwords?

The chief merit of language is clearness, and we know that nothing detracts so much from this as do unfamiliar terms.

Galen, *On the Natural Faculties*

There are a number of items you can set to control access to remote data. Some of them apply only with SPT, while others affect views as well. Naturally, all of them come with long-winded terminology. Most of these settings apply to a connection, but some are properties of individual views or cursors.

A word of caution here. Several of the authors have run into situations where a developer has tweaked so many of these options that it's impossible to figure out what's causing performance or operational problems. As a general rule, the defaults are the right settings. Change these with care, and only one at a time, testing before and after the change to ensure that you're seeing the effect you desire, and aren't breaking other parts of the application with your change.

Everything in Synch

The first choice you have (for SPT or named connections only) is whether to use synchronous or asynchronous processing. In English, this means whether you have to wait for the command to finish or you get control back right away.

Synchronous processing is what we're all pretty much used to. You issue a command and when it's done, you go on. With asynchronous processing, you have to keep asking the server if it's done. So why would you want to do this? If the command will take a long time, asynchronous processing lets you update the display (or even do other stuff) while you wait. It's like taking a book along to the doctor's office.

With asynchronous processing, you keep issuing the same command over and over until it returns a non-zero value. The bonus is what else you put in the loop that issues the command.

A Nice Big Batch

The next option is relevant only when you're dealing with a server that lets you send multiple commands at once. (SQL Server does this; Access doesn't.) When you do that, you have a choice of waiting for the whole group of commands to finish (batch processing) or starting things off with the first command and then coming back to ask for results of the others (non-batch). This one also applies only to SPT and named connections.

As with asynchronous processing, non-batch lets you do things in between and keep the user updated on progress. In this case, you start the commands and then use SQLMoreResults() each time you want results from a command after the first.

Although synchronous/asynchronous and batch/non-batch sound just about the same, they're really not. Synchronous/asynchronous relate to a single command; batch/non-batch control a group of commands.

In fact, you can mix and match the two. Any of the four combinations of these two settings is permitted. Here are the choices and what they do:

- Synchronous batch processing means you can start a group of commands, and control doesn't return until all the commands have been processed. When control returns, a cursor has been created for each result set generated by the commands.

- Asynchronous batch processing means you start a group of commands and keep reissuing the original call (SQLExec()) until it returns something other than zero. At this point, there's a cursor for each result set generated.

- Synchronous non-batch means you start a group of commands. Control returns when the first command is done and there's a cursor containing that result set. You call SQLMoreResults() for each subsequent result set.

- Asynchronous non-batch is the most complicated, but gives you the most control. You start a group of commands. You reissue the original command until you get a non-zero value, at which point you've got the first result set. Then, you issue SQLMoreResults() repeatedly for each additional result set. Each time SQLMoreResults() returns 1, you know you've got another result set. When it returns 2, you know you're done.

But Wait, There's More

Progressive fetching—sounds like something a new-age kind of dog would do. Actually, it means you get control back while the server keeps on sending the rest of the records. This one's easy to test. Just create a view with a few thousand records in it (say, based on the OrderDetails table in Northwinds). When you USE the view from the Command Window, watch what happens in the status bar. You get control back with only 100 records in the cursor, and you can go right ahead and Browse that cursor right away. But if you keep watching the status bar, you'll see the record count going up and up until it's reached the actual table size.

You can set the number of records that get fetched at a time. You also control whether data in memo and general fields is retrieved up front, or not until you need it. Waiting until you need it speeds up the initial query at the cost of a slight delay when you want to edit a memo or general field. Another setting lets you control the maximum number of records returned by the server. You get back the first however many records the server finds; the rest are ignored.

The complete list of properties for remote data access is covered under the DBSetProp(), CursorSetProp() and SQLSetProp() functions.

It's Been a Pleasure Transacting Business with You

Visual FoxPro's built-in transactions let you protect your data when storing it. For example, you can wrap storage of an invoice and its detail records in a transaction. If storage of any one record fails, the whole transaction can be rolled back, preventing partial data from being stored.

FoxPro's transactions don't affect storage of remote data. If the server you're dealing with supports transactions natively, use SQLSetProp() to set Transactions to Manual; without that setting, each individual SQL statement is wrapped in an individual transaction. It's far more likely that you'll want to ensure that whole batches of updates happen together. You can control the remote transactions with the SQLCommit() and SQLRollBack() functions. Remember, though, if you've assumed the responsibility of controlling transactions, you'd better remember to finish them! An uncommitted transaction is automatically rolled back if it's not completed before the connection is lost. Also, transactions typically place a heavy burden on servers, forcing them to hold locks on a number of records and slowing processes for other applications accessing the server. Get in there, start your transaction, make your data changes and get out as quickly as possible, in order to get optimum performance from your server.

To Err is Human

SQL Pass-Through functions handle errors somewhat differently than most FoxPro commands. In fact, error handling for SPT functions is similar to that for the low-level file functions they resemble. Unlike the LLFFs, though, the SPT functions don't have their own dedicated error function—instead, they cooperate with the AError() function.

Rather than triggering a FoxPro error (or the specified error handler), the SPT functions return a negative number when they fail. According to Help, they return -1 when there's a "connection-level" error and -2 when there's an "environment-level" error. We haven't been able to generate an environment-level error, but maybe we just haven't tried the right destructive things.

We've also run into a few situations where an SPT function does go to the FoxPro error handler rather than returning a negative result. Passing bogus SQL sometimes generates error 1526 (a connectivity error). Check out a few of the errors in the 1520's and 1530's for items you'll need to beware of. SQLDisconnect(), in particular, yells for help when you try to shut down a nonexistent connection or a connection that's in use.

It looks like you usually get FoxPro's error handler when FoxPro itself can detect the error, and you get a negative result when ODBC or the server finds the error. We sure wish it were uniform. This hybrid mix makes writing an error handler much harder.

Your overall error handler has to be prepared to deal with some client-server errors, but any SPT code has to check each return value and call on an error handler if a negative value pops up.

In spite of this weakness, we're very satisfied with Visual FoxPro's client-server capabilities. We see a lot of client-server work out there and are really glad that Visual FoxPro can now jump right into the fray.

n-Tiers of a Clown

If you talk to a cutting-edge developer about client-server work, you're likely to get the reaction "Bah! Client-server? Way too limited! We're into n-tier applications now." It sounds way cool, but what does this mean?

The tiers in application development refer to the different independent processes performing data manipulations in an application. A one-tier application, like classic FoxPro applications using DBFs, Access applications with MDB files, or even Word or Excel, involves a client application that reads and writes to a file. While there might be a "server" somewhere out on the network providing file services, there is no other intelligent process intervening between the client and the data. Two-tier applications, on the other hand, have a client application, one that typically interacts with the user, talking to the server application that processes the queries and allows (or disallows) updates to the data. Client-server allows centralized processing of data queries and the centralization of all logic that is needed to determine whether an update should be applied to the database.

What more could we possibly ask for? A two-tier application sounds like it has solved all problems. Client applications perform the locally intensive work of presenting the user interface, while a "big-iron" server can do heavy-duty queries with—what is to the server—local data. In addition, the server can provide a "firewall" of protection to make sure that bad data doesn't get into the system, maintaining referential integrity and perhaps security as well.

Well, there are a few chinks in the armor. First, server products typically each have their own proprietary languages, usually extensions to SQL, and well, frankly, they stink. While they're good at protecting their data and performing routine tasks like queries and triggers, they aren't built for processing complex business logic ("If the customer has ordered more than $X from categories A, B and C within the last 90 days, not counting closeouts and specials, their shipping is free, unless…"), nor is there any easy way to transmit complex messages from the back end to the client. No client likes to be told "Update rejected," but that's about what you can get from a lot of client-server systems.

The other problem with client-server is that the problem model they were designed to solve—big, hefty servers with dumb little terminals—is outdated. While a large shop can field a symmetric multi-processing, RAID-5 server with a couple of gigabytes of RAM and 100 gig of drive space, it's most likely being hit by Pentium III workstations with 256 MB of RAM themselves—not shabby machines. The idea that one box, even with eight processors on it, can do all of the heavy lifting for hundreds of high-powered users is a very poor use of resources.

Enter n-tier. The idea of an n-tier model is that the database server just serves the data. Its job in life is downsized from a one-stop shop to a big, dumb brute that serves data as rapidly as possible, performs queries, fires triggers and ensures relational integrity. Middle tiers come into play—*tiers* with an 's'—there might be more than one, hence we're not talking about three tiers, but *n*, in the sense of 1, 2, 3, 4, ... *n* objects between you and the data. A middle-tier object is where the business rules get placed—an object with clearly defined interfaces and a specific task to which it's been assigned. By creating multiple objects through which the data passes, we can simplify the tasks of each object, and by using an object technology that lets us manage these objects, we can field the individual objects on whichever platform makes the most sense in terms of efficiency and distribution of processing.

So now we need a technology that can create objects with simple interfaces, manage them across an enterprise and allow us to do distributed processing. Is this possible? Ta-da! Microsoft to the rescue with COM and DCOM. Check out "It was Automation, You Know" and "Active Something" for some ideas on where these technologies are and where they are going.

Much ADO About Nothing?

As we mentioned earlier, Microsoft has gone ga-ga over data. We're somewhat glad for the attention, but a little concerned whenever the Microsoft Marketeers get an idea. And lately, they've been getting a lot of them.

For a while, Microsoft pitched Universal Data Access (UDA) as the solution for all things data. The key technologies behind UDA are (get your acronym seat belt on!) ADO, OLE DB and ODBC. What are these? ADO, ActiveX Data Objects, are high-level COM components that provide basic data services within the familiar COM programming model. OLE DB is the underlying technology that ADO uses to reach data. OLE DB, in turn, uses either native OLE DB providers or ODBC to reach the data sources. VFP 7 includes an OLE DB provider for VFP, which is more scalable and provides more capabilities than using the ODBC driver (which is now in "support mode," so it won't be upgraded any more).

So why would we want to go to all this trouble to get to data when we can already do it quite well natively? Well, there are a number of situations where ADO has a distinct advantage over the built-in FoxPro one-tier and two-tier models. First, ADO presents a very simple model. Second, ADO recordsets are COM objects that can be passed from one object to the next with no dependence on work areas or knowledge of how to manipulate a cursor. Not only can ADO be passed between local objects, but these lightweight objects can be transferred over a variety of network protocols, including the Internet.

In addition, languages that lack a native database engine, like Visual Basic or Visual C++, have flocked to this technology, which effectively gives them a data engine to work with. If we want to play in the exciting world of components with these tools, we need to learn to speak the lingua franca as well.

Other pieces in this puzzle include MTS (for Windows NT) and COM+ (for Windows 2000 and later). Now that we have this gaggle of objects slinging ADO recordsets from place to place and attempting complex transactions, how do we coordinate all of this? Microsoft Transaction Server, MTS, was the piece Microsoft came up with to handle all this stuff. This server, running on a Windows NT Server machine, allows us to parcel out and load-balance resource dispensers of middle-tier objects and back-end connections in a manner somewhat akin to the TP monitors of the mainframe model. With the release of Windows 2000, MTS was no longer a bolt-on but became an integrated part of some new technology called COM+. MTS and COM+ are the crown jewels that link all of the ADO, DCOM, COM and OLE DB technologies into a grand whole. They're the star players of their Digital Nervous System (DNS) and Distributed interNet Architecture (DNA). (We're pretty nervous ourselves about the idea of a digital *nervous* system. Wouldn't want trembling fingers on the red button.)

Whew! Had enough acronyms yet? Sorry, but there are more to come.

Can You Spell XML? We Knew You Could

Like it did with the Internet, one day, Microsoft woke up and discovered XML, decided it was the wave of the future, and so started adding support for it into everything they build. Okay, maybe not everything; we're still waiting for the XML version of Monster Truck Madness.

XML, which stands for eXtensible Markup Language, is to data as HTML is to presentation. It provides a simple way of working with data: The data elements are just text stored between "tags" that identify what the elements are. With some nice formatting, the average human can even read this stuff! That's a far cry from DBF, Access MDB and SQL Server storage.

So what's the big deal about storing data as text rather than in proprietary (or even standard) binary formats? The big deal is transportation. A cursor in VFP can't go anywhere outside the VFP application (you can't even pass it to another data session in the same application). While ADO has built-in mechanisms for transport over a wire (whether via DCOM to a server or HTTP over the Internet), some Internet sites have firewalls that prevent objects from getting in or out. And even if you can get the ADO recordset through, the receiver may not be running Windows (think Mac, Unix, or Linux) so it can't do anything with the recordset it gets.

On the other hand, you can easily pass a text string pretty much anywhere. It doesn't matter whether you pass it to another component running in the same language on the same machine, to a server running a component on the other side of your office, or to a Unix box somewhere behind a firewall on the other side of the planet—everything understands text.

For this reason, Microsoft says that XML is the preferred means for transporting data. Okay, okay, we've heard it all before. "No, really, *this* is the way you should do it. Forget about that stuff we told you to use last year that was supposed to replace the stuff we told you about the year before. Trust us!" This time, however, we think they're on to something (as opposed to *on something*, which we've occasionally wondered about in the past). For one thing, you can't get much simpler than text. Although you can use a fancy XMLDOM object to create and consume XML, you can also just generate and parse it using straight VFP code if you wish. For another, Microsoft (for once) isn't alone in this. XML is becoming the foundation in almost every vendor's plans. For example, within a few years, XML will replace EDI as the means of exchanging information between customer and supplier or business partners.

VFP 7 adds several new functions that allow it to play nice in the XML world. See the Reference section for details on XMLToCursor(), CursorToXML(), and XMLUpdateGram().

But Wait, There's More!

The pace at which new technology comes out of the offices in Redmond seems to accelerate every year. The next new thing is .NET, Microsoft's framework for building applications. It includes yet another new data access technology, this one called ADO.NET. While it sounds like an updated version of ADO, it doesn't bear a lot of resemblance to its predecessor. The good news is that, underlying the ADO.NET object model (which is actually pretty cool), is plain-old XML. So, transporting an ADO.NET dataset over the Internet means you're actually just sending a bunch of text to someone, formatted so the receiver can either use it as is (if they're not using Windows or .NET) or use it as an object-oriented set of data.

Sadly, VFP can't use ADO.NET; it's available only to languages based on the Common Language Runtime (CLR) of .NET, such as Visual Basic.NET and C# (although you could create a subclass of the ADO.NET classes, using a CLR language, that exposes ADO.NET to VFP or other COM clients). However, that doesn't mean VFP can't play in the .NET world. VFP can create and consume XML, or expose COM objects for consumption by a .NET application, so exchanging data with .NET applications won't be a big deal.

Where Do You Want To Be Dragged Kicking and Screaming Today?

I fear we have awoken the sleeping giant.

Admiral Yamamoto, on hearing of the success of his Pearl Harbor attack

Microsoft has noticed data. Having all but cornered the market on office productivity software, on an uphill climb to take over network operating systems, and skirmishing to make the Internet its own, Microsoft has chosen to open yet another war front by attempting to wrest the enterprise applications from the mainframe and mini-computer crowd. To do that, Microsoft has been getting a lot better at working with data, and the efforts in DNA, ADO, XML and .NET are signs that Microsoft is making its move. Considering Microsoft's track record, we have little doubt they'll succeed. So we'll keep an eye on their progress, and think you should, too.

In the meantime, we'll continue using FoxPro to deliver the most powerful desktop applications on the planet.

"It Was Automation, You Know"

Besides black art, there is only automation and mechanization.

Federico García Lorca, 1936

Have you ever been working in one application and really needed some capability from another? Say you were creating a report in FoxPro, but really needed Word's formatting prowess? Or maybe you needed to do calculations on a few items of data contained in a set of spreadsheets? We sure have, more times than we can count.

In the real world, many of the things people want to do aren't segregated into discrete kinds of tasks. Sure, sometimes all you want to do is write a letter or total some numbers. But more often, you want to create a complex report with pictures and maybe some spreadsheet data and so forth. (Heck, even our kids do this sort of thing starting in middle school these days.)

Finding a way to handle interaction among applications has been computing's equivalent of searching for the Rosetta Stone since not too long after the PC was introduced. Various approaches have been tried over the years.

First, we had applications that could read data in other formats or write their own data in a format another application could read. That helped, but didn't solve the problem.

Next up, we got the integrated applications, like Framework, Q&A, ClarisWorks and Microsoft Works. These tried to throw all the apps you might need into a single package. The price was that none of the apps inside was particularly powerful, and they could only talk to each other through common file formats, though they knew something about each other's formats.

Until the Windows world, that was pretty much it. Windows brought us Dynamic Data Exchange (DDE), which let one application order another around. Progress, but it was awfully hard to use. Windows also introduced Object Linking and Embedding (OLE). That gave us a way to combine data from different applications into a single document, but still didn't quite solve the problem.

Then along came Automation (called OLE Automation at the time, until Microsoft decided that the term "OLE" wasn't snazzy enough for them, so they dropped it). Automation lets one application speak directly to another in a simple object-based way, and makes it easy to work with data from multiple applications at the same time.

We love Automation! In fact, this book was assembled using Automation. We wrote it using Word (a word processor did seem like the most appropriate choice). Each chapter, as well as each entry in the Reference section, was stored in a separate document. (That's 900-odd documents, if you're counting.) Of course, being FoxPro programmers, we tracked the progress of each document using a set of VFP tables.

Eventually, we finished, though not by the time that we're writing this. (That was a sentence only Raymond Smullyan could love.) But how do you turn over 900 documents into a book and a CHM file? Automation to the rescue. Focusing on the hairiest part of the book, the Reference section (which is not in the printed book, so go download it from www.hentzenwerke.com if you haven't already), we told Word to open each of the documents, convert them to HTML, and put them in the proper location for the CHM file. We used Automation for the previous editions of this book, too, and were amazed how easily, accurately and quickly an error-prone, tedious operation was completed.

As Automation itself has become more common, Microsoft has morphed OLE into ActiveX and, more recently, ActiveX into COM (Component Object Model). COM gives us the ability to talk not just to other applications, but to an assortment of operating system objects as well. Clearly, Automation brings us much closer to the lingua franca. But how do you use it?

Putting Automation to Work

Far and away the best prize that life offers is the chance to work hard at work worth doing.

Theodore Roosevelt, 1903

The good news is that if you're comfortable with VFP's object-oriented syntax, where one object calls another's methods, and you can manipulate behavior by changing properties, Automation is easy. It's just another set of objects, each with its own properties and methods.

The bad news is that, for each application you want to talk to, you have to learn a new object model. Each one has its own objects in their own hierarchy, and some of it is pretty obscure (not to mention underdocumented).

You may have already won a million dollars. No, wait a minute! That's Ed McMahon's line. Let's try again. You may have already worked with some Automation objects. The Project object introduced in VFP 6 is an Automation object, as are the DataObjects used in OLE drag and drop, and the Objects collection found in the VFP container classes.

Most Automation objects, though, don't make themselves available quite so transparently. You have to go out and grab the object you want (using CreateObject(), GetObject(), or CreateObjectEx()). Once you have a reference to it, though, you can do all kinds of things, from opening documents with the application to saving them to sending data from VFP to the other application to bringing the other application's data into VFP.

But Where Did Automation Come From?

Automation offers the opportunity to start moving our applications away from the one-app-does-it-all method of writing huge applications, toward an application design where more of the components are pulled off the shelf and the job of the application developer becomes one of identifying the correct components and providing the glue to bring them together. Much of the productivity gain of the Industrial Age came from the availability of cheap, interchangeable parts available in large quantities from many vendors. Automation may lead to a similar availability of component parts for our applications.

Automation is similar in many ways to the DDE (Dynamic Data Exchange) protocol it's eclipsing. Both require applications on each end to carry on a conversation. Both require one of the applications to initiate the conversation (the client), and one to respond (the server). (This is an unfortunate choice of terms, as client-server means something completely different in the world of database management systems.) There are also differences—Automation is implemented by a new engine, and in a different way, than DDE is. Automation has the opportunity of being a visible as well as invisible participant in the ongoing events.

Automation is a replacement for DDE, but a far richer and more visual replacement. In exchange, it also tends to be far more resource-intensive. Automation allows direct dialogue between applications, giving the programmer the opportunity to take advantage of the strengths of the different applications making up the total client solution. In this way, Automation can be thought of as an inter-application or Windows batch language.

Automation was introduced in the OLE 2.0 standard. The Microsoft Office Development Kit for Office 95 states that "Different applications expose different objects in different ways." This is an understatement. Every application we've worked with has its own unique implementation of Automation. We are seeing improvement, however: Microsoft has standardized on VBA for their Office applications, and is trying to bring similar object models to other applications as well. VBA has been licensed by a number of third-party vendors, too. But many tools, both within and outside Microsoft, lag behind, with weird implementations, actions that fire on setting property values, strange callback schemes, and hard-to-decipher error messages. Nonetheless, despite the frustrations of having to learn to speak a new language with each application, the power of Automation promises to bring new levels of functionality and features to our applications.

I'd Rather Fight Than Switch

So is DDE dead? Nope, not by a long shot. While Automation has supplanted DDE in many applications and has become the more stable and reliable of the two, many third-party applications are just now getting on board the Automation bandwagon. Other applications may never need to make the switch, so the older DDE means of communication will still be needed for some time. If you have an application running satisfactorily using DDE, we can't recommend that you switch. On the other hand, if you have a DDE link to an application that keeps failing or crashing or just not working, press the vendor for an Automation solution (or shop for a vendor offering one) and see if that makes for a more solid solution.

Using FoxPro as a Client

Visual FoxPro works quite well as the client in an Automation conversation, directing the work of other Automation servers. It's quite impressive to see the database-processing power of Visual FoxPro augmented by the features of Word, Excel or Visio (or whatever Automation server you need to use). There are four commands to initiate Automation: CreateObject(), NewObject(), GetObject() and CreateObjectEx().

CreateObject() is used to create new objects (surprising, huh?) based on either Visual FoxPro class definitions (base classes or class definitions in programs, procedures or VCXs) or from OLE objects defined in the Windows Registry.

```
oObjectHandle = CreateObject(cClassName)
```

NewObject() sure sounds similar to CreateObject(), doesn't it? It does essentially the same thing for COM objects. Its main advantage for VFP-coded classes is that the class library can be specified as part of the NewObject() call.

```
oObjectHandle = NewObject(cClassName, cClassLibrary)
```

GetObject() is used to access a pre-existing object, and is used only for Automation, unlike the overloaded CreateObject() above.

```
oObjectHandle = GetObject(cFileName, OLEClassName)
```

In most cases, only the file name must be supplied—COM matches the file up to its appropriate server. In the case where a file might have more than one server that could work with it, or where the file has a non-standard extension that doesn't specify the server, cClassName should be used to indicate which class to use.

Finally, CreateObjectEx() is the extended version of CreateObject(), though used only for COM objects. You give it the class name, and optionally the name of a remote computer, and you can take advantage of Distributed COM (DCOM) objects. A feature new to VFP 7 is that you can also optionally specify the interface for early binding (see the Reference section).

Once you've instantiated an object, you can manipulate it by using the properties and methods it "exposes" through COM. The next section illustrates the kind of interfaces that may be presented.

In addition to manipulating the properties and methods, you may want to respond to events raised by that control. It wasn't until VFP 6 that you could use VFPCOM, a separate free utility from Microsoft, to react to events in another COM object. While it generally worked well, it was a separate DLL that needed to be shipped and installed with your application. VFP 7 has incorporated event binding right into the product with the EventHandler() function.

One note on the syntax you'll encounter below. Some commands and property references use the Object property. This isn't really a Visual FoxPro property; it's a means of clarifying that you want to speak to the server contained within an OLE control, rather than the OLE control itself. This syntax is required only when an OLE server object and the OLE control have a property or method with the same name— use Object to make it clear that you mean the contained OLE server's property or method, and not that of the container.

Automation with the Office Applications

> When I give a man an office, I watch him carefully to see whether he is swelling or growing.
>
> Woodrow Wilson, 1916

Word 97 changed everything from the challenges we described in our original *Hacker's Guide.* Where Word 6.0 exposed only a single "Word.Basic" object and you had to manipulate all of the Word features through a difficult interface, Word 97 introduced a rich object model that made it easy to work with a specific feature set.

We've heard many complaints that every example of Automation anyone can find uses the same example: Open Word, load and print a document, and close Word. It's not only boring, it's trivial and useless. So we've got a better solution: We won't show you an example at all. The easy examples are, well, easy, and the tough ones are way too specific. Here's a little bit of advice instead.

First, take advantage of the Help provided with the product. Search for "Visual Basic" in your version of Word for instructions on installing and running the help for VBA. Other Office products have similar topics. These are your best friends as you stick your toes into the waters of automating the Office applications.

If you're going to get into Office Automation in a big way, get the best references out there. In our opinion, there's no better reference than the Hentzenwerke book, *Microsoft Office Automation with Visual FoxPro* (we should know, as Tamar and Della wrote it, and Ted edited it). See www.hentzenwerke.com for more information about the book. In addition, Microsoft publishes a monstrous set of books detailing every nook and cranny of the interface. Start slowly, and build your way up. A number of other authors have written killer books on using the Office tools. Our litmus test is pretty easy: Recall a problem you encountered in automating Office that took a while to resolve. Go to your local bookstore and check the indexes and tables of contents of the books to see if you can solve the problem. Read the section involved. If you understand the solution and like the writing style, buy the book. If they can't solve a problem you've already run into, what are the chances they'll solve any others? Take a pass.

Our favorite way to start an Automation programming session is to start in the tool we want to automate and record the sequence of actions. The easiest way to learn to program Word, Excel or PowerPoint is to record a macro of the steps you need to take, and then translate it into matching VFP code. Unfortunately, there isn't a one-to-one correspondence from the VBA code into the code VFP uses via Automation because VBA allows the use of named arguments. However, the translation isn't that difficult. Here's the trick.

In languages that support only positional arguments (like FoxPro), parameters are passed to a function in a specific order, and elements not needed for that call are left empty or placeholders are supplied, as in this example:

```
Do MyFunc with "One","Two","Three", , , , "Seven"
```

But in languages that support named arguments, you can pass only those parameters that are needed, by preceding each with the parameter name, like this:

```
MailMerge CheckErrors = 0, Destination = 3, MergeRecords = 0
```

While somewhat more self-documenting, this notation is wordier and is more difficult to work with using Automation, which supports only the positional form. Versions of Office prior to Office 97 didn't always document the correct positional form, and additional documentation needed to be dug out of the Microsoft documentation dungeons. With the later versions, they seem to have done a much better job of covering the language.

Digging Into Other Servers

You will no doubt be called upon to automate other servers. The good news is that, even if the books supplied with a server seem lacking in essential details, most of what you need to know to automate a server is built in to the server and its supporting files. With Visual FoxPro 7 and later, IntelliSense should automatically provide much of this information to you. In earlier versions, using the Class Browser, Office's Object Browser, or another OLE-snooping tool (see below), you should be able to determine the interface of the server, the constants it uses, and the parameters it requires in its method calls. Type Libraries, typically with extensions of TLB and OLB, are the files an application uses to register itself on your machine. The libraries contain the definitions of method names, parameters and constants added to the Registry and made available to calling programs to validate their method calls. You, too, can access this information, with a variety of tools.

The first tool in your Automation toolbox is the IntelliSense feature in VFP 7. Provided that you've used *early binding* when you declare your variable (the AS clause in the LOCAL command, below), IntelliSense can prompt you for the members in the object. Imagine you are typing in the following code:

```
LOCAL oWord AS Word.Application
oWord = CreateObject("Word.Application")
oWord.
```

Just after you hit that period on the last line, a popup appears, showing you the list of available members. You can scroll down the list to find the Visible property, or the Documents collection. You won't find the Font object, as it's not a member of the Application object. Since many of the resources available list the PEMs in alphabetical order, IntelliSense is a wonderful tool for making sense out of what you're actually able to use for the object. See "Intellisense and Sensibility" for more information on IntelliSense.

Should you need a little more help than IntelliSense provides, your second tool is VFP 7's Object Browser. This cool tool is even an improvement on the Object Browsers provided with VBA, as it sorts the members into categories, such as properties, events, methods and constants. Click the Open icon, and you're presented with a dialog listing all the registered COM objects. Choose the appropriate one, and the list of members (PEMs, constants, interfaces, etc.) is displayed. You can examine constant values, see the syntax to the methods, and determine which objects the method or property belongs to. The Object Browser also provides an easy way to solve the constants problem: Just drag the Constants node into a program file, and VFP #DEFINE's are created for all the constants.

If you haven't upgraded to VFP 7 (what are you waiting for?), you can view type libraries with the Class Browser. It can open and examine Type Libraries. Click the Open icon, and drop down the listing of file types—note that both TLB and OLB files are listed. You can also use the Visual Basic or VBA Object Browsers. (In Word, Tools | Macro | VB Editor gets you to the Visual Basic editor. Select Tools | References, pick the COM component you want to examine, and then press F2 to bring up the Object Browser).

If these tools aren't enough, you can really get down and dirty with the OLE View tool that comes with Visual Studio (assuming you have access to Visual Studio). It's normally installed as part of the standard Visual Studio install. It lets you examine OLE interfaces in some detail, down to the GUID numbers and the Access and Assign interfaces for each exposed member. Several third-party tools are available that expand on the Microsoft tool; you'll easily find a wide variety of free and inexpensive utilities by searching the Internet.

Turning the Tables

It is not real work unless you would rather be doing something else.

J. M. Barrie, 1922

Like so much else these days, Automation looks at the world in terms of clients and servers. The application that starts the conversation and says, "Hey, you! I want to talk to you!" is the client. The application on the other end of the line, the one saying "Yeah? What's up, man?" is the server. In our various examples above, VFP was always the client, telling Word to assemble our book or telling Excel to hand over some data so it could be stored in a table for further processing. And, in fact, in VFP 3, that was your only choice. FoxPro could be an Automation client only.

In VFP 5, Microsoft added an interesting capability. They allowed VFP to be used as an Automation server. So, other applications can call on VFP to hand over some data or whatever's called for. You can even call on the VFP Automation server from inside VFP, using the built-in Application object (or the system variable that references it, _VFP). The application object's DoCmd, Eval and SetVar methods let you execute a VFP command, evaluate an expression, and assign a value to a variable, creating it if necessary, respectively.

For fun, call on VFP 7 from VFP 3 by issuing:

```
oVFP = CreateObject("VFP.Application")
```

Then, use the oVFP reference and its methods to execute VFP 7 code in VFP 3. Well, it's not really in VFP 3, any more than a command you send to Word through Automation is executing in VFP. But it is fun. However, there's not much practical use for this particular ability, because you have to have VFP 7 to do it. Why would you bother with VFP 3 when VFP 7 is available?

More importantly, because VFP is an Automation server, other applications can call up and say, "Run this query and hand me the results" or "Here's some new data for you. Please store it where it belongs." We're also fairly certain that, without the ability to act as an Automation server, VFP couldn't play with OLE drag and drop, one of the coolest additions back in VFP 6.

Would You Care for a Custom Server?

He serves his party best who serves his country best.

Rutherford B. Hayes, *Inaugural Address*, 1877

However, working with VFP through its Application interface can get a little tedious. You can manipulate properties and even objects in an OOP way, but to execute any custom code, you're stuck with the DoCmd, Eval and SetVar methods. While you can do just about anything, it doesn't take too long to get tedious this way.

If the goal is to have access to a fixed set of operations, there's another way to go. Instead of working with the whole VFP Automation object, use VFP to build a custom class with methods for the things you want to do. Have VFP build it into a server for you (by declaring it OLEPublic). Then, you can instantiate your server object from other applications, and call on its methods to do what needs to be done.

An Automation server is a DLL or EXE created in FoxPro. It presents COM interfaces that can be manipulated by other programs. So how do you create those interfaces? How do you create the DLL or EXE? How do you choose between DLL or EXE, for that matter? And finally, once you've solved all that, how do you distribute your Automation server to the world?

All objects you want to make accessible through COM must be created as part of a VFP project. The process of building a project into an EXE or DLL creates the appropriate registry entries and the additional files needed to turn a VFP program or class into a COM object.

COM interfaces are nothing more than method calls, just like the ones we're used to making. It's the packaging that's different. All classes containing interfaces you want to make public must be declared with the keyword OLEPUBLIC. For classes defined in code, this keyword is used in the DEFINE CLASS statement; for visually designed classes, the OLE Public check box must be checked in the Class Info dialog.

Once you've defined a class as OLE Public, you'll probably want to tweak the class definition a bit so only those PEMs you want accessible to the outside world are visible via COM. In the Class Designer, check Protected on the Members tab for all those PEMs you want to keep internal to the object. Public members are exposed as part of the COM interface. If you're defining the class in code, use the Protected keyword for the properties and methods to hide. For greater control of the visibility of PEMS, you could use the Session object, which exposes only custom PEMs. Still greater control is obtained by using VFP 7's new _COMATTRIB flags on the DEFINE CLASS command. These flags follow the method definition, and designate whether the method is restricted, hidden or non-browsable—these are varying forms of hiding the method from other developers looking at it through property and object browsers. The _COMATTRIB flags can also be used to make properties read-only and write-only. See DEFINE CLASS in the Reference section for details on how to use these features.

In your method, it's pretty much business as usual. You define the parameters for the method to receive, perform the processing code, and return a result. Essentially, there's no difference in the behavior of FoxPro code within a COM server; it's just running in the runtime as far as it is concerned. Since you're running as a COM object, however, there are a few additional considerations you need to keep in mind.

First, most developers who use COM objects are used to seeing a brief description of what the method does, what parameter and expected data types are passed to the method, and what is returned from the method. VFP 7 offers some new enhancements to the DEFINE CLASS command to help out developers who use your COM objects. The HELPSTRING keyword sets the help string displayed in an object browser. For example:

```
PROCEDURE GetCustomerName(tcCustID) ;
  HELPSTRING "Accepts the customer ID and returns the customer name."
ENDPROC
```

DEFINE CLASS now has strong typing, too. Visual FoxPro has notoriously been a weakly typed language, meaning that all variables are seen as *variant* types. You don't have to explain to FoxPro what the variable contains, nor does it always have to contain a certain type of data. Weak typing can have its place, but not in writing COM objects. The DECLARE CLASS command has an AS clause that can be added after each parameter. Likewise, you can add the AS clause after the parameter list, to assign a type to the return value. It looks like this:

```
PROCEDURE GetCustomerName(tcCustId AS String) AS String
```

See the DEFINE CLASS topic for more information on these new features.

Another thing to consider when creating COM servers is to make sure that your code doesn't attempt to interact with the user. Since a COM object is instantiated invisibly, there is nowhere to ask the user "Are you sure?" questions. Make sure your code doesn't call any dialogs. You also need to turn off the implicit ones. Remember to SET SAFETY OFF if you're deleting or overwriting files. Scan your code carefully. Some statements will surprise you. SET HELP TO, for example, will probably work fine on your development system but hang on your client's workstation. Why? SET HELP TO tries to set help to the default FoxHelp.CHM—what you probably mean to do is SET HELP OFF. Visual FoxPro 6.0 introduced a new function, SYS(2335), which prevents your server from invisibly hanging when a dialog appears. Instead, it generates an error, which your error handler should be able to record. Then, you can safely and cleanly terminate your server, if appropriate.

Face to Face with COM Interfaces

But wait, didn't we just say that you shouldn't call any dialogs in your COM objects? Isn't that an interface? Yes, that's a user interface; but here we're talking about COM interfaces. A COM interface is how the client talks to the COM server. It's just a bunch of methods. Of course, it's not quite that simple, because the interface must meet a stringent binary definition. Visual FoxPro automatically creates a default COM interface for you, so this business of dealing with interfaces can be simple.

Of course, interfaces can get more complex, too. First of all, once you've published your COM component, you cannot change its interface, because this breaks all of the code based on this component. Instead of changing an interface, COM, and now VFP 7, supports multiple interfaces, meaning that you can add interfaces to your control to keep existing applications happy while providing new features to future applications. (Of course, you can also regenerate the COM control with a different GUID, and change whatever you'd like, because it's no longer the same control. But that wouldn't lead us into a discussion of multiple interfaces.) Another example of multiple interfaces is to provide several different event interfaces that other applications (or different facets of the same application) can hook into.

An interface is a related group of methods that define a behavior. There's always a default interface, which is named "I" plus the name of the class. So an Employee class has a default interface of IEmployee. Managers are a special kind of employee, so you might define an interface called IManager that adds or augments features of the IEmployee interface. Many different interfaces can be added; carrying this theme a little further, you might have IInfoTechs, IHumanResources, or IAccounting.

Now, what if you want to implement the interface of a COM object? VFP has had *implementation inheritance* since it was released. That's where the PEMs in the class and the code behind them are inherited, and something we're quite fond of. However, when you DEFINE CLASS using the IMPLEMENTS keyword pointing to a COM object's interface, COM does not support implementation inheritance. What they do support is *interface inheritance*, meaning that the public methods are inherited, without any code behind them—you get the interface only, and you supply the code. So using IMPLEMENTS gets you interface inheritance, not implementation inheritance (is this OOP terminology overloaded, or what?).

Without any code, what's the value of interface inheritance? Plenty! First is polymorphism—different objects responding differently to the same commands. Do you use abstract classes (classes that contain PEMs with no code behind them) as templates? That's like using interface inheritance. And interface inheritance is absolutely required if you want to venture into the COM+ world.

This is actually quite a complex topic, and we recommend that you look at other sources. One that we know is a Hentzenwerke Publishing book, *What's New in Visual FoxPro 7.0*, by Tamar, Doug, and Kevin McNeish. There are five chapters devoted to creating COM components, understanding and implementing COM+, and understanding Web services.

EXE or DLL? Only Your Hairdresser Knows for Sure.

I am not an adventurer by choice but by fate.

Vincent Van Gogh, 1886

The Build dialog in the Project Manager includes options for building both EXEs and DLLs. Both of these apply to COM. (Of course, BUILD EXE also applies to other applications.) An EXE, known as an *Out-of-Process* server, runs in its own memory space, while a DLL, or *In-Process* server, shares memory space with the application that instantiates it. You need to create your COM server as an EXE if you're going to make it available remotely. For other machines to invoke the COM server on a server machine, the COM server must run on that server machine in its own memory space.

Another reason for choosing an EXE over a DLL is stability. If a COM server runs into problems and errors out, hangs, or just plain dies, an EXE usually crashes its own space, but causes an error only in the client calling it. A crash in a DLL-based server usually brings down the whole process—client, server and all.

There's a down side to using EXEs, of course. Since the client application and the server are in different processes, there is a significant amount of overhead in the interprocess communication that takes place. Also, if the EXE needs to load from disk and start each time it is called, there can be a significant wait (called a "latency period") before the EXE is ready to serve. Under heavy loads, this latency can become a bottleneck.

A DLL has the opposite benefits, with equivalent liabilities. Because a DLL is running in the same memory space, the communication carries far less overhead. But running a FoxPro DLL, especially inside a FoxPro application, does introduce some tricky issues. The Fox DLL shares the same VFP runtime with its hosting client, which means that they share the same DEFAULT, TALK and other global settings. Be very careful to preserve and restore any settings you change when crafting a FoxPro DLL. Like a guest in someone else's house, make sure you put back what you move and disturb as little as possible. (Of course, that's always good advice when programming.) Take advantage of scoping and privatizing your behavior, using private data sessions and minimal variable scope to minimize the effects on the host application.

The other advantage of DLLs is that they can run within the Microsoft Transaction Services (MTS in NT 4.0) or Component Services (Windows 2000). These DLLs can be pooled, so that more of them are available to handle heavy bandwidth demands, and can be kept alive when not in use for rapid startup. This topic, too, tends to get beyond what we need to cover in a VFP-specific book, but check the documentation for your particular OS and Microsoft's online resources for a lot more information.

Distributing Your COM Server

> Our society distributes itself into Barbarians, Philistines and Populace; and
> America is just ourselves with the Barbarians quite left out, and the Populace
> nearly.

> Matthew Arnold, *Culture and Anarchy*, 1869

If you're using VFP 6 or earlier, a COM server can be bundled up and shipped using
the Setup Wizard, just like any other application. In the second step of the wizard,
pick "COM Components" and follow the prompts to add your servers to the list
displayed. In-Process (DLL) servers have no options, but with Out-of-Process (EXE)
servers, you can specify several options as to how the install should proceed. Check
the help file for more details.

VFP 7 replaces the Setup Wizard with a VFP-specific version of InstallShield
Express. Check its help file for more details on how to install your COM server.

How to Troubleshoot

> People struggled on for years with "troubles," but they almost always
> succumbed to "complications."

> Edith Wharton, *Ethan Frome*, 1911

Troubleshooting COM components can be a bear because they don't have a visible
interface you can use for direct debugging. A DLL produces a "Feature not available"
error if you attempt to suspend or debug in the middle of one of its procedures, even if
you've instantiated it in the FoxPro development environment. Our advice: Debug in
advance as much as possible, and set up a robust error handler to dump all of the
environmental information you can find into an error log when an error occurs. That
way, even though live debugging is unavailable, you should have sufficient evidence
to deduce the source of the problem. You should also consider adding a simple
logging feature to your base COM classes (textmerge and the new file-handling
functions are ideal for this), so you can log "Step 1 start", "Step 1 end" if you're in one
of those sticky debugging situations where things just seem to stop.

COM, DCOM, and COM+

DCOM, or Distributed COM, is simply a term meaning that the location of the COM
server doesn't matter. Termed *location transparency*, this ability to access a COM
server on your local machine, on another machine on your local network, or on some
machine who-knows-where on the Internet, is what DCOM is. So, what does DCOM
give us?

Distributed COM is built into all versions of Windows, beginning with Windows NT 4.0 and Windows 98 (if you're still using Windows 95, there's a free download from the Microsoft site). DCOM allows you to call for a service, using the same terminology you would for any object invocation, but the service actually runs on another machine! This opens up some great possibilities for distributed computing—where a few fast, powerful machines, or machines with special resources, could provide their services to other clients.

So what's COM+? Well, with the advent of DCOM, the developers had to roll their own solutions for a number of things, such as managing all the resources, data transactions and security. Microsoft created Microsoft Transaction Server as an add-on for Windows NT to provide developers some relief from writing these things themselves. In this latest incarnation of COM, COM+ merges COM and MTS, improves on them, and builds them right into the Windows 2000 and later operating systems.

But What About .NET?

Microsoft is at it again, developing more acronyms for us to learn. The latest of these is .NET, the integrated development environment for creating Internet applications. Does it spell doomsday for COM/COM+? Of course not. Microsoft knows that software companies have a significant investment in COM/COM+, so they're not going to yank it out from under them in the near future. In fact, Microsoft's own .NET Enterprise servers, including SQL Server 2000 and BizTalk Server 2000, have COM/COM+ at their core. Instead of mandating a move to .NET, Microsoft has made it easy for the two technologies to co-exist.

How does VFP play in the .NET arena? Pretty well, actually. Since .NET has XML Web Services at its core, VFP 7 has new features that allow developers to write and consume Web Services. Visual Studio .NET is Microsoft's premier toolbox for writing .NET applications, and much has been made of taking VFP out of the Visual Studio box. This is a Good Thing: We have the best of both worlds. We can write and consume Web Services, thereby playing in the future .NET arena, and we can write the "old-style" COM/COM+ objects (old? didn't we just learn how to write COM objects?), supporting the current software technologies. .NET has some cool features, one of which is the Common Language Runtime, or CLR, which replaces the separate C, C++, and VB runtimes. No, VFP won't take advantage of the CLR or other VS.NET features (which is another Good Thing, as we would have lost our local database engine and significant backwards compatibility—both hallmarks of the FoxPro product). So, we get to have our cake and eat it, too, taking advantage of .NET when it is available, but retaining the ability to develop independent, stand-alone applications. The Fox team has enabled us to be compatible with .NET without losing features we've come to love.

Using VFP in an n-Tier Architecture

Microsoft's recent marketing pitch, COM+, is an application architecture that uses COM components and the COM interface for all layers of an n-tier application model. (See "n-Tiers of a Clown" in "Your Server Will Be With You in a Moment" for more on the n-tier model.) We welcome these developments, and feel that VFP has a place to play, both as a heavy-duty front-end tool and as a middle layer serving business rules between the client and the data services. However, we advise caution before leaping into this new solution.

Before you dive in head-first, you want to make sure that your application really needs the power of an n-tier solution. While the architecture seems attractive, we've discovered that the complexity of design, management and testing of our applications is proportionate to the number of interfaces we need to support. As more components are introduced into the mix, it becomes more complex to anticipate and properly code the ability to handle failures of single components, error passing between layers, and many other issues.

Once you've determined that your application needs the n-tier model, Visual FoxPro provides a rich array of tools to help you create your COM components.

"Ah, What a Tangled Web We Weave"

The Internet. Unless you've been hiding in a cave for most of the past decade, you know that the Internet, and particularly the World Wide Web, has captured the lion's share of the publicity in the computer world. What is it about the Web that has attracted so much attention? What can we FoxPro developers do to capture some portion of this market? And what *should* we do?

This is not a primer on the technologies of the Internet—there are many fine books on that subject. Nor is it an in-depth examination of the techniques needed to assemble a robust VFP Web-based application—that's well covered in other volumes in the Essentials series, which includes the fine volume you're reading now. Check out Rick Strahl's awesome *Internet Applications with Visual FoxPro 6.0,* and also *WebRAD: Building Database Websites with Visual FoxPro and Web Connection*, by Harold Chattaway, Randy Pearson, and Whil Hentzen, both available from Hentzenwerke Publishing. Our goal is to give you a brief overview of the stuff that's involved, and then we'll dig into the stuff you can do with Visual FoxPro.

HTML is Just Text!

The idea behind the Web is that specially formatted, plain old text can be used as the communication medium between any two computers. With special formatting marks to designate relative font size, italics, font strength, and so forth, each computer application can read the text and render it in a means appropriate for its display device. The basic language involved is Hypertext Markup Language, HTML. It consists of *tags*, usually in begin-end pairs, set off from the main text with greater-than and less-than brackets, which set the format of the text between them. Tags are typically reduced to a few mnemonic characters, so <I> stands for italic and <BR> for line break. When paired, the ending tag begins with a slash. So, text wrapped in the <STRONG> and </STRONG> tags appears as strong text (usually represented by bold).

Right away, you should be realizing that HTML itself is pretty plain vanilla, and that, if text manipulation is all that's involved, well, Visual FoxPro's textmerge capabilities, as well as functions like StrToFile(), make VFP an ideal language for generating HTML. True enough. But wait, there's more …

HTML was designed as a language primarily to let viewers on different computers with different capabilities see a document as similarly as could be rendered by their software and hardware. HTML serves adequately as a markup language for generating static pages. It isn't a typographer's dream, being limited to a few relative font sizes and a couple of simple enhancements—bold, italic and so forth. In addition, basic HTML supports simple input via text boxes, command buttons, option buttons and combos. But that's about the limit of the language. In order to get much further than that, you need to look into extensions to the basic language and into scripting languages.

We love standards. That's why we have so many. HTML is no exception. Over its short lifetime, it has gone through a number of revisions, with version 4.01 the currently accepted standard. HTML was reformulated to include many of the rules within the eXtensible Markup Language, XML, resulting in XHTML 1.0.

It's important that you know what your customers will be using to access your Web pages so you can ensure that your pages don't present content your customers can't read. Different browsers and different versions of the same browser support different versions of HTML and the various extensions. HTML 4.01, XML 1.0, and XHTML are the latest in languages and standards—if you're dealing with an in-house application, or can limit your customer base to those with the latest compatible browsers, this is what you'll want to code in. But plan on testing, testing and more testing, as every variation may work differently. For example, Internet Explorer 5.x on the Macintosh platform is very nearly 100% standards-compliant, while IE 5 on Windows platforms widely missed the mark.

Script Me a Part

The technologies discussed to this point generally have more to do with static layout. For more sophisticated work than layout, enter scripting languages. Scripts are blocks of code in HTML that run within their interpreter. Java, JavaScript (no relation), VBScript and ECMAScript (the European Community standard of JavaScript) are among the more popular. These scripts perform many of the interesting things that go on within a displayed page, such as highlighting areas as the mouse floats over them. Scripts can be client-side—that is, run in the user's browser—or server-side, running on the Web server to modify the HTML before it's sent to the client browser.

There are a bunch of scripting languages, and they present many of the same compatibility issues as do the varied versions of HTML. Java is considered to be the "universal" language for browsers. Developed and licensed by Sun Microsystems, Java took the world by storm a few years ago. We're a little envious of the Java language, because it was built from the ground up as a new language with the latest technological bells and whistles and none of the baggage of supporting legacy applications that many languages suffer from today. At the same time, it's faced great challenges in being developed to run within a Java Virtual Machine (JVM) on any number of otherwise incompatible platforms, running on each platform securely and efficiently. Quite a task. With Java, Sun likes to claim you can "Code once, run everywhere." If you are coding an application for a limited number of platforms, Java may be the leading choice.

Whether Java is or is not included with Microsoft platforms is the ping-pong ball of the moment. Microsoft and Sun have been batting things back and forth in court for most of a decade, with Sun claiming that Microsoft is trying to destroy Java's universality with proprietary extensions, and Microsoft counter-claiming that Sun doesn't really mean to allow licensing of the platform. If it doesn't come pre-installed on your clients' machines, you can count on being able to download Java from Sun's site at http://java.sun.com.

Serve It Up!

Okay, you've got some idea of what you want to present and what languages you'll use to present it. Now, how do you get that cool Web site up onto that World Wide Web? First, obviously, you need a connection into the Internet. While many larger firms have full-time Internet access in-house, a number of smaller firms depend on an outside vendor, an Internet Service Provider (ISP), to host and maintain their Web sites. Choosing whether to use an ISP or supporting a Web server in-house is primarily an economic decision, but whichever way you go, make sure the server you are using can support the server-side work you'll want to perform. Many ISPs run their machines on UNIX or other operating systems that won't support FoxPro runtimes or

ISAPI interfaces. Others have a policy against anything but Active Server Pages (ASP). Make sure you find an ISP who understands what FoxPro is, or is willing to let you rent a machine and do whatever you want on it. Everyone's policies are different, so shop around.

In a typical Web site scenario, clients connect to your Web site, requesting a particular Web page via a Uniform Resource Identifier (URI). Your server receives this request, finds the specified page, and returns it. The actual mechanism for finding the page depends on the request. If it was just for "somepage.html", the server may just pull a static page off disk. If the request includes specific keywords, it triggers the server to run certain programs and return the HTML those programs generate. Like every other aspect of Web technology we've talked about so far, yes, there are many techniques to choose from, and yes, different solutions have advantages and disadvantages, compatibility issues and limitations.

As we've said before, we can't possibly go into all of the details of all the ways a server can interact with data, but here are some basics to give you an idea of what's out there.

CGI—Common Gateway Interface—really is the common way to interact with Internet servers. You've probably seen "cgi" in URIs while browsing the Internet. CGI is a standardized interface to communicate with servers—you can count on it being available on pretty much any server out there. If your site is hosted on an ISP, there's very little chance this interface is not supported, whether they run IIS on Windows NT or the Apache server on Linux, or JoeBob's WonderServer on some operating system you've never heard of.

ISAPI, the Internet Server Application Programming Interface, is a proposed Microsoft standard; it requires a far more intimate connection between the application and the server. CGI scripts run as individual executables for each request made of the server, potentially bogging down the server under very heavy traffic. ISAPI is a single DLL running in the server's space, and is capable of handling multiple requests and queuing results. While performance may be improved by eliminating inter-application communication and multiple EXE startups, you trade this for a DLL capable of crashing the server if it misbehaves. ISAPI interfaces (yes, that's redundant) are supported by more than a dozen commercial and open-source Web servers.

What Does the Fox Do?

Okay, by now we expect you're totally dazzled and frazzled on this whole Internet thing. There are clients and servers, scripts and protocols, lots of things to consider. But FoxPro's end of this thing is pretty simple: Generate HTML and XML. That's easy. Here's a trivial sample to generate an HTML document:

```
* MakeHTML

SET TEXTMERGE ON TO main.html NOSHOW
\<HTML>
\<HEAD>
\<META NAME="Generator" CONTENT="Microsoft Visual FoxPro">
\<META NAME="Date" CONTENT="<<DATETIME()>>" >
\<TITLE>Demonstration HTML</TITLE>
\</HEAD>
\<BODY>
\<H1> This is a demonstration of HTML </H1>
\</BODY>
\</HTML>

SET TEXTMERGE OFF
SET TEXTMERGE TO
```

This program generates a small file named Main.HTML, which displays "This is a demonstration of HTML" in large letters, when opened in a browser. Ho-hum. It's hard to get clients to pay you for this sort of stuff. But notice the seventh line of the routine, where DATETIME() is automatically evaluated by the textmerge process, as part of generating the text file. No, clients won't pay you for the time of day, either (though wc hope they'll give you the time of day), but they will pay you for converting their data into HTML, and that's exactly what you can do with Fox and textmerge (or Fox and XML; more on that in a moment).

There are two things the client might want to consider, with two different solutions and levels of difficulty and expense. If the client is interested in posting information on its Web site in "real enough time" (last month's sales figures, a list of items in inventory, relatively static information), it probably makes sense to consider generating the static information offline and transferring it to the Web server as Web pages. If, on the other hand, the client needs information online and up-to-date, FoxPro is up to working as part of an online Web service. We'll look at both of those options in the next few sections.

We'll take on the static items first—the capability of generating HTML for transfer to a Web site. Then, we'll look at the options for generating HTML live and on-demand.

"Save as HTML" Menu Option

You may have noticed that, starting in VFP 6, the File menu has the welcome addition of a Save As HTML option, but it seems to be disabled much of the time. This option is available only while creating or modifying menus, forms or reports, but much of the underlying engine is available to developers at any time. Let's take a look at what it does first, and then look at the how.

When editing a menu, selecting Save As HTML generates a file listing all prompts and messages for the menu. We're really not sure why. We can't see a lot of use for such a thing, unless a developer was then to go in and edit all of the HTML into links to various parts of the application. But it doesn't strike us as a particularly appealing user interface.

With a form, the Save As HTML option generates an HTML file that closely matches the layout of the original form. When translating a program from network-based VFP runtimes to an Internet-based Web design, we can see this as an attractive step. However, the Save As option doesn't support a number of VFP controls: Container, Grid, Image, Line, PageFrame, Shape or Spinner. For those, you have to go in and edit the generated HTML manually to get what you want, or consider writing your own modifications to the supplied GenHTML.

The Save As HTML option also works for reports: The option appears to generate an ASCII output file and then converts that by adding the required HTML headings, wrapping <PRE> formatting tags around the displayed text, and converting spaces to their equivalent non-breaking spaces by adding the code . The ugly   codes take up a lot of space and probably aren't necessary if the reports already use a non-proportional font—the default seems to set it to Courier.

How do these functions work? Setting a breakpoint on PROGRAM() = "GENHTML" gives it away. Each of these options calls the program set in _GENHTML; by default, it's GenHTML.PRG in the VFP home directory.

The Magic of GenHTML

With code like this, there's no need for comments—NOT!

```
oSaveEnvironment=NEWOBJECT("_SaveEnvironment")
lcProgramPath=JUSTPATH(LOWER(SYS(16)))+"\"
lcHTMLVCX=IIF(VERSION(2)=0,"",HOME()+"FFC\")+"_HTML.vcx"
lcOutFile=IIF(VARTYPE(tcOutFile)=="C",LOWER(ALLTRIM(tcOutFile)),"")
IF NOT EMPTY(lcOutFile) AND EMPTY(JUSTEXT(lcOutFile))
    lcOutFile=FORCEEXT(lcOutFile,"htm")
ENDIF
lnShow=IIF(VARTYPE(tnShow)=="N" OR ;
       VARTYPE(tnShow)=="I",MIN(MAX(INT(tnShow),0),5),0)
lcSourceVarType=VARTYPE(tvSource)
```

We suspect GenHTML is a slick and elegant program with a whole bunch of real cool features. We say "suspect" instead of "know" because no one but the whiz kids at Microsoft who wrote it have a clue what it does! There's a lovely header at the beginning of the file that describes the various parameters that can be passed to the function, and we suspect that with a few months of testing and tweaking, we will find GENHTML to be a handy tool. But, our past few months have been spent documenting the other 1,575,498 topics for this book. We hope some other hackers will come along and do the same for this tool.

We can see some real power in this tool and wish it were better documented.

A few hints: The program uses the various _HTM* classes that are part of the FoxPro Foundation Classes found in HOME()+"\FFC". It also depends upon styles and directives stored in GenHTML.DBF in the FoxPro root directory. Good luck, spelunkers! Let us all know what you find!

But FoxPro is going to interact with the Internet in many more ways than just being a passive server of text data! First, we anticipate the need to have our applications call up a browser directly. We also can see situations where our application may be running *within* a browser. The Hyperlink control, covered next, solves the first problem, while Active Documents and the remainder of this section look at various ways we can interact live with the Internet.

HyperLink Control

The HyperLink control can be placed on a FoxPro form or within a FoxPro class in order to access the Web by passing an address to its Navigate method. We can see many good uses for these, such as linking tech support information on Help or About forms directly into your technical support Web site. Other uses include providing additional navigation within Active Documents, or starting up a browser to display other information—see "HTML is Not Just for Web Pages Anymore!" below.

Active Documents

Active Documents were all the rage when the Fox team started putting together the list of goodies for Visual FoxPro 6. "Tahoe," as it was known in those days, would have Active Documents as well, catching up with the ActiveDocs of Visual Basic 5.0. Not only that, but ActiveDocs in Visual FoxPro would not just be VFP forms running in a browser, but entire Visual FoxPro *applications,* capable of doing everything their network-bound apps could do.

Well, it sounded good in theory. And in fact, Active Documents have some remarkable features. But don't give up your favorite HTML editor just yet— ActiveDocs are not going to become the Next Big Thing on the Internet. The good news is that a properly constructed VFP application that can run as a stand-alone network application can also run as an ActiveDoc. With careful negotiation with its hosting browser, the app can share menu items and give the browser clues as to how to handle various requests from the user.

The bad news? First, Active Documents have no special way to handle data. They require a network connection to the data just like regular applications. Without a special means of transferring data over HTTP, such as ADO or streams of XML, these applications must have some sort of a network attachment to the data source. If your users are willing to set up a bunch of network mappings while they're on the Internet, it is feasible to use ActiveDocs over the Internet, but what's the point? You can do the same thing without the browser container, and with a little less overhead. Finally, and perhaps more importantly, running an ActiveDoc is the same as running a FoxPro executable—the client workstation needs to have the FoxPro run-time files loaded. Very few casual browsers to your site are going to be interested in a multi-megabyte download. On the other hand, customers who could gain significant benefit from this, or "roaming users" who can be configured in the office before going on the road, could find this mechanism to be a useful one.

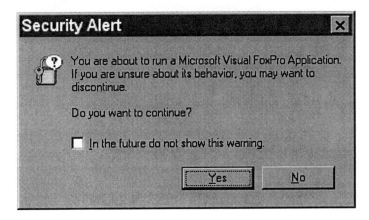

Figure 1-1: Is there an app whose behavior you are sure of?

We can live with the warning the application gives us on startup (shown in Figure 1-1), rude as it is. But without a means of transferring data or running on client machines without the VFP runtime, ActiveDocs have ended up as curiosities used only in a few very specialized applications. They certainly haven't had the general usage we hoped they would.

Web Publishing Wizard

We often think of wizards as simplistic programs with few options that generate basic documents, but usually not as tools powerful enough to use for "real" production work. The Web Publishing Wizard may be the exception that proves this rule. This cool tool lets you pull data from the application of your choice and generate HTML to display it as you wish. In addition, the wizard can generate a PRG to re-create the HTML on demand with updated data. Cool!

This wizard is a pretty slick device. It starts out in the usual fashion with the "pick a table, select your fields, select the order" routine that most developers can do in their sleep. But in step 3, the power of this little tool begins to shine. In addition to being able to pick from a set of five data layout templates, you can apply one of 26 styles to them. Each of the data layouts has an option dialog with a pageframe full of settings. Using the Advanced dialog, you can go even further, specifying a Cascading Style Sheet, background image, or even additional HTML elements you want to add to the page. Finally, step 3 also has a Preview button. Whew! This page is like an applet unto itself, with three levels of modal dialogs sometimes appearing.

 Something happened in VFP 7. Selecting certain backgrounds in step 3 gives an error when previewing, but still generates a valid HTML document, just without the specified background. Also in step 3, selecting any of the tabular data layouts generates a page with code fragments in the place of the data.

They all worked fine in VFP 6.

If you survive the gauntlet of step 3, you're almost done. Step 4 gives you the usual "finish line" options of running the page, viewing the code, or saving it for later. Choosing the last option saves code that looks something like the following:

```
* -- Generated Web Wizard Script File --
*
* A unique record has been created in GENHTML.DBF with your settings.
* This record can be referenced by the ID specified in the
* DO (GENHTML) command below.

LOCAL lnSaveArea
lnSaveArea=SELECT()
SELECT 0

SELECT Topic,Ngroup,Version FROM "E:\HACKFOX7\STATUS\ALLCANDF.DBF" ;
  ORDER BY Ngroup INTO CURSOR webwizard_query

IF EMPTY(_GENHTML)
  _GENHTML='GenHTML.PRG'
ENDIF
DO (_GENHTML) WITH
"E:\HACKFOX7\STATUS\ALLCANDF.HTM",ALIAS(),2,,"_RXL0WSC1J"

IF USED("webwizard_query")
  USE IN webwizard_query
ENDIF
SELECT (lnSaveArea)
```

The Web Publishing Wizard offers us some really powerful capabilities. By saving all of our preferences in the GENHTML table, the wizard is, in effect, a What You See Is

What You Get (WYSIWYG) editor for publishing Fox data on the Web. Rather than settling for the feeble Select statement generated by the wizard, we can substitute any generated query, filtered table or parameterized view request to populate the source table, even perhaps receiving our search parameters from another Web page. Then, we can leave it all to GenHTML to format and generate the HTML.

A few cautions are in order. If you're using the Tabular Hierarchical data layout, the Web page is generated with an ActiveX control (the Tabular Data Control, Tdc.OCX) and a comma-separated value (CSV) version of the table. You'll need to install the TDC on those client machines that don't already have it, and make sure that you put the CSV file in a place accessible to the Web site. Finally, for any of the Web pages, the wizard seems to generate the graphics with unique names but leaves them in the Wizards\Graphics\ subdirectory of the FoxPro home directory. Plan on moving them, and updating the HTML, when installing them on your Web server.

Don't confuse FoxPro's Web Publishing Wizard with the same-named Microsoft Web Publishing Wizard. The first is an application that runs within FoxPro and gives us HTML and the PRGs to create them. The latter is a program for uploading Web pages to a remote Web server.

HTML is Not Just for Web Pages Anymore!

Just because HTML was originally designed for Web pages doesn't mean that its use should be restricted to that purpose. The Web browser technology provides us with widgets that are ideal as viewers, not only as stand-alone applications, but also as *components* within our applications. For example, it's easy to put Internet Explorer right on your form: Simply drop the Web Browser control on it. Two tricks are needed to bind Internet Explorer to a VFP form: Ensure that VTable binding is off (it's the default, but issue SYS(2333) if you've tinkered with the setting) and add NODEFAULT to the Refresh method of the control. Then, you can call the control's Navigate2() method and pass it the URI you want it to display. The URI does not have to be a Web page—it can be an HTML page on a local disk (called with the FILE:// protocol), a GIF or JPG, or any file for which a viewer add-on has been installed—you could let the user preview Word documents, Acrobat files, or any other files with viewers available. Figure 1-2 should give you some ideas.

Hacker's Guide to Visual FoxPro 7.0

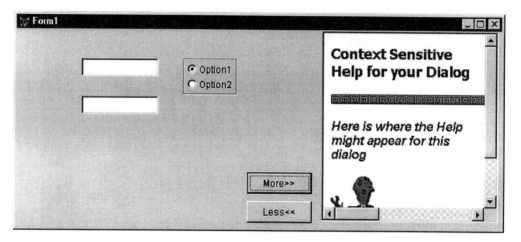

Figure 1-2: A Web Browser control added to your form gives you the ability to display richly formatted materials within your forms.

FoxISAPI

Buried deep down in the samples is the FoxISAPI sample—check under HOME(2) + "Servers\Foxisapi." This provides yet another newer, more modern way to access Fox logic from the Web. Unlike many Microsoft technologies, though, this one is available from other Web server vendors as well. The idea behind ISAPI is that a product that runs in the same process space as the Web server itself can eliminate much of the interprocess communication overhead of a Web application.

FoxISAPI.DLL runs within the Web server and it talks to FoxPro Automation servers. Two server samples are included. There's FoxWeb, a simple demonstration of Automation in code. Then there's FoxIS, a pretty slick sample of how an Automation server can have both a FoxPro front end and generate HTML for a Web-based view. It uses the classic employee table example, but the Web interface is pretty impressive. (See Figure 1-3.) Studying the source code can give you lots of ideas about how to implement similar technologies to solve your own problems. You can use the FoxISAPI.DLL as a tool for your own custom FoxPro Web server applications.

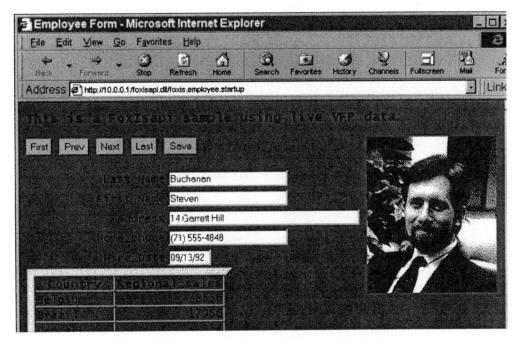

Figure 1-3: The FoxISAPI sample pulls out all the stops to demonstrate VFP as a legitimate Web server database engine.

Make sure to read the section of the VFP help file titled "FoxISAPI Automation Server Samples" in order to understand all the capabilities of this cool tool.

XML: Made for Data

We've mentioned XML a little in this chapter, but it deserves more ink. XML seems to be everywhere. It's prominent in the marketing of VFP 7.0. So what's the big deal? It's the hottest technology for moving data across the Internet, mostly because it has been nearly universally accepted.

Like HTML, XML is just text. Specially formatted text, in a standard format (or one of several formats, as we'll see below) allows data to be transmitted to other systems— systems that might be running completely different operating systems or languages— in an easy-to-read manner. XML can easily be integrated into HTML applications, and fits just as well in the components of any application that need to receive or send data to other components.

Let's look at a small XML document, in the element-centric XML format:

```
<?xml version = "1.0" encoding="Windows-1252" standalone="yes"?>
<VFPData>
  <products>
    <product_id>1</product_id>
    <prod_name>Chai</prod_name>
    <eng_name>Dharamsala Tea</eng_name>
    <no_in_unit>10 boxes x 20 bags</no_in_unit>
    <unit_price>18.0000</unit_price>
    <unit_cost>16.3800</unit_cost>
    <in_stock>39.000</in_stock>
    <on_order>0.000</on_order>
    <reorder_at>10.000</reorder_at>
    <discontinu>false</discontinu>
  </products>
  <products>
    <product_id>2</product_id>
    <prod_name>Chang</prod_name>
    <eng_name>Tibetan Barley Beer</eng_name>
    <no_in_unit>24 - 12 oz bottles</no_in_unit>
    <unit_price>19.0000</unit_price>
    <unit_cost>17.2900</unit_cost>
    <in_stock>17.000</in_stock>
    <on_order>40.000</on_order>
    <reorder_at>25.000</reorder_at>
    <discontinu>false</discontinu>
  </products>
</VFPData>
```

The first line is the declaration. While this is optional, it is highly recommended, because it identifies the document as an XML document.

You might recognize the rest of the file as data from the first two records in the Products table from the VFP sample data (in fact, this example was built from the Products table using the CursorToXML() function added in VFP 7). We, as database geeks, plainly see this as a depiction of a table, with rows and fields delimited by pairs of appropriately named delimiters. We see the <products> and </products> pair of delimiters separating rows, while the fields have delimiters named after their field names.

XML sees this as a series of elements. Each element has delimiters. There must be one root element, and in this example, it's named VFPData. Note that all delimiters are case-sensitive. The convention is to always use lowercase to avoid case-sensitivity issues, but for some reason, VFP's CursorToXML() function names its root element in camel case. It really doesn't matter, so long as the case is consistent throughout the document.

While this isn't exactly a compact method of describing data, because it is entirely text, it makes it easy for developers to look at the data and debug it. Besides, disk space is cheap, and you can zip the file before sending, and unzip it upon receipt, or use other techniques to save bandwidth. XML is designed to send small packets of data—say, enough to fill an HTML table on a Web page—quickly over the wire in a standardized, easy-to-parse format.

What this gives us is a series of elements that have names, and, just as we can extract rows and fields from tables in VFP, we can extract the named elements from the XML data.

There are actually three kinds of XML formats. The first is the element-centric format, shown above. There's also an attribute-centric format, and a raw format. The attribute-centric format is a little more compact, and uses attributes within the tags. These attributes correspond to what we consider as fields:

```
<?xml version = "1.0" encoding="Windows-1252" standalone="yes"?>
<VFPData>
    <products product_id="1" prod_name="Chai" eng_name="Dharamsala Tea"
    no_in_unit="10 boxes x 20 bags" unit_price="18.0000"
    unit_cost="16.3800" in_stock="39.000" on_order="0.000"
    reorder_at="10.000" discontinu="false"/>
    <products product_id="2" prod_name="Chang" eng_name="Tibetan Barley
    Beer" no_in_unit="24 - 12 oz bottles" unit_price="19.0000"
    unit_cost="17.2900" in_stock="17.000" on_order="40.000"
    reorder_at="25.000" discontinu="false"/>
</VFPData>
```

Notice that all elements are formatted as strings, even if they represent numeric data. The last format is the raw format. It's very similar to the attribute-centric format, except that the tag is always named "row."

```
<?xml version = "1.0" encoding="Windows-1252" standalone="yes"?>
<VFPData>
   <row product_id="1" prod_name="Chai" eng_name="Dharamsala Tea"
   no_in_unit="10 boxes x 20 bags" unit_price="18.0000"
   unit_cost="16.3800" in_stock="39.000" on_order="0.000"
   reorder_at="10.000" discontinu="false"/>
   <row product_id="2" prod_name="Chang" eng_name="Tibetan Barley Beer"
   no_in_unit="24 - 12 oz bottles" unit_price="19.0000"
   unit_cost="17.2900" in_stock="17.000" on_order="40.000"
   reorder_at="25.000" discontinu="false"/>
</VFPData>
```

XML can also have a schema that explains the data contained within the XML file. A portion of the schema for the Products XML examples looks like this:

```
  <xsd:schema id="VFPData"
xmlns:xsd="http://www.w3.org/2001/XMLSchema"
      xmlns:msdata="urn:schemas-microsoft-com:xml-msdata">
    <xsd:element name="VFPData" msdata:lsDataSet="true">
      <xsd:complexType>
        <xsd:choice maxOccurs="unbounded">
          <xsd:element name="products" minOccurs="1"
               maxOccurs="unbounded">
            <xsd:complexType>
              <xsd:attribute name="product_id" use="required">
                <xsd:simpleType>
                  <xsd:restriction base="xsd:string">
                    <xsd:maxLength value="6"/>
                  </xsd:restriction>
                </xsd:simpleType>
              </xsd:attribute>
              <xsd:attribute name="prod_name" use="required">
                <xsd:simpleType>
                  <xsd:restriction base="xsd:string">
                    <xsd:maxLength value="40"/>
                  </xsd:restriction>
                </xsd:simpleType>
              </xsd:attribute>

  [In the interest of brief examples, we've omitted
   the definitions for the attributes eng_name, no_in_unit,
   unit_price, unit_cost, in_stock, on_order, and reorder_at.]

              <xsd:attribute name="discontinu" type="xsd:boolean"
                   use="required"/>
            </xsd:complexType>
          </xsd:element>
        </xsd:choice>
      </xsd:complexType>
    </xsd:element>
  </xsd:schema>
```

As you can see, the schema tells a lot about the structure of the XML file, including data type, whether it's required, and so on. Schemas can be inline with the XML file, or stored in an external file.

VFP 7 has added support for XML. XMLToCursor() and CursorToXML() are the means to read and write XML strings. For communicating changes to buffered tables, look at XMLUpdateGram().

Want to do more with XML? Microsoft has a COM object, MSXML.DLL, that's Microsoft's interpretation of the XML Document Object Model (XMLDOM), an XML parser. It ships with Internet Explorer 5.0 and later; updates and documentation can be found at www.microsoft.com/xml. XMLDOM parses XML strings (much like

VFP's XMLToCursor() function), and can be used to render the XML into a viewable HTML document.

Web Services

Web Services are the latest and greatest way to program for the Web. Web Services are integral to the .NET architecture, as applications are built from a series of Web Services. But, Web Services aren't just for .NET. They are a nicely defined way to distribute applications over the Internet.

So, what's a Web Service? To cut to the chase, it's a function that works on the Internet. OK, that's oversimplifying things a bit, but to look at all the acronyms associated with Web Services, you'd think it was some sort of complex, esoteric *something* that's so complicated that only the brainiest of geeks can understand it. Not so. We've seen this kind of intimidating jargon before: Think way back to programs, functions, methods, COM objects, OCXs, DLLs ... these are all names for "some code that does something." Now you can add *Web Service* to that list.

A Web Service has some specifications that differentiate it from the other kinds of "code that does something." There are five specifications:

1. It uses XML to represent data.

2. It uses Simple Object Access Protocol (SOAP) to define the way messages are exchanged. There are several parts to the SOAP specification, which include rules for representing data in XML, conventions for representing remote procedure calls, and bindings to the HTTP protocol.

3. It uses Web Services Description Language (WSDL) as a standard way to document what messages the Web Service can accept and generate (more terminology that basically means, "What functions can I call?"). Think: Internet equivalent of a Type Library.

4. A way to find out what Web Services are out there to be consumed (the technical term for "used"). There's a Discovery Protocol, nicknamed Disco (and we thought disco was dead!) that helps developers find services at a particular URI.

5. A way to tell others about your Web Service, since they might not know your exact URI. This mechanism is the Universal Description, Discovery, and Integration (UDDI) specification, where you can advertise your Web Service.

So, in a technical nutshell, a Web Service is a special kind of program that uses enough acronyms so that your bowl of alphabet soup now looks like it makes sense.

To fully appreciate a Web Service, you need to see one. There's a wonderful Web site, www.foxcentral.net, which has all kinds of news for the FoxPro community displayed using Web Services. It consumes various vendors' Web Services, and likewise, you can consume its Web Services. This site has detailed explanations on consuming and setting up a Web Service to access information from this site; it's a great site to visit, not only for learning about Web Services, but also for keeping abreast of the FoxPro community's news.

Web Services are the Next Big Thing in the programming world, and you'll likely need to brush up on them if you're in a shop that's moving to .NET (and you can tell your supervisor that you can write Web Services in VFP 7, which shipped months before .NET was even at the Release Candidate stage).

Tell Me More, Tell Me More

When you're ready to know more about working with VFP and the Web, there are plenty of resources out there. Before you leave the comfort of your office, take a look at all the information that comes with FoxPro. Check out the Solutions sample for good examples of Active Documents, hyperlinks and HTML generation. Read through the documentation on HTML, the wizards and the new XML capabilities of Visual FoxPro. If you're testing out the servers, read through the documentation a few times, and make sure you do your testing on a machine other than your production server. Until you have mastered the intricacies of working with Web servers, it is likely you'll need to start and stop the machine a few times, and you'll also want to make sure you've worked the bugs out of updating data before you go live.

A browse through the Internet can give you more high-quality materials on HTML, Web design and Web applications than we could possibly list here.

Other Commercial Fox Application Tools

Finally, you need to realize that the tools Microsoft supplies with Visual FoxPro most likely are missing some capabilities you will need. The Web Publishing Wizard and the FoxISAPI samples are not intended as end-alls and be-alls as much as demonstrations of technology—proof that the ability to do the work of Web programming is present and feasible in Visual FoxPro. In order to develop Web applications capable of supporting large commercial applications, it's reasonable to look outside the Visual FoxPro box for commercial applications or frameworks capable of providing many of the foundation pieces and the key technical support needed to deliver world-class applications.

Several vendors advertise in the FoxPro magazines and frequent the FoxPro forums, newsgroups and Web sites. A simple search of the Web will get you dozens of hits.

Finally, there is life beyond Microsoft. We're really not qualified to talk about a lot of it, but searches of the Web should lead you to many other vendors with many nifty products to sell. Since FoxPro comes with an OLE DB provider, and since an ODBC driver is still available (at http://msdn.microsoft.com/vfoxpro/downloads/updates.asp at press time), nearly any Web development environment should be able to access FoxPro tables directly. With Visual FoxPro's capabilities for creating COM components, you should be able to achieve mixed development environments that include the business rules and processing you developed in FoxPro.

> We stand today on the edge of a new frontier—the frontier of the 1960s, a frontier of unknown opportunities and perils, a frontier of unfulfilled hopes and threats. ... The new frontier of which I speak is not a set of promises—it is a set of challenges.

John F. Kennedy, July 13, 1960

The frontier of the Web may truly turn out to be as earth-shaking a change as the changes of the 1960s. The promise of ubiquitous access and the ability to gather information from widely disparate sources may have a profound effect, not just on us nerds cranking code, but on the entire civilization. Who'd have thought that PTAs and scout troops would have Web sites and private discussion rooms, and would communicate almost exclusively by e-mail? School kids, even as young as elementary school, can get their homework from a Web site, and submit their assignments via e-mail (in Della's home, e-mailing assignments has almost eliminated the problem of papers left at home, and also works when the printer conveniently runs out of ink at 10:00 p.m.). Teens now shun the phone, talking with their friends using instant messaging—finally, parents can have the phone! But now we're negotiating with our kids for computer time. We send e-greetings (great for procrastinators); purchase items from computer accessories to groceries, gifts and even cars; research topics for work, homework and hobbies; check the weather for our destination as we book our travel; keep up with the news and our favorite sports teams; all of this—and more—on the Internet. Magazines, television commercials, the local news, and even cereal boxes are emblazoned with Web sites, inviting us to find out more information. So far, it's a pretty earth-shaking change on all of civilization. Just ask anyone how important it is when their high-speed access line is down.

Section 2: Ship of Tools

Man is a tool-using animal ... Without tools he is nothing, with tools he is all.

Thomas Carlyle, *Sartor Resartus*, 1833-1834

Section 2 discusses in brief the Power Tools—the key to using Visual FoxPro effectively. You'll find our favorite tips and tricks for using the Power Tools here, too, and an introduction to integrating source control with VFP development.

When Should You Use the Power Tools?

Always.

Okay, would you believe:

Almost Always.

We used to say (and believe) "always" as the answer to "When should you use the Power Tools?" But some changes, both in the product and, more importantly, in the development world, mean that there are some valid reasons to write code by hand. Let's look at what the Power Tools are, and then we'll come back to the question of when not to use them.

What's a Power Tool?

Long, long ago, in a land far away, Xbase was a command-line language. A not-very-user-friendly dot greeted you on an empty startup screen, and you were left to your own devices to create screens, reports, menus and other interface elements. Programmers spent their hours with graph paper, trying to calculate how many fields could be fit on a page, how many characters in each prompt. Hours were wasted drawing, erasing and redrawing these prototype screens, and more hours consumed trying to transfer them from paper to screen.

Evolution brought primitive tools—first to reports, then to menus and screens. Like many of the innovations introduced into the language, third-party add-on tools were first on the scene, adding desperately needed features into the product. These third-party tools allowed you to develop a sample screen, perhaps in a template language, and offered a method to translate these templates into your Xbase language of choice.

FoxBase was one of the first Xbase languages to add template generation into the product. The first attempt, with the FoxCode product, introduced yet another template language and a generator to write FoxBase code. Although it worked quite well, learning yet another language just to code screens was a burden, and acceptance was not universal. The FoxPro product broke new ground, in bringing everything under the FoxPro language's domain. Design tools built FoxPro tables (in the standard DBF format) and then generation programs, also written in FoxPro, read these tables and created executable FoxPro code. Although this may seem like an inefficient and time-consuming process, in fact, the open nature of the generation process allowed FoxPro programmers to intervene in the process, customizing the underlying tables and generation programs to extend the results of the generated objects in ways that Fox Software, and later, Microsoft, never anticipated. One of the most famous of these, Ken Levy's GENSCRNX program, allowed additional capabilities within screen programs, such as screen elements becoming visible under only certain conditions, or 3-D effects added without programmer painting.

The overall concept behind the Power Tools is pretty straightforward. You use a visual design tool to lay out the form, label or report you want. The tool saves your design into a series of DBF records. These DBF records can then either be generated into code, in the case of 2.x forms or menus, or interpreted at run time, in the case of labels and reports. The open nature of this design-generate cycle leaves the doors open to innovative developers who can take the core "engines" and drive them in ways not anticipated (or perhaps needed) at the time the tools were designed. This idea of allowing extensibility of the core product in new ways was a key concept behind FoxPro 2.x, and it continues in Visual FoxPro with its accessible design storage, user-extensible data structures, and open Wizard and Builder engines.

With Visual FoxPro, Microsoft turned the tables a bit, but still leaves us with lots of room to customize the process to our own ends. In the 2.x model, we used built-in objects, placed them on an input or output form, and then added code to get them to behave the way we wanted them to. We needed to intercept the generation process to customize the objects beyond the basic options that were provided for us. In the VFP model, we are not limited to using the objects that Microsoft wants us to use. Rather, we can create our own powerful custom controls, pre-programmed to do what we need them to do, and use them on our forms. We don't need to create our objects by handcrafting them; they can come from pre-built Visual Class Libraries. We don't even have to set their basic options ourselves—we can build our own Wizards to do that. After creating these objects, we can run our custom Builders on them to tweak them the way we'd like them. (See the "Wizards and Builders and Bears, Oh My" section, which details these wonderful tools.)

"I hand-coded it myself before, and I'll hand-code it now," a few diehards out there say. Well, let's see if we can give you a few more reasons to reconsider your stand...

Cross-Platform Transportability

Most VFP developers snicker at the thought of cross-platform transportability, now that it has become clear that Microsoft intends to release and support Visual FoxPro on its Win32 platform only. But cross-platform does not mean all the versions of Windows. The tables of the Power Tools are not just for the use of the Power Tools, but can be used by developers as a repository of design information. Having forms, menus and reports designed with the Power Tools gives us access to their designs, in our FoxPro programs, so that we can generate the HTML, SGML, XML, or whatever-ML an application may call for. Power Tools store design metadata, a commodity that promises to become more valuable over time.

Upgradability

There have been numerous versions of Fox to date, and we hope to see quite a few more. Each upgrade has added capabilities, features, language enhancements, and has also occasionally required some changes to the basic structure of some of the Power Tools' tables. This can be performed automatically as part of the upgrade; but don't expect Microsoft to come out with a code parser to graze through your volumes of code and try to introduce new features into it. Processing tables, on the other hand, is far easier. A Power Tool user will find it easier to get to the next upgrade.

Enhancements

There are a number of third-party add-ons (some for sale, some for free) for Visual FoxPro. Many of them—new custom visual classes, business rules managers, Builders, Wizards, and so forth—expect and perhaps require your code to be properly encased in the Power Tool format. Don't miss out on the great work of others. Avoid the 'Not Invented Here' syndrome and leverage the work of others into delivering the best application for your clients. See "Resource File" in "Back o' da Book" to get an idea of what kind of tools are available.

So Why Not Use The Power Tools?

> Men have become the tools of their tools.
>
> Henry David Thoreau

The ability to build COM components, added to VFP 5, lets FoxPro play with the big boys. We can build objects that other applications can just plug in and use. In Service Pack 3 of VFP 6 (a really strange place to introduce something new and monumental), the Session base class was added.

Session was born to be the basis for COM components. It's a lightweight class with a private data session. Session got even better in VFP 7. When it's used for a COM object, its native PEMs are protected by default, so you decide which of them to expose to the outside world.

What does this have to do with the Power Tools? Well, Session is one of the base classes that can't be subclassed in the Class Designer, but can be subclassed in code. On top of that, several other features (such as specifying COM attributes) added in VFP 7 apply only to code classes.

The result is that, while we still believe that the Designers are the right place to create your forms and any classes that are meant for use within VFP, manual construction is your best bet for building COM components. The good news is that VFP 7 introduced several new tools and features that make working with classes in PRG files a whole lot easier. Be sure to check out Document View, shortcuts and bookmarks.

The rest of this section digs into the Power Tools, including the ones that ease manual construction.

These Are Not Your Father's Power Tools

> Civilization advances by extending the number of important operations which we can perform without thinking about them.
>
> Alfred North Whitehead, *An Introduction to Mathematics*, 1911

When you walk into a hardware store, there's generally no question about what's a power tool and what's not. If it has a cord or uses batteries or gas, it's a power tool. If you make it go by the sweat of your brow, it's not.

In Visual FoxPro, the lines aren't quite as simple. There are a number of items that could be called "power tools" or not. We choose to take a fairly broad view and include in our list anything that at least partially automates a task you'd otherwise have to do by hand.

We're not going to give you step-by-step (or even general) instructions on using each of the Power Tools. We assume you've read the documentation or an introductory book. Instead, we concentrate here on the stuff you might have missed—shortcuts, neat tricks, and new ways of working.

As with everything else in FoxPro, there are various ways the Power Tools can be categorized. It turns out that, for the most part, the design team has done a pretty good job of pigeonholing the tools just by assigning them names, so we'll use that breakdown.

Designers

Generally, Designers are tools that let you point and click to create something for which you'd otherwise have to write code. They let you work visually instead of worrying about syntax. They also let you see results as you go, although you might be seeing intermediate results (as in the Form Designer, where you can tell what the form looks like, but not how it works).

By our count, Visual FoxPro has 11 designers: Form, Class, Report, Label, Menu, Database, Table, View, Query, Connection and Data Environment. The Form and Class designers are quite similar, as are the Report and Label designers, and the View and Query designers.

There's one more tool that's not named "designer," but we think belongs in this category. That's the Expression Builder, which lets you design an expression. It's certainly not a builder, and in some ways it's just barely a Power Tool. (It's kind of like a cordless screwdriver. It has power, but not much.) But, if we call it a Power Tool at all, it's more of a designer than anything else.

Wizards

Not quite as magical or entertaining as Harry Potter, wizards are useful helpers to automate some of the more mundane tasks. They serve the same purpose as the Experts and Assistants that those other big software companies provide.

Wizards walk you through a task, taking care of the details so you don't have to remember all the steps. They're a one-shot deal—once you've run a particular wizard, you can't rerun it on the results.

Different versions of VFP have different numbers of wizards. They cover a wide range of tasks, from laying out a form to documenting your code to preparing an app for distribution to scaling data up to SQL Server or Oracle. Rather than listing all of them here, we'll point out that you can find out which ones you've got by examining the table Wizard.DBF in the WIZARDS subdirectory of the main Visual FoxPro directory.

The wizard system in Visual FoxPro is extensible in two ways. You can add your own wizards. You can also add formatting styles to be used in those wizards where it's relevant (the various form and report wizards). Both of these topics are covered in "Builders and Wizards (and Bears, Oh My!)".

We think the wizards are an area neglected by too many developers. Those of us who have grown up (and grown old) using the product dismiss them as "training wheels for newbies." But, in fact, the wizards present simple, automated ways to perform some complex tasks. The Application Wizard and Application Builder, coupled with foundation classes, provide some real power. Project hooks also offer opportunities for wizard and builder creators, since it's now easy to hook right into project management.

A couple of other notes about wizards. The Documentation Wizard is the replacement for the old FoxDoc application documenter. The Setup Wizard was eliminated in VFP 7, in favor of a special edition of InstallShield.

In all versions of VFP, the source code for the wizards and builders is provided with the product, so you can make changes if you don't like the way they work. All the code is in a ZIP file in HOME() + "Tools\Xsource\".

Builders

Builders are like wizards, only much better. We can't figure why wizards got the flashy name while "Builders" is so prosaic.

The simplest definition of a builder is a "re-entrant wizard." They're similar to wizards, in that they guide you through a complex task, letting you focus on the desired result rather than how to get there. Unlike wizards, though, you can go back again. You can apply the same builder to the same object over and over, until you get it just right.

Like wizards, builders are extensible; you can add your own. "Builders and Wizards and Bears (Oh My!)" explains how.

As with wizards, the exact set of builders supplied varies from one version to the next. However, in all versions, all but one of the supplied builders relate to creating forms and their controls. The exception is the Referential Integrity Builder, which helps you set up appropriate triggers in your databases.

As with wizards, you can find the list of installed builders by examining a table—in this case, Builder.DBF. It's also found in the WIZARDS subdirectory.

On the whole, we find we're using builders a lot less than we anticipated when we first saw them introduced into VFP. We suspect that's generally true, and that most people who use builders regularly are using homegrown builders, not the ones that come with the product.

It's actually quite easy to write simple builders that use SYS(1270) or AMouseObj() to get a reference to an object and then do something to it behind the scenes. The hard part is putting on an attractive interface and making them work in general, rather than specific, cases.

Managers

Actually, that should read "manager"—there's only one of these, the Project Manager. But it's a humdinger. The Project Manager is where you'll live when you're working on an application. It organizes the components of your application and gives you quick access to the other Power Tools. And, of course, it lets you build an APP or EXE file.

System Dialogs

There are a whole bunch of FoxPro dialogs you can incorporate into your applications. We think of these as Power Tools because they save you from having to write your own dialogs. We mentioned the Expression Builder above—it's accessible via the oddball GETEXPR command. The rest of these are, more sensibly, function calls. Here's the list. Before you spend too much time trying to write your own dialogs, you might want to look through this list and consider using one of these. See the Reference section for details on using each.

- GetColor() displays a variant of the Windows Color Picker.

- GetCP() displays the Code Page dialog.

- GetDir() displays the Select Directory dialog.

- GetFile() and LocFile() both display the Open File dialog, but LocFile() looks for a specified file first and displays the dialog only if that file can't be found.

- GetFont() displays the Font selection dialog.

- GetPict() displays the Open dialog specially configured to choose pictures. Starting in VFP 6, support was added for most graphic formats.

- GetPrinter() and SYS(1037) both display printer dialogs. SYS(1037) displays the Print Setup dialog, which lets you choose a printer and paper type and orientation. In VFP 5 and later versions, GetPrinter() displays the printer selection dialog.

- PutFile() displays the Save As dialog.

Doing It the Windows Way

Back in FoxPro 2.x and even in VFP 3, using the system dialogs through the GetWhatever functions listed above seemed incredibly forward-thinking. But the proliferation of ActiveX over the last few years means that, for a lot of those tasks and a whole bunch more that aren't listed above, there are better ways. For example, the Common Dialogs control gives you access to the native Open File, Save File and Printer dialogs, with a lot more control than is offered by GetFile(), PutFile() and SYS(1037).

ActiveX controls are available for all kinds of things. You can replace the status bar, put a calendar onto a form, use treeviews and listviews (the main interface elements of Windows Explorer), or even put a Web browser into your application. A lot of ActiveX controls come with Visual FoxPro, more get installed by other things you might have on your system, and thousands are available for sale, usually in packages of related items.

The fact that ActiveX controls get installed on your development machine by just about every application you install these days does raise one problem. Most controls have pretty strict rules about licensing and redistribution. When you're designing a form, it's hard to know whether you have a particular control because it came with VFP and, therefore, you can distribute it with your apps, or it's there because the last applet you downloaded brought it along, and you have rights to use it only on your machine. Be sure to check this stuff out before you base your whole interface metaphor on some cool control you found lurking. (You can look at the help file that comes with a control by dropping the control on a form and right-clicking, and then choosing Help. At least some of them give you a clue about what can be distributed and what can't.) Also, check the root Visual FoxPro directory for a file called Redist.TXT that indicates, in accordance with your license agreement, which files can be redistributed. We found the VFP license as Eula.TXT in the Visual FoxPro 7.0 Professional – English subdirectory of the VFP root.

OOP Tools

One of the most powerful of the Power Tools is the Class Browser, which lets you explore and manage the contents of class libraries. VFP 6 brought us the Component Gallery, which organizes not just class libraries, but all kinds of files. The big secret is that the Class Browser and the Component Gallery are really the same tool (which is why there's a button in each that switches to the other). Properties control which face it puts on when you call it.

In its Class Browser guise, this tool lets you look at the structure of classes as well as perform maintenance on class libraries. The Component Gallery provides tools for organizing all kinds of files into logical groups. For more on these tools, see "Hacking the Class Browser and Component Gallery" in "But Wait! There's More!"

The Object Browser is a long-awaited tool that makes its debut in VFP 7. The Object Browser peers into a COM object's type library, and displays the properties, events, methods, interfaces, constants and other information needed to work with COM objects, whether you created them in VFP or they are a shrink-wrapped application. This is a real boon to those of us who have been automating Microsoft Office—you don't have to rely on the Object Browser in the Office application (and the VFP version is a nicer implementation).

It's worth noting, by the way, that the Browser/Gallery and the Object Browser are written in VFP. (In VFP 6 and later, source code is provided.)

Odds and Ends

The remaining Power Tools can't be easily categorized. In fact, we're not exactly sure what they are. But they add power to our development efforts, so here they are:

The updated Debugger probably ranks as a Power Tool, though the old one available in VFP 3 certainly doesn't. For sure, the Coverage Analyzer is a Power Tool. Both the Debugger and the Coverage Analyzer are discussed in "Productive Debugging."

The tools we're not sure have power are GENDBC (which generates code to re-create a DBC), the Converter (to bring FoxPro 2.x projects and screens into VFP), and the Data Session window (the window formerly known as "View").

Some of the Power Tools are helpful to use while working in the code editor. The Document View window displays all the procedures, functions, #DEFINES and preprocessor directives in the code window. Making its debut in VFP 7, Document View replaces the Procedures/Function feature. The Document View is a dockable window, and offers more display options than its predecessor. However, unlike its predecessor, it's available only from the Tools menu, and is no longer on the right-click menu—an oversight we're none too happy about.

Also added in VFP 7, IntelliSense is another feature that makes life easier while coding. IntelliSense is that wonderful feature that we've been drooling over in other Visual Studio products: It automatically completes code, offers syntax help, displays object members, slices, dices, chops and makes julienne fries. It's such a robust tool, we've given it its own chapter, "IntelliSense and Sensibility."

Another couple of tools useful while coding are bookmarks and shortcuts. Still more Power Tools added in VFP 7, these tools let you mark code to come back to later. You can cycle through them using a variety of methods, including keyboard combinations and right-click menus. Bookmarks are temporary and go away when you close the editing window. Shortcuts are persistent, and also add a record into the Task List database (FoxTask.DBF by default, but you can change that with the _FoxTask variable). The Task List application (TaskList.APP, or you can point to your own app with the _TaskList variable) lets you post a due date, track whether you've read or completed the item, and opens the appropriate editing window with the cursor set to that line. For more information on the Task List feature, see "Using the Task List Manager" in the Visual FoxPro Help.

The Tools subdirectory of VFP contains a number of other goodies, including Ted's favorite, Filer, which gives you a cousin of Explorer's Find dialog inside VFP. There's also HexEdit that provides a hex editor (surprise), letting you twiddle bits and bytes by hand. Be careful with that one. The Tools directory also contains the Transformer, which lets you move older applications to VFP.

VFP 7 adds a few more tools. The Accessibility Browser is a tool to help you develop applications that are more accessible to people with disabilities. The Automated Test Harness is a tool to create and play back scripts so you can test your application. Both of these use Microsoft's Active Accessibility technology (MSAA) to perform their functions. Find the Accessibility Browser, AccBrow.APP, in the Tools\MSAA directory, and the Automated Test Harness, AATest.APP, in Tools\Test; both directories are under the VFP installation directory.

In addition, definitely not Power Tools, but more like a filled toolbox, VFP 6 and later include a ton of classes for all kinds of tasks (the FoxPro Foundation Classes, in the FFC subdirectory of the VFP home directory) and an extensible application framework. Use the Component Gallery to check out the parts that Microsoft has supplied. One of the most overlooked tools in the toolbox is the Solutions samples (found in the Samples\Solutions subdirectory of the VFP home directory). This application is really a series of programs that demonstrate many of the features and intricacies of Visual FoxPro. There's a ton of code there to examine; it covers most controls, forms, Foundation Classes, reports, toolbars, the Windows API, and much more.

A Tip O' the Hat

Here are our hints for working more productively. We start out with those that apply pretty generally, then hone in on tool-specific tips.

Right-click

Just about everywhere in VFP, in just about every mode, right-click brings up a menu of context-specific choices. Beginning in VFP 5, that context menu even lets you do things like highlight a block of code and run it on the fly. Wherever you go, try a right-click and see what happens.

Do be careful—on many of the right-click menus, the first choice is "Cut" and it's pretty easy to choose it by accident. Worse yet, Undo doesn't always undo the cut. If you've created an ON KEY LABEL RightMouse in some of your routines, you'll probably want to ditch it about now, especially if it ends with KEYBOARD "{ENTER}".

If you're having problems with right-click menus always coming up as "Move Here/Copy Here/Cancel," instead of something context-appropriate, the problem is that FoxPro is detecting your click as a MouseDown-Drag-MouseUp. Try rearranging your mouse setup, tweaking on the driver, or being really, really careful not to move the mouse as you press the button. There really are more options on the menu!

Drag and Drop

Again, drag and drop is widely supported in VFP and, beginning with VFP 6, even between VFP and other applications. You can drag a class from the Project Manager to the Form Designer to put an instance of that class on the form. You can even drag a table from Explorer into the Command Window, and it gets opened and BROWSEd. As with right-clicks, try dragging and dropping all over the place and see what you get.

Layout Toolbar

The Form, Class, Report and Label designers all work with the Layout toolbar. This handy contraption lets you line things up neatly and match object sizes. It sounds so easy, but was so hard to do in 2.x.

Always On Top

The Property Sheet, the Class Browser/Component Gallery, and torn-off tabs in the Project Manager can be made "always on top." In VFP 3 and with torn-off tabs in all versions, push in the pushpin and you can't put anything on top of that window. In later versions, right-click and select "Always on Top." If you're still working in 640x480 mode and probably even in 800x600, you'll never want to do this. As we mention in "Hardware Recommendations," 640x480 is probably an unrealistic video mode for working in Visual FoxPro, and this nice feature illustrates the problem well.

Sittin' on the Dock of the Tray

Dockable windows take on new features in VFP 7. In addition to the pushpin "Always on Top", now you can dock many of the windows just about anywhere you want to dock them. The Command Window, Property Sheet, Data Session, and Document View windows are all dockable. So are the various Debugger windows. There are three kinds of docking modes: normal, linked and tabbed.

Normal docking docks the window to any boundary of the VFP window. Drag the title bar of the window to any of the boundaries of the VFP window, and it docks there.

Linked docking links two windows together so they are both viewable, but share the same window. You might dock the Command Window to the Project Manager and display them side-by-side. Drag the title bar of one window to a boundary of the other window to stack them or display them side-by-side, depending on which boundary you select.

Tabbed docking maximizes your space on the screen by docking windows together but making only one visible at a time through the use of tabs. Since you probably don't use the Project Manager at the same time as the Property Sheet, you can dock these two together and tab between them. Drag the title bar of one window to the title bar of the other to get a tabbed dialog with the tabs at the bottom of the window.

If you happen to find this behavior annoying (because you keep docking windows when you simply want to move them out of the way), you can turn this behavior off for each window by right-clicking the title bar and unchecking the Dockable option.

Note that in VFP 7, the Project Manager uses the VFP 6 version of docking, and still uses the pushpin to keep it always on top.

That's One Option

The Tools | Options dialog includes an amazing array of choices for configuring both your working environment and the results. Spend some time experimenting there.

Be aware that the changes you make in this dialog are in effect only for the current session (except for Field Mapping and the IDE page, which are persistent). To make the others stick, click on Set As Default in the dialog. But watch out! Even though you can see only one page at a time, Set As Default stores the current settings for all the pages. (This stuff is stored in the Registry.) We haven't found a way to store just a few settings, short of editing the Registry, which is not one of our favorite tasks. Also, check out the SYS(3056) function for rereading those settings.

Query/View Field Lists

You almost never need to visit the Fields page in the Query and View designers. Instead, use the top pane, which shows the tables in the query or view. You can double-click on fields there to choose them. Beware—the result depends on which page is on top. With the Join, Filter, Update Criteria or Miscellaneous pages on top, fields are added to the Fields list. With Order By topmost, the field is added to both the list of selected fields and the ordering list. When Group By is on top, the field is added only to the grouping criteria. (The set of pages is different in VFP 3, but the results are the same.)

You can also add fields to the various lists by dragging and dropping. You can add multiple fields by highlighting them, and then dragging them into the destination list.

Double-clicking in the Selected Fields list of the Fields page removes the field from the Selected Fields list.

Class Browser Tricks

The Class Browser isn't just for classes. You can open forms there, too. Just choose Form or All files from the List files of type dropdown in the Open dialog. If you choose Project or Application and then pick one of those, the class libraries and forms for that project are opened. You can also browse objects of other types, such as ActiveX controls.

It might not be obvious that you can use the keyboard to navigate through the Class Browser (and its symbiotic twin, the Component Gallery), but in fact, a combination of tabs and arrow keys does let you get pretty much everywhere.

You can test VFP classes while you're looking at them. Highlight the desired class in the hierarchy, and then drag the icon that appears just above the hierarchy onto the screen. An instance of the class is created as a member of the screen. You can access it as _SCREEN.<classname>1. For example, if you drop the icon for a class called Yowza onto the screen, you can address it as _SCREEN.Yowza1.

The Class Browser gets close to providing Visual FoxPro with "two-way tools." Click the View Class Code button and a window opens, showing an equivalent class definition in code. Although the code generated isn't always executable as-is (it takes some shortcuts), it's great for debugging and documentation, not to mention its value as an aid to help you understand how things get put together.

The Browser is itself an object with properties, events and methods. You can change all kinds of things about its behavior by modifying its properties or invoking its methods. Check out the various Class Browser topics in Help to see what properties are available.

Like so much about Visual FoxPro, the Class Browser is extensible. The button that looks like it's got blocks on it gives you access to "add-ins"—programs that you register with the Browser and can then activate from inside it. Use the Browser's AddIn method to register an add-in—check Help for the details.

Take a really good look at the Browser itself. It's a tremendous example of what you can do with Visual FoxPro. (Try resizing it—notice how everything gets neatly rearranged. Also, in VFP 6 and later, note the splitter that lets you size each panel as you like.)

Report/Label Designer changes

The Visual FoxPro Report and Label designers look an awful lot like their FoxPro 2.x counterparts, but there are some neat features hidden inside.

First, although the RD and LD haven't been OOP-ified, they do have a data environment. We're not real clear on how a non-object can contain an object, but when data environments initially were introduced, we didn't complain because it meant we didn't have to write driver programs for reports. Instead of using a program to set up the data for a report, you could do your setup in the data environment. Like forms, reports can operate in a private data session. However, after having time to work with this feature for a while, we find that we still write a driver program/form to build a cursor from which the report is run. This is mostly to create de-normalized tables to exploit the features of the Report Writer and overcome some of its limitations.

Again, although report objects don't have PEMs like their form counterparts, reports and labels themselves have acquired a set of events. Each band of the report now has the ability to execute a function "On Entry" and "On Exit." Think of these as GotFocus and LostFocus for report bands—they'll let you display thermometers (without resorting to tricks like FOR UpdateTherm() in the REPORT FORM command that actually runs the thing) or update data as the report executes. Double-click on the band bar (the gray bar with the name of the band on it) to bring up the dialog that lets you specify these.

Perhaps the most welcome change to the Report Designer in VFP is the ASCII keyword to the TO FILE option of REPORT FORM. Finally, you can send reports to a text file without worrying about printer-driver garbage!

Project Manager Mania

You'll spend a lot of time in the Project Manager. It's incredibly versatile.

You can choose whether double-clicking an item opens the item for editing or executes it. The Tools | Options dialog's Projects page has option buttons for the two choices. It also lets you decide whether you want to be prompted to use wizards every time you create something new. That page also lets you configure your interaction with a source code provider. (See "A Source is a Source, Of Course, Of Course" for more on source code control.)

The Project Manager can be collapsed into something resembling a toolbar. In that state, you can open a single tab or tear off the tabs to put them where you want them. In either case, the tab can be resized. The PM remembers each tab's size. It can also be docked to any of the edges of the FoxPro window, and VFP 7 adds the ability to dock it to another dockable window, like the Command Window—either side-by-side with the Command Window or with each one as a tab that takes up the full size of the window. See "Sitting on the Dock of the Tray" for more information on docking.

You can provide a description for any item in the project using the Edit Description option on the Project menu (and the PM's context menu). The description you enter appears in the bottom panel of the PM when the item is highlighted. No more frantically trying to remember what "Arpmt02.PRG" does. For classes, the description shown in the Project Manager is the same one you can enter in the Class Designer's Class Info dialog. You can enter it either place and see it in both. (Consider using a project hook to force you to add a description at the same time you add an item to the project.)

The Version button in the PM's Build dialog gives you access to the same version information used by commercial applications. You can set up your app with version number, copyright, and so forth that'll show up when the user chooses Properties in Explorer. You can also grab this version information to use in your application's About dialog using AGetFileVersion() in VFP 6 and later or the FoxTools' GetFileVersion() function in VFP 5.

Expression Builder Tricks

The Expression Builder has its own set of preferences, hidden away under the Options button on the misnamed "Builder." These preferences are saved in the current resource file, and allow the Builder's popups to be restricted to just those functions you'd like the user to be able to manipulate. You can also specify whether system memory variables are visible, and how aliases get added to expressions. Because anyone can access these options, it's not exactly foolproof security, but it can be an aid to guide the user. See the Reference section's entry on GETEXPR for more on this command.

You can also replace the Expression Builder with your own dialog by setting the _GETEXPR system variable. The program you specify runs any time the built-in Expression Builder would be called and when GETEXPR is executed.

Toolbar Techniques

Right-click in any toolbar and you get a list of system toolbars. Choose one and it appears.

Double-click in a docked toolbar to undock it. Double-click in an undocked toolbar and it redocks wherever you last docked it (by default, at the top).

Toolbars sometimes seem to disappear. Usually, the problem is that they are docked somewhere off-screen (or far enough off that you can't find them). We haven't found a command to fix this, but you can do it by brute force. Use the View menu to close the toolbar in question. SET RESOURCE OFF and open the resource file. Find the record for this toolbar (Id="TTOOLBAR" and Name is the toolbar's name). Delete the record and pack the file. Close the resource file and SET RESOURCE ON. When you bring up that toolbar again, it'll be in its initial, default location.

Toolbars are customizable. Bring up the Toolbars dialog from the View menu, and click the Customize button. You can drag the standard buttons onto any toolbar to customize it to your liking.

Form Designer Hints

If you're designing forms for users who work at a lower video resolution than you, make sure you don't make things too big. The Forms page of the Tools | Options dialog lets you set a maximum design area to any of the most common Windows video modes. Limiting a form to 640 x 480 doesn't prevent you from creating forms with insufficient room because of all of your added menus, status bars, toolbars and other miscellaneous ornamentation, so you should still test your application in the lower resolution for ease of use. (Try to keep form height to 390 pixels or less to account for all these factors.)

Always test your applications in both large and small fonts so that, no matter which way your users set up their machines, things look right. (We're pretty sure Microsoft doesn't always remember to do this, since Tamar habitually uses large fonts and frequently finds graphic glitches in MS apps.) On this front, don't ever, under any circumstances, use 8-point MS Sans Serif or any other non-scalable fonts in your forms. They don't scale properly between large and small fonts. Stick to TrueType or OpenType fonts.

If you're always annoyed by the Prompt to Save Changes dialog when you run a form right from the Designer (well, gee, what else would you want to do?), get rid of it by unchecking that item in the Tools | Options dialog. (Thanks to our good friend Mac Rubel for this one.)

There are two ways to set the tab order for controls. One is by clicking on each control in the order you want it. The other is by using a list with movers. You choose which method you want in the Tools | Options dialog—again, the Forms page is used.

Know the grid of lines that appears on the background in the Form Designer (or for form classes in the Class Designer)? You can control that. By default, the grid lines are 12 pixels apart in each direction. In VFP 7, they really are 12 pixels apart. In VFP 6 and earlier, the grid was drawn at double the scale. You can change that for a particular form by using the Set Grid Scale item on the Format menu, or for all new forms using the Forms page of the Tools | Options dialog. This option is not only used for the Snap to Grid feature, but it is also used when you copy and paste an object with the Ctrl+C, Ctrl+V shortcuts—the copy appears one grid increment to the right and below the original.

When you're writing code in a method window, right-click and choose Object List to avoid having to type long object references. Just choose the object you're interested in and an appropriate reference is added at the cursor position. In VFP 7, you can still use the Object List, but IntelliSense helps you choose not just object references, but also helps to select its members. VFP 7 adds some new options to the right-click menu. You can toggle a breakpoint from within the code window (or double-click in the selection bar on the right of the code window), add a bookmark that persists for only this VFP session (or Shift+double-click the selection bar), or add a task list item (or Ctrl+double-click the selection bar).

You can run a form directly from the Form Designer using the ! button on the Standard toolbar. If you're like Tamar and prefer the keyboard to the mouse, use Ctrl+E. In VFP 3, that was it for this capability, but it keeps getting better and better. In VFP 5, another button was added that lets you go back to the Designer from the running form. In fact, anytime you run a form from the Form Designer, closing it takes you back to the Designer. But, in VFP 5, you had to make sure that the form window itself was on top in order to click the ! button. Not anymore. In Version 6 and later, not only can you click ! no matter which window is on top (the form, the property sheet, or a method code window), but when you return to the Form Designer, the last method code window you were working in is still open and it's on top.

Speaking of methods, the METHOD keyword of MODIFY FORM and MODIFY CLASS is a real time-saver, too! If you're repeatedly in the run-test-crash-code cycle, consider using MODIFY FORM YourForm METHOD YourMethod if you keep going back to tweak on the same chunk of code.

Draw Me a Map

One of the truly powerful changes in VFP 5 was the addition of field mapping. In VFP 3, when you dragged a field from the Data Environment or the Project Manager onto a form, you got a text box based on the VFP base text box class. When you dragged a table, you got a grid based on the base grid class.

However, using the base classes is a bad idea. It's always better to use a subclass at least one level down the hierarchy in case you need to make some global changes (like getting rid of MS Sans Serif, 8).

Field mapping lets you specify the classes used when you drag a field or table onto a form. It also lets you specify the form class used by default when you issue CREATE FORM. You set up your mappings in, where else, the Tools | Options dialog, save them as defaults, and forget about it. (We tend to forget about it so much that we're occasionally surprised to find ourselves working with a test form that isn't based on VFP's form class.) You can use a project hook to swap the settings you want in and out when a project is opened and closed. However, if you open multiple projects at the same time and they have different settings, there's no way to ensure that the right settings are in place as you move among the forms. VFP 7 offers a workaround with the new Activate method of the project hook. You can swap every time you switch projects. The only problem is that Activate doesn't fire if the project is docked.

A View To Kill For

The Data Session window was formerly called the View window, way back in FoxPro 2.x. You can bring up this window by using the SET command, which used to bring up a View window with all the SETtings, which were moved to the Tools | Options dialog.

Opening a table through the Data Session window opens it in a new work area, even if an alias is already highlighted. Open tables are listed in reverse order of being opened—that is, the most recently opened table appears at the top, and the one you opened first shows up last.

The Properties button gets you to the Work Area Properties dialog, which can change such properties as buffering and indices. You can even modify the table from here.

Color Us Happy

Another big change introduced in VFP 5 was syntax coloring. This means that, as you type code, whether in an editing window or the Command Window, it gets colored based on VFP's interpretation of it. You can control the colors used with the Editor page of the Tools | Options dialog.

The syntax coloring mechanism appears to be a simple lookup, not a sophisticated parser. So, it can't tell that you're using a keyword as a table name. For that matter, it can't even tell that a comment has been continued to a new line. Nonetheless, we love it, and when on occasion we're forced to use older versions of FoxPro, we find it hard to read the dull black code we see there.

Edit Me This

Aside from syntax coloring, the editor was seriously enhanced in VFP 5. The context menu includes the ability to comment or uncomment a block of code, as well to indent and unindent a block of code. Starting in VFP 7, you can set the character string used to denote a comment, through the Tools | Options dialog. VFP 5 and 6 require you to edit the Registry—the key you're looking for is:

```
HKEY_CURRENT_USER\Software\Microsoft\VisualFoxPro\7.0\Options\EditorCo
mmentString
```

Substitute the appropriate version number in there. It works for VFP 7, too.

VFP 7 added a number of other options to the context menu, such as changing the case, and toggling bookmarks, tasklist items, and breakpoints.

In VFP 5 and VFP 6, a dialog is available on the context menu to teleport you instantly to any function or procedure within the code. In VFP 7, this was replaced with the Document View tool, available only through the Tools menu. The Document View window has some enhancements over its predecessor, most notably being modeless, allowing you to sort by type of entry, and displaying preprocessor directives. The nice color icons really help you zero in on exactly which item you're searching for.

In the last version of this book, we said that if you hate having BAK files all over your disk, right-click in an editing window and choose Properties. You can still do that, but you're better off using the IDE tab of the Tools | Options menu (more on that in a bit). The dialog there lets you decide whether backups should be created on every save. (This one is a bit of a toss-of-the-coin. We rarely go back to those files, but when we do, we're really glad they're there. Of course, more often, we don't realize that we've fouled up until we're several saves beyond the critical mistake. That's just one feature of Visual SourceSafe that we love: It steps in as a backup on steroids, even in a single-developer environment.)

The IDE tab also lets you decide what font your editing windows use, so you can blow things up if, like us, you're starting to find 10-point type a little hard to work with. You can also decide whether to show line and column positions while editing. We like them on for PRG files, but off for TXT, where we generally have word-wrap on. You can even set the size of a tab for indentation. In versions prior to VFP 7, that one's a mixed bag because the Tab key inserts actual tabs, not spaces. You might not want those in your code. However, VFP 7 offers an option to insert spaces when the Tab key is pressed.

The right-click dialog saves your settings to the FoxUser table. This is nice because you can save different settings for each program. You can choose to save BAKs for IWantBaks.PRG and leave it off for IllNeverBotchThis.PRG. Okay, so you can do that, but do you want to? You can override these local settings by using the IDE tab of the Tools | Options menu. Anything you set here will take precedence over what's set in FoxUser. So, when you keep setting line and column positions on, but forgetting to set them as defaults for PRGs, you can go to Tools | Options | IDE, and set it the way you really want them. And you don't have to blow away your FoxUser file to do it.

Another VFP 7 addition is the ability to display white space. Just what do they mean by displaying space that's already white? If you've used Word, and clicked the button with the paragraph symbol on it, you're familiar with this idea. When white space is displayed, you see a representation of each unprintable character, such as tabs, spaces and paragraph markers. Now you have the same option in VFP. You'll see that "·" represents a space and "»" represents a tab. Note that what you see varies with whether word-wrap is on or off. Paragraph markers (¶) display when you have word-wrap on. As with the Tools | Options dialog, it's a good idea to check out Edit Properties every now and then to remind yourself what's there.

Macro and Cheese

Visual FoxPro includes a keyboard macro recorder that lets you record, edit, play back, store and retrieve sets of keystrokes that you can use to speed the development process. Many old geezers like Ted still have macros for some of their favorite WordStar commands like {SHIFT+END}{BACKSPACE} for Ctrl+K (clear to the end of the line), and {HOME}{SHIFT+END}{DEL}{DEL} for Ctrl+Y to erase the current line. Tamar once created a macro that replicated her favorite feature from a long-ago word processor—it switches the last two characters typed, so that you can quickly change MOID to MODI. The keystrokes you need are {SHIFT+LEFTARROW}{CTRL+X}{LEFTARROW}{CTRL+V}. Other clever ideas are to minimize the keystrokes you have to type for common sequences—for example, storing "CreateObject()"{RIGHTARROW} so you need only one key to get there. Play with the macro recording tool, available on the Tools menu, and check out the commands PLAY MACRO, SAVE MACROS and RESTORE MACROS for some ideas on what to do with these.

IntelliSense, introduced in VFP 7, can take the place of many of these macros. See "IntelliSense and Sensibility" for more information.

Keep Exercising the Interface

We are all creatures of habit, to one extent or another, and we all tend to get into routines. Click here, drag there, call up the menu for this. And occasionally we'll gripe that it takes too many keystrokes to get some common task done. Inevitably, a coworker will point out a button on a toolbar that does exactly what we need, without the clicking and dragging. For example, many developers use the Form Controls toolbar, but miss the Form Designer toolbar that gives you access to the Data Environment, the Code Window, the Color Palette, and many of the other tools you need to build forms.

Consider, too, developing your own toolbars or menu pads to provide the features you need. If you are constantly calling up a particular tool, consider creating a toolbar button for it. Add it to the Standard toolbar or write your own. This is your development environment—spiff it up to make your coding its most productive.

Productive Debugging

Error is a hardy plant: it flourisheth in every soil.

Martin Farquhar Tupper, *Proverbial Philosophy*

Our programs run correctly the first time, every time. Yeah, right—if you believe that one, we have a bridge in Brooklyn we'd like to sell you. We figure we spend at least as much time debugging our programs as we do writing them in the first place.

If your programs do run correctly the first time, every time, you can skip this part of the book. In fact, you should write a book and tell us how to do it. For the rest of you, we'll take a look at the kinds of errors that occur in programs, give you some ideas on how to root them out, and show how VFP can aid your efforts.

"Whatever Can Go Wrong, Will"

I will not steep my speech in lies; the test of any man lies in action.

Pindar, *Olympian Odes IV*

Errors in programs fall into three broad categories. One of them is pretty easy to find, the second usually isn't too bad, and the third is the one responsible for most of our gray hairs (at least a few of those have to be credited to our respective children).

The first group of errors, the easy ones, is the syntax errors. These are the ones that come up because you typed "REPORT FROM ...", forgot the closing quote on a character string, and so on. These are easy because FoxPro will find them for you if you ask. (In fact, VFP 5 increased the strictness of syntax checking so even more of them than before can be found just for the asking.) In addition, the new VFP 7 enhancements to the editor, such as IntelliSense and parenthesis matching, help you avoid quite a few of these bugs. Here's a tip just for that forgotten closing quotation mark: Set the syntax coloring for strings to something different (say, magenta), and your strings magically turn magenta when you type the matching quotation mark.

If you just start running a program, it crashes as soon as an error is found. Not bad, but you can do better. Use the COMPILE command or choose Compile from the Program menu, and FoxPro checks the whole program for syntax errors and gives you an ERR file (with the same name as your program). One shot and you can get all of these. The Build option in the Project Manager gives you the same errors for all of the code within a project. We regularly select Recompile All Files as an easy "smoke test" for the project—just make sure to also check Display Errors to see the resulting ERR file.

The next group is a little more subtle. We call these "run-time errors" because they don't turn up until run time. These errors result from comparing variables of different types, dividing by 0, passing parameters when none are expected, and so forth. They're things that FoxPro can't find until it actually runs the code, but then they're obvious. Again, your program crashes as soon as one of these turns up.

Because you have to tackle them one at a time and you have to actually execute a line of code to find an error in it, these are more time-consuming to deal with than syntax errors. But they're manageable. In VFP 5 and later, they're even more manageable because you can use assertions to test many of these things, so you can find them before VFP crashes. The task gets easier again in VFP 6 because the Coverage Profiler can help you figure out what's been tested, so you can test the rest.

The truly terrible, difficult errors are what we call "correctness errors." Somehow, even though you knew what the program was supposed to do and you carefully worked out the steps necessary to do it, it doesn't do what it should. These are the errors that try programmers' souls.

Tracking down correctness errors requires a planned, systematic, step-by-step attack. Many times, it also requires you to take a fresh perspective on the symptoms you're seeing—take a break or ask someone else to look at your code. (Tamar has solved countless correctness errors by talking them out with her non-programmer husband. Ted's favorite method is to try to explain the problem in a CompuServe message—invariably, two-thirds of the way through explaining it, the problem explains itself.)

Don't You Test Me, Young Man

> None but the well-bred man knows how to confess a fault, or acknowledge himself in an error.
>
> Benjamin Franklin, *Poor Richard's Almanac*, 1738

So now you can categorize your errors. So what? What you really want to know is how to get rid of them.

Let's start with a basic fact. You are the worst possible person to test your code. It's fine for you to track down syntax and run time errors, but when it's time to see if it works, anyone else will do it better than you.

Why's that? Because you know how it's supposed to work. You're going to test the system the way it's meant to be used. No doubt after a little work, you'll get that part working just fine. But what about the way your users are really going to use the system? What happens when they push the wrong button? When they erase a critical file? When they enter the wrong data?

Understand we're not picking on you personally—we're just as bad at testing our own applications. The psychologists call it "confirmatory bias." Researchers find that a programmer is several times more likely to try to show that a program works than that it doesn't.

So how can we avoid the problem? The answer's obvious: Get someone else to test our code. That's what all the big companies do. They have whole testing departments whose job it is to break code. If you're not a big company, you could try what one of our friends used to do—he hired high school students to come in and break his code. We've been known to sit our spouses or kids down in front of an app and let them bang on it.

A second problem we've found is that clients are almost as bad at testing as we are. Not only do they have an investment in the success of the application, but very typically they hired you because they did not have the resources to develop the application—they won't find the resources to test it, either! The ideal situation is one in which the testing person's interest, motivation and job description is to find flaws in the program.

No matter who's testing the code, you need a structured approach to testing. Don't just sit down and start running the thing. Make a plan. Figure out what the inputs and outputs should look like (or should never look like!), then try it.

Here are some things you need to be sure to test (and it's easy to forget):

- Every single path through the program. You need to figure out all the different branches and make sure every single one gets tested. Change your system date if you have to, to test the end-of-decade reporting features or what happens on February 29.

- Bad inputs. What if the user enters a character string where a number is called for? What if he enters a negative invoice amount? What if she tries to run end-of-month processing on the 15th?

- Extreme values. What happens if the patient was born on January 1, 1901? What if someone's last name is "Schmidgruber-Foofnick-Schwartz"?

- Hitting the wrong key at the wrong time. We've seen applications that crash dead when you press ESC.

In larger projects, you should generate a set of test data right up front that handles all the various possibilities, and use it for ongoing testing. It's easy to figure out the expected results once, then test for them repeatedly.

With large projects, it's also much more likely for a change in one place to cause problems in another. Plan for regression testing (making sure your working system hasn't re-exposed old buggy behavior due to changes) for these applications. Your test data really comes in handy here.

You need to test your error handler, too. The ERROR command makes it easy to check that it handles every case that can occur, and then does something sensible. When you design the error handler, keep in mind that every new version of FoxPro that's come along has introduced new error codes—be sure it's easy to add them.

Harnessing Your Tests

Thy horses shall be trapp'd,
Their harness studded all with gold and pearl.

William Shakespeare, *The Taming of the Shrew*

Visual FoxPro 7 includes the Active Accessibility Test Harness, so you can record and play back test scripts. This helps you standardize your testing, especially the regression testing part. It relieves the tedium of trying to remember exactly what you typed in last time so you can test it again (and again and again).

The test harness is an application found in the Tools/Test directory in the VFP 7 installation directory. It's called AATest.APP. Like most tools in VFP, it is written in VFP, and the source code is included. Run the Test Harness app with the following command:

```
DO (HOME() + "tools\test\aatest")
```

A tabbed dialog appears. The Scripts page shows the stored scripts in a grid. You can access and modify all the script information here. You'll likely want to start by recording your own test script. The Test Harness toolbar has a set of VCR buttons; press the circle button to begin recording a script.

A dialog box appears, asking you to choose the VFP/Application window. It shows all (and we do mean "all") open windows on the desktop. While it offers you any window, VFP or not, you must select only a VFP window, or you get an error. Your application should be up and running before you start recording the script.

Next it asks you for the name of your script. Type the name, press Enter, and you're ready to record your script. If you've ever recorded a macro in another language or in a Microsoft Office document, you know exactly what to do. Just test your application by clicking on menu items or typing in the information. The Test Harness records the location of mouse clicks as well as recording every keystroke. When you're done, go back to the Test Harness app and press the Stop button (the square).

To play back your script, check the check box in the Select column on the Scripts tab, and then press the Play button. Be sure you've started your application and know what window it's running in. Select this window, and then watch as your script executes. When it finishes, you'll see a modal dialog that indicates it's done. You can look at the Test Log tab to see what passed or failed, a reason why it failed, how much memory was used, and how long it took.

 Sometimes the mouse clicks aren't always accurate. While they always seem to fire, they don't always click in the same place. Lists and grids are particularly difficult; don't count on always selecting the same list member or grid cell as was selected while running the recorder.

Brand new in VFP 7, the Test Harness has a few bugs in it, and the interface—well, it could be a little (or a lot) more intuitive. You do have access to the source, if you care to dig into it. In spite of the bugs and the unintuitive interface, this is a tool that can really help test your programs much more thoroughly. Since you (the developer) are the worst person to test your apps, you can have somebody test your application while recording the test script, then run these scripts until your program works flawlessly.

Extreme Programming

One of the newest methodologies, extreme programming, makes testing an integral part of the development process. In a nutshell, extreme programming involves two developers working side-by-side, focusing on the simplest solution to the design and coding tasks at hand. Developers integrate and test their code often to ensure any defects are found early. It also mandates that software be delivered early and often, so as to get feedback from the client. With two developers cross-checking each other's design and code (not to mention the peer pressure of not wanting to let one's peers down), far fewer flaws are introduced. And by delivering early and often, if the team's understanding of the problem is off-base, it can be corrected quickly with as little impact on the project as possible.

Sometimes it's hard enough to justify the one-programmer approach; who's going to buy into two programmers working on the same code simultaneously? Studies have shown that extreme programming can produce applications in less time, with fewer defects (hence fewer maintenance hours), and a minor increase in total programmer hours. This reduction in errors generally more than offsets the increase in hours. It's a topic worth looking into.

Where the Bugs Are

Truth lies within a little and certain compass, but error is immense.

Henry St. John, Viscount Bolingbroke, *Reflections upon Exile*, 1716

Once you figure out that the program's broken, what next? How do you track down those nasty, insidious bugs that haunt your code?

FoxPro has always had some decent tools for the job, but starting in VFP 5 (that's getting to be a theme in this section, isn't it?), the task is much easier. We'll talk only about the debugger introduced in that version. If you're using VFP 3, check out the *Hacker's Guide to Visual FoxPro 3.0* for suggestions on debugging using the older tools.

Assert Yourself

Let me assert my firm belief that the only thing we have to fear is fear itself.

Franklin D. Roosevelt

The way to start debugging is by keeping certain kinds of errors from happening in the first place. The ASSERT command lets you test, any time you want, whether any condition you want is met. Use assertions for any conditions that can be tested ahead of time and that don't depend on user input or system conditions. If it can break at run time even though it worked in testing, don't use an assertion. We use ASSERT the most to test parameters to ensure that they're the right type and that they contain appropriate data.

Give your assertions useful messages that help you hone right in on the problem. One trick is to begin the message with the name of the routine containing the assertion. A message like:

```
MyRoutine: Parameter "cInput" should be character.
```

is a lot more helpful than the default message:

```
Assertion failed on line 7 of procedure MyRoutine.
```

or, the worst, a custom message like:

```
Wrong parameter type.
```

Liberal use of assertions should let you get your code running faster and help to track down those nasty regression errors before they get to your clients.

Debugger De Better

Error is the contradiction of Truth. Error is a belief without understanding. Error is unreal because untrue. It is that which seemeth to be and is not. If error were true, its truth would be error, and we should have a self-evident absurdity—namely, erroneous truth. Thus we should continue to lose the standard of Truth.

Mary Baker Eddy, *Science and Health*, 1875

Before VFP 5, FoxPro could just barely be said to have a debugger. The Watch and Trace windows worked as advertised and gave you tools for seeing what was going on, but they were pretty limited. Fortunately, as so often happens with FoxPro, the development team heard our pleas and VFP 5 introduced "the new debugger," so called because it doesn't really have any other name.

The debugger is composed of five windows and several other tools. It can run inside the VFP frame (meaning that the windows are contained in the main VFP window and are listed individually on the Tools menu) or in its own frame, with its own menu and its own entry on the taskbar. On the whole, we much prefer putting the debugger in its own frame. Then we can size and position both VFP and the debugger as we wish (someday we hope to have a monitor big enough to make them fit together nicely without compromises—perhaps our best hope is using two monitors side by side), minimize the debugger when we're not using it, and so forth. In addition, when the debugger has its own frame, tools like Event Tracking and Coverage Logging appear in the debugger's Tools menu. When the debugger lives in the FoxPro frame, those tools appear only on the debugging toolbar that opens when any of the debugger's windows are opened. We should point out that, even when in its own frame, the debugger is still not totally independent of VFP. It closes when VFP closes, and you can't get to it when you're in a dialog in VFP. (Well, actually, you can get to it by bringing it up from the taskbar, but you can't do anything there.)

The five main debugger windows are Trace, Watch, Locals, Output and Call Stack. Whichever frame you use, each of them is controlled individually.

You can open or close whichever windows are useful at the moment. If you open the debugger in its own frame, you can move the windows around within the frame, and dock them along the edges of the frame. In the FoxPro frame, the debugger windows are also dockable. You can dock them along each of the edges, and you can even dock them to each other, using either tab docking or link docking. So what do these windows let you do? Trace lets you view code, and Watch lets you keep an eye on values of expressions. The Locals window saves on putting things into the Watch window—it lets you see all the variables that are in scope at the moment. Call Stack shows you the (nested) series of calls that got you to the current routine. Output, also known as Debug Output, holds the results of any DebugOut commands, as well as things you consciously send there, like events you're tracking. We'll take a look at each one, and point out some of the cooler things you can do.

Before that, though, a quick look at the Debug page of the Tools | Options dialog. This is one of the strangest dialog pages we've ever encountered. Near the middle, it has a set of option buttons representing the different debugger windows. Choosing a different button changes the dialog, showing options appropriate only to that window. Figure 2-1 shows the dialog when the Trace window is chosen. Figure 2-2 shows the dialog when the Output window is chosen. Each window also has its own font and color settings.

One last general point: Since you're likely to be working on a number of programs and each probably has different debugging needs, you can save the debugger's current configuration and reload it later to pick up where you left off.

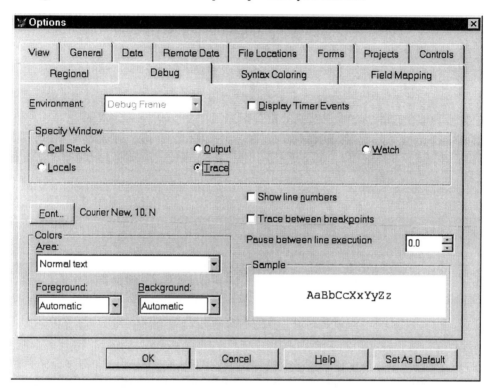

Figure 2-1: Tracing Paper—When the Trace window is chosen, you can specify whether to trace between breaks and how long to wait between each line executed.

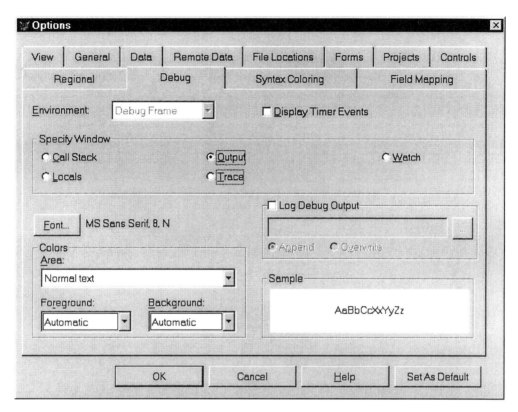

Figure 2-2: Putt-Putt Output—With the Output window chosen, you can indicate whether to store any output sent to that window to a file, and if so, where.

The Trace of My Tears

> Well had the boding tremblers learned to trace
> The day's disasters in his morning face.

> Oliver Goldsmith, *The Deserted Village*

The Trace window shows you code and lets you go through it at whatever pace you want. You can open programs ahead of time or wait until a Suspend in the code or a breakpoint stops execution. Once a program is open in the Trace window, you can set a breakpoint on any executable line. When you run the program, execution stops just before running that line.

In an application, the Trace window (together with the Call Stack window) gives you quick access to any program or object in the execution chain. You can also open up others and set breakpoints by choosing Open from the Debugger menu or using the Trace window's context menu.

Several commands let you execute a little bit of the program while still retaining control. Step Into executes the next command, even if it calls another routine. Step Out executes the rest of the current routine, stopping when it returns to the calling routine. Step Over executes an entire routine without stepping through the individual lines within; if you use it when you're on a line that's not a call to a subroutine, it's the same as choosing Step Into. Run to Cursor lets you position the cursor in the code, then execute all the code up to the cursor position. All of these options have menu shortcuts, so you can use a single keystroke (or a keystroke combination) to move on. (If some of the keystrokes don't work for you, check your development environment. Even if the debugger is running in its own frame, On Key Labels you've defined intervene and prevent keystrokes from executing debugger commands.)

When you run the debugger in the FoxPro frame, the F7 (Run to Cursor) and Shift+F7 (Step Out) keystrokes don't work. They're fine when the debugger lives in its own frame.

The Set Next Statement choice on the Debug menu is a little gem. While stepping through code, you can position the cursor, and then choose this one to skip over some code or go back and execute some again. This is probably one of the most overlooked options in all of VFP. Thanks to our friend Christof Lange for pointing it out to us.

The "Pause between line execution" option on the Trace portion of the debugger options (see Figure 2-1) is pretty cool. Sometimes you want to step through a program, but the simple act of doing so changes the results. This setting to the rescue—it lets you slow the program down (not one of our usual goals, but handy for debugging). Set it to a speed where you can see each line execute without growing a beard in between. The dialog simply changes the system variable _THROTTLE.

"Trace between breakpoints" is also controlled from the Tools | Options dialog, as well as from the Trace window's context menu. It can make a big speed difference when you're trying to get to a particular trouble spot. It determines whether all code is echoed in the Trace window on the way to a breakpoint. If you turn it off, Trace stays the same until you reach a breakpoint, then the code there is updated—this can be a lot faster.

Opening a form or class in the Trace window is a pain. You can't just use File | Open as you can with a PRG. However, the Breakpoints dialog makes it easy to set a breakpoint in a form, so you can stop execution quickly when you get there. See "Break It Up Out There" later in this section.

Once a form is open, though, the Object and Procedure drop-downs let you get to the various methods in the form and set breakpoints as needed (or you can do it with the Breakpoints dialog).

Just Watch Me!

Oh! death will find me long before I tire
Of watching you.

Rupert Brooke

The Watch window is the successor to the old Debug window of FoxPro 2.x and VFP 3 fame. You put expressions in and you can see their values. But it does much more than that, too. You can set breakpoints (as you could in the old Debug window) and you can change the values of variables, fields and properties on the fly.

Unlike the old Debug window, the Watch window lets you look at objects and arrays. Just put the object or array name in and it shows up with a "+" next to it to let you expand it and drill down. Very handy.

Over the years, we've run into some problems using ActiveX objects. Some of them didn't interact so well with the Watch window and can hang VFP or make it play dead until you destroy the object. (Doug also reports that he can crash VFP 5 under Windows 95 by putting a reference to a Word object in the Watch window.) The debugger seems to be much more stable in VFP 7.

You can also drag and drop into the Watch window. If you want an expression that's almost the same as one that's already there, drag the one you have into the text box, edit it and hit Enter. You can drag from other windows as well, so you could drill down in the Locals window to find the property you want to watch, then drag it into the Watch window. When you do it that way, you don't even have to drop it in the text box first; just drop it right into the main part of the Watch window. You can do the same thing from the Trace window or even from VFP itself. No more typing long expressions and hoping you can get them right.

The Watch window lets you know what's changed recently. When the last command executed changed one of the items you're watching, the color in the Value column for that item changes. (Actually, it seems to stay changed for more than just the next command. We haven't figured out exactly when it changes back.)

To set a breakpoint in this window (as in the Trace window), click in the gray bar on the left. (As in the Trace window, a red dot appears next to the item with the breakpoint.) As soon as the value of that expression changes, program execution is suspended and you can get a look at the current state of affairs. (Note the difference between breakpoints in Trace, which happen before the marked line, and breakpoints in Watch, which happen after the value has changed.) With objects, you don't always know the name of the thing you want to look at. Say you want to see what's going on with a check box on a form. But the same form might be running several times. Instead of trying to figure out the name of the form, just refer to it via _Screen.ActiveForm—this expression always references the form that has the focus (unless it's a toolbar). Use _Screen.ActiveForm as a way of getting to the controls on the form. The nicest thing is that the Watch window is very forgiving—if the property or object you reference doesn't exist, no error is generated; you just have the message "(Expression could not be evaluated)" in the Value column for that expression. SYS(1270) is also a handy way to get a reference to an object so you can watch it. See that topic in the Reference section for details.

Protected and Hidden properties are a special problem in the Watch window (they don't show up at all in the Locals window)—you can only see their values when you're in a method of the object. When you're executing other code (or even just sitting on a form), they show up as unable to be evaluated.

The columns in the Watch window can be resized. Just put the mouse over the divider between the columns. Voila, a sizer. We haven't yet found a good way to size things here so that we can always read everything that's showing, short of maximizing the debugger (and maybe the Watch window, too). But you can click into an item (click once on the line and again in the section you're interested in) and use the arrow, Home and End keys to see the hidden part.

Clicking into the Value section that way also lets you change the value, if it's possible. That is, you can change variable, field and property values, but you can't change the value of computed expressions. Very handy when you're 20 minutes into a complex test and you find you failed to initialize a counter to 0.

Local Hero

> The evil which assails us is not in the localities we inhabit but in ourselves.
>
> Seneca, *Moral Essays, "De Tranquillitate Animi" (On Tranquility of Mind)*

Just when you're convinced that the Watch window is the greatest thing since sliced bread, along comes the Locals window. This one cuts down dramatically on what you need to put into the Watch window. It shows you every variable that's in scope and, in fact, lets you choose the scope whose variables you want to see. Unlike the Watch window, you can't set breakpoints in Locals, but you can drill down in arrays and objects.

The context menu for this window gives you some control over which variables show up. The choices are a little strange, since they're not mutually exclusive. The Local and Public options do what they say—indicate whether variables declared as local and public, respectively, are shown. The Standard choice appears to really mean "private" and indicates whether private variables currently in scope are displayed, whether or not they were created by the current program. The Objects choice is independent of the other three and indicates whether variables holding object references are displayed, regardless of scope.

Call Me Anytime

> She was not quite what you would call refined. She was not quite what you would call unrefined. She was the kind of person that keeps a parrot.

> Mark Twain, *Pudd'nhead Wilson's New Calendar*, 1897

The Call Stack window lets you see where you are and where you've been. It shows the sequence of calls that got you to the current situation. However, it only shows call nesting—that is, if routine A calls routine B, which finishes, and then A calls C, which contains a breakpoint, the Call Stack window at the breakpoint shows only A and C. It doesn't show you that you visited B along the way.

Call Stack interacts with Locals and Trace. When you're stopped, you can click on any routine in the Call Stack window, and the Locals window switches to show variables for that routine, while Trace shows the code for that routine.

At first glance, Call Stack isn't as useful as it should be, because it works only when "Trace between breakpoints" is on. Fortunately, though, as soon as you turn on Trace between breakpoints, the complete call stack does appear. Breakpoints also make the call stack appear. You can change the Trace between breakpoints setting with the context menu in the Trace window or the SET TRBETWEEN command, as well as in the Tools | Options dialog.

Here Comes Debug

We use the last of the debugger windows a lot—it's the Debug Output window, and you can send all kinds of information there. By default, anything in a DebugOut command goes there, of course. The Event Tracker likes to send its output there. And finally, the output of _VFP.LanguageOptions = 1 goes there, too.

Use the DebugOut command and the Debug Output window for the kinds of testing you've always done with WAIT WINDOWs or output sent to the screen. DebugOut interferes with your running program much less.

If you want to examine the output at your leisure, you can also redirect it to a file (either from Tools | Options or the SET DEBUGOUT command). If you forget to do so, the context menu for the window contains a Save As command. (You might want to think of it as a "save my bacon" command.)

Break It Up Out There

A prince never lacks legitimate reasons to break his promise.

Niccolò Machiavelli, *The Prince*, 1514

Breakpoints are one of the key weapons in the fight to make code work right. They let you stop where you want to see what's going on. As with so much else about debugging, breakpoints got much better in VFP 5.

In the old debugger, you could set breakpoints at a particular line of code or when a specified expression changed. With some creativity, you could stop pretty much anywhere, but it wasn't easy.

The new debugger makes it much simpler. First of all, you can set breakpoints while you're looking at the code in the development environment. The context menu for all the code editing windows includes a Toggle Breakpoint option ("Set Breakpoint" in VFP 6 and earlier).

Once you're working with the debugger, the Breakpoint dialog is available from the Tools menu and has its own button on the Debugger toolbar. In VFP 7, it's also on the Tools menu all the time. In addition to the same old choices, it has options to stop at a specified line when a particular expression is true or after you've executed it a certain number of times. You can stop not only when an expression has changed, but also when an expression is true. Each breakpoint you specify can be turned on and off independently. Finally, breakpoints are among the things saved when you save the debugger configuration.

In an OOP world, it can be difficult to specify just where you want to put a breakpoint. What a pain to type in "_Screen.ActiveForm.grdMain.Columns[3].Text1.Valid". Fortunately, you don't have to. If you don't mind stopping at every Valid routine that contains code, just specify Valid. If you do mind stopping at all of them, maybe you don't mind stopping at each Valid in that form—specify Valid for the Location, and specify the form's name (including the SCX extension) for the File. And so forth. And so on. Be creative and you'll get just what you want.

Some things are obvious candidates for breakpoints. If a variable is coming out with a value you don't understand, set a "Break when expression has changed" breakpoint on it. Similarly, if a setting is being changed and you can't figure out where, set the same kind of breakpoint on SET("whatever").

You can get even more clever than that. Wanna find out when a table is being closed? Set a breakpoint on USED("the alias"). When a window is being defined? Set a breakpoint on WEXIST("the window name").

You get the idea—you can set breakpoints on any change at all in program state as long as there's some way to express it in the language.

In fact, you can take advantage of this flexibility to set breakpoints in the Watch window as well. Put an expression like "CLICK"$PROGRAM() in the Watch window and set a breakpoint (by clicking in the left margin next to the item) to make VFP stop as soon as it reaches any Click method. You can use the same approach to set breakpoints on things like the line number executing. While the Breakpoint dialog gives you tremendous flexibility in describing your breakpoints, turning them on and off is much easier in the Watch window.

VFP 7 offers still more ways of setting breakpoints right from the code editor. At the left side of the editor window is a selection bar (provided it's turned on). Double-clicking in this bar sets a breakpoint, denoted by a red circle. Double-clicking again removes the breakpoint. The shortcut menu displayed by right-clicking on any line includes the Toggle Breakpoint option, just in case you need yet another way to set breakpoints.

The Toggle Breakpoint option (as well as several others) is displayed only if the code editing window you're working in has already been saved at least once. Specifically, the program, form or class must have a name. That's because the name is used in specifying the breakpoint.

We don't have any problem with this, except that we don't understand why those options simply disappear rather than being dimmed.

Boy, What an Event That Was

Men nearly always follow the tracks made by others and proceed in their affairs by imitation, even though they cannot entirely keep to the tracks of others or emulate the prowess of their models.

Niccolò Machiavelli, *The Prince*, 1514

One of the trickier aspects of working in an OOP language is that events just happen. For programmers used to controlling every aspect of an application's behavior, this can be disconcerting to say the least. Event Tracking is one way to calm your rapid breathing and get your blood pressure under control.

Like the Breakpoint dialog, event tracking lives in the debugger's Tools menu and on the Debugger toolbar. It lets you choose whichever events you're interested in and have a message appear whenever that event fires (for any object at all). The messages go into the Debug Output window by default, but can also be sent to a file.

Be careful. Tracking an event such as MouseMove can generate a tremendous amount of output. Choose only the events you're really interested in, so the output is manageable. SYS(2801), added in VFP 7, can make the log even larger and more unmanageable, because now you can track not only VFP events, but also Windows events. However, you can control whether the tool tracks VFP events, Windows events, or both, depending on what you're looking for. The nice thing about this SYS() function is that sometimes you really want to see what Windows events are lurking about behind or interspersed within the VFP events. Though it tracks only mouse- and keyboard-related events, this function lets you see a lot more about what events are firing when.

One thing about event tracking is one of our least favorite aspects of the debugger. The button for it on the Debugger toolbar is a toggle. In fact, it's not really a button at all; it's a graphical check box. So, when you have event tracking in place, clicking the "button" doesn't bring up the dialog for you to change it—it turns it off. Then, when you click again to make changes, the check box in the dialog that actually controls tracking is unchecked. Yuck. This wouldn't be such an annoying problem except that there's no menu shortcut for event tracking, either. So you can't just hit a key combo to bring up the dialog. We sure hope someone at Microsoft notices how aggravating all this is soon. (We've told them.)

You can also use SET EVENTTRACKING and SET EVENTLIST in code or the Command Window to control how event tracking works.

Cover Me, Will You?

> We gaze up at the same stars, the sky covers us all, the same universe compasses us. What does it matter what practical systems we adopt in our search for the truth. Not by one avenue only can we arrive at so tremendous a secret.
>
> Quintus Aurelius Symmachus,
> *Letter to the Christian Emperor Valentinian II*, 384

The last of the debugger's tools is Coverage Logging. This gadget creates a file (generally, voluminous) containing one line for each line of code that executes. It includes the file name, the routine name, the line number, the object containing the code, how long it took, and the nesting depth of the routine.

The file is comma-delimited, so it's easy to pull into a table. However, by itself, the file isn't terribly informative. Unfortunately, in VFP 5, that's all we had.

VFP 6 and later include the Coverage Profiler, an application that analyzes coverage logs and gives you information such as how many times a given line was executed. If you point it to the right project, it'll tell you which files in that project were called and which ones weren't.

The Coverage Profiler that's provided is actually just a front end on an incredibly extensible coverage engine. You can enhance it in two different ways. The first is by specifying Add-Ins, similar to those you can specify for the Class Browser. The second alternative is to subclass the coverage class and define your own front end for it. Check the Microsoft Visual FoxPro Web site for some solid information on extending the Coverage Profiler.

The Coverage button on the Debugger toolbar has the same annoying behavior as the Event Tracking button, but we find it bothers us a lot less because we're far less likely to need to make changes and keep going. Also, all it takes to turn on Coverage Logging is a valid file name—there's no check box you have to remember to check.

The Coverage Profiler can generate a lot—a whole lot—of output. If you want to run the Coverage Profiler for only a portion of your code, you can set it programmatically. See SET COVERAGE in the Reference section for more information.

Doing It the Old-Fashioned Way

You've set breakpoints, you've put everything you can think of in the Watch window, you tracked events until they're coming out of your ears, and you still can't figure out where it's going wrong. Time to step back and try another approach.

Grab a sheet of paper and a copy of the code (could be online or on paper). Now pretend you're the computer, and execute your program step by step. Use the paper to keep track of the current values of variables.

These days, we don't use this technique a lot, but when we do, it's invaluable. This systematic attack, or any method of logically proceeding through the possibilities, whether splitting the problem in half or bracketing it from input to output, is vastly superior to the panicked "change this, change that, change the other thing, try it again" mentality typical of amateurs. If you can't explain why it works, you haven't found the problem yet.

Staying Out of Trouble

> Nobody knows the trouble I've seen.
>
> *Anonymous Spiritual*

These are techniques we use to minimize our troubles. They're mostly pretty straightforward, once you know about them.

Get Me Outta Here

Always have an escape valve. Sometimes programs crash really badly and leave you with lots of redefined keys and all kinds of other trouble. Keep a cleanup program around, which at a minimum should include:

```
ON ERROR
ON KEY
SET SYSMENU TO DEFAULT
CLOSE ALL
CLEAR ALL
```

Give it a simple name like Kill.PRG and set some obscure key combination (like CTRL+Shift+F12) to DO this program. If your applications use an application object of some sort, put all the cleanup code in the application object's Destroy method and you'll cut way down on the number of times you need the escape hatch, since Destroy should run even if the application crashes.

Step By Step

Testing a whole application all at once is guaranteed to fail. Build it piece by piece and test each piece as you go. It's much easier to get a 20-line function working than a 20,000-line application. But if the 20,000-line app is made up of 20-line functions that work, it's a whole lot easier.

When you're testing, take it one thing at a time, too. For that 20-line function, see what happens if you forget the parameters, if you pass the wrong parameters, or if you pass them in the wrong order. Once all that stuff is working, get to the heart of the thing and see if it works when you do hand it the right data. Try each endpoint; try typical data; try bizarre, but legal, data.

When building a complicated routine (especially parsing sorts of things), we've even been known to test one line at a time from the Command Window until we get it right, then plunk it into the routine. The ability to highlight several lines of code in the Command Window or a MODI COMM window and execute them (added in VFP 5) makes this technique more valuable than ever.

You Deserve a Break

When your hair is all gone and you're pounding your bald head against the wall and you still can't see what's wrong, take a break. Go for a walk, talk to a friend, anything—just get away from your desk and let the other part of your brain kick in. The folk wisdom of "sleeping on it" really works for many difficult troubleshooting problems.

That's What Friends Are For

If a break doesn't work, ask somebody else. We've all worked in project teams, where it's easy to wander down the hall and ask someone. And we've all worked alone, but we're not afraid to pick up the phone and call a friend to say, "What am I doing wrong here?" If we don't need an instant answer, we'll post a message in the FoxPro forum on CompuServe, on the Universal Thread, or the other wonderful online Fox communities—we've never failed to get some ideas there, even if no one knows the exact answer. (See "Back o' da Book" for some other places to get VFP help online.)

So What's Left?

> When you have eliminated the impossible, whatever remains,
> however improbable, must be the truth.

> Sir Arthur Conan Doyle, *The Sign of Four*, 1890

So, you're sure the file exists or that the variable is getting properly initialized. If you've tried everything else and you can't find the problem, question your assumptions. Go up a level and make sure things are as you expect when you get to the problem point. Sherlock Holmes knew what he was talking about.

Do It Right in the First Place

A lot of the things we mention elsewhere in this book will help to keep you from reaching the hair-pulling stage. It's a lot easier to realize you've initialized a variable incorrectly when you see something like:

```
cItem = 7
```

than when it's:

```
MyChosenItem = 7
```

Good documentation makes a difference, too. If you've declared cItem as LOCAL and commented that it contains "the name of the chosen item," you're not likely to make the mistake in the first place.

Watch out for undeclared and PRIVATE variables. They can often cause hard-to-find errors. VFP 7 adds a new feature to help find problems in poorly written code you've inherited. (You wouldn't write it this way in the first place, would you?) The _VFP.LanguageOptions property checks for undeclared and PRIVATE variables when set to 1. It won't produce an error, but it does send information about the errant variable to the Debug window.

These are a Few of our Favorite Bugs

> Nothing is more damaging to a new truth than an old error.
>
> Johann Wolfgang von Goethe, *Sprüche in Prosa*

There are certain bugs we find ourselves fixing over and over and over again. Since we make these mistakes a lot, we figure other people do, too. (Check out "It's a Feature, Not a Bug" for more items along these lines.)

Is That "a AND NOT b" or "b AND NOT a"?

It's easy to mess up complicated logical expressions. Back to paper and pencil to get this one right. Make what logicians call a "truth table"—one column for each variable and one for the final result. Try all the possible combinations of .T. and .F. and see if you've got the right expression.

If the expression's really complex, break it into several pieces and check each one separately.

But I Changed That Already

Change begets change. Nothing propagates so fast.

Charles Dickens, *Martin Chuzzlewit*, 1844

You find a bug. You figure it out and fix the code. You run it again and nothing's different—the exact same problem you will swear you just fixed replays again and again. What gives? There are a couple of possibilities here.

One is that you're running an APP, and though you changed an individual routine, you didn't rebuild the APP file. Do.

Another is that you're not running the copy of the program you think you are. Check around for other copies in other directories and figure out which one you're actually running. Try deleting the FXP file, if you're dealing with a PRG. If you don't get a new FXP, you'll know you're not pointing at the program you think you are.

There's one more subtle case that can happen. FoxPro keeps stuff in memory to speed things up. In some situations, it doesn't do a good job of cleaning up when you need it to. If all else fails, try issuing CLEAR PROGRAM before you run again. Really desperate? QUIT and restart.

What is This?

In moving to object-oriented programming, we often forget to include the full reference needed to talk to an object. Writing FOR nCnt = 1 TO ControlCount doesn't do a bit of good—it needs to be This.ControlCount or ThisForm.ControlCount or This.Parent.ControlCount or something like that. We've found we're most likely to forget when dealing with array properties.

There are no easy solutions for this one—we all just have to learn to do it right.

I Really Do Value Your Input

Here's another one that you just have to learn, but it's pretty common for VFP newcomers and we still do it ourselves occasionally, especially when working with unfamiliar objects. The problem is referring to the object when you want one of its properties. Probably, this happens most with the Value property. Somehow, it seems appropriate that ThisForm.txtCity should contain the city that the user just typed in, but of course, it doesn't. You need ThisForm.txtCity.Value in this case.

Frequently Asked Power Tool Questions

Actually, some of these are frequently asked questions and others are "we expect these to be frequently asked" questions about things. There's a mix here of stuff we're tired of answering already (we hope putting it here will cut down on the number of times we're asked) and things we think will *be* like that.

If you don't see your question here, check out "It's a Feature, Not a Bug"—more of this kind of stuff is there. Some other items that might be on your "how do I" list may be covered in the other chapters in Section 2 of this book. And if you still don't see your question, try one of the public support forums for VFP. (See the appendix for a list of places where kind folks answer questions and chat about FoxPro.)

Q: I'm using the Component Gallery to organize all my stuff. But the built-in catalogs don't really cover all the bases. I'd like to create some new catalogs. I've tried right-clicking everywhere I can think of and I can't find a way to make a brand new catalog.

A: We think the design of this particular feature is terrible. Like you, we figured we'd be able to right-click in the right pane of the Component Gallery while it displays the list of catalogs, and then create a new one. But the Add Catalog option there doesn't let you create a new one; it just adds a catalog that already exists. There's a New option that appears sometimes, too, but it doesn't include catalogs. Instead, you have to click the Component Gallery's Options button and then choose the Catalogs page. That page has a New button that lets you create a new catalog. Click that button and specify a table to contain the information for the new catalog. If, like us, you're not big fans of embedded spaces in file names, you can name the table with your preferred naming convention, exit the dialog, right-click the new catalog in the Component Gallery's left pane, and then choose Rename to give it a useful name. The associated table retains the original name, but the Component Gallery shows the new name. Figure 2-3 shows the Options dialog with the New button. Frankly, we can't think of a much worse way to handle this.

Q: At conferences, I've seen speakers grab a class from the Class Browser and drop it somewhere else to create an instance. But I can never make this work when I try it. What's the secret?

A: This is one of those things that demos really well, but is just complex enough to be hard to find on your own. It's really a two-step process. First, click the class you're interested in. Then, grab the icon that appears above the listview (just below the Browser's title bar). That's what you have to drag. The mouse pointer in Figure 2-4 is pointing at the appropriate icon.

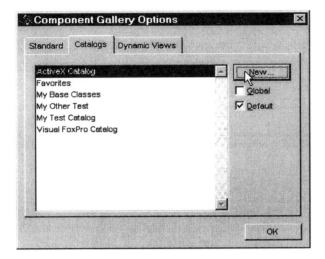

Figure 2-3: New Options for Old—Since when does creating a new one of anything belong in an Options dialog?

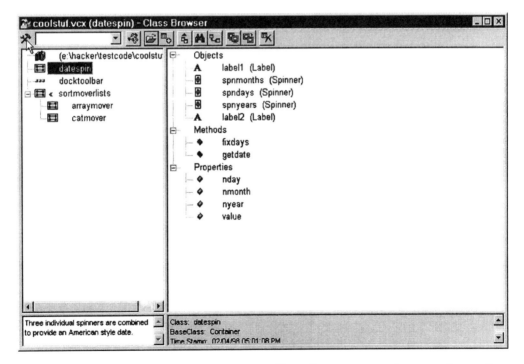

Figure 2-4: To drag an instance from the Class Browser, you have to choose the class, then drag the icon at the upper left. In this case, it's a hammer and wrench.

Q: I want to add an array as a property of a class. But I can't figure out how to get FoxPro to understand that the property is an array.

A: In coded classes, this one is very simple. Just put the DIMENSION statement in the class definition along with other properties. For example:

```
DEFINE CLASS Demo AS Custom

  DIMENSION aAnArray[7]
  cCharProperty = ""

  Name = "Demo Class"
ENDDEFINE
```

When you're creating classes in the Class Designer (or forms in the Form Designer), it's not really any harder—you use the New Property dialog. There are two ways to get there. The first works in all versions of Visual FoxPro. Use the New Property item on the Class menu (or the Form menu in the Forms Designer). In VFP 6 and later versions, you can choose Edit Property/Method from the Class or Form menu, and then choose New Property from that dialog. Once you reach the New Property dialog, when you enter the array name, be sure to follow it with brackets (our preference) or parentheses and the array dimensions. That's how FoxPro knows it's an array. Figure 2-5 shows the New Property dialog with an array.

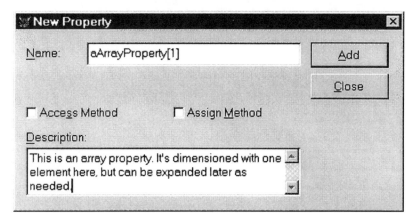

Figure 2-5: Adding an array property—don't forget the dimensions.

You can either specify the exact dimensions when you create the array property, or you can redimension it in a method of the class. In forms, we often use array properties to hold the items for a list or combo box. In that case, we dimension the array as [1], and then redimension and populate it with a query in the list or combo's Init method.

Properties you add to a class are listed on the Other tab of the Property Sheet. When you add an array property, you can see on the PropSheet that it's an array, but you can't specify an initial value (as you can with other properties you add). You have to do it in a method.

The thing we keep forgetting when dealing with array properties is that, like other properties, you can't just refer to them by name. You have to specify the containing object along with the property, or use This or ThisForm. So, for example, if we use an array property of a form as the RowSource for a combo on that form, the assignment looks like:

```
* This would be in the combo's Init:
This.RowSource = "ThisForm.aComboContents"
```

Q: I've specified hotkeys for all my menu pads by preceding the hotkey in the prompt with "\<" (like "\<File"). But when my users press ALT+F, it doesn't activate the File menu.

A: Windows has two ways to let users press keys and make things happen in the menu. You're already using hotkeys, which let a user quickly choose an item when focus is already on the menu. The other approach is menu shortcuts, which can be pressed at almost any time to choose a menu item.

In VFP, hotkeys are specified by putting "\<" in front of the letter you designate to choose the item. Pressing that letter chooses the item when the menu is already highlighted. Actually, it's a little more complicated—the exact effect of pressing any letter depends on whether any menu popups are open. (A hotkey for a menu pad works only if no other popups are open.)

Shortcuts work when focus isn't on the menu or when the popup containing the shortcut is open. Windows has a number of pretty standard menu shortcuts, like CTRL+C for copy and CTRL+Z for undo. ALT+underlined letter, used to open a menu popup, is also a shortcut (not a hotkey). It's pretty standard to use ALT+some key for menu pads and CTRL+some key for menu items.

In the Menu Builder, you specify shortcuts by clicking the Options button for an item. In the dialog that appears, there's a section labeled Shortcut. In the Key Label text box, press the key combination you want to use as a shortcut. Then, if necessary, tab to the other text box and type the description of the shortcut you want on the menu. Figure 2-6 shows you the Prompt Options dialog. For a menu pad, you may want to make the description empty, since no description appears anyway. For menu items, typically you use something like CTRL+A. (VFP is smarter about this than it used to be, and the default Key Text is usually what you want.)

One of the hardest tasks in an application can be finding enough unique, yet meaningful, key combinations for all the menu shortcuts.

In code, you specify shortcuts with the KEY clause of the DEFINE PAD or DEFINE BAR command. (We had to look that one up because it's been years since we've defined a menu with code.)

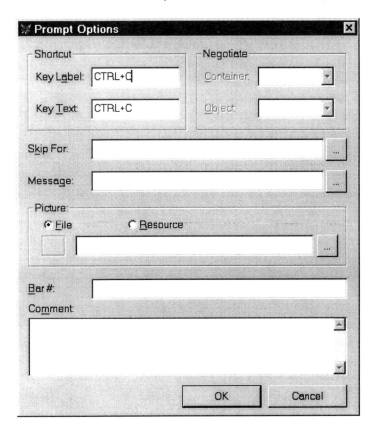

Figure 2-6: Specifying menu shortcuts—just click Options in the Menu Designer.

Q: Whenever I try to add controls to a page of a page frame, they wind up on top of the page frame instead. I've been going to the Property Sheet and choosing the page I want first, but that's really tedious. There must be a better way to do this!

A: Your question can be generalized to a broader question: How do I edit the contents of a container and not just the container itself? It applies to page frames, grids and any other container objects.

As you've discovered, you can do it by brute force. Use the combo in the Property Sheet to select the object you want to edit. But, as you note, that's pretty tedious. We'd scream bloody murder if that were the only way to do it.

Right-click to the rescue. Right-click any container object, and the menu that appears includes Edit as one of its options. Choose Edit and you have access to the items inside the container. Click on a page and it comes to the top. You can then drop controls on it.

You can tell when you have access to the items inside a container because there's a diagonally striped border around the container. Figure 2-7 shows a page frame with page 3 selected for editing.

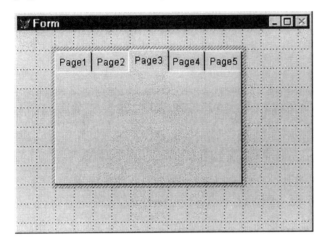

Figure 2-7: The striped border (reminds us of a college tie) indicates you're editing the contents of a container, not the container itself.

With grids, it's a little more complicated. The Edit option doesn't even appear in the right-click menu unless ColumnCount has a value greater than 0. Once you choose Edit, you can click the header of a column to select the header, or anywhere else in the column to select the column.

In VFP 7, this became much easier. Hold down the Ctrl key while you click on a container object to automatically put it into "edit" mode. But wait, it gets even better. To directly select a contained object, put the mouse pointer over the object, hold down the Shift and Ctrl keys, and click. This really saves right-clicking and choosing Edit when you've got multiple levels of containership (say a text box inside a container which sits on a page in a page frame).

Again, grids are a little different. Holding down Shift and Ctrl while clicking on a column header of a grid doesn't select the column header; it selects Column1, even if the mouse pointer was over the header of Column3. Also, you can't select the control (usually a text box) inside a column by clicking on it (with or without using the Shift or Ctrl keys). All that happens is that you select the column. You have to use the combo box in the Property Sheet to select any controls inside the column.

Q: If I change a property in the Property Sheet, then decide I didn't really mean it, how do I get rid of my change so that it inherits from the parent class again? When I delete the value I entered or put back the old value, I still see the property value in bold—that means I'm not inheriting, right?

A: Yep, boldface in the Property Sheet means you're getting a custom value, not the inherited value from the parent class. To get back to inheriting, choose the property in the PropSheet. Then right-click. The first option is "Reset to Default."

We think this is a really good item for the right-click menu. It's easy to find and use. But we think it's really dumb that right-click is the only way to get at this important item through the interface. What if your mouse isn't working? What if you have a handicap that makes it hard to use a mouse?

By the way, restoring a method to inherit is even easier than for a property. Just delete all the custom code for the method and it'll inherit from the parent class. One more "by the way"—you can restore defaults programmatically by calling the object's ResetToDefault method and passing the property or method you want to reset. For properties, it even works at run time.

Q: I'm trying to figure out where the code for the Click method of a command button is located. The command button on the form is an instance of a class that's a subclass of a subclass of a VFP CommandButton. (For example, cmdOK is an instance of OKButton, which is a subclass of MyCommandButton, which is a subclass of VFP's CommandButton.)

A: There are three ways you can determine the location of the code that executes when you click the button.

First, the brute force way: Open the Click method of the button and look there. If the code isn't there, check the Class and ClassLibrary properties of cmdOK to see what class the button is an instance of, close the form, open that class, and look at its Click method. If the code isn't there, check the ParentClass and ClassLibrary properties to see what the parent class of this class is, close the class, open the parent class, and look at its Click method. Continue this process until you've found the code, or until you find that the ParentClass is a VFP base class (which you can't open and look at).

The brute force way gets old fast, especially because you have to close the class you're currently looking at before you can open the parent class.

The second way, new in VFP 7, is to look at the method in the Property Sheet. If the method doesn't contain any code but there is some code in this method somewhere in the class hierarchy, you'll see something like "[Inherited MyCommandButton c:\projects\vfp\controls.vcx]", telling you exactly where to look. You still have to close the form or class to open the source class, but at least you don't have to check every class along the way to find the right one.

The third way, added in VFP 6, is the best. If you open the Class Browser or Component Gallery, a new toolbar with a single button is created. This toolbar sticks around even after the Class Browser or Component Gallery has been closed. The tooltip for the button, "Edit ParentClass method", pretty much describes what it does for you. Open the editor window for a method of an object or class, and then click on the button in this toolbar. A text window appears, showing the code for this method from the first class in the class hierarchy that has code in it (the one that VFP 7 shows you that the method was inherited from). There's no syntax coloring, but you can edit the code in the window if necessary. (When you close the window, you're asked if you want to save the changes back to the parent class method.)

If, for some reason, you're stuck using Visual FoxPro 5.0 or 3.0, take a look around for Ken Levy's SuperClass utility. This will give you the same functionality.

Q: When I create a grid, it has a text box in each column. When I add the control I really want in a column (say, a check box for a logical field), the default text box is still there. How do I get rid of it so I don't have the overhead of an extra control I'm not using?

A: This is one of those things that's pretty clumsy. We keep hoping the Microsofties will come up with something better.

In the Property Sheet, use the drop-down list to choose the control you want to delete. Then click on the *title bar* of the form or of the Form Designer. Be careful not to click on the form itself—that'll change the focus.

Now press Delete to remove the control you don't want.

Fortunately, adding a different control is much easier. Just right-click and choose Edit on the grid to get inside, and then click the column to give it focus. Click the control you want in the Form Controls Toolbar and then click in the column to drop it.

 We were astonished to find that the Grid Builder doesn't handle this stuff automatically. If you specify a control other than a text box for a column in the Builder, the new control is added automatically. But the text box isn't removed. Why not? In our opinion, this is just plain bad design.

Q: The Command Window is starting to annoy me because it's always on top of every other window. How can I turn that off?

A: VFP 7 added the ability to dock certain "system" windows, such as the Command, Data Session, and Properties windows, just as you would a toolbar. This feature is kind of cool, especially tab docking, which allows you to combine multiple windows and select which one should be on top with a tab button.

However, this feature can also get in your way, especially if you prefer that these windows behave the way they did in earlier versions. Fortunately, it's very easy to turn off this behavior: Right-click in the title bar of the window and choose "Dockable" from the shortcut menu. That unchecks the item (selecting it again checks it and turns the behavior back on) and the window reverts to the behavior it had in previous versions of VFP.

Q: I do a lot of demos at my user group. It's a pain to have to change the font every time I open an editor window or browse a table so everyone in the room can see it. How can I change the default font and size that VFP uses for these windows?

A: Another feature added in VFP 7 is the IDE tab in the Tools | Options dialog. This tab allows you to specify the appearance and behavior of the different types of windows available in the development environment. As you can see in Figure 2-8, there are a lot of settings here!

The way this tab works is a little weird. (Actually, there is a precedent for this behavior: the Debug tab works similarly. So, at least they're consistently weird.) You have to select the window type you want to change; the rest of the controls then reflect the settings for that window type. Any controls that aren't applicable to the window type are disabled.

You can change all kinds of things in this tab, including font and size, indentation, word wrapping, and save options. "Override individual settings" is an interesting item. If it's unchecked, the settings will only apply to windows you haven't yet opened in an editor (such as new PRG files). For windows you have previously opened, the existing

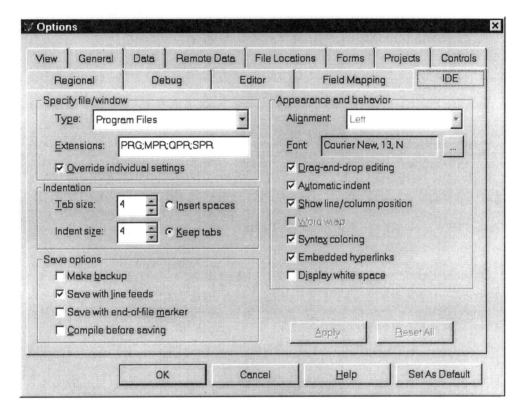

Figure 2-8: The IDE tab of the Tools | Options dialog allows you to control the appearance and behavior of VFP windows.

settings, which are stored in your FoxUser resource file, are used. If you check "Override individual settings", the settings in this tab are used for all windows of a given type, regardless of any settings that were previously used for individual windows.

To answer the question, change the font and size for each window type (you have to do them one at a time), check "Override individual settings", and click on Apply. When you're done changing all the window types, click on Set as Default if you want to make these settings permanent.

If you do a lot of demos, you might want to create another Windows user login to use strictly for presentations. Use the same procedure above, and Set as Default, to keep the settings for this user. Not only can you set up VFP for presentations, you can also set up the desktop appearance (you might look at the Windows Standard – Extra Large scheme on the Appearance tab of the Desktop Properties dialog). You can also set it for the resolution of your projection device, and clean up the menus to show only those shortcuts and menu options you need for your demo (and you can clean off those shortcuts to Microsoft Monster Truck Madness so nobody knows how you spend your free time).

Q: How do you know all this stuff?

A: We'd like to point out that it involves years of hard work, perseverance, perspiration and brilliance, but no one would believe us.

The *Hacker's Guide* itself is a labor of love that's consumed an incredible amount of time over the years, but we haven't mastered VFP by locking ourselves away in a cave. There are lots of people (we thank a lot of them in the Acknowledgements in the front of the book) who spend time online sharing their expertise with others. They have helped us or taught us many of the answers we share. CompuServe, the Universal Thread, Microsoft's newsgroups, Usenet newsgroups and hundreds of Internet resources are invaluable. In addition, we own many books on FoxPro, read a number of periodicals and a fair number of non-FoxPro-specific books on subjects from project management to user interface design (check out the Appendices for some recommendations). We regularly attend conferences to keep up with what's going on. We often resort to the Microsoft Knowledge Base (online or available on the TechNet and MSDN CD-ROMs) to find out the latest documented anomalies. So, while we all have pretty good memories, we keep our resources (especially the *Hacker's Guide*) within reach so that we can answer those tough questions.

A Source is a Source, Of Course, Of Course

Private information is practically the source of every large modern fortune.

Oscar Wilde

Wait! Don't flip that page! Source code integration in Visual FoxPro is not just for team development! If you're a solo developer, or work in a group where each of you has your own project, source code control is for you, too.

The additions that came in Visual Studio 6 offered greater possibilities for tight integration of Visual FoxPro projects with the other tools supplied in the Visual Studio package. Now that Visual FoxPro 7 is no longer in Visual Studio, we see no need to panic; it still works with the other tools, especially Visual SourceSafe. However, the integration with Visual SourceSafe started with Visual FoxPro 5.0, and SourceSafe has been a tool useful in coordination with FoxPro since before Microsoft bought either tool.

"Why Should I Bother with Source Control?"

> Integrity without knowledge is weak and useless, and knowledge without integrity is dangerous and dreadful.

Samuel Johnson

Source code control can be a very useful tool to the solo developer as well as a key tool for multi-developer teams. For the solo developer, source code control provides backup facilities and the ability to perform a "grand undo" as well as retrieve early builds or versions. With a multiple-developer team, source code control can ensure that all members of the team work with the latest revision of source code, protect the members of the team from inadvertently overwriting each others' work, and can provide a simple method to keep track of multiple releases of the software to the same or different clients.

Source code control programs have been around for quite some time but, like difficult backup programs, programs that prove too hard to use are too easy to avoid. With the increasing complexity of projects and the improved accessibility of these products, they are tools worth the effort to learn. Integration of source code control directly into the development environment is a relatively recent feature that makes these programs easier to use.

Bear in mind that Visual SourceSafe, or any other source code control program, is a separate product and you must learn its terminology and operations to get the greatest benefit from it. While many operations can easily be performed from within the FoxPro interface, you should become familiar with the less frequently needed maintenance functions that may only be available within the program itself.

With SourceSafe, we'll caution you that many of the "features" are well hidden. SourceSafe, like FoxPro (and many other Microsoft products) was not created by the boys and girls of Redmond, but rather was purchased. The original product was developed primarily as a command line utility and supported clients on DOS, Macintosh, UNIX and Windows platforms. Many of the utility programs are available only from the command line. When you install SourceSafe as described below, make sure you check out the Administration tool and read through both the user's and administrator's sections of the help file. The help file recommends that tools like Analyze, used to check the integrity of the SourceSafe data store, should be run on a *weekly* basis. We've worked with clients with gigabyte-sized data stores who weren't aware that the Analyze tool exists!

 Visual Studio 97 Service Pack 2 causes "Invalid Page Faults" in VFP if you're using integrated SourceSafe projects! Avoid Service Pack 2. You can find Service Pack 3 for Visual Studio 97 on the Microsoft Web site.

This is a killer bug, because VSS crashes the machine about 10 minutes *after* you close a project that's under source code control. Uck.

(One of Ted's sessions on benchmarking at the 1997 DevCon included a close-up and personal demonstration of this bug. Ouch.)

Getting SourceSafe Ready

But their determination to banish fools foundered ultimately in the installation of absolute idiots.

Basil Bunting

Follow the prompts of the Visual Studio install (or the Visual SourceSafe install, if you purchased it separately) to install the full "server" installation of VSS to a section of your network where it can be accessed by all workstations. Each workstation needs to be able to access the shared SourceSafe install to run the NetSetup.EXE, which in turn installs client software on the local machine. If you're installing on a stand-alone machine, you still need to go through these steps. The server install creates the data structures needed to store the SourceSafe information; the client install sets the Registry settings so VFP and other source-code control-enabled applications can recognize that the service is available.

A couple of additional settings need to be tweaked before the product is ready for use. In the Administrators tool, under Tools | Options, you should enable the multiple checkouts option (see Figure 2-9) to allow all developers to jointly check out the PJM file that serves as the ASCII equivalent of the Project Manager. Some developers have reported success with leaving multiple checkouts disabled, and requiring each developer to individually and manually check out the PJM file (via the native VSS interface) in order to synchronize their project changes to the shared project. We haven't tried this, but suspect that a process that cumbersome is done less often than one that can just be picked from the VFP menu.

If you're working with VSS 5.0, you also need to add .PRG to SourceSafe's list of file extensions for Visual FoxPro (see Figure 2-10). Each workstation needs to turn on Visual SourceSafe from the Tools | Options dialog, using the Active source control provider drop-down (see Figure 2-11). For the other options on the Projects tab, we've found that different developers are happier with them in different configurations. You'll need to experiment to determine which settings best fit your work style. Finally, note that the last SourceSafe option on the page is one for the text generation program. As we explain below, binary files are stored both in their native format and a text equivalent, to make comparisons easier. The source for the program that generates the text, SccText.PRG, is included with Visual FoxPro; you should consider modifying it to meet your needs if necessary.

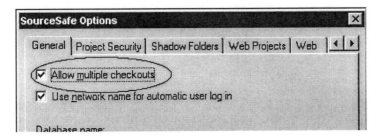

Figure 2-9: Administrator option for multiple checkouts must be turned on.

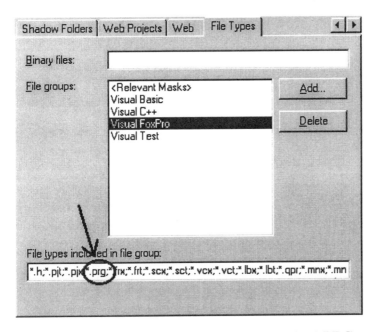

Figure 2-10: For VSS 5.0, you'll need to add the *.PRG to VFP's File Types. They got it right in VSS 6.0.

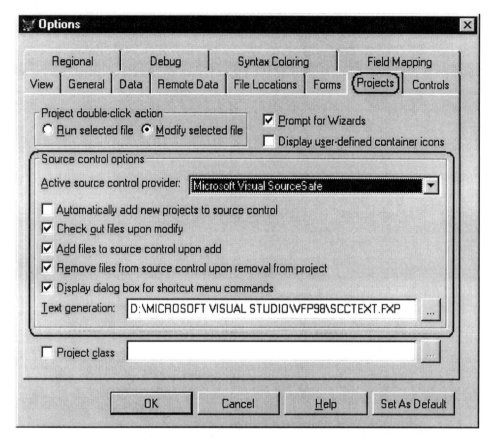

Figure 2-11: The Tools | Options | Project dialog provides SourceSafe options.

The Intricate Dance of the Source and the Fox

I do not know what the spirit of a philosopher could more wish to be than a good dancer. For the dance is his ideal, also his fine art, finally also the only kind of piety he knows, his "divine service."

Friedrich Nietzsche, *The Gay Science*

Once VSS is installed, the developer who creates a project can select "Add Project to Source Control" (if he hasn't set things up to do this automatically via the Options dialog). All other developers can now access the project by selecting "Join Source Control Project" from their File menu.

Each developer maintains her own copy of the shared project, and each has a complete copy of all of the source code. By default, all of the source code is flagged read-only to prevent inadvertent code changes. After checking out an individual file, additions and modifications to the source code are made by each developer on his local machine. When the changes have been tested and are ready to be shared with the rest of the development team, the developer chooses "Update Project List" from the Source Control submenu of the Project menu. This option updates a text version of the project, a PJM file, with the changes this developer has made to her local project file. When other developers choose to update the shared project list, they see the changes made by this developer. Figure 2-12 shows the dance of files from place to place.

Source code control works best on text files, because differing versions of text files can be visually compared. Since FoxPro keeps a lot of its designs in table format (SCX, VCX, MNX), these files cannot be compared directly. Instead, the integrated source control creates an ASCII version of each of these files (with corresponding SCA, VCA and MNA extensions) so that changes can be "diffed" (checked for differences). The SccText.PRG program creates and interprets these ASCII files; this program can be modified (or replaced) to suit your needs.

Integrated Source Code Control in Visual FoxPro

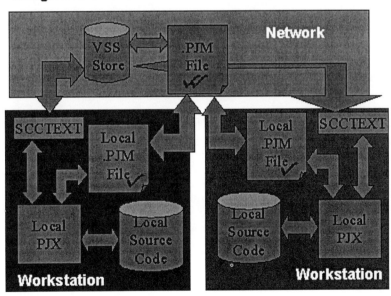

Figure 2-12: Source code control using VFP's Project Manager makes developers play nicely together.

Visual SourceSafe at Work

You have a new source of doubt and apprehension.

Charles Horton Cooley, *Human Nature and the Social Order*

When source control is in use, the Project Manager displays icons to show the status of each file (see Figure 2-13).

The PJ* Project files and database and table files should not be checked in. The project file is generated for each developer by the FoxPro-to-SourceSafe interface by reading the PJM file, which is checked out by each developer who joins the project. The PJM file contains the "header" information for the project—name, address, icon, generator options, and a line for each file within the project. Figure 2-14 shows a typical PJM file.

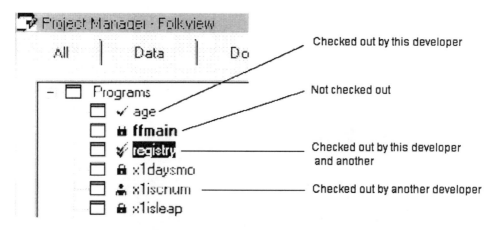

Figure 2-13: Icons within Project Manager tell us the status of each file. Even though a file might be available, there are no icons for "married," "single," or "just wants to be friends."

```
CompanyName=Ted Roche
FileDescription=FoxFolk Viewer
LegalCopyright=©1997 Ted Roche. Portions © MaxTech, Inc.
LegalTrademarks=
ProductName=FoxFolk Viewer
Major=1
Minor=00
Revision=16
AutoIncrement=.F.
[OLEServers]
[OLEServersEnd]
[ProjectFiles]
         0,i,graphic\foxfolk.ico,.F.,.F.,0,,,
 574386657,x,graphic\tbrbotth.bmp,.F.,.F.,0,,,
 574386657,x,graphic\tbrbottv.bmp,.F.,.F.,0,,,
 574386657,x,graphic\tbrdel.bmp,.F.,.F.,0,,,
 574386657,x,graphic\tbrexit.bmp,.F.,.F.,0,,,
 574386657,x,graphic\tbrfind.bmp,.F.,.F.,0,,,
 574386657,x,graphic\tbrnew.bmp,.F.,.F.,0,,,
 574386657,x,graphic\tbrnexth.bmp,.F.,.F.,0,,,
 574386657,x,graphic\tbrnextv.bmp,.F.,.F.,0,,,
 574386657,x,graphic\tbrprevh.bmp,.F.,.F.,0,,,
 574386657,x,graphic\tbrprevv.bmp,.F.,.F.,0,,,
 574386657,x,graphic\tbrprint.bmp,.F.,.F.,0,,,
 574386657,x,graphic\tbrsave.bmp,.F.,.F.,0,,,
 574386657,x,graphic\tbrtoph.bmp,.F.,.F.,0,,,
 574386657,x,graphic\tbrtopv.bmp,.F.,.F.,0,,,
```

Figure 2-14: The PJM file is the text file equivalent of the Project Manager's PJX table. Not something we'd want to have to read regularly.

The Sourcerer's Apprentice

> In the world of knowledge, the essential Form of Good is the limit of our inquiries, and can barely be perceived; but, when perceived, we cannot help concluding that it is in every case the source of all that is bright and beautiful.

> Plato

Once you have succeeded in using Visual SourceSafe with the Visual FoxPro Project Manager, there are a number of ways in which the collaboration between the two products can be enhanced and your life, thus, made easier.

Automate It!

Rather than using the internal source code control mechanism, it is possible to control Visual SourceSafe using Automation directly from FoxPro. You can scan the contents of a project (PJX files are just data tables), or you can iterate through the files in a Project object and process the contents directly against the SourceSafe back end.

An extract of Visual SourceSafe's object model is shown in Figure 2-15.

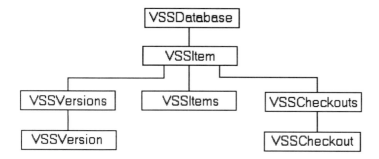

Figure 2-15: The Visual SourceSafe Object Model—Cindy Crawford is a lot more interesting to look at, but this one is informative.

The object model is pretty much like other OLE objects and collections (including the VFP Project, Server and Files objects), only this time, the objects are files, *versions* of those files, and records of checkouts. The objects are:

VSSDatabase: A SourceSafe database.

VSSItem: A project or file. Note there is also a VSSItems object that's a collection of all the children in one project.

VSSVersion: One way of representing a specific version of a file or project. VSSVersions is a collection of all the versions of a particular file or project.

VSSCheckout: A checkout record for a file. Note once again there's a collection, since one file may have many simultaneous checkouts.

Here's a routine that lists the files available along the path specified in a tree format:

```
*******************************************************************
* Program....: LISTTREE.PRG
* Abstract...: Recursively displays VSS tree
*******************************************************************
LPARAMETERS lcPath, lcPrefix, lcINIFile, lcUser, lcPassword
IF TYPE("lcPath") <> "C"
  lcPath = "$/"
ENDIF
IF VARTYPE(lcPrefix) <> "C"
  lcPrefix = SPACE(0)
ENDIF
IF VARTYPE(lcINIFile) <> "C" or EMPTY(lcINIFile)
  lcINIFile = "D:\VS98\Common\VSS\SrcSafe.INI"
ENDIF
IF VARTYPE(lcUser) <> "C" or EMPTY(lcUser)
  lcUser = "troche"  && Substitute your own VSS login here
```

```
ENDIF
IF VARTYPE(lcPassword) <> "C"
  lcPassword = SPACE(0)
ENDIF
LOCAL loSSafe, loVSSItems, loRoot, loNode
loSSafe = CREATEOBJECT("SourceSafe")
loSSafe.Open(lcINIFile, lcUser, lcPassword)
loRoot = loSSafe.VSSItem(lcPath)
loVSSItems = loRoot.Items()
FOR EACH loNode IN loVSSItems
  ? lcPrefix + loNode.Name
  IF loNode.Type = 0   && project
    * Use recursion to drill down VSS tree
    do listtree with lcPath + loNode.Name + "/", ;
                     lcPrefix + "+", ;
                     lcINIFile, ;
                     lcUser, ;
                     lcPassword
  ENDIF

NEXT
RELEASE loNode, loVSSItems, loRoot, loSSafe
```

This second sample opens a database, displays a few properties, and then checks out a specific file. Properties of the file are then displayed. Note this sample has the file paths, login information and file names hard-coded for demonstration purposes; a general-purpose routine would accept these as parameters.

```
**********************************************************************
* Program....: TESTVSS1.PRG
* Abstract...: Demonstrate VSS Automation
* Changes....:
**********************************************************************

oSSafe = CREATEOBJECT("SourceSafe")

* Syntax is object.open(path to srcsafe.ini, username, password)
oSSafe.Open("D:\VS98\Common\VSS\SrcSafe.INI","troche","")

* The following lines show some of the object's properties
? oSSafe.UserName          && Troche, no surprise there
? oSSafe.CurrentProject    && $/simpserv, the last project opened
? oSSafe.SrcSafeINI        && the file and path above

* The next line assumes Sys2335 is a Visual SourceSafe project and
* Sys2335.PRG is a program of that
oFile = oSSafe.VSSItem("$/sys2335/Sys2335.PRG")
oFile.Checkout()
? oFile.IsCheckedOut = 2  && returns .T.
? oFile.Binary            && returns .F.
? oFile.IsDifferent       && returns .F.
? oFile.VersionNumber     && returns 1, 2, etc for your file
oFile.Checkin()
```

That Annoying SCC Window

Under Visual FoxPro 5.0, whenever a SourceSafe check-in, check-out, or "get latest" operation is attempted from within FoxPro, a top-level window appears to report any messages from SourceSafe, but more likely just blocks your access to the FoxPro application and occasionally intercepts keystrokes. Thanks to Christof Lange for pointing out that you can get rid of this annoying window with HIDE WINDOW "SOURCE" or HIDE WINDOW "Ergebnisse der Quellcode-Kontrolle", if you're using the German version of these tools.

This annoying behavior was replaced in VFP 6.0 by the less annoying feature of echoing actions to the Command Window. It didn't change in VFP 7.0. We still wish we could just have the ability to turn this stuff off!

Files Outside of the Project Tree

SourceSafe doesn't allow you to include files outside the project directory tree; attempting to do so generates an error. There are several workarounds, depending on the situation. If the file is used in this application only, the simplest thing to do is just to move it into the directory structure. If the file is used in multiple projects, one alternative is to add it to a separate project within the SourceSafe native interface. Use sharing in VSS to add the file to the current project, and use "Get Latest Version" to copy a version to the appropriate project directory. Within FoxPro, add the shared file to the project, and when FoxPro protests that the file already exists under source code control, select "Overwrite" to update the file to the most recent version.

Pinned to the Wall

While it's way beyond the basic introduction this section is meant to give you, SourceSafe can do some cool things. Look at sharing between projects to maintain control of common files (FoxTools, framework source code). Consider "pinning" to lock in versions for shared branches. A "pinned" file is a branch of the file versions that's locked at a particular revision until "unpinned." The idea is that common files can get updated, but the code you've shipped to a particular client doesn't reflect those changes until you open the safety pin.

Label Maker

Look at the labeling options within Visual SourceSafe to control and document versions sent to testing or released to clients. This is a big help when the client calls and reports some problem in their Outer Mongolia office with code three revs back. With labeling on each released version, you can use the native SourceSafe interface to produce a snapshot of the code at that label point.

SccText.PRG—Sort of Right

The October '97 issue of *FoxPro Advisor* has an excellent article by Mark Wilden with several suggestions for changes to SccText.PRG, the text generation program. One issue he identifies is that SCX and VCX files jumble the order of methods each time they're saved. When SccText generates the method code to go in the corresponding SCA or VCA file, the methods are put in their order in the SCX or VCX and are not sorted. Since each version can have the methods in a different order, viewing differences in the files is difficult. Mark proposed a simple change to the SccText program to sort the methods before writing out the text file. Amazingly, Microsoft did not integrate these changes into the 6.0 version of SccText—it is byte-for-byte identical with the version that shipped with 5.0! And a few minor changes were made in VFP 7, but not changes we were looking for. If you ever find the need to compare versions of SCXs or VCXs (we'd be surprised if you didn't), this change is well worth making.

Mark Wilden, Advisor Publications and Microsoft did give Ted permission to reproduce and distribute the SccText.PRG with his book, *Essential SourceSafe,* also published by Hentzenwerke Publishing. If you're serious about source code control, this is one book you ought to, er, check out.

Sharing Ought to be Easier Than This

The Project | Source Control | Share option on the VFP Project menu allows you to add controlled files from any other project directly into your project. Unfortunately, there's no option to specify where these files are stored—all are dumped into the project root directory. You can move the file using the SourceSafe interface. In version 5.0 and earlier, you do this by dragging and dropping into the correct folder, and then deleting the file from the root. (Yes, this is how you have to do a "move"— copy and delete—there's no native move functionality in versions of SourceSafe before version 6.0.) In version 6.0 or later, drag using the right mouse button and select "Move" from the menu. Finally, modify the PJM file directly to point to the new location of the file.

Source Control—It's Not Just for Code Anymore!

By default, the VFP-VSS interface doesn't put data files under source code control, nor does it include the database container. Consider adding data files that are more control files than end-user data. Take a look at the GenDBC program, included with Visual FoxPro in the Tools\GenDBC directory, to generate a program containing all of your database container properties and methods; once you create the program, put it under source control. Consider a tool like xCase or Stonefield Database Toolkit to generate the design metadata for preservation within SourceSafe.

Microsoft Office Developer editions, beginning with 2000, ship with Visual SourceSafe 6.0 to add a SourceSafe menu to those products. Consider maintaining all project documentation under source code control as well.

Troubleshooting Speed Problems

Under some circumstances, the Project Manager takes *forever* to do anything with projects under source code control. Make sure you're using the latest versions of FoxPro and SourceSafe—each version and Service Pack has improved on the previous one. Ensure your network is performing correctly by checking the configuration of your clients and server, monitoring performance at the server, or using a packet sniffer to watch network traffic. Use the SourceSafe admin tools like Analyze.EXE to test and correct problems with the SourceSafe data store. You'll also want to check the Microsoft Knowledge Base (see the appendix for details on the Knowledge Base) for updated information on this—we've heard of anecdotal cases, but haven't managed to chase down a cause yet.

Mother Said We Should Share

There's no concept in the SourccSafc model of "synching" between two SourceSafe repositories, nor is there significant support for remote sites or developers who want a separate SourceSafe installation for their laptop. The solutions at this point are manual: Check the files out from the "master" database and check them in to the "slaves." The process is arduous and requires close attention by the operators.

When duplicating SourceSafe-controlled projects between machines, a number of errors can be generated if the project's status, as stored in the PJX, doesn't match that of SourceSafe. For example, if you attempt to open a SourceSafe-controlled project on a machine connected to a different SourceSafe database, you can receive the error 'SCC API error "Project created" occurred. The project will be opened without source control.' This is proof positive that two wrongs don't make a right.

Two fields in the PJX table appear to determine how files are controlled within the project: the LOCAL field is a logical to determine whether the file is only used locally (.T.) or if it's controlled via source code control (.F.). In the project header record (the first record in the table), SCCDATA stores path names and SourceSafe control information. In the records for the individual files, the SCCDATA memo field appears to contain flags for the status of the associated file. Thanks to fellow MVP Christof Lange for hacking his way through this one: Bytes 260 and 261 (or 0x104 and 0x105) determine whether the file is checked in or out, by this developer or another, within this project or another project. These flags seem to be updated automatically by the Project Manager, but only if the LOCAL switch is set.

Give Me That Remote Control

There's no native support for remote access, and Visual SourceSafe over RAS is significantly slower than LAN speed. However, the VSS team worked hard at improving the performance of VSS over dial-up lines in the 6.0 product and its Service Packs. Look for significant performance improvements, especially in SP5. You should also consider alternatives such as using a shadow directory structure to allow developers to "get" all current source code without invoking VSS, using a store-and-forward process, like e-mail, to transfer files to and from remote users, or setting up an Automation server locally with a better remote interface.

One third-party product, SourceOffSite, by SourceGear Corporation (www.sourcegear.com), has gotten rave reviews by many of our fellow developers. If you are working on a project with remote or home-based teams, check this one out.

Control That Source!

There is no such source of error as the pursuit of absolute truth.

Samuel Butler

Microsoft has provided us with hooks into the Project Manager and source code control to allow us to reliably maintain source code shared among multiple developers. A little time spent understanding how the mechanism works and how it can be used to your best advantage can pay off for the multi-developer team.

This chapter presents an overview of Visual SourceSafe. For an in-depth look, we suggest you obtain Ted's book, *Essential SourceSafe*, published by Hentzenwerke Publishing (www.hentzenwerke.com). It covers just about anything you'd want to know about Visual SourceSafe.

Section 3: Franz and Other Lists

To criticize is to appreciate, to appropriate, to take intellectual possession, to establish in fine a relation with the criticized thing and to make it one's own.

Henry James

Section 3 contains a bunch of stuff that didn't fit in anywhere else in the book. Most of it can be viewed as lists of one sort or another. You'll find our hardware recommendations, our opinionated list of useless commands to avoid, optimization tips, and a collection of weird items that make you think you've found a bug.

Hardware and Software Recommendations

(From a group of hardware haters)

We hate hardware. Let's get that one fact out from the beginning. IRQs and memory locations, obscure settings and incompatibilities are the bane of our existence. We're FoxPro hackers, not wire weenies, and it saddens us that FoxPro requires any hardware at all—a virtual machine would be so much nicer to work on! However, this is the real world, and it's a fact.

In the years since we first wrote this section for the *Hacker's Guide to Visual FoxPro 3*, much has changed, and yet much remains the same. We've seen a number of flavors of Windows ship, from Windows 95 to the just-released (as of this writing) Windows XP.

Hardware

"The faster and the bigger, the better" is a pretty good rule for FoxPro's use of hardware. More CPU power and faster clock speeds mean faster performance; swifter video performance makes FoxPro shine; and a well-tuned operating system is icing on the cake. However ...

> Moderation in all things.
>
> —Thornton Wilder, *Our Town*

A real fast processor isn't worth much if it's right only 98.997979% of the time. Blazing video performance that occasionally blazes into an inferno is useless. Whizzy new CD-ROMs ain't worth a darn if they sometimes spit out your still-spinning disk when you need to read them. (Ted had a "compatible" machine that actually did this.) They don't call it the "bleeding edge" for nothing. Unproven, version 1.0 technology is not the kind of thing that we bet the mortgage on, and you should probably consider these factors yourself. With proper backup and a consideration of the risks involved, investment in new technologies pays off for many hearty pioneers, but make sure when you're purchasing hardware that there is a conscious decision when to buy a workhorse and when to buy a new thoroughbred colt.

> It's always something.
>
> —Roseanne Rosannadanna

Our cut on things: Read the books, read the magazines, ask online. Make sure that what you're purchasing is compatible, especially if a client is going to be running it.

At a minimum, Visual FoxPro claims it requires a Pentium processor and 64 megabytes of RAM. That's pretty much the minimum configuration for Windows 2000, too, and Windows XP requires a Pentium or equivalent processor running at 300 MHz or better with 128 MB of RAM. Obviously, the faster the processor, the better the Fox will run. With machines available at 1 GHz and faster, it shouldn't be difficult to find inexpensive hardware to develop on. As far as RAM goes, more is better. A minimum is 128 MB, though 256 MB gives good performance.

Your users might be able to get away with the minimum configuration, but be careful cutting corners. Test your app on one of their machines regularly to ensure that the app will run acceptably on their hardware.

Hard Disks

You can never be too rich, too thin, or have too much hard drive space.

Anonymous

Hard disk space is an issue for both developers and end users. A full installation of Visual FoxPro requires an enormous amount of space, easily half a gigabyte. Disk space is cheap; buy the biggest disk you can. Even a 10 GB drive on a laptop isn't always roomy enough for a machine dedicated to FoxPro development. All that data to process can eat up space quickly!

One tip: If you're installing the common components onto a FAT drive, each file will take up a minimum of one disk cluster. Clusters are sized based on the total capacity of the partition divided by 65535. So the bigger the partition, the more space is wasted for the dinky bitmaps, cursors and icons supplied with the package. Consider formatting the partition as FAT32 if you are running Windows 98, or using NTFS under Windows NT/2000/XP to minimize the wasted space.

A second hard disk issue you need to be aware of is that Visual FoxPro's installation requires not only space on the volume where you want to install Visual FoxPro, but also free space on the drive where Windows is installed. Visual FoxPro comes with updated DLLs and Windows support files that will be installed in the main Windows and System subdirectories. These can take significant space. Obviously, overwriting these files will also require appropriate rights in the case of a network install.

In that same vein, use the Custom option of the Visual FoxPro install to determine which portions of Visual FoxPro may be reinstalled, uninstalled, or ignored. If you are installing workstation copies on multiple developers' machines, you might want only the network administrative copy to be a full copy, while each developer can get by with a smaller subset.

For end users, besides the space for your application and its data files, you need to plan on over 4 MB for the run-time VFP7*.* files.

Video

A good video card with plenty of resolution and memory is a necessity for working with Visual FoxPro. What with dozens of toolbars, as well as property sheets, tabbed options dialogs, drop-downs, OLE objects, OCX Outline controls and what-have-you, a powerful video card can make an enormous difference in your productivity. 256 colors is the minimum, with many running in High Color (24 bit) and True Color (32 bit) modes. The minimum resolution we'd even consider for running Visual FoxPro is 800 x 600, provided we're working on a system designed for 640 x 480. A good working ratio is at least one resolution higher than the system being designed, and even better (given good eyes) is the highest resolution that the hardware will support.

Why one resolution larger than the screens you're designing, you ask? It's not too hard to place a full-sized 800 x 600 form on a 1024 x 768 screen, with enough room to access the necessary tools like the Property Sheet (about 200 pixels wide, placed to the side of the Form Designer) and the Command Window. On the other hand, if you try to edit an 800 x 600 form in an 800 x 600 mode screen, you'll spend your life pushing scrollbars, moving dialog boxes, and cursing at Visual FoxPro. If you want to be able to interact with all parts of a form while you're designing it, with the appropriate toolbars and property sheets also visible, you'll want to use at least one resolution higher than you're designing for (design "6 by 4" forms in "8 by 6", design "8 by 6" forms in "10 by 7" and so on). Even better, design two resolutions higher: Design 800 x 600 forms in 1280 x 1024. Stop us if you've heard this before—more is better.

While we're on the subject of video, the monitor is the other element that makes a huge difference. 1024 x 768 or greater resolution is impossible to read (at least with our aging eyes) on a small 14" or 15" monitor. Seventeen inches is the least we'll work on, and 19", 20" or even 21" monitors make viewing an absolute pleasure. You're going to spend an awful lot of your life in front of this tube—do yourself a favor and get the largest and clearest display you can afford. Even the new flat-screen monitors are coming down in price, and the benefit is that they don't take up your entire desktop. For laptops, the newer 14.1" displays handle 1024 x 768 quite well.

A caution, however. While we feel that justifying the costs of a large monitor is a no-brainer for a developer, it may not be as easy for dozens or hundreds of operators using your application. Just as with processing speed, make sure that you check out your application frequently on one of the lower-powered, lower-resolution machines it will run on, to ensure that the interface is easy to use for the operators as well.

Operating Systems

You have four choices for an operating system on which to run Visual FoxPro for Windows, and you shouldn't be surprised that they all have the name "Windows." They are Windows 98, Windows NT, Windows 2000, and Windows XP. We suppose you can add Windows ME, if you're brave. Here are our somewhat biased opinions.

Windows 98—The OS for the Rest of Us?

Windows 98 is looking more and more like a legacy operating system; however, you'll find that many corporations are still running it. We wouldn't want to develop on it, as it's not as stable as its successors, but VFP runs just fine on it. Depending on your situation, it might still be your only option for the client operating system.

Windows NT—Nice Try

When Microsoft planned the FoxPro DevCon '95 in January, they hoped to show a late beta or perhaps even an early release copy of Visual FoxPro. Alas, a miracle did not come to pass, and instead they showed a late alpha/early beta copy of Visual FoxPro that crashed in nearly every session. But because they were running under NT, a simple double-click of the Visual FoxPro icon was all that was necessary to restart the app—NT cleaned up the mess very nicely, all by itself. That alone sold us. This is why we develop on Windows NT or a successor, because developers tend to try things that might (will?) crash their machines.

Windows NT is solid, but that robustness comes at a price. Performance is comparable to Windows 98 only on the higher-end processors, and NT demands more RAM than 98 (of course, as a developer, you're hopefully running a higher-end machine). In addition, managing the Windows NT domain model, setting up security or maintaining a large network does not come easy. For more than a few machines, the assistance of a Microsoft Certified System Engineer becomes less of a luxury and more of a necessity.

One caveat—ensure that your machine is *100%* NT compatible. This was more of an issue when we wrote the last edition of this book, but if you have clients running on old hardware, this can really bite you. The Hardware Compatibility List (HCL) is available from a number of Microsoft sources, and you should make sure that *all* of your peripherals are listed. Unlike DOS and earlier Windows incarnations, if it's not listed, it probably won't work. We've spent more than a few hours trying to shoehorn NT onto a machine that "should be" able to run NT, but some little part, perhaps a serial port or a video card, just wasn't compatible enough. Don't frustrate yourself. Only attempt upgrading to NT if the machine is *really* compatible.

Windows 2000

Windows 2000 improves upon Windows NT. Of course, it needs a little more RAM, a little faster processor. But you get a little more stability, and a few more features. Performance is a little better (though booting still seems to take as long or longer than the other operating systems). Of course, none of your earlier Windows drivers will work on Windows 2000, so some older hardware is just not supported (nearly anything you buy today is supported), and upgrading a machine from 98, NT, or even ME can be an Internet scavenger hunt for drivers.

Windows ME

For a while, this was the operating system of choice to be factory installed on most new computers. Most developers immediately wipe it out to put on Windows 2000 (and then go on the Internet scavenger hunt for Win2K hardware drivers that don't ship with the Windows ME machines). Windows ME was designed for home use, and incorporates lots of cool things like digital video, easy networking and lots of support for the Internet. Tight security and robustness was not a part of this operating system's design.

Windows XP

Windows XP comes in three flavors: the Home edition, the Professional edition, and a special 64-bit version for technical workstations (we don't think you'll see that one too much). Windows XP launched on October 24, 2001, while we were writing this book. Some people love the new features, one of which is ClearType for LCD screens, which makes 1600 x 1200 very readable on a 15" notebook display. It also is supposed to be "crash-free" (yes, they really say that on their Web site), and has plenty of support for huge hardware configurations.

There's one real drawback. It's called Windows Activation. This is Microsoft's brilliant scheme to prevent softlifting, or software piracy. Upon installation, after typing in the product key, you're assigned an installation ID. It's based on information about the hardware configuration being passed into a one-way hash, and coming up with the installation ID. (Microsoft guarantees this ID contains no private information.)

This installation ID is automatically sent to Microsoft if you have an Internet connection or modem; otherwise you must call it in within 30 days or only the activation portion of the operating system will work. Successive installations for this product key calculate the installation ID, and if the hardware is identical or "similar" (as in, you've added or removed some hardware), XP will activate again and run just fine. It will squawk only if the hardware is substantially different.

Developers swap out hardware with incredible frequency, sometimes swapping out enough hardware to make it look like a different machine. Microsoft's answer is that you simply need to call and get another installation ID, and you're on your way. Not something we'd like to do several times in a week for testing various hardware, or several times between 1 and 3 a.m. (the best hours for development).

DOS, Windows 3.x, Warp-OS/2, Linux, Palm, WinCE, and the Mac OSes

No doubt, someone's out there, even as you read these words, oh, faithful reader, picking up their poison pen to write us a flaming, screaming, bombastic letter on how we have ignored the most powerful operating system in both the known and unknown universes: (fill in the blank). This next paragraph is for them. You can skip it.

We know. It's not our fault. VFP 5.0 and later run on 32-bit Windows and that's all. No dice. Sorry. Call Microsoft.

So, Where Should You Want to Go Today?

We do call this section "Recommendations," so we should name our operating system of choice. Well, life is not always that easy.

Della runs Windows 2000 Professional, and has one machine that dual boots into Windows 98 for testing (and for some old software and hardware that isn't supported by Win2K). Doug runs Windows 2000 Server, and likes it, although he pines for the DOS days every time he waits for it to restart (ain't that the truth!). Tamar also runs Windows 2000 Professional on her development machines. Her test machine runs NT4, but soon it may be upgraded to Windows XP, in her elusive free time. Noted for liking the simplicity of running the same operating system on all machines, she's feeling a little less stubborn about it these days. Ted runs a heterogeneous network of Win2K Pro (x3), WinNT 4.0 Server (IIS and SQL Server Development), Win2K Server (Intranet), Win95 (one print server, one utility terminal), and Win2KPro on two laptops.

So what should you choose?

It does depend to some extent on your client base: If they are all running Windows 9X (or NT), you probably should be, too, or at least have one machine available and used regularly that squawks if you are writing software your clients can't run.

For a development machine, Windows 2000 wins hands down. Win2K Professional works fine if licensing is a problem.

What about Windows XP? As we've shown you, none of us have upgraded to WinXP yet. Why? It probably has something to do with it shipping while we were writing this book, and every experienced developer knows not to change the configuration of a working development machine in the midst of a project. It also has to do with the experienced developer's wait-and-see attitude of hearing the experiences of other developers who like to live on the edge. We've heard things ranging from "VFP runs the best on WinXP," to "XP is a bad nightmare added on to Win2K, primarily an advertisement for Microsoft services like MSN, Messenger, Media Player and Passport." It's new enough that it hasn't really proven itself in the marketplace yet. Few corporations seem to find a compelling reason to upgrade. But they will, 'cause Microsoft ain't shipping anything else. We're all cautious, waiting until at least the first Hot-Fix or Service Pack, which, as of this writing, hasn't happened yet.

BUT, if your new whiz-bang box comes from the manufacturer (OEM) with Windows XP on it, you'll likely want to stay with it. Microsoft and their hardware vendors are constantly innovating new standards, and you'll find that new machines may be incompatible, or they won't have drivers for legacy (last week's) operating systems. Stick with WinXP if you get it. If you get WinME or Win98SE from the manufacturer, you could be in for compatibility nightmares—or at the very least, an Internet scavenger hunt trying to find drivers. (Della's laptop, shipped with Windows ME, needed nine separate files from several Web sites, and 26 reboots to install them, to get to Win2K compatibility.) Insist on Win2K or WinXP from the factory.

"Oil Change, Tune-up and a Freemanize, please"

If you've run computers for a while, you recognize they need regular maintenance. The case needs to be opened yearly and the dust blown out. Backups should be done regularly to prevent loss in case of hardware failure ("regularly" means daily to weekly, not quarterly to annually). Hard disks need to be defragmented—perhaps weekly. Directories storing temp files should be purged. But here's one you may not have considered:

Format your hard drive regularly.

"What!?" you scream. "It took me days to install all this stuff and now you want me to blow it all away?"

Yup. The Freeman treatment (named in honor of Dan Freeman, a Prince Among Men, and guru extraordinaire) is the only reliable cure we've found for all those little aches and pains: The Registry that just doesn't seem right anymore. The weird DLLs with names you can't fathom. The bloat of the System directory to hundreds of megabytes.

Blow it all away.

Radical as the idea seemed to us at first, it does make some sense. Developers who install, test and remove a bunch of stuff from their machines are likely to get machines that bog down after a while. Downloading lots of goodies from the Internet and installing beta packages ensures that some "stuff" gets left lying around on your hard drive. Finally, the occasional misbehaving application will overwrite a key system file with an older or less stable one, and that's it—you're out of business.

But doesn't that take a lot of time? Sure. But utilities like Ghost or DriveImage make this process much less painful. First, get a good installation (maybe the one that came from the manufacturer), and make an image. Then, install all the software you need. Make another image. Don't forget all the tools you can't live without (WinZip comes to mind). Maybe even a couple more iterations. Then, when Freeman day comes, you don't really reformat the hard drive; instead, you restore the appropriate image, then install whatever else you need to, and find your data backups (which not only include your development work, but also extremely important data like your address book and Internet bookmarks). Plan for the inevitable. Log the files you install on your machine. Keep a network directory available with the "goodies" you can't live without. Get a serious backup device for the stuff you need to restore regularly: digital tape, ZIP, Jaz and SysQuest are worth considering. Archive the CDs with your key development tools on them. And, of course, make lots of backups.

"It's a Feature, Not a Bug"

It's not surprising that a language with as many different roots as FoxPro has a number of odd behaviors—things that make you say "hmmm." Some of them, of course, are bugs. But this section is dedicated to those that really aren't bugs—the ones for which there's a legitimate explanation. You'll also find a number of these items in the Reference section. Often, you'll find a design icon next to them.

We'll Continue to Try

Comments and continued lines can get you in trouble. On the whole, the trouble isn't as severe as it used to be (before VFP 5), but you can still get yourself in trouble.

The problem comes up when you put the continuation ";" after a comment. The next line is still considered part of the comment, even if it doesn't start with a "*". So, the following:

```
* This is the comment before the command ;
SELECT Something FROM SomeWhere INTO SomeOne
```

is actually treated as a comment. The query never executes.

Personally we like to put a "*" at the beginning of each line of a comment, but there is a situation in which we find the above behavior pretty handy. Sometimes, we need to comment out a command for testing purposes or because we've replaced it with a new version. If the command is continued onto multiple lines, it's sufficient to just stick a "*" in front of the first line. Of course, starting in VFP 5, it's easy enough to highlight, right-click, and choose Comment, too.

In VFP 3 and FoxPro 2.x, there's another situation where continuation can get you in trouble. You can't put in-line comments on a continued line. That is, lines like:

```
SELECT Something  ;  && here's the fields
   FROM SomeWhere ;  && and the table
   INTO SomeOne      && put it here
```

fail because FoxPro just drops the ";" and concatenates the whole thing into a single line. This behavior was changed in VFP 5 to our great relief.

But There Didn't Used to Be a Syntax Error There!

When people started running existing applications in VFP 5, lots of them started seeing syntax errors in code that had been running for years. The code hadn't changed, so what was going on?

Way back in Xbase history days, someone decided that you should be able to put comments on the same line as the structured programming commands without having to use the comment indicator. That is, you could write:

```
IF x<3    Fewer than three remain
   ...
ENDIF
```

The rule applied to each of the components of the branching and looping commands (IF, DO CASE, DO WHILE, FOR and SCAN). In fact, we have little doubt it was really set up this way so you could write stuff like the following (by the way, the dots used to be required around the Boolean logical operators .AND., .NOT. and .OR.):

```
DO WHILE .NOT. EOF()
   * process records
ENDDO WHILE .NOT. EOF()
```

It looks real nice, but it turned out to cause a rather nasty, subtle problem. When FoxPro parsed one of these lines, it stopped as soon as it reached something syntactically incorrect. That's right, as soon as the parser found a syntax error, it figured it had a comment and gave up. Consider, for example:

```
IF x<3 .AND y>7
```

As far as versions of FoxPro through VFP 3 are concerned, that line only checks whether x is less than 3. The second part of the condition was totally ignored.

VFP 5 changed the rules. You're still allowed to include comments without an indicator on lines that don't have any executable code (like ENDDO, ENDIF, DO CASE and so on), but if a line contains code (like IF or DO WHILE), the whole line is checked. Since we think the original design decision was terrible, we're delighted by the change. Anything to help root out stubborn hidden bugs is welcomed.

By the way, the parser got stricter in other ways as well. Used to be that extra right parentheses at the end of an expression were ignored. No more. Starting in VFP 7, spaces are no longer allowed to separate variables in LOCAL, PUBLIC, PRIVATE, LPARAMETERS, or PARAMETERS statements (for example, "LOCAL MyVar1 MyVar2" is now a no-no). In general, from VFP 5 forward, the compiler does a better job of finding syntax errors and ensuring that you're running the code you think you're running.

The Single Letter Blues

On the whole, the designers of Visual FoxPro have done a tremendous job marrying object-orientation to Xbase. But there are places where the marriage seems a little rocky. The use of single-letter identifiers is one of them.

Traditionally, the letters A through J are alternate names for the first 10 work areas. (When the number of work areas went up to 25, Fox Software didn't extend this convention. It's just as well—they'd have a heckuva time finding 32,767 different characters to represent the work areas in Visual FoxPro.) In addition, the letter M was reserved to indicate that what followed was a memory variable.

So, how would this cause you any trouble? Well, what if you have a table named C.DBF? When you open it with USE C, you'd expect it to have the alias of "C", right? Only if you're really lucky. Because "C" is reserved for the third work area, the only way C.DBF will have an alias of "C" is if you open it in the third work area. Otherwise, it'll have an alias of the work area it's opened in ("A" through "J" if it's opened in one of the first 10 work areas, or "W" followed by the work area number if not). So, when you use code like SELECT C to select the table, you'll really be selecting the third work area, which may have an entirely different table open or no table open at all.

OOP makes it even worse. Object-orientation uses the same type of "dot" notation that fields in tables do to spell out the complete name of an object, like frmMyForm.grdMainGrid.colName.txtName. So what's the problem? There is none, unless you try to use one of the letters A-J or M for the name of an object. Code like the following:

```
a=CreateObject("form")
a.Caption="My Form"
```

is doomed to failure. You can create the form, but the assignment blows up on you as VFP goes looking for a field named Caption in the first work area.

Of course, single-letter variable and table names are a lousy idea anyway (most of the time—we're still fond of variables like x, y, z and o for quick and dirty testing), so the workaround for this isn't terribly painful. It's like the old joke—"Doctor, it hurts when I do this."—"Then don't do that." Use names longer than one character and you'll never run into this problem.

Why Won't You Validate Me?

Here's a behavior that drove people nuts in FoxPro 2.x and, even though the whole context surrounding it has changed in Visual FoxPro, it continues to drive people nuts.

Say your user is entering a new record and is sitting on a field that requires validation. After entering bad data for that field, but before moving focus to another field, the user clicks the Save button on your toolbar or chooses Save from the menu. Whoosh—the data is saved, including the bad data. What happened?

In VFP, as in FoxPro 2.x, the Valid routine for a text field doesn't execute until focus leaves that field. Clicking a button on a toolbar or picking a menu item doesn't change focus and therefore doesn't fire the Valid method or the LostFocus method, of course. (In fact, a toolbar never has focus, which lets you do pretty cool things.)

Why does it behave this way? Because we want it to. It feels wrong in this situation, but suppose the toolbar or menu item the user chose was Select All or Paste. We sure wouldn't want the focus to change (and the Valid and LostFocus methods to fire) in that case.

So how do we make sure the data gets validated? Simple—make sure focus changes. One way to do this is to reset focus to the same field:

```
_SCREEN.ActiveForm.ActiveControl.SetFocus()
```

Since menus and toolbars don't get the focus, _SCREEN.ActiveForm is still the same form as before. We just set the focus back to the object that had it, which triggers that control's Valid, LostFocus, When and GotFocus methods.

You Want To Print That Where?

Letting users choose the printer for a report at run time and having it automatically adjust itself for that printer's settings ought to be a piece of cake. Isn't that one of the things Windows is supposed to handle for us? Unfortunately, VFP tries to be too smart and ends up making things a lot harder than they need to be.

When you create a report with the Report Designer, information about the currently selected printer and its settings is stored in the first record of the report table (FRX). When you print the report, VFP checks that information and uses it. If the selected printer was the Windows default, VFP is smart enough to use whatever printer the user chose. But if the selected printer was something else, VFP assumes that you meant it when you created the report with that printer chosen, and it expects to print to that printer.

Why does it behave this way? Well, we think the developers were trying to be helpful. They figured that, if you'd gone to the trouble of configuring a printer especially for the report, they ought to pay attention. The problem with this is that the people using your application probably don't even have the same printer you do. The other problem is that this is such a non-intuitive way of arranging for special settings that we can't imagine anyone doing it on purpose.

So how do you get VFP to print to the user's chosen printer and honor that printer's settings? Easy—throw out the stored settings. The information is in the Tag, Tag2 and Expr fields of the first record of the report. Just blank 'em out.

Our friend Brad Schulz, who knows more about printing from FoxPro than anyone else, suggests making a copy of the report at run time, blanking the Tag, Tag2 and Expr fields of the copy, then stuffing the Expr field (which is plain text in an INI-file type format) with the settings you really want. Then, use the copy to run the report. Another friend, Rick Schummer, is a wiz at application deployment. He uses a ProjectHook for his projects that, when an EXE is built, automatically opens every report in the project and blanks the necessary fields. That way, he doesn't have to worry about forgetting this important step when he's preparing to send the application to his client.

But It Ran Okay in VFP 5!

Normally, the folks at Microsoft (and, before them, the folks at Fox Software) go out of their way to make sure that, whatever they change in a new version of FoxPro, code that ran in the old version will still run in the new one. But in VFP 6, they broke that rule. Not only that, they did it on purpose. Say what?!

Because the year 2000 was looming, the Fox team figured it was about time to really make FoxPro developers aware of the bugs lurking in their old code. So they added the SET STRICTDATE command to help us find problems and to keep us from making them in the first place. When you turn STRICTDATE on, VFP lets you know if any of your code contains ambiguous dates. Great, that sounds good.

But here's the catch. By default, it's set to moderate strictness in the development environment. That means that any date or datetime constants that don't use the long unambiguous format (that is, {^1958-09-01} rather than {9/1/58}, the latter of which could be either January 9 or September 1, depending on what SET DATE is used) cause an error. (See the Reference section for the details.)

Well, it's nice that they can find our errors for us, but why they heck didn't they make the old way the default? Because if they had, we'd keep going along in our misguided belief that our old code was Y2K-compliant. They're forcing us to pay attention.

About now, you're probably wondering how you're supposed to upgrade your users to newer versions of VFP if all your dates are going to fail. That's easy. By default, STRICTDATE is set to 0 for them (that is, at run time), but you'll want to set it to 2 on your development machine so you can catch and squash these bugs.

But It Ran Okay in VFP 6!

As with VFP 6, some things were changed in VFP 7 that might break code written in earlier versions (although that's much less likely than the changes made in VFP 6).

A couple of changes were made to the _DBLCLICK system variable. First, it no longer contains both the interval necessary for two clicks to be considered a double-click *and* the interval during which keystrokes will perform incremental searching (which seems like a daft combination in hindsight). Starting in VFP 7, the latter interval is contained in the _INCSEEK system variable. Second, rather than the default of 0.5 seconds that previous versions had, _DBLCLICK now defaults to the value set by the user in the Mouse Control Panel applet. That means we can now create applications that are more respectful of the user's wishes (what a concept!). Thus, there's very little reason for you to touch _DBLCLICK in your applications anymore. For lack of a similar system setting for incremental searching, _INCSEEK also defaults to the user's specified double-click setting. We recommend you add this one to the Options dialog of your applications and let the user set it there.

Another change is that the Top, Left, Height and Width properties of _VFP and _SCREEN are no longer identical. The properties of _VFP now reflect the entire VFP window, while those of _SCREEN contain the values of the "client" area of the window, the white area of the window that doesn't include the title bar, menu bar, toolbars, status bar, and so forth. This is a Good Thing, since we can now determine how much actual space we have to work in without having to adjust for the size of the title bar, menu bar, toolbars, status bar, and so forth. However, if you have code that subtracts these sizes from the _SCREEN properties, you'll end up with values that are much too small. Be sure to look for any such code and either use _VFP instead of _SCREEN or (a better idea) don't make any adjustments to the values of the _SCREEN properties.

The spelling checker included with earlier versions was dropped in VFP 7. Since you couldn't legally distribute it with your applications, the only code this should break is developer tools. If it breaks any client code, you need to check REDIST.TXT in the

VFP home directory to see what other files you might be distributing in violation of the VFP license agreement!

The CENTRAL, FOXCODE, FOXGEN, FOXGRAPH and FOXVIEW commands were removed in VFP 7. Since these had no place in any application and have been obsolete for years, that shouldn't break any code.

Commands Never to Use

Our fellow developers amaze us. Never have a group of such clever people created so many amazing applications. And how they do it is equally stupendous, using commands or features of this remarkable language that we knew of only peripherally, or with capabilities we only suspected. However, there are a few commands whose use should be relegated to legacy code. These commands have been replaced by better, newer or safer commands; never really had a reason to exist in the first place; or they just plain break the machine.

We divide our list into two parts: commands that should never, ever be used, and commands that should only be used from the Command Window. Some commands are just useless, and we have a few favorites that we recommend you avoid altogether. But then, there are some commands that do useful things but have too many side effects to let us feel comfortable bringing them into a client's application.

Never, Ever Use These Commands:

ACCEPT, INPUT

These commands are two of the original Xbase commands. They were a pain to work with then, and they're a pain now. ACCEPT and INPUT have no place in our visually designed, event-driven applications. You can't assign picture clauses, valid routines or events to them. They're not objects, nor can they be subclassed. Leave 'em alone.

DEFINE BOX

An odd duck of a command to begin with, DEFINE BOX doesn't work in Visual FoxPro at all.

INSERT

Not to be confused with the very useful SQL INSERT INTO command, the INSERT command forces a record to be physically placed between two others, forcing FoxPro to rewrite the remainder of the table. Now, before you get out your poison pens and inform us that in order to run the XYZ Personal Information Manager, you must pass it a DBF sorted in physical order, think about some alternatives and whether you really need to rewrite all those records, which is asking for trouble from I/O errors or power interruptions. Consider using a SQL SELECT statement with an ORDER BY clause to create an output file in a programmable order when needed.

JOIN

JOIN creates a new table by merging two tables, potentially adding all of the records from the second table for each record in the first—a condition referred to as a "Cartesian join." Why would you want to do this? Beats us. Although you can control exactly which records of the second table are matched with which records of the first, there is a far easier way to do this—use a SQL SELECT. In addition to the advantage of working with more commonly understood syntax, SELECT offers many more capabilities in terms of the order of output records, the join conditions, and the form of output. This command is one for the bit bucket. Avoid it.

SET COMPATIBLE ON

This dangerous command is made much more so because it's accessible through the General tab of the Tools | Options dialog, represented by a check box labeled "dBASE Compatibility". Sounds innocuous enough. After all, we all just want to get along, right? Don't we want to be compatible?

But SET COMPATIBLE ON is an oxymoron, as we discuss in the Reference section. Not only does it make the language less compatible with anything else out there, it also breaks code left and right in ways you can't even imagine. Originally, in the FoxBASE days, this was a way to have your cake and eat it, too: fast Fox code wrapped within an IF FOX ... ENDIF routine, and compatibility if you needed to compile with other Xbase languages as well. But there are so many places where dBASE and FoxPro have parted company that this command will give you much more grief than it's worth.

SET DOHISTORY ON

This precursor to the Trace Window allowed you to record commands as they occurred for later dissection. Like core dumps, they were useful for dissection once the patient was well dead, but this forensic style of debugging has been replaced with the interactive real-time diagnostics tools of the debugger—in particular, the Trace Window. Also, as we mention in the Reference section, dumping this file can slow down performance to a crawl. Skip it. Check out Event Tracking or the Coverage Profiler for newer, better, faster ways to do what you want.

SORT

Same deal as INSERT and JOIN. Fast and efficient indexing makes the physical order of the database almost irrelevant. If you must create a table in a particular order for output, consider using SQL SELECT to generate the table. Using a Rushmore-optimizable query, output will be far faster, and much less disk space will be consumed.

SYS(12), SYS(23), SYS(24), SYS(1001)

These functions provide a suite of memory-reporting functions. In MS-DOS days, we needed to check to make sure that EMS memory was allocated and available, that we had the room to create our objects, and that we weren't going to crash on creating the next object. Now, with the Win32 virtual memory system, this is far less likely, even on marginal machines, and these functions can, on the whole, be ignored.

UPDATE

UPDATE (not the SQL version, the Xbase one) is a close relative of the JOIN command, and works with a similar logic. This command updates the contents of one table based on the contents of a second. The logic is a bit loopy, and should your orders or indexes not match, really bad things can happen. There are too many commands that will let you avoid attempting this nightmare function to list them all, but let's give you an idea of a few. If you're updating multiple records interactively, set table buffering to update them all at once. Try SCATTER and GATHER and their cool ARRAY keyword to batch a group of records programmatically. Update from a cursor with a SCAN...ENDSCAN logical structure. See? Many workarounds exist and there's no need to use (or even to try to understand) this old behemoth of a command.

Commands for Development, Never for Production

Despite the section heading, a few of these might even belong in test code, not just in the Command Window. But, for sure, none of them belongs in an application.

These commands don't have as many poor side effects as the killers listed above, and sometimes they can speed the development process. As developers, we should be able to understand their bad or unintended side effects, and use them only in appropriate circumstances.

VALIDATE DATABASE RECOVER

This is an indispensable command for fixing database containers gone bad. Of course, our idea of "fixing" is somewhat different than the Fox team's—instead of repairing the bad parts, this command cuts them out of the DBC (with your permission, of course). But it's a start to a process of fixing up problems.

Prior to VFP 7, there was no way to use VALIDATE DATABASE RECOVER anywhere but from the Command Window (not even in a PRG in a development environment). VFP 7 added the capability to use this command in a run-time environment. However, we don't think this is something you should ever do in an application. It displays dialogs with messages such as "Object #7 (Table 'orditems'): The fields in table 'd:\myapplication\data\orditems.dbf' did not match the entries in the database. Would you like to delete this object or cancel the validation?" Not exactly the kind of question we like to ask our users! And do you really think things will be better when they choose either one of those options? (Doug likes to think of "cancel" as "leave me hosed" and "delete" as "hose me worse than I already am.")

The best way to fix a client's DBC is to restore it from backup or send them your copy. (After all, while the contents of their tables will obviously differ from yours, the DBC itself shouldn't.) VALIDATE DATABASE RECOVER should be a tool you use to fix *your* database.

APPEND

APPEND was intended primarily as an interactive command. APPEND gives you a raw view of a file, suitable for dumping data into a system. If you're testing from the command line and you just need to pop one record into the table with a negative balance, this is an easy way to do it. But this is not an end-user interface. It gives raw field names, no help on the status bar, no tooltips, and worst of all, no application logic ("save this record only if..."). APPEND is good for quick-and-dirty data entry by a programmer; it's unsuitable for end users.

BROWSE/EDIT/CHANGE

Interactively, these are a fast way to change your data on the fly and get back to troubleshooting. Database container rules and triggers keep you from shooting yourself in the foot too badly, but you don't have to endure the overhead of starting the entire app, logging in and getting going if all you want to do is test a routine for one condition in the data.

On the other hand, the same capabilities that make these functions attractive to us can make them a killer in the hands of an end-user. BROWSE is not really an easily trappable part of the event loop (though we know many developers who have made it work), meaning that "On Selection" and "Upon Leaving" events are difficult to fire with reliability. Sequencing of data entry is not enforced—you can jump all over the BROWSE fields if you'd like.

These commands provide too many capabilities and too little control to hand to our end-users. Use forms and grids in your application instead.

CREATE

We find it astounding that the Table Designer is available in applications distributed with the FoxPro run-time files. What on earth are they thinking up there in Redmond?

If your users want to be able to create tables on their own, guide them through their choices with your own dialogs (perhaps even a custom Wizard), then use one of the CREATE commands to make the table. Check to make sure they're not overwriting the main tables of your application—you can bet they won't check!

FIND

FIND was also intended more for interactive use, and is included "for backward compatibility." It locates the first record whose index value matches the parameter passed with the FIND command. It's really nice to be able to type FIND GATES in the Command Window, but use SEEK or LOCATE instead in your apps.

MODIFY STRUCTURE

This is as dumb as the CREATE command above. Why on earth do you think your users would be interested in learning all the rules of good table- and field-naming conventions? Don't include it in your apps. If tables need to be changed on the fly, use the ALTER TABLE command instead.

Never Say "Never": Use With Caution

The commands in this final set are dangerous but may occasionally be used in an application, as long as precautions are taken to avoid the potential disasters that can occur.

ZAP

While it's the fastest way to blow away all the records in a table, one big problem is that ZAP fails to fire the delete trigger of tables contained within a database. With SET CONFIRM OFF, ZAP, to paraphrase the immortal words of a sneaker commercial, just does it, with no confirming dialog. There is no "undo" within the language to recover the lost records.

So what's wrong with using ZAP when you know what it is you mean to do? There are too many scenarios where some event can trigger a change to the current work area in such a way that ZAP can blow away your hard-earned data. For example, an

ON KEY LABEL routine that changes work areas as part of its processing, and sloppily fails to change it back, can work under most circumstances within your system. If most of your data-manipulation routines check to make sure they are in the right area before performing their tasks, the OKL will probably work fine and could go undetected for years. But, if that OKL fires between the lines of code (ON KEY LABELs can occur between any two lines of code), say between SELECT TEMP and ZAP, well, we hope you have made good backups. Starting in VFP 7, you can use ZAP IN to ensure the correct work area is zapped, so this problem has gone away.

The one place we think ZAP belongs in a production application is to empty cursors that hold temporary data, especially those bound to a grid, since you can't just re-create the cursor in that case.

PACK

PACK works by copying all records not marked for deletion to a temporary file. It then renames the old file to a new name, the new file to the original name, blows away the old file, and, if the table belongs to a database container, fixes the header of the new file so it properly points to the DBC.

Some gurus maintain that there exists a critical portion of time between the first rename and the second when a catastrophic system failure (such as the complete loss of power) could leave us with no data files whatsoever. Since in fact we've never heard a single person ever say they lost their data by packing (the window for failure is extremely small) and since issuing the equivalent commands ourselves essentially duplicates the internal process using slower VFP code instead of faster C code, we think this belongs in the realm of "urban myth." However, we feel due caution is wise, considering how painful such a loss could be. You might want to squirrel away a copy of the table just before issuing PACK so if something horrible occurs, you can get the data back.

Faster Than a Speeding Bullet

Speed is where it's at. No client is going to pay you to make his app run slower. Fox Software's initial claim to fame was that FoxBASE (and later, FoxBASE+ and FoxPro) ran faster than its competitors. Fox's reputation for speed was well deserved. However, the speed gain has never been automatic. You have to do things right to make your code "run like the Fox."

The Rushmore optimization technology introduced in FoxPro 2.0 is based on indexes. Rushmore examines index files to determine which records meet the conditions for a particular command. So, in order to make things fast, it's important to create the right indexes and to write code that takes advantage of those indexes. The difference between the lightning-fast code your client uses to make crucial strategic decisions and the plodding code his competition uses might differ by no more than an operator or two, so listen up!

There are also some other tricks, not related to Rushmore, that can speed up your applications considerably. This section discusses both Rushmore and non-Rushmore optimization techniques.

Scared by a Mountain in South Dakota?

Fox Software always claimed that Rushmore was named after Dr. Fulton and the development team watched Hitchcock's *North by Northwest*. But we have no doubt the name caught on due to the phrase "rush" embedded in it. In fact, some of the FoxPro documentation and advertising used the phrase "RUSH me some MORE records."

As we mentioned above, the key to getting the most from Rushmore is to create the right indexes and take advantage of them. So how do you know which are the right indexes, and how do you take advantage of them?

Rushmore can optimize the SET FILTER command, and any command involving a FOR clause, as well as SELECT-SQL. The secret (not really a secret—it is documented) is to make the left-hand side of each expression in the filter, FOR or WHERE clause exactly match an existing index tag. For example, to optimize:

```
SUM OrderTotal FOR state="PA"
```

you need an index tag for state. If your tag is on UPPER(state), instead, you'd want to write the command as:

```
SUM OrderTotal FOR UPPER(state)="PA"
```

Suppose you want to find everyone named Miller in a table of Clients and that you have a tag on UPPER(cLastName+cFirstName) to put folks in alphabetical order. You optimize the BROWSE by writing it as:

```
BROWSE FOR UPPER(cLastName+cFirstName)="MILLER"
```

even though you're really interested only in the last name.

It's All in What You Index

We've answered the second question—how to take advantage of existing tags—but we still haven't tackled the first: What are the right indexes to create? That's because it's not always straightforward. There are a few clear-cut rules, but to a great extent, you'll need to use your judgment and test your theories against your data, on your hardware.

Here are the rules:

- Create a tag for your primary key, the field that uniquely identifies the record. (Do this whether or not you define it as a primary key in the database.) You'll need it to look up particular records and for setting relations. (If your table is in a database, you'll want a tag for the primary key anyway for creating persistent relations.)

- Create a tag for any field or expression you expect to search on frequently.

- Create a tag for any field or expression you think you'll want to filter data on frequently. (This is to let Rushmore kick in.)

- Make sure the tags you create exactly match the conditions you'll need to search or filter on.

- Don't automatically create tags on every field. (That's called inverting the table.) It can make adding and updating records slower than necessary, especially if you have a lot of fields in your table. On the flip side, if you have a table, especially one that is rarely changed, where you do use every field in filters, then go ahead and invert the table.

- Do not create indexes with a NOT expression for Rushmore optimization. Rushmore ignores any tag whose expression contains NOT. If you need the NOT expression, say, for a filter, create both indexes, one with and one without the NOT.

- Don't filter your tags. That is, don't use the FOR clause of the INDEX command. Rushmore ignores tags that are filtered. If you need a filtered tag for some reason, and you're likely to filter on that tag's index expression as well, create an unfiltered tag, too.

In general, you'll be trading off update speed for search speed. So, think about what you expect to do with this table. If it's going to have lots of additions but few searches, keep the number of tags to a minimum. If it'll be used for lots of searching, but rarely updated, create more tags. You have other middle-of-the-road options, too: If you do an intensive filtering process once a month, but primarily do updates the rest of the time, consider creating temporary tags (in their own CDX, or as stand-alone compact indexes) for the process. On the flip side, if you primarily handle queries against the data, but add large batches of the data infrequently, consider dropping all of the tags for the bulk load (after saving their definitions, of course) and then re-creating them afterwards.

To Delete or Not to Delete

For many years (and in the earlier editions of this book), one of the mantras of optimization advice was to index every table on the DELETED() function, if an application was to run with SET DELETED ON. This advice was accepted by virtually everyone who knew anything about Rushmore.

Here's the way we explained it in the VFP 6 edition of this book:

"Even in many complex queries and FOR clauses, Rushmore performs its magic almost entirely on the relatively small and compact CDX file, a file structured with nodes, branches and leaves to be searched efficiently. When DELETED is ON, FoxPro has to check each and every record in a result set (whether from a query, a filter, or FOR) to see if it's deleted—even if no records are actually deleted. This sequential reading of the entire cursor or file completely defeats the benefits of Rushmore. Don't do it!

"By creating a tag on DELETED(), you let Rushmore do the checking instead of looking at each record sequentially, which makes the whole thing much faster. The larger the result set, the more speed-up you'll see."

Sounds really good, doesn't it?

The walls came crashing down on this piece of wisdom with an article by Chris Probst in the May '99 issue of *FoxPro Advisor*. Probst was working with an extremely large data set in a network environment and found that some of the queries were just too slow. Monitoring network traffic found the problem: The portion of the index file related to the DELETED() tag was huge (at least in some cases), and transferring it across the network was bogging down the whole query.

Probst's experiments determined that, when an expression has only a few discrete values (like .T. and .F.), and the values are unevenly distributed (as is typically the case with DELETED(), since in general, few records are deleted), queries run faster without a tag on the expression. In those cases, it's better to let VFP narrow things down first based on the other expressions involved, and then do a sequential check of the remaining records.

The phenomenon Chris witnessed is not unheard of in the database world. The index with few values is called one with "low selectivity" and is considered suspect in most database designs. But this was the first documented case of the low-selectivity issue appearing in FoxPro's remarkable optimization.

What does all this boil down to for you? For small tables in a desktop or LAN situation, we generally think having a tag on DELETED() is a better choice. As tables get larger or when operating in a WAN situation, skip it. And just for good measure, you should test the performance, in your specific production (as opposed to development) environment, with and without the DELETED() tag.

Going Nowhere Fast

Another common problem goes like this. In troubleshooting sessions we attend, someone complains that a filter should be optimized, but it's dog slow. He's asked to show the filter and the tags. Everything looks good for Rushmore to optimize the filter. Puzzling.

Then he shows the code he's using. Typically, it looks something like this:

```
SET FILTER TO <something optimizable>
GO TOP      && Put filter in effect
```

and the light goes on. GO TOP and GO BOTTOM are not optimizable commands. They move through the records sequentially, attempting to find the first record matching the filter.

Without a filter (and with SET DELETED OFF), this isn't generally a problem. Moving to the top or bottom of the current order is pretty quick. FoxPro can either locate the first or last record in the index or, if no tag is set, move directly to the beginning or end of the file.

But when a filter is set (or DELETED is ON, which is like having a filter set), once GO gets to the first or last record in the order, it has to search sequentially for the first record that matches the filter condition. This is what's so slow. Smart like a fox, eh? What a dumb idea! This is like you writing code to go to record 10 by issuing a SKIP, asking if this is RECNO()=10, and if not, SKIPping again.

What can you do about it? Don't use GO TOP and GO BOTTOM. How do you avoid them? By using a neat trick. It turns out that LOCATE with no FOR clause goes to the first record in the current order. So, for GO TOP, you just issue LOCATE, like this:

```
SET FILTER TO <optimizable condition>
LOCATE    && Same as GO TOP
```

Okay, that works for finding the first record. What about the last record? You have to stand on your head for this. Well, almost. You really have to stand the table on its head. Try it like this:

```
SET FILTER TO <optimizable condition>

* Reverse index order
lDescending=DESCENDING()
IF lDescending
   SET ORDER TO ORDER() ASCENDING
ELSE
   SET ORDER TO ORDER() DESCENDING
ENDIF
* Now Top is Bottom and Bottom is Top
LOCATE   && Same as GO TOP

IF lDescending
   SET ORDER TO ORDER() DESCENDING
ELSE
   SET ORDER TO ORDER() ASCENDING
ENDIF
```

After setting the filter (or with a filter already in effect), you turn the index upside down. If it was ascending, you make it descending; if it was descending, you make it ascending. Then, use LOCATE to go to the first record. Since you've reversed the order, that's the last record in the order you want. Then, reverse the order again. Voila! You're on the bottom record.

By the way, the code above works only if there is an index order set. If there might be no order, you have to check for that.

One more warning. Under particular circumstances, the work-around can be very slightly slower than just using GO. In most cases, though, it tends to be an order of magnitude faster. We think it's worth it.

We should also comment that, in VFP 7, we've seen some cases where GO TOP and GO BOTTOM seem to be behaving in a more optimized way. But enough of our tests still show the LOCATE technique to be faster for us to stick with it.

HAVING noWHERE Else To Go

SQL-SELECT has two clauses that filter data: WHERE and HAVING. A good grasp of the English language might lead us to believe that these are synonyms, but SQL is not English, and mixing these two indiscriminately is a sure-fire disaster in the making! It's not obvious where a particular condition should go at first glance. But getting it wrong can lead to a significant slowdown.

Here's why. The conditions in WHERE filter the original data. Wherever possible, existing index tags are used to speed things up. This produces an intermediate set of results. HAVING operates on the intermediate results, with no tags in sight. So, by definition, HAVING is slower than WHERE, if a query is otherwise constructed to be optimized.

So, when should you use HAVING? When you group data with GROUP BY and want to filter not on data from the original tables, but on "aggregate data" formed as the result of the grouping. For example, if you group customers by state, counting the number in each, and you're interested only in states with three or more customers, you'd put the condition COUNT(*)>=3 in the HAVING clause.

```
SELECT cState,COUNT(*) ;
    FROM Customer ;
    GROUP BY cState ;
    HAVING COUNT(*)>=3
```

A simple rule of thumb: Don't use HAVING unless you also have a GROUP BY. That doesn't cover all the cases, but it eliminates many mistakes. To make the rule complete, remember that a condition in HAVING should contain one of the aggregate functions (COUNT, SUM, AVG, MAX or MIN) or a field that was named with AS and uses an aggregate function.

Unfortunately, simple rules aren't always the best rules. There's one other situation where you may choose to use HAVING rather than WHERE. That's when you're specifically trying to avoid having Rushmore come into play. When would that be? When you have an index on a field (presumably because you need it elsewhere), but there are only a few distinct values for the field. If the query has other optimizable fields that narrow the result set down to a small percent of records, the cost of reading the relevant part of this index may be greater than the cost of sequentially checking the records isolated by the other conditions. In that case, moving the condition to the HAVING clause means that Rushmore ignores it, and the index isn't read.

The Only Good Header is No Header

FoxPro lets you store procedures and functions in a variety of places. But using the Project Manager gives you a strong incentive to put each routine in a separate PRG file. We generally agree with this choice.

But, if you're not careful, in versions through the original release of VFP 6, there's a nasty performance penalty for doing so. It turns out that having a PROCEDURE or FUNCTION statement at the beginning of a stand-alone PRG file increases the execution time by a factor of as much as 10!

You read that right. It can take 10 times as long to execute a PRG that begins with PROCEDURE or FUNCTION as one with no header. Hearing about this goodie (no, we didn't discover it ourselves), we tested a couple of other alternatives. It turns out that using DO <routine> IN <PRG file> cuts the penalty down some, but it's still twice as slow as simply eliminating or commenting out the header line.

SETting PROCEDURE TO the PRG, then calling the routine, speeds things up if you only have to do it once, but issuing SET PROCEDURE TO over and over again (as you'd need to for many different PRGs) is about 20 times slower than the slow way. That is, it's 200 times slower than omitting the header in the first place. Even issuing SET PROCEDURE TO … ADDITIVE repeatedly is slower than just setting it once.

But wait, there's more. Not surprisingly, if the routine you're calling isn't in the current directory, but somewhere along a path you've set, it takes a little longer. For an ordinary routine with no header, the difference isn't much. Same thing if you're using SET PROCEDURE. However, the other two cases get a lot slower when they have to search a path. Using DO <routine> IN <PRG file> when the file isn't in the current directory is just about as slow as doing a SET PROCEDURE. But that's only the bad case. The horrible situation is calling a routine with a PROCEDURE or FUNCTION header directly—it can be as much as 1000 times slower than calling the same routine without the header!

The good news is that the path penalties go away as soon as you add the routines to a project and build an APP or EXE. That is, unless you're running in a very unusual setup, your users are unlikely to pay this price.

The better news is that the penalty seems to be gone in VFP 6 SP3 and later, where the differences in the way you set up and call a routine are small enough to matter only in situations where you need to squeeze the last drop of performance out. In those cases, you'll need to test all the alternatives in your configuration to see what produces the best results.

Watch Out for Breakpoints

When we were testing the procedure header issue in VFP 7, we ran into some results that didn't match our expectations at all: wide variations in test speeds across our different machines, and major differences between VFP 6 and VFP 7.

It took quite a while (and a pointer from Mike Stewart of Microsoft) to pin down the difference: What mattered was whether any breakpoints were set in the testing environment. It turns out that, in VFP 7, even with the debugger closed, having breakpoints set slows down execution significantly. In earlier versions, you pay the penalty for breakpoints only if the debugger is open.

We're not sure why Microsoft changed this, and we'll reserve opinion on its wisdom until we know. What we are sure about, though, is that before you do any performance testing in VFP 7, make sure you clear all breakpoints. (It's not enough to uncheck all the breakpoints listed in the Breakpoints dialog. You actually have to remove them.)

Fortunately, this slowdown won't affect most end-users, since they don't have the development version of VFP.

Loops Aren't Just for Belts

FoxPro offers three (well, really, four) different ways to write a loop. Choosing the right one can make a big difference in your program. So can making sure you put only what you have to inside the loop.

Let's start with the second statement. Every command or function you put inside a loop gets executed every time through the loop. (Big surprise.) Put enough extra stuff in there and you can really slow a program down. The trick is to put each statement only where you need it. This is especially true when you've got nested loops—putting a command farther in than it has to be might mean it gets executed dozens more times than necessary.

Bottom line here: If the command doesn't depend on some characteristic of the loop (like the loop counter or the current record) and it doesn't change a variable that's changed elsewhere in the loop, it can probably go outside the loop.

Here's an example:

```
* Assume aRay is a 2-D array containing all numeric data.
* We're looking for a row where the sum of the first three
* columns is greater than 100.
lFound = .F.
nRowCnt = 1
DO WHILE NOT lFound AND nRowCnt<=ALEN(aRay,1)
   IF aRay[nRowCnt,1]+aRay[nRowCnt,2]+aRay[nRowCnt,3]>100
      lFound = .T.
   ELSE
      lFound = .F.
      nRowCnt=nRowCnt+1
   ENDIF
ENDDO
```

The version below eliminates repeated calls to ALEN() and the need for the lFound variable. Our tests in VFP 7 show that it's about an order of magnitude faster than the original code.

```
nNumofRows = ALEN(aRay,1)
DO WHILE aRay[nRowCnt,1]+aRay[nRowCnt,2]+aRay[nRowCnt,3] <= 100 and ;
         nRowCnt < nNumofRows
  nRowCnt = nRowCnt + 1
ENDDO
```

We find we're most likely to make this particular mistake when we're dealing with nested loops, so scrutinize those especially carefully.

What's This Good FOR?

In the case of loops that execute a fixed number of times, FOR is a better choice than DO WHILE. Because the counting and checking feature is built into FOR, it just goes faster than DO WHILE. In a simple test with a loop that did nothing at all except loop, FOR was more than 10 times faster than DO WHILE. Never write a loop like this:

```
nCnt = 1
DO WHILE nCnt <= nTopValue
   * Do something here.
   nCnt=nCnt+1
ENDDO
```

Always use this instead:

```
FOR nCnt = 1 TO nTopValue
   * Do something here.
ENDFOR
```

SCANning the Territory

Guess what? DO WHILE isn't the best choice for looping through records either. SCAN was designed to process a table efficiently and does it faster than DO WHILE. Our results show that SCAN is one-and-a-half to two times faster to simply go through an unordered table one record at a time.

To give full disclosure, we have found that with some index orders, DO WHILE was as much as 20 percent faster. With other indexes, SCAN is faster, although it doesn't appear to have the same advantage as in an unordered table. (It's also worth noting that, with large tables, if the memory allocation to FoxPro isn't property tuned—see below—DO WHILE can be faster than SCAN.)

A word to the wise here: When you're tuning existing code, don't just globally replace your DO WHILE loops with SCAN...ENDSCAN. SCAN has a built-in SKIP function—if your code already has logic to perform a SKIP within the loop, you can inadvertently skip over some records. Make sure to pull out those SKIPs.

FOR EACH, his own

There's one more special-purpose looping construct: FOR EACH. It's designed to go through the elements of a collection or an array, giving you access to each in turn. We like it a lot for working with collections, where it makes the code more readable.

We're sorry to say that using FOR EACH doesn't seem to offer any performance improvement over a counted FOR loop. On the other hand, it doesn't seem to be measurably slower either, so use whichever gives you the greatest readability in any given situation.

To Wrap or Not to Wrap

One of the capabilities that OOP gives us is "wrapper classes." These classes let us take a collection of related capabilities and put them all into a single class— "wrapping" them all up into one easy-to-use package. The class gives us a more consistent interface to the functions involved and generally presents a tidy package.

The Connection Manager class described in the Reference section (see SQLConnect()) is pretty much a wrapper class, though it adds some capabilities. We've seen folks suggest wrapper classes for the FoxTools library (which desperately needs a consistent interface despite the addition of lots of its residents to the language). During the beta test for VFP 3, we played around on and off for months with a wrapper class for array functions that would let us stop worrying about things like the second parameter to ALEN().

On the whole, wrapper classes sound pretty attractive. Unfortunately, they also add a fair amount of overhead.

There's another way to do the same thing—just create an old-fashioned procedure file. Since SET PROCEDURE has an ADDITIVE clause, it's no big deal to have lots of procedure libraries around. It turns out, of course, that procedure libraries also carry an overhead penalty.

So, if there's significant overhead with wrapper classes and procedure files, what do you do? Because the contents of the class or library matter so much, it's hard to produce benchmarks that give you hard and fast rules about this stuff. We tested with our embryonic array handler class, using only some of the simpler methods included (aIsArray, aElemCount, aRowCount, aColCount, aIs2D—all of which do exactly what their names suggest). We set it up as a class and as a procedure library. Then, we wrote a program that made a sample series of calls. We also wrote the same functionality in native code (ALEN() for aElemCount, ALEN(,1) for aRowCount and so on).

The sad result is that either a procedure library or a class is an order of magnitude slower than using the built-in functionality. In this example, the procedure library was pretty much always faster than the class, but the exact difference varied and wasn't enough to worry about.

We also tested the same functions as stand-alone programs. The timing came out pretty much the same as the procedure library and the class. (Well, mostly. One of us found the stand-alone programs uniformly another order of magnitude slower. We're not sure what was going on there, perhaps the problem described in "Watch Out for Breakpoints.")

Our guess is that, as functionality becomes more complex, the overhead counts less. Given the other, overwhelming benefits of using modular code, we don't recommend you stop writing procedures. But, at this point, we can't recommend wrapper classes where a procedure library would do. The key question to answer is whether you're creating an object that has behaviors. Typically, behaviors need some common data, such as a set of properties to store the initial values of SET commands in an object that uses the Init and Destroy methods to push/pop the SETtings. If all you need to do is perform some function (transform some data, for example), use a function. But when you need more than that, go for the wrapper class.

There are benefits to a wrapper class, of course. The biggest benefit is the ability to subclass to provide specialized behaviors. Where this is a possibility, it's worth the overhead.

What's in a Name?

You wouldn't think that a little thing like a name would matter so much. But it does. The name we're referring to is the Name property possessed by almost every object you can create in Visual FoxPro. (A few of the weird marriages of Xbase to OOP, like SCATTER NAME, produce objects without a Name property.)

For code-based classes, when you CreateObject() an object whose class definition doesn't assign a value to the Name property, Visual FoxPro makes one up for you. That's nice. Except, prior to VFP 7, it insists on making it unique (usually, the class name or a variant thereof, followed by one or more digits, like Form3 or Text17). The problem is, as the number of objects of that class grows, making sure a name is unique takes longer and longer. The Microsoft folks say the time grows exponentially. We suspect that's an overstatement and that it's actually geometric. What it ain't is linear. What it really ain't is fast enough. (Before we go any further with this, we should point out why this applies only to code classes. All VCX-based classes have an implicit assignment of the Name property, so there's never a need to assign a name at instantiation time.)

We tested in VFP 6 with a pair of very simple classes based on Custom. One contained nothing. The other contained an explicit assignment to Name. With 10 repetitions, the explicitly named class would instantiate so fast it couldn't be measured, but the nameless class was fast, too. By 100 repetitions, explicit naming was more than four times as fast. At 1000 repetitions, the explicit version was eight to 10 times faster. At 5000 of each class, explicit names are about 18 times faster than nameless objects to instantiate.

The moral of the story here is easy. In VFP 6 and earlier, always assign a value to the Name property for any class you write in code.

The happy ending is that Microsoft changed this behavior in VFP 7 and now, newly instantiated classes simply take the class name as their Name.

Looks Can Be Deceiving

But, in this case, they're not. The form property LockScreen lets you make a series of changes to a form without the individual changes showing as you go. When you set LockScreen to .F., all the changes appear to occur simultaneously. Visually, it's far more consistent.

We were all set to tell you that this is one of those times where the user's eyes will play tricks on him. He'll think the update is faster because he doesn't see the individual changes take place.

But guess what? The update really is faster this way. We tested a simple form with just a few controls. We changed about 20 properties of the form and the controls. With LockScreen set to .T., the updates were very slightly faster in each case. Surprise—the version that looks better is faster, too. We're fairly certain it's because Windows has to redraw the screen only once—and screen redraws aren't the fastest thing that the operating system can do.

What Type of Var are You?

Testing the type of a variable or field is one of those things we do a lot in our code. Starting in VFP 6, it's something we can do faster than ever. The VARTYPE() function is significantly faster than its predecessor, TYPE(). How much faster? With both variables and fields, we consistently find VARTYPE() two to three-and-a-half times faster than TYPE(). The smallest differences occurred when checking non-existent variables. (A code maintenance and debugging tip here: Not only is VARTYPE() faster, but you don't have to pass the quoted variable name to VARTYPE(), eliminating one more of those needless development errors. VARTYPE(MyVar) is functionally equivalent to TYPE("MyVar").)

One warning here: VARTYPE() is appropriate only for fields, variables, properties and the like. If you use it with expressions to find out what type the result will be, be aware that you actually evaluate the expression (in fact, it's evaluated before it's even passed to VARTYPE()). In addition, VARTYPE() is useful only for items that can be evaluated. In particular, you can't use it to check whether a particular property exists, which you can do with TYPE(). For example, VARTYPE(oObject.Name) fails if oObject doesn't exist or doesn't have a name property. However, TYPE("oObject.Name") works, returning "U" in that case. So, don't throw TYPE() out of your toolkit quite yet.

Stringing Along

Building up strings has become increasingly important, as we need to create HTML and XML and who-knows-what-else-ML. Fortunately, VFP has been tuned to make construction of large strings extremely efficient.

However, there's one important trick you need to know. Building a string from left to right is fast; building it from right to left isn't. What does that mean? It means that a series of assignments in the form:

```
cString = cString + cMoreStuff
```

is much faster than:

```
cString = cMoreStuff + cString
```

regardless of the actual contents of the variables.

How much faster? That does depend on the contents of the variables or, more specifically, the length of the strings involved. As the string gets larger, the first version gets better and better. To build a string of 30,000 characters, adding three at a time, the first version runs about two orders of magnitude faster than the second.

How to Create an Object and Other Mysteries of Life

VFP 6 also introduced a new way to create objects. The NewObject() function lets you instantiate objects without worrying about whether you've pointed to the class library ahead of time—instead, you just include the library name in the call. CreateObject(), of course, needs the library in the current list with either a Set ClassLib or SET PROCEDURE ahead of time.

So which way is faster? As usual, the answer is "it depends." With VCX-based classes, if you can issue Set ClassLib just once and then instantiate classes from that library repeatedly, CreateObject() is the way to go. It's anywhere from four to 10 times faster than calling NewObject() with the class library. On the other hand, if you need to load the library each time, the Set ClassLib/CreateObject() pair is in the same ballpark as NewObject().

How about for classes written in code? In that case, issuing a single SET PROCEDURE and calling CreateObject() repeatedly is five to 10 times faster than either NewObject() or the SET PROCEDURE/CreateObject() pair, which are pretty similar.

In the VFP 6 version of this book, we reported that instantiating a coded class was a little faster than instantiating a VCX-based class, but not enough faster to wipe out the benefits of developing classes visually. In VFP 7, we see varying results: Sometimes the coded class instantiates faster, while at other times, the VCX-based class is faster. Bottom line: We'll stand by our advice to develop visual objects visually.

We're not really surprised that NewObject() is generally slower than CreateObject(). It's doing a lot of work behind the scenes. Here's the sequence: Save the names of all open class libraries, then close them. Next, open the specified class library, instantiate the object, and close the class library. Finally, reopen all the formerly open class libraries. Whew, that's a lot of files to find and mess with. Of course, we don't understand why VFP doesn't check whether the specified library is in the current list before going to all that trouble—seems to us it could speed up NewObject() considerably, in most cases.

We tested and found no performance penalty for having a lot of class libraries open, no matter where in the list the class you're instantiating is found. So the rule here is to think about how you're going to do things before you write the code and, if possible, just keep open the class libraries you use a lot. Then use NewObject() for the one-shots, the classes from libraries you need only once in a while.

Can You Have Too Much Memory?

It turns out that, in VFP, the answer is "yes." When you start VFP, it figures out how much memory it ought to be able to use, if it needs it. The number is generally about half as much as the machine actually has. Often, the amount that VFP picks is too much.

How can you have too much memory? Like this, according to our buddy Mac Rubel, who knows more about this topic than anyone else—more even, we suspect, than the folks who wrote VFP. However much memory VFP grabs, it assumes it has that much *physical* memory to work with. But, because it takes so much memory, it often doesn't—some of the memory it's working with is really disk space pretending to be memory, and that's slow. By decreasing the amount of memory VFP thinks it has available, you ensure that it uses only physical memory. VFP knows what to do when it needs more memory than it has available, and it's good at that. The last thing you want happening is the operating system swapping virtual (disk) memory for real memory while FoxPro thinks it is using RAM. So, as long as you restrict it to using physical memory, things are fast, fast, fast.

Okay, so how do you that? Use the SYS(3050) function. SYS(3050,1) controls foreground memory, the memory VFP has available when it's in charge. SYS(3050,2) is for background memory—how much memory FoxPro should have when you're off doing something else. In either case, you pass it a number and it rounds that down to a number it likes (multiples of 256), and that's how much memory it uses. It even tells you how much it really took.

We've been amazed how much of a difference this setting can make. Unfortunately, getting it just right is a matter of trial and error, so try a bunch of different settings until you find the one that seems suited to the way you work.

Practice, Practice, Practice

All of the tips we've given you here should speed up your code, but *your* application on *your* network with *your* data is the true test (and "*your*" refers to the final production environment, not necessarily your development environment). Differences in network throughput, the architecture of your system, the design of your tables, your choice of indexes, the phase of the moon, what's on TV that night, and so forth, all make significant differences in the performance you see. Our advice is always to examine and benchmark how a particular change affects your system. Keep in mind that a single test isn't conclusive unless it can be repeated, and you need to repeat tests with caution because FoxPro and the operating system and the network and even your disk controller might be caching information. Also, don't forget to shut down background processes like your virus scanner and your e-mail client while doing performance testing.

Finally, now that we've given you all this advice, keep in mind that most of the time, you don't need to worry about a few milliseconds here or there. Don't spend a lot of energy optimizing until you know there's a problem. Of course, when there's a clear choice and it's also good practice (like using SCAN instead of DO WHILE to process a table), write your applications using the better choice. But, your first task is to get the application working and producing the right results.

If there's a speed problem at that point, use the Coverage Profiler to help you figure out where the bottleneck is. Then, follow longtime Fox guru George Goley's advice and "take out the slow parts." That's where the information here should be most useful.

Section 4: Visual FoxPro Reference

"But 'glory' doesn't mean 'a nice knockdown argument'," Alice objected.
"When I use a word," Humpty Dumpty said, in rather a scornful tone, "it
means just what I choose it to mean—neither more nor less."
"The question is," said Alice, "whether you can make words mean so many
different things."
"The question is," said Humpty Dumpty, "which is to be master—that's all."

Lewis Carroll, *Through the Looking-Glass*, 1872

Section 4 is the meat of the book. You'll find a listing for every command, function,
property, event, method and system variable. We've grouped them logically so that
you can find several related topics in one place.

For an explanation of the syntax we use for commands, see "How to Use This Book,"
back in the Introduction.

In the printed version of this book, you'll notice that this section is, well, missing. We've had plenty of requests to cut down on the size and weight of this book. Here are a few of those reasons:

- Conservationists, from those saving the trees to those saving the habitats for animals living in the trees, have expressed a desire for us to reduce the amount of paper used.

- Workers in the Hentzenwerke stock room and our shipping companies are complaining about back pain and exhaustion from moving copies of the *Hacker's Guide* around, and they keep muttering things like "worker's compensation."

- It costs too darn much to ship such a large book, especially to our overseas readers.

- Nobody wants to purchase it at a conference, because they'd need another suitcase just to bring it home, and it may put them over the airline's cargo limit.

- We're tired of the jokes about it being a great monitor stand (though the advent of 17" and larger monitors has drastically cut down on that one), that it makes a great doorstop, and that it provides more exercise than a membership to a fitness center.

- Nobody reads the paper version anyway; we all use the .CHM version instead.

So, dear reader, we have listened to your comments, and we've provided this section in an electronic format only. "How do I obtain this wonderful file?" you ask. Very simple. Point your browser to www.hentzenwerke.com. Somewhere on the main page is a link to Downloads. Click that. You'll be given instructions from there on how to get the CHM file. If you purchased this book directly from Hentzenwerke Publishing, you were e-mailed a user ID and password, and can log in and download the files you want. If you bought the book from another source, you need to have the book in front of you (like now), so you can answer some questions to prove you own it.

See the section "How to Use the Help File" for lots of useful information, including keyboard shortcuts, how to put the *Hacker's Guide* into your FoxPro menu, tips on searching, and much, much more.

Feel free to copy the help file onto the hard drive of each of your own computers, but please do us the courtesy of not sharing it with everyone you know, even the other folks in your office. (Think of the book as having a single-user license. You will find appropriate copyright notices in the help file.) We've put a tremendous amount of time into this book, and illegal copies deprive us of the income to pay for that time.

Section 5: But Wait, There's More!

We will now discuss in a little more detail the Struggle for Existence.

Charles Robert Darwin, *The Origin of Species*, 1859

We've sliced, we've diced, we've chopped Visual FoxPro into little pieces. But there's still more to say. A few features are so cool, they warrant their own chapters. This section goes into detail on the ActiveX technologies, the Object Browser and Component Gallery, Wizards and Builders, and IntelliSense, all of which provide opportunities for extending your use of VFP.

Active Something

True contentment is a thing as active as agriculture.

G. K. Chesterton, *A Miscellany of Men*, 1912

In the original *Hacker's Guide to Visual FoxPro 3.0,* we included a chapter "OLE, OLE, Oxen Free!" that talked about the brave new world of OLE. Even at that time, OLE was not that new, but it was just catching on in the developer community. FoxPro 2.x provided support only for OLE 1.0 in its implementation, and that was pretty weak. Visual FoxPro supported OLE 2.0 but, like many "point zero" releases, there were a lot of incompatible products released under the 2.0 banner.

We've made a somewhat arbitrary decision to divide the ever-expanding subject of OLE, er, COM, into several pieces. "It was Automation, You Know" covers those technologies formerly known as OLE Automation, now simply Automation, as well as the brave new world of Automation servers created with Visual FoxPro. In this section, we take on a few of the other aspects of the technology, and look at the Registry, linking and embedding, and ActiveX controls.

OLE History

"In the beginning, there was DOS. And it was good ..."

Well, maybe not that good. People wanted computers to be able to do more and more, and DOS just didn't cut it. So then GUIs (Graphical User Interfaces) were invented, to allow users to create better-looking documents in an easier-to-use environment. And it was good. Well, maybe not that good. Users now wanted to be able to copy a portion of one document and place it in another. Cut-and-paste was invented to fill this need. And it was ... okay, but not enough. Now that users could create an item in one application and paste it into another, they wanted to go back to the first document, update the data, and have the second document reflect the changes made in the first. So DDE, with its hot-links, cold-links, warm-links and lukewarm-links, was invented to fill this gap. And DDE was ... well, it was ... anyway, we learned to work with it.

OLE was next in this genesis—Object Linking and Embedding—a method used to actually embed the data and a link to the originating document in a final document in a visual manner. OLE 1.0 was a clumsy and error-prone architecture. OLE 2.0 introduced far more stability into the structure. And with OLE 2.0, sounding like Monty Python's Knight Who Says "Ni," Microsoft declared that OLE was no longer "Object Linking and Embedding" but should henceforth be referred to only as "OLE."

Not long after that, "OLE Automation" became simply "Automation" and OCXs (which started as OLE Controls) were declared to be "ActiveX Controls." More recently, the term "OLE" was considered too passé, and "COM" became the new rage.

In the last edition, we asked, "Who knows what Microsoft will be calling this technology by the time you read this book?" Well, it's still COM. It's been extended to support distributed applications, cleverly called Distributed COM, or DCOM (sounds like something to rid your house of mice, doesn't it?). And now we have COM+ (if Microsoft doesn't call it Active something, they'll put a plus or two at the end of it). COM+ came about when Windows 2000 combined COM technologies with Microsoft Transaction Server (both of which were previously add-ons), and integrated them into the operating system.

There really and truly is something to COM and its successive technologies that's different from ActiveX or OLE. COM, the Component Object Model, has been at the very base of all of Microsoft's designs for object interaction. OLE and all of the Active technologies are built on the base of COM object design.

We've all heard the hype for .NET as the next solution, so does that mean COM is dead? Hardly. Microsoft has hyped COM for around seven years, so there must be six bazillion COM apps out there by now. (Actually, a Web page at Microsoft's site touts that COM is in use on "well over 150 million systems worldwide." And that page was last updated in August 1999, so six bazillion apps isn't too far off the mark.) All the developers in the world working 24/7 couldn't convert these COM apps to .NET anytime soon after .NET is released, especially given the less-than-blazing speed with which many firms upgrade (remember that call last week to support FoxPro 2.6 code? That Windows 95 app? That Office 95 installation?). COM's going to be around for quite a while. Fortunately, COM objects can play in the .NET world, so developers don't have to instantly rewrite bazillions of COM objects when .NET 1.0 is finally released—furthering the life of COM.

Windows Registry

> I know not anything more pleasant, or more instructive, than to compare experience with expectation, or to register from time to time the difference between idea and reality. It is by this kind of observation that we grow daily less liable to be disappointed.
>
> Samuel Johnson

The Windows Registry is the source of all information linking applications together. The Registry is a structured collection of "key" values, each of which may have one or more settings. Understanding how to read and work with Registry entries is crucial for understanding the nuances of COM.

The Registry can be viewed with a Microsoft-supplied viewer program, RegEdit.EXE (on Win9x platforms) or RegEdt32.EXE (for Windows NT/2000/XP)—see Figures 5-1 and 5-2. Tracing your way through the networked set of keys can tell you the verbs appropriate to use with a server, the paths to the server, and how to match extensions to their executables. A set of registration keys can be exported from the registration file to an editable text format (usually with a .REG extension) and imported into the same or a different Registry.

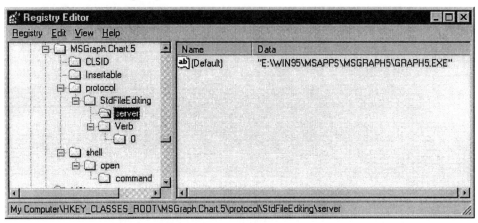

Figure 5-1: A view of the Windows 95 Registration Editor, showing entries for the MSGraph 5.0 applet.

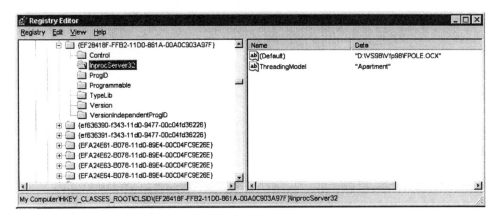

Figure 5-2: The Windows NT 4.0 Registration Editor, showing the settings for VFP's FPOLE interface.

Two words of caution (based on painful experience!) for working with the Registry: Make backups! A badly planned entry in the Registry can cause your applications or even Windows itself to fail. Some backup programs fail to back up the Registry, because the file is always open while Windows is running. Make sure your backup program knows how to back up the Registry. In addition, look for utilities specifically designed to restore the Registry when the operating system is no longer bootable. Rdisk.EXE comes with Windows NT. Emergency startup disks can be made for Windows 98, 2000, ME or XP. In addition, the Resource Kits for each operating system come with additional Registry tools. Check 'em out.

Linking and Embedding

There is no object so soft but it makes a hub for the wheel'd universe.

Walt Whitman

The simplest form of OLE is the ability to place data and images from one application into another. This ability to embed or link objects within FoxPro is cleverly called "Object Linking and Embedding." Bet someone stayed up all night thinking that one up! Linking and embedding objects is a feature that was available in FoxPro 2.5 and 2.6 for Windows, but there have been significant enhancements in Visual FoxPro.

FoxPro stores the object, or the links to the object, in a general field. General fields are nothing more than enhanced memo fields, and they share many characteristics with them. Among other things, for a given table, they're both stored in a single FPT file. A general field is made of several components. First, there's the binary data needed to tell FoxPro what this data is. This key refers FoxPro to the Registry, which stores the name of the server (originating) application and the capabilities of the server. Also stored within the general field is the "display data," a bitmap or metafile that gives FoxPro an image to display when the general field is shown in a MODIFY GENERAL window or an OLEBoundControl. Finally, if the data is linked from a file on disk, the path and file name of the original file are stored in the general field. If the data is embedded rather than linked, the actual data is also included within the general field.

When should data be embedded and when should it be linked? The answer, as with most things in the design of a FoxPro application, is "it depends." Some OLE servers, like MSGraph, don't have the ability to store freestanding files, but can operate only within another application. For these servers, the decision has been made for you. On the other hand, if you're working with data that needs to be accessed and manipulated from another application, such as a Paintbrush file that will change over time, the data should be linked so the other applications will be able to find it on disk. The flip side of the same coin is that embedding data within a general field protects it from unauthorized changes, so it's editable only within your application or another application with appropriate access to your data.

Disk space is another consideration. Since OLE generates display data as well as storing embedded data within a file, large, high-color, detailed graphic images can consume enormous amounts of disk space. Display data is typically stored in a bitmap-type format: several bytes of color information for each pixel. So, even if the original image is deeply compressed, like a JPG or PNG image, the resulting display data can take megabytes of space. We know of some applications where the decision was made to bypass general fields for storing the image altogether. The path to the actual data is stored in a character or memo field, and the data is brought into the general field of a temporary cursor when it needs to be manipulated. So the decision to link or embed, either permanently or temporarily, or none of the above, is one that needs to be made based on the best compromise of your application's need for access, security and disk space issues.

Data is attached to a general field with the APPEND GENERAL command. It can be displayed with the legacy MODIFY GENERAL or @ ... SAY commands, or preferably with the more capable and controllable OLEControl and OLEBoundControl. See the Reference section for more on these commands.

Like memo fields, general fields suffer from "memo bloat." When changes are made to information stored within the memo file, new blocks of information are written at the end of the file, and then the original blocks are marked as no longer in use. These blocks are never reused. It is necessary to PACK MEMO (we dislike PACK—see "Commands Never to Use" earlier in the book for some good workarounds) or COPY the table to eliminate the wasted space.

In-Place, er, In-Situ Activation, er, Visual Editing

> To a philosopher all *news*, as it is called, is gossip, and they who edit it and read it are old women over their tea.
>
> Henry David Thoreau, *Walden*, 1854

The confused topic title is typical of this confused topic. Microsoft fumbled the ball in a major way when rolling out this feature, changing its name three times in the process. "In-situ" is wonderful for those Ivy League Latin scholars among us, but we can't see this catching on with the MTV crowd—it sounds more like a sneeze than a feature. "In-Place" says what it does and will probably be popular with programmers for years to come, because it tells us what it is. Visual Editing, however, is what Microsoft decided to call it, a phrase that flows off the tongue of the sales reps easily enough, and one that looks good in print. But what does it mean to do "visual editing"—that you look at the screen while you type?

What it does is far easier to explain than trying to come up with a name for it. Visual Editing is a better user interface to allow users to manipulate data from one application while running another. Microsoft has discovered through usability studies that users are uncomfortable and disconcerted when they're working in an application and a second application's interface—a new window, menu and toolbars—leaps to the front when the second application's data is called up. For example, a user might want to place a graph of quarterly sales on a page in the annual report. In earlier versions of OLE, placing a graph in a document and calling it up for editing brought up the entire MS Graph interface, with its own menus, toolbars and separate graph and datasheet windows. The document the hapless user was working on was shoved far to the back, out of the way and inaccessible.

With Visual Editing, the graph doesn't come up with its own window, but rather is activated in place (get it?), maintaining its position and relative size within the document. The toolbars of the host application are replaced with the toolbars of MS Graph, in a manner similar to the way that Visual FoxPro brings up and removes its own toolbars as the various power tools are called into play. The menus also change. Those menus that are more the concern of the containing application remain the same. That includes the File menu, with its options to Open, Close and Exit, and the Window menu, with its choices for arranging the various windows on the screen. The remaining menu pads are up for negotiation between the contained application and its container. The Edit menu is a good candidate for replacement, so that it can offer features unique to the application. The Help menu is taken over by the embedded application, allowing it to offer context-sensitive help. Any menus you create that should participate in this negotiation process should include the NEGOTIATE keyword (see the Reference section on DEFINE PAD for details). Figures 5-3 and 5-4 illustrate the menu negotiation with before-activation and after-activation pictures of an MS Graph application.

One significant limitation of this method is that Visual Editing is available only for embedded objects. Microsoft claims this is to avoid having multiple users attempting to make changes to a file simultaneously. We find it astounding that no one considered implementing a locking scheme as part of the logic of Visual Editing. So, you need to either embed data you want to allow your clients to edit, or run the linked application directly, rather than use Visual Editing.

Last words of warning before you leap into implementing this feature: Visual Editing, like most of OLE, is resource-intensive. Ensure that you test and evaluate the features on a minimally acceptable system before committing to a large project dependent on this feature. OLE is very cool, but that coolness comes at a cost. While it may be theoretically possible to implement a Visual FoxPro system with Visual Editing on a 64 MB, low-end Pentium III system, it would not be a pretty thing. Data-entry clerks

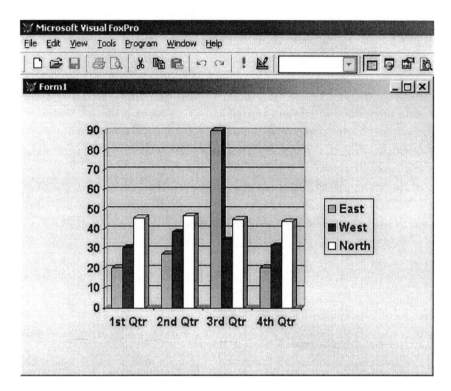

Figure 5-3: The native FoxPro menu before OLE activation.

would get into the habit of calling up a Visual Editing situation just before going to lunch, so it might be ready for them upon their return. Something along the lines of 128 MB is probably a good minimum system for OLE work, and more is better. For more of our hardware recommendations, check out "Hardware and Software Recommendations" in the earlier part of the book.

ActiveX Controls, aka OLE Custom Controls, aka OCXs

> Any technology sufficiently advanced is indistinguishable from magic.
>
> Sir Arthur C. Clarke, *Clarke's Law*

Sometimes it's hard to believe things accomplished by our computers are not simply magic. ActiveX Controls often seem to take on that aura. An ActiveX Control is an add-on for Windows32 applications that gives our applications capabilities not imagined by the authors of Visual FoxPro (or sometimes just better versions of the ones they did imagine). ActiveX Controls, or, more familiarly, OCXs (named for their usual extension), can be added to a development environment like Visual FoxPro in such a way that they seem like just another control. They have properties, events and

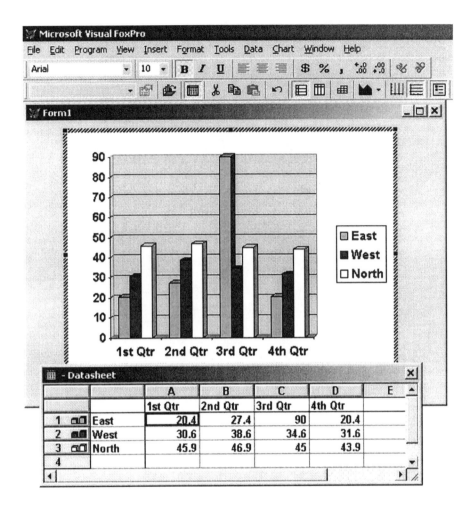

Figure 5-4: After In-Place Editing. Note new toolbar and menu pads and bars.

methods. They can be selected from the Form Controls toolbar and placed on forms. They can be manipulated in code through the usual Formset.Form.Object.Property addressing scheme. Events and methods can be initiated as with any native control. But the ActiveX Control can be written by a third party. This is a tremendous avenue of possible add-on tools for Visual FoxPro.

Not only that, but ActiveX Controls are designed to be available to any tool that supports the OLE Custom Control interface. ActiveX Controls developed for other tools, such as Visual Basic, Access, or Visual C++, should be compatible ("should be" is the key here—see below) with the FoxPro environment. This larger market for selling tools can only help to bring more and better developers into this field. ActiveX

Controls from a variety of manufacturers are already available for graphing, displaying calendars and acquiring analog data. We continue to see new and interesting controls.

ActiveX Controls originated with the VBX, or Visual Basic eXtension, feature added in Visual Basic 3.0. These add-ons were specifically designed to take advantage of the VB environment, and had a number of limitations that made them difficult to use in other development environments or to add to other platforms. Access 2.0 featured the ability to use the second generation of VBXs, 16-bit OCXs. However, this still wasn't enough, and 32-bit ActiveX Controls were developed to address those needs. 32-bit ActiveX Controls are the only format supported by Visual FoxPro, and VFP was the first released application to use them. Since the release of Visual FoxPro, additional platforms for 32-bit ActiveX Controls have appeared—most notably, Visual Basic 4.0 and later.

With the proliferation of ActiveX Controls for the much larger developer market, the reality behind the promise came to light. ActiveX Controls *should* be the same, the interfaces *should* all work the same, and everybody *should* just get along fine. Uh-huh. Well, the ugly truth is that VFP, first out of the gate with OCX support, was developed with a preliminary specification. Last-minute changes defeated some of the compatibility the VFP team tried so hard to achieve. Developers of VB, in an effort to make OCXs most useful on their platform, interpreted the specification to let them introduce some custom interfaces, rendering controls that used those interfaces inoperable in other platforms. Finally, OCXs shipping to support the interface in VB lacked key elements needed to support the faster VTable binding, forcing the VFP development team to create the SYS(2333) function to turn off that feature.

Like many other features of OLE 2.0, ActiveX Controls are a mish-mash of feature sets and optional APIs. Visual Basic, Access and other development platforms supporting ActiveX Controls reveal incompatibility problems, with controls running with one and not other platforms of this "standard." We really hope that Microsoft gets their act together on this one and finds a way to deliver the same support, using the same APIs across their entire product line of development systems. If Microsoft can't even do this internally, third-party vendors stand no chance of supporting the OCX specification.

The number of OCXs bundled with Visual FoxPro is pretty dazzling, and really beyond the scope of what we want to cover here. In the following sections, we'll talk a little bit about how ActiveX Controls are used in VFP, and some important controls VFP provides.

How to Use ActiveX Controls in Visual FoxPro

Just as with FoxPro's base class controls, the first thing you want to do with these controls is to subclass them, and use your subclasses in forms. The reason for this is that it's not possible to add custom properties and methods to the base classes. There will come a time when you have designed the coolest form and realize that you need to add some feature to the control. With subclassed controls, this is easy.

The properties of these controls are accessible in curious ways. Right-clicking on most ActiveX Controls will bring up a context-sensitive menu with two "Properties" options: one labeled just "Properties" that brings up the native VFP property sheet, and a second one, usually labeled "*Control* Properties" that brings up the control's property sheet. The control's own property sheet is often the only way to see some of the properties of the control. If they appear at all, many of the control's properties show up only on the All tab and not on the Other tab of VFP's property sheet. However, the VFP team has made it easier to find the control's PEMs by showing them in color in the VFP property sheet. The actual color used is configurable from the property sheet's context menu. In addition, the method editor puts the string "*** ActiveX Control Method ***" at the beginning of each method that belongs to the control.

You'll also note that few ActiveX Controls have data binding features. If you need to add, say, a table of data, you'll have to use AddItem to do it one record, or even one field, at a time. This can seriously limit the capacity of the controls to work with large data sets. We have seen a few controls with data binding features, using ODBC or ADO to link to the underlying data sources. These can be problematic, because their implementation really makes them stand-alone data applications plunked in the middle of our apps—they're not sharing data with the host VFP application. That means these controls are usually pretty heavy consumers of resources, and aren't going to recognize changing data within the application until it's committed to the data source and the control's data is requeried. If you need to data-bind an OCX, you might have to write the code yourself, perhaps in a data-binding wrapper class definition.

Almost all of the controls we discuss below have an AboutBox method, which displays a dialog crediting the authors. They also have help files, stored in the Help directory under the Windows installation directory.

MSComCtl.OCX

The MSComCtl.OCX library contains a number of very useful controls, including the ProgressBar, Slider, StatusBar, Toolbar, and TreeView controls. There's also an ImageCombo control that's similar to the VFP ComboBox control, except that pictures can be attached to each item in the list. (Actually, you can do that with VFP's combo box, too. See the Picture property in the Reference section.) Ever want to change the look of the tabs on a PageFrame control? The TabStrip control has a number of different looks to try; implement it by having it activate the pages of your PageFrame control on which you've turned off the tabs. Also available is the ListView control, used to give an Explorer-like interface to your apps. And finally, the ImageList control is a collection of images, used by other controls to set their image properties. You can find help for all of these controls in CmCtl198.CHM.

Don't forget that when you use any one of these controls, you must ship MSComCtl.OCX with your application.

Note that in previous releases, this library shipped as ComCtl32.OCX (the version 5 controls), so don't forget to take this into account with your older apps.

MSComCtl2.OCX

This library contains some cool controls. The Animation control lets you run .AVI files (without sound) on your buttons when the button is clicked. There's a DateTimePicker and a MonthView control that make entering dates and times much easier. The UpDown control works just like the arrows on a spinner, but updates an associated control (ever want to use a spinner with character data?). And the FlatScrollBar control looks like the scrollbar in Internet Explorer. You can find the help for this library in CmCtl298.CHM.

MCI32.OCX, a Multimedia Control

This is the Multimedia MCI control, which manages the recording and playback of multimedia files. It's a set of VCR buttons that can be programmed to do whatever you need. Its help file is MMedia98.CHM.

MSChrt20.OCX, the MsChart Control

MSChart is a control that creates graphs (aka charts). Its help file is MSChrt98.CHM.

MSComm32.OCX, the MSComm Control

This control provides communications over the serial port. You can manipulate the settings of the port, and then send and receive data. Its help file is Comm98.CHM.

MSINet.OCX, Microsoft Internet Transfer Control

This control implements HTTP and FTP protocols in your application. There are Username and Password properties to let you connect to private sites, as well as an Execute method to perform common FTP commands. The help file is INet98.CHM.

MSMAPI32.OCX, MAPI Controls

You can provide e-mail support with the Messaging Application Program Interface (MAPI) controls. There are two controls: the Session control opens (and closes) the MAPI session, while the Message control works with individual messages within a MAPI session. MAPI services must be installed on the computer running your application in addition to providing this OCX. The help file is MAPI98.CHM.

MSMask32.OCX: Masked Edit Control

The OCXs mentioned in this section are also shipped with the other Visual Studio tools, which explains this control's inclusion. It's like a text box with an InputMask property. Unless you're matching interfaces with another language that uses this control, we think you'll stick with InputMask. Its help file is MASKED98.CHM.

MSWinSck.OCX, WinSock Control

The WinSock control lets you connect to another computer to exchange data using TCP and UDP protocols. See MSWNSK98.CHM for more details on how to use this control.

PicClp32.OCX, PictureClip Control

The PictureClip control takes a single bitmap and divides it into rows and columns, making each clipped region available for use by a button or other control requiring a picture or icon. You can put all of your icons in one bitmap and reference the location in this control, instead of using a multitude of files shipped with your application. Its help file is PicClp98.CHM.

RichTx32.OCX, Rich Textbox Control

Here's the tool to format text with all the various font properties. You'll need to create an interface that sets these properties (an Italic button, a Bold button, a font selector, etc.), but all the tools are here to let the user see or choose text formatting in your application. See RTFBox98.CHM for much more information.

SysInfo.OCX, SysInfo Control

The SysInfo control responds to system events, like changes to the system time or date, power status, and plug-and-play events, and it monitors system properties like OSVersion and WorkAreaHeight. Its help file is SysInf98.CHM.

Filer

Filer used to be a handy "desktop accessory" tool built into FoxPro, great for finding all those times you misspelled "license" and opening all the programs in the native FoxPro editor. Alas, time and politics killed poor Filer, eliminated from the feature list for VFP 5. Rumors abound as to the real cause of its demise. We can't say for sure, but we suspect it wasn't really long file names that killed it.

Filer returned, not too long after the shipping of VFP 5.0a, but in a new guise: as a FoxPro form and a COM object containing the core file-searching capabilities. The source code for the Filer form is provided, and we've seen several variations of the Filer form in *FoxPro Advisor* magazine as well as out on the Web. In VFP 6 and later, you'll find the form and DLL in HOME() + "\Tools\Filer".

Did we say DLL? Yes, the Filer functionality comes to us as a DLL. But, you might ask, is a DLL an ActiveX Control? Well, no, strictly speaking. By Microsoft's definitions this month, ActiveX Controls are COM components with a design-time user interface: an OCX. But this chapter is "Active Something" and, like many of the other Active technologies Microsoft is shipping these days, Filer is a COM component accessible from many languages but lacking a design-time user interface. We feel the control needs to be featured, and this was the best place for it.

Here's a quick idea of what Filer can do for you:

```
oFiler = CREATEOBJECT("filer.fileutil")
oFiler.SearchPath = "C:\Temp"  && path can be separated with commas
oFiler.FileExpression = "*.*"  && wildcards and multiple file
                               && expressions, separated with semicolons
oFiler.SubFolder = .T.         && search subfolders
oFiler.SearchText1 = ""        && the text to search for
oFiler.SearchText2 = ""
oFiler.SearchText3 = ""
oFiler.IgnoreCase = .T.        && ignore the case
oFiler.WholeWords = .T.        && find only whole words
oFiler.Find(0)                 && 0: new search, 1: add to results
oFiler.Files.Count             && returns count of files found
oFiler.Files[2].Name           && returns name of file
oFiler.Editor = "notepad"      && specify an external editor
oFiler.IsHostedByFox = 0       && use the specified editor, not internal
```

Now, you could probably write all of the code to perform the searching functions in VFP—ADIR() and a little recursion get you most of the way there. Processing the text searching is easy with FileToStr(); ANDing and ORing results would be tiresome but manageable—but why bother? You've already got the functionality you need, in a compact little utility, listed as being freely distributable.

FoxTLib

The FoxTLib OCX is a handy utility for reading and parsing ActiveX Type Libraries. A Type Library describes the functionality of its associated component, going into detail on the interface. It can be important to browse type libraries, as we discuss in "It Was Automation, You Know," to determine the method names, parameters and constants required by a function. FoxTLib supplies all of the information in an easy-to-use format. Check out the VFP Help for the details on FoxTLib, and check out the sample class Typelib.VCX (original, huh?) included in the _SAMPLES + "Classes\" directory.

FPOLE

Some people are still out there programming in a language not capable of working with all of Microsoft's technologies (actually, come to think about it, we suspect we all are). For them, the VFP team included a DLL in VFP 5, and a DLL-OCX pair in VFP 6 and later, that allows them to access FoxPro's internal functionality even if their language is not capable of using Automation directly. It is called FPOLE, and it presents several methods. FoxDoCmd allows you to pass a single command to FoxPro and have it execute it. Other methods include FoxEval to evaluate an expression, SetOLEObject to specify the class used in the methods above, and several other methods for error handling.

Wrap it Up

There is not a fiercer hell than the failure in a great object.

John Keats

ActiveX offers some great challenges. Integrating the functionality available only through OLE can allow you to create easier-to-use, easier-to-maintain, richer interfaces with less coding and maintenance. Embedded and linked data can maintain the inter-application links from one session to the next. Visual Editing allows the presentation of data from foreign sources within the comfortable context of your own application.

But the reality of the situation is that many of these new capabilities are still being worked out. The perfect OCX for the job might work well under Visual Basic but may not have been tested under Visual FoxPro. Your clients might be surprised to hear that some functionality is available only under specific variations of the operating systems, or that 128 MB of RAM is good for a "starter" system. Each and every application you work with will require a different command set, different syntax, perhaps a different sequence of steps. Be prepared to face these challenges, and you will create some very cool COM/OLE/ActiveX-based systems.

One final tip: In many cases the OCX is just a wrapper for underlying technology available through COM or DECLARE-DLLs, and by using the lower-level access, you can often avoid problems with OCX hell. A case in point is the CommonDialogs control, contained in ComDlg32.OCX, which provides a number of Windows dialogs, such as Open and Save As. Starting in VFP 7, one of the classes (_ComDlg in HOME() + "FFC_System.VCX") included in the FoxPro Foundation Classes (FFC) provides Open and Save dialogs by calling the same Windows DLL functions the ActiveX control does. You can use this class rather than having to worry about distributing and registering ComDlg32.OCX.

Hacking the Class Browser and Component Gallery

Visual FoxPro's Class Browser and Component Gallery (or just "Browser" and "Gallery") are valuable development tools; most self-respecting VFP hacks will want to know them well.

Most of Visual FoxPro's ancillary tools, like Browser and Gallery, are actually written in Visual FoxPro. (Surprised?) Starting with VFP 6, the source code for all the VFP-coded tools is included. This is great news for VFP developers because the source for these tools provides some great (and occasionally not so great) examples. If you search carefully, you may even find an astonishing feat of software prowess: a comment in the source code.

Lack of comments aside, if you've ever wondered just how a particular wizard or service works, you can now easily and legally reverse-engineer it.

The source for VFP's tools is kept in a ZIP file in the HOME()+"Tools\XSource" directory. If this directory doesn't exist on your system, it's possible that you chose to omit some tools during installation. The Browser and Gallery source can be found in the HOME() + "Tools\XSource\vfpsource\Browser" directory. The most interesting file in this directory is the form Browser.SCX. The Browser and the Gallery share the same SCX file, and many of the methods therein serve both the Browser and the Gallery.

Let's look first at the Browser, and then we'll explore the Gallery.

The Class Browser

The Browser is useful for a variety of development purposes. These include, among others:

- Managing classes and class libraries, including adding, deleting, renaming and redefining classes.

- Generating equivalent code for visual classes.

- Creating running instances at design time.

- Browsing all the classes and libraries used by a project.

- Browsing the interfaces of ActiveX and COM components.

Starting the Class Browser

There are three ways to start the Browser. From the Tools menu, select Class Browser. Another way is to use the _BROWSER system variable. _BROWSER defaults to "Browser.APP", which is located in the Visual FoxPro home directory. Issuing the command:

```
DO (_BROWSER)
```

is equivalent to using the menu. In addition, you can pass a parameter containing the name of the class library to load. For example, this code:

```
DO (_BROWSER) WITH HOME(2)+"tastrade\libs\about"
```

loads About.VCX from the TASTRADE sample application. Add a second parameter to the command to select a particular class in the list. For example, this code:

```
DO (_BROWSER) WITH HOME(2)+"tastrade\libs\about", "aboutbox"
```

loads the About library and selects the class called AboutBox. Specifying a form file name directly works, too:

```
DO (_BROWSER) WITH HOME(2)+"tastrade\forms\customer.scx"
```

starts the Browser with the form Customer.SCX loaded.

Finally, if the Gallery is running, you can just click the Browser button to show the Browser.

The Browser Interface

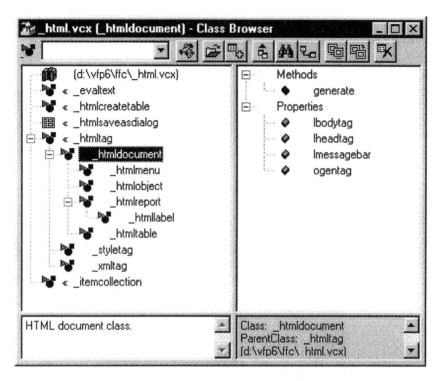

Figure 5-5: Just browsing, thanks. The Class Browser interface.

Figure 5-5 shows the Browser. Here are a few things you should know about the Browser to increase your productivity with this tool.

 Click this button to see the class code. Note that in some cases, the code shown can't be executed correctly. (This happens if the class is a container of other classes.) Right-click this button and see the class code in HTML format. This isn't obvious, but the window that appears is actually an instance of your HTML browser. You can right-click in the window and choose View Source to display the HTML source for the display.

 Use this button to create a new class. This new class can be a subclass of the currently selected class, a subclass of any other class, or a subclass of a VFP base class.

You can redefine classes (that is, change the parent class) in the Browser with this icon. Starting in VFP 6, you can even redefine a class to use a different base class, after being warned that some intrinsic methods and properties will understandably be lost in the process.

 When you have a method code window open, this button (which floats or docks independently of the Browser on a one-button toolbar) allows you to view the code up the class hierarchy in parent class methods. This button is available even after you close the Class Browser.

View More Than Class Libraries

In the Browser's Open dialog, note the different types of files that are supported. Figure 5-6 shows the Browser's Open dialog with the drop-down expanded to show the sorts of things you can display in the Browser.

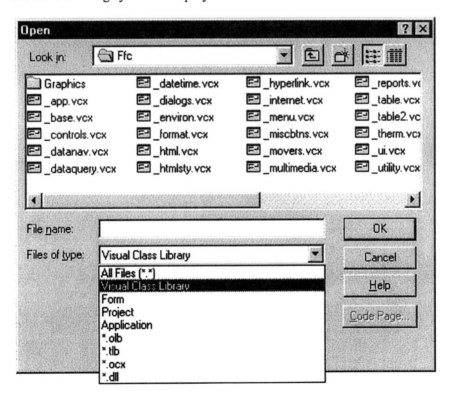

Figure 5-6: Open sesame! The Class Browser's Open dialog shows that you can view more than just class libraries in the "Class" Browser.

You can open VFP forms in the Browser; many of the features, such as showing code, work as you might expect. This is very handy for communicating your code examples with other users via e-mail.

If you open a VFP project file, all the class libraries in that project are visible in a single view. This is great if your project contains hundreds of classes and you have no idea which library a particular class belongs to. This view is a lifesaver when you inherit (or join) a new project.

You can open all manner of EXE and OLE files, and the Browser displays their public interfaces. If help is available, double-clicking an item or pressing the spacebar invokes it.

Clever Tricks

To add controls to a form or class, in the Browser open the VCX (class library) containing the class of the object you want to add to the form, select the class, and then drag and drop the class icon to the design surface. You can also drop a control on the desktop, and you'll get a running instance of that class.

To quickly get to a class you're using, in the Form or Class Designer select an object. Open the Browser. It opens with the class library of the selected class loaded, and with the selected class highlighted.

Class Management

Table 5-1 shows what you can do with classes using VFP commands or the Browser.

Table 5-1: The class-management functions of the Class Browser.

Action	VFP Command	Class Browser Action
Clean up a class library	COMPILE CLASSLIB or open the VCX as a table and issue a PACK command.	Highlight a class or class library file in the Browser and click the Clean Up Class Library button.
Copy a class from one class library to another	ADD CLASS	Open two copies of the Browser, with one pointing to the class to be copied and the other containing the destination class library. Ctrl+drag the class's icon from one Browser instance to another.

Action	VFP Command	Class Browser Action
Create a class library	CREATE CLASSLIB or CREATE CLASS using a new class library.	Click the New Class icon and specify the new class library name in the New Class dialog.
Create a new class	CREATE CLASS	Select the parent class in the Browser and click the New Class button.
Move a class between class libraries	No single command exists to move a class. Instead, copy the class to a second library (ADD CLASS), and then remove it from the first.	Drag the class's icon from one Browser instance to another. If subclasses of the moved class are open in any open Browser instances, the subclasses are automatically remapped to the parent class's new class library. If subclasses of the moved classes aren't open in another Class Browser instance, you've just corrupted your class hierarchy. Watch out!
Open a class in the Class Designer	MODIFY CLASS	Select the class in the class library. Then double-click it, select Modify from the shortcut menu, or press the spacebar.
Remove a class from a class library	REMOVE CLASS	Select the class, and then select Remove from the shortcut menu.
Rename a class	RENAME CLASS VFP does not adjust classes below the renamed class in the class hierarchy.	Select the class, and then select Rename from the shortcut menu. The Browser adjusts classes below the renamed class in the class hierarchy if they're displayed in any open Browser window (not just the current one).

Action	VFP Command	Class Browser Action
View class code	There's no command or series of commands to do this, short of a complex program.	Select the class and click the View Class Code button.
Add an instance of a class to a container (such as a form or _SCREEN)	Container.AddObject() or Container.NewObject()	Click on the Move icon (the top-left icon in the Browser form, which changes based on the highlighted item) and drag it to the container.
Change the icon for a class	There's no command for this. Instead, open the class in the Class Designer, choose Class Info from the Class menu, and change the Container Icon setting.	Right-click on the Move icon and select an image file in the GETPICT() dialog that appears. There's a nice touch here: When you select Cancel in the dialog, you get the option to reset the icon to the default for that item.

Programming the Class Browser with Add-Ins

The VFP Browser is designed for extensibility. It has a rich programming interface, and it exposes its complete object model. The usual way to program the Browser is by hooking its events and methods with Browser add-ins.

An add-in is a program that you create (or download) and then register with the Browser. Once registered, the add-in can be invoked automatically by Browser events or methods. If the add-in is not assigned to a particular event or method, the user can invoke it.

Here is an example Browser add-in that demonstrates some of the most important qualities of add-ins.

```
* Program Add-InSample1.PRG
* This program echoes class information
* to the Debug Output window

#DEFINE DEBUGWINDOW  "Debug Output"

LPARAMETERS oBrowser
```

```
IF ! oBrowser.lFileMode AND !EMPTY(oBrowser.cClass)
 ACTIVATE WINDOW DEBUGWINDOW

   *-- Output the class name
   DEBUGOUT "Class Name: "+ oBrowser.cClass

   *-- Output the class library name
   DEBUGOUT "Class Library: "+ oBrowser.cFileName

   *-- Output the class's timestamp
   DEBUGOUT "Timestamp: "+ PADR(oBrowser.nTimeStamp,25)

   *-- Display the entire class pedigree
   DO WHILE oBrowser.SeekParentClass()
      *-- Output the parentclass name
      DEBUGOUT "Parent Class: "+ oBrowser.cClass
   ENDDO
ELSE
   WAIT WINDOW "Please select a class and try again"
ENDIF
```

Observe the following points about the sample add-in above: The Browser passes a reference to itself as a parameter to the add-in. This means that all of the Browser's members are available for reference. The example demonstrates the Browser's cClass, cFileName, and nTimeStamp properties, and its SeekParentClass method.

Now, with the Browser running, register the add-in as follows:

```
_oBrowser.AddIn("Sample Add-In", "Add-InSample1.PRG")
```

While the Browser form is running, you can refer to it with a memory variable named _oBrowser.

The Browser's AddIn method registers add-ins. The syntax shown here specifies a name for the add-in and the program to run. An optional third parameter specifies the event or method to which the add-in gets assigned.

If a Browser event is assigned to the add-in, then the add-in is invoked automatically near the beginning of that event's execution. If a Browser method is assigned to the add-in, then the add-in is invoked near the end of that method's execution.

In the example above, since no method or event is specified, the add-in is listed in the Browser's add-in shortcut menu.

 The Add-In option doesn't always appear on the shortcut menu. When the mouse is over the Classes or Members panes, right-clicks don't show add-ins among the choices. You have to right-click on either of the description pages or the top of the Browser, where the buttons are, or over the Browser form itself, to see the add-in item.

Alternately, passing the name of an add-in to the Browser's DoAddIn() method runs that add-in.

Tell me more! Tell me more!

The Browser is extensively documented under "Class Browser" in VFP Help. Also take a look at the following topics: "Class Browser Buttons", "Class Browser Methods", and "Class Browser Properties." For more information on add-ins, see also the white papers section of the Visual FoxPro pages on the Microsoft Web site.

Having Trouble with the Class Browser's ActiveX Controls

Some people complain that earlier versions of the Class Browser crashed a lot. Although that's not much of an issue in later versions, if the Browser is prone to instability on your system, try invoking it with the optional third parameter set to .T.:

```
DO (_BROWSER) WITH FileName, , .T.
```

This opens the Browser in "listbox" mode with the TreeView control replaced by a VFP listbox. It's not as pretty looking, but it may work better for you. (This is a legacy feature from VFP 3, which had a Mac version; the listbox is a substitute for the outline OLE control, which doesn't have a Mac counterpart.)

The VFP Component Gallery

The Gallery is the Browser's companion. Both share the same display surface, and you can toggle between them with a handy command button.

The Gallery is a flexible and programmable shortcut manager. Because it works with shortcuts, you can't hose a file using the Gallery; when you delete a shortcut from the Gallery, the underlying file is not deleted.

The Gallery can be used to categorize and display almost anything, and its strength is in grouping the various resources used in software development. With the Gallery, you can create and display your own abstractions, organized as you wish, with event behavior—such as click, right-click, double-click—that you can innovate and control. Moreover, the Gallery also has *dynamic folders*, which we'll discuss in a minute, which have the ability to hold all the contents of VFP projects, class libraries and directories.

Now, you could use the Other Files section of the Other tab in Project Manager to do some of this, but that's primitive, inflexible, and—let's face it—low tech.

What's What in the Gallery

It's probably a good idea to explain a few things before going further.

A **catalog** is both a DBF table and the highest-level element of the Gallery. A catalog's records define the shortcut items you see in the right-hand pane in the Gallery.

A **folder** is simply a logical package of items and possibly other folders. (Folders look just like subdirectories and that abstraction works for us.) Folders are either *static* or *dynamic*. A static folder contains predefined shortcuts to items. A dynamic folder determines its contents each time the Gallery is refreshed. A dynamic folder could be defined as a directory ("C:\Projects*.*"), a VFP project, or a class library.

An **item** is a shortcut to a particular file or URL.

An **item type** defines the behavior of particular items in the catalog. Item types are stored in the HOME()+"Gallery\VfpGlry.VCX" class library, and are configurable through the Properties dialog for each catalog. The root catalog, named "Catalogs", contains the default item types that apply to all catalogs. See "Understanding Item Types" below for more on item types.

Start Me Up!

VFP has a system memory variable named _GALLERY to identify the Gallery application. By default, it's called "Gallery.App" in your HOME() directory. You can replace or "wrap" the Gallery application by changing the value of _GALLERY.

You can use the _GALLERY memory variable to invoke the Gallery, like this:

```
DO (_GALLERY)
```

In addition, you can pass a parameter containing the name of the catalog to load. For example, this code:

```
DO (_GALLERY) WITH HOME()+"Gallery\Vfp Catalog"
```

loads Vfp Catalog.DBF.

You can also start the Gallery from the Tools menu, or click the Gallery button in the Browser.

The Component Gallery Interface

If you're comfortable with Explorer-type interfaces, the basic features of the Gallery (see Figure 5-7) will work pretty much as you'd expect.

The Gallery is segmented into two panes. The Catalog pane, on the left, lists the folder hierarchies within the currently open catalogs. The Items pane, on the right, shows the items in the current catalog or folder. Both panes are endowed with item-sensitive context menus to do the usual useful things such as cut, copy, paste, rename, and so on. You can also invoke item-sensitive property dialogs for selections in the left or right panes. Moreover, the entire Gallery is enabled for both regular and OLE drag and drop.

As in the Browser, the Move icon—the top-left icon in the Gallery form (which changes based on the highlighted item)—can be used to drag the currently selected item to the desktop, a design surface, or a project. Right-clicking the Move icon invokes a GETPICT() dialog to change the icon. There's a nice touch here: When you select Cancel, you get the option to reset the icon to the default for that item.

The View Type drop-down lets you choose among different views of the Gallery. For example, in the VFP Catalog, selecting "Internet" filters the catalogs to display Internet items only. To create your own custom views, use the Dynamic Views tab in the Gallery Options dialog—we'll look at that in more detail a little later. The Browser button toggles the view back to the standard Browser. Neat touch here: Right-clicking the Browser button brings up a nice long list of the previously opened folders.

The Open button is for opening new catalogs. The Open dialog (see Figure 5-8) is a little unconventional and merits explanation. In the process, we'll take our first look at the Gallery internals.

This isn't your garden-variety Open dialog. The catalog drop-down control displays the catalogs currently registered on your system. The catalog names are kept in the Browser.DBF table. If you ever clean out or lose Browser.DBF, you can click the Browse button to select an existing catalog file that isn't listed in the Catalog drop-down. The "Add catalog" check box control adds the contents of the catalog to the current view (the default is to close the current catalog and open the one you specify).

The Options button brings you to a three-tabbed dialog (see Figure 5-9) where you can set certain Gallery properties.

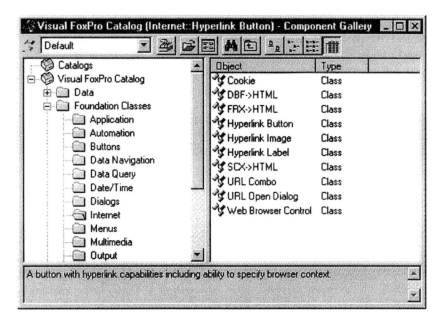

Figure 5-7: The Component Gallery interface—yet another Explorer-type interface.

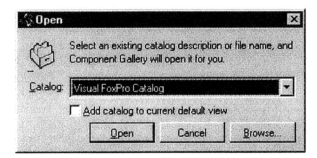

Figure 5-8: An Open dialog like no other. The Component Gallery's Open dialog is different because it offers catalog tables, and those references are kept in Browser.DBF.

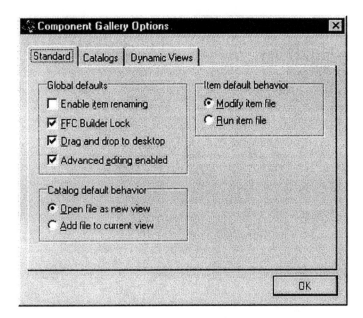

**Figure 5-9: I need options. The Component Gallery comes
with its own options; this figure shows the Standard tab.**

The Standard tab displays the general defaults for the Gallery itself. Like some of the
Tools | Options dialog options, these brief labels can be pretty obscure until you
understand the product well:

• The "Enable item renaming" check box determines if clicking and then hovering
  over the item puts you in a name-edit mode, just as it works in Explorer.

• The "FFC Builder Lock" check box will, if checked, automatically invoke builders
  for new objects you create with the Gallery. If they have a builder, that is. Some
  do, some don't.

• The "Drag and drop to desktop" check box enables dragging and dropping to the
  desktop, just like it works in the Class Browser.

• Checking "Advanced editing enabled" gives you access to advanced features of
  Gallery property dialogs. This is where the Gallery really starts to shine!

 The "Advanced editing enabled" check box is a killer. If this option isn't checked, that explains why you can't do half the stuff we're talking about in this chapter.

- The "Catalog default behavior" option determines whether new catalogs are appended to, or replace, the current visible collection of catalogs.

- The "Item default behavior" option determines whether double-clicking on an item opens or edits an item by default. This applies only to items that can be edited in VFP, of course. Otherwise, the selection will simply run regardless of what you've specified here.

Use the Catalogs tab (see Figure 5-10) to maintain the list of catalogs that appear in the Catalog drop-down in the Catalog Open dialog.

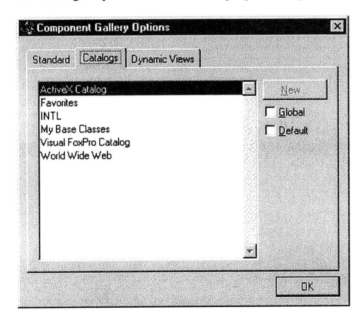

Figure 5-10: What, no underwear ads? A catalog page suitable for family viewing.

The New button is enabled only when at least one catalog is loaded in the Catalogs pane. We don't know why we need to load a catalog before we can create a new one, and frankly this behavior seems wrong. Nonetheless, that's the way it is.

The Global and Default check boxes let you set the persistent visibility of each catalog. A Global catalog is always visible in the Catalogs pane, regardless of which catalogs you open for display. You may want to mark the Favorites catalog as a global catalog so you always have access to your favorite things. A Default catalog is the one that's active and current whenever the Gallery is invoked programmatically. You can have any number of default catalogs.

When you invoke the Gallery from the Browser, it always comes up empty. The only way the Gallery appears initially populated with the default catalogs is when it's originally opened with DO (_Gallery) or with Tools | Component Gallery.

The Dynamic Views tab lets you create your own custom, live views of your catalogs. Figures 5-11 and 5-12 show how to create or edit a new dynamic view called "Excel Spreadsheets" that displays all items of type "file" that contain ".XLS" in their names.

We think dynamic views are ultra cool. This adds a second powerful dimension to the Gallery. The first dimension is the obvious one: catalogs and folders that logically segment things as you choose. But dynamic views permit you to see all the items of a particular type (you define), regardless of their logical placement within a catalog.

Figure 5-13 shows the Keywords dialog, accessible from a button in the Edit View dialog. This dialog lets us create dynamic views based on keywords used to describe them. The keywords displayed in this list are stored in a table called Keywords.DBF. You can use keywords to further expand the power of the Gallery's dynamic views.

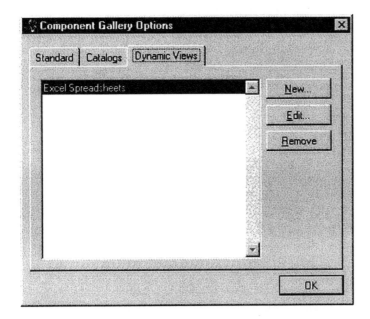

Figure 5-11: Click the New button to create a new view, or the Edit button to bring up the dialog below.

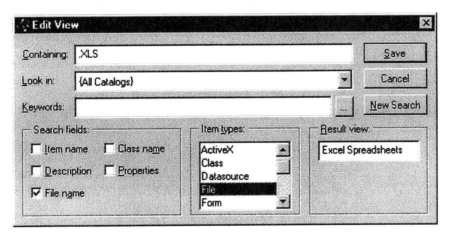

Figure 5-12: A different view of things. This is where you define and edit dynamic views.

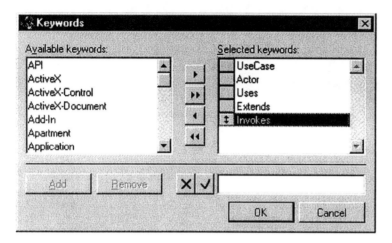

Figure 5-13: Views can be based on keywords you specify.

In order to add a keyword, you must first have a catalog loaded in the Gallery. When we instructed the underpaid workers at Hacker Laboratories to take the screen shot shown in Figure 5-13, we forgot to mention that, so that's why the Add and Remove buttons look disabled.

We think all the things you can do in the Options dialog are a good idea. But we cannot fathom why the Catalogs page is in that dialog. More specifically, we can't understand why the New button is in that dialog. This isn't an option, it's an action. Options are choices you make about how things look or operate. It's as if the New button in the Project Manager could only be accessed from the Project Info dialog. We'd feel the same way about the Dynamic Views page, except for one thing.

Surprise! The Find button works just like choosing New on the Dynamic Views page! In effect, when you choose Find, you create a new persistent view. We're not really crazy about this; after all, cluttering our dynamic views every time we go searching is a bit much. However, it's easy enough to clean up the list of dynamic views using the Dynamic Views page.

Understanding Item Types

So, how does the Gallery work internally, you ask? The behavior of a Gallery item, like what happens when you click or drag it, is defined by its item type. The class library Gallery\VfpGlry.VCX stores the item types supplied by Microsoft, and you can modify, subclass, or simply copy these classes to create your own types. If you develop your own custom item types, it's probably a good idea to store them in some other VCX, such as *My_VfpGlry.VCX*. This allows you to later update the Gallery's class libraries without fear of clobbering your work.

Figure 5-14 shows the hierarchy of the Gallery item types as supplied by Microsoft. The _item and _folder classes live in _Gallery.VCX. All other classes are defined in VfpGlry.VCX.

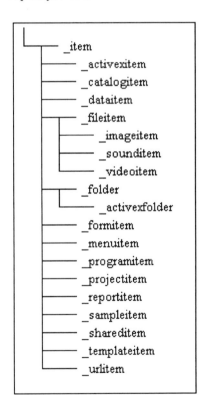

Figure 5-14: Type-o-rama! The Item Types hierarchy provided by Microsoft.

When creating your own item types, the most flexible base type is the _fileitem. In fact, _fileitem should serve most of your needs because its behavior is to simply invoke the Windows file associations. Moreover, the _fileitem type has the ability to redirect popular file extensions to other file types. We'll talk more about redirection in a minute.

Item types can be tied to particular catalogs. The root catalog, which is always named "Catalog", serves as the basis for all catalogs. If you select the Item Types tab of the properties of the root catalog, you'll get something like the dialog in Figure 5-15 once you've turned on the Advanced Editing option on the Class Browser's option dialog. Do it now! C'mon, you're reading the *Hacker's Guide*! That alone qualifies you as "Advanced!"

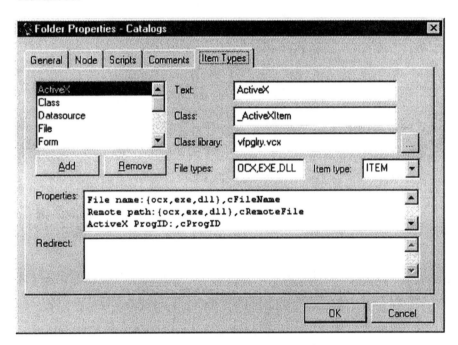

Figure 5-15: Catalog Properties, Item Types.

Note the following things about the Item Types page in this dialog:

- The list of item types matches the item types you see in the New Item shortcut menu. To modify the New Item shortcut menu, simply edit this list.

- Each item type can be associated with display text, a class, and a class library. In this case the display text is "ActiveX", the class is _ActiveXItem, and the class library is VfpGlry.VCX.

- The lines in the Properties edit box specify what's displayed in the final page of the item's Properties dialog. For example, for the ActiveX item type pictured in Figure 5-15, when you examine the properties of an ActiveX item in the Component Gallery you'll see the following:

  - File name: with an associated Open dialog initialized with OCX, EXE, and DLL files, and the file name specified will be stored in the item's cFileName property.

  - Remote path: with an associated open dialog initialized with OCX, EXE, and DLL files, and the file name specified will be stored in the item's cRemoteFile property.

  - Other lines in the edit box can't be seen in Figure 5-15. They include entries for Class, Class Library, Source project and Associated file; these all work the same as described above for the corresponding text box entries.

- If you create your own item types, you make them available by clicking the Add button and filling in the specifics of your new item type.

The properties for the _fileitem item type are worth a look because, in addition to showing custom properties, they show an example of item redirection. See the Redirect field in Figure 5-16.

Here is the full list of redirections:

BMP=_imageitem, ICO=_imageitem, JPG=_imageitem, GIF=_imageitem, WAV=_sounditem, RMI=_sounditem, AVI=_videoitem, DBF=_dataitem, SCX=_formitem, MNX=_menuitem, FRX=_reportitem, LBX=_reportitem, PRG=_programitem, APP=_sampleitem, OCX=_activexitem, HTM=_urlitem, HTML=_urlitem, PJX=_projectitem, TXT=_programitem, LOG=_programitem, H=_programitem.

You can probably guess how redirections work: When an item with any of those file extensions is created, the designated item type is created instead. For example, if you try to add a PRG as a file item, the Gallery notices the PRG redirection and creates a _programitem instead of a _fileitem. This is why the _fileitem item type is so flexible; it has the ability to properly redirect new items to the correct item type.

Note that dragging VCX or PJX files from Windows Explorer just creates a regular file shortcut, and not a dynamic folder. We think VFP's Gallery should be able to recognize VFP's own components.

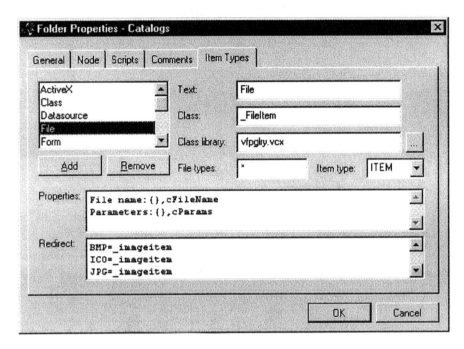

Figure 5-16: Item Types.

Programming the Component Gallery with Add-Ins

Since the Gallery and Browser are really the same application, you can hook into the Gallery's events and methods with add-ins in the same way you can with the Browser.

I Never Metadata I Didn't Like

Here's a brief description of the data structures used by the Browser and the Gallery.

Browser.DBF

The Browser stores all its metadata in a table named Browser.DBF found in the VFP home directory. The Gallery also uses Browser.DBF to store its catalog-related information. Table 5-2 shows a field-by-field description of Browser.DBF.

Table 5-2: The structure of Browser.DBF.

Field	Description	Used by (B)rowser (G)allery
PLATFORM	"WINDOWS" or blank when Type="ADDIN". We suspect this is left over from the VFP 3 days when there was something other than Windows, and that it was retained for backward compatibility.	BG
TYPE	Records with type field value "PREFW" store Browser and Gallery preferences. Records with type field value "ADDIN" store add-in information.	BG
ID	"FORMINFO" records are used by the Browser to store form preferences and by the Gallery to store information about your catalogs. The only way to tell the difference is that Gallery records contain the string ".dbf" in the Name field. "BROWSER" records contain default settings for the Gallery (not the Browser!). See the Properties field for this record to see these default properties. These get set in the Gallery Options dialog. "METHOD" records store Browser add-ins that are tied to a particular Browser event or method. "MENU" records store Browser add-ins that are not tied to a particular Browser event or method, and are thus available on the Add-ins shortcut menu.	BG
DEFAULT	True for the default Gallery catalog.	G

Field	Description	Used by (B)rowser (G)allery
GLOBAL	Applies to Gallery catalog records. True if the catalog is global. By default, new catalogs are not global. To make a catalog global, check the appropriate check box in the Catalogs tab in the Gallery's Options dialog.	G
BACKUP	When Gallery opens a catalog or a VCX, this field in the associated Browser.DBF record is queried. If the value is True, the Gallery checks to see if a file of the same name exists in the backup subfolder below that one. If the backup file doesn't exist, it is automatically created (as is a subfolder called Backup if needed). Then the Backup field is set to .F. This field can be set programmatically to force the Gallery to automatically back up a file the next time—and only the next time—that file is opened. You can set this field via add-in hooks, or with a program that opens and updates Browser.DBF. Note that Gallery doesn't automatically back up your work. You can force a backup at any time by selecting Backup on the catalog item shortcut menus. This feature is used internally in one special case. When Browser.DBF is first created after VFP is installed, it's set up with the default catalogs (around five or so). The Backup field is set to .T. so that each catalog gets backed up the very first time it is opened, since VFP doesn't install the associated backup catalog tables. Beyond that special function, it can be used at will by developers for their own purposes.	G

Field	Description	Used by (B)rowser (G)allery
NAME	The file name that relates to this record. For a Browser record, the file type could be, among other things, VCX, PJX, SCX, OCX, DLL, EXE, or APP. For Gallery records, the file type is DBF. In the case of Browser and Gallery add-ins, the Name field stores the name of the add-in. This is what appears in the Add-ins shortcut menu if the add-in is not tied to an event or method.	BG
DESC	Used only by the Gallery, it stores the description of the catalog referred to in the Name field.	G
METHOD	Stores the name of the method to which an add-in is tied. If the Method field equals "*", the add-in executes for all methods.	BG
PROPERTIES	Used by the Browser to store default settings.	B
SCRIPT	According to our sources at Microsoft, this field is used by code deep within the Gallery and is for internal use only.	G
PROGRAM	Stores the name of the program to executein the case of a PRG-based add-in.	BG
CLASSLIB	Stores the name of the class library in the case of a VCX-based add-in.	BG
CLASSNAME	Stores the name of the class to execute in the case of a VCX-based add-in.	BG

Field	Description	Used by (B)rowser (G)allery
FILEFILTER	Used by add-in records to specify file masks for which the add-in applies. The FileFilter is specified in the fourth parameter of the AddIn method.	B
DISPMODE	Hierarchical/alphabetic listing display mode for the Browser (numeric).	B
TOP	The stored top coordinate for the Browser/Gallery form. All stored coordinates and sizes apply only if you include the file name when you open the Browser/Gallery. When you use the Open button, you get whatever settings are currently in effect.	BG
LEFT	The stored left coordinate for the Browser/Gallery form.	BG
HEIGHT	The stored height of the Browser/Gallery form.	BG
WIDTH	The stored width of the Browser/Gallery form.	BG
HEIGHT1	The stored height of the Class and Member description panes in the Browser.	BG
WIDTH1	The stored width of the Class and Member description panes in the Browser.	BG
HEIGHT2	The height of the Item Description pane in the Gallery.	G
WIDTH2	The width of the Item Description pane in the Gallery.	G
WINDOWSTAT	0—Window is zoomed normal; 1—Window is minimized; 2—Window is maximized.	BG

Field	Description	Used by (B)rowser (G)allery
PROTECTED	True if protected members are to be displayed in the right-hand Browser pane.	B
EMPTY	True if empty methods are to be displayed in the right-hand Browser pane.	B
HIDDEN	True if hidden members are to be displayed in the right-hand Browser pane.	B
DESCBOXES	True if description panels are to be displayed.	BG
AUTOEXPAND	True if hierarchical items are to be displayed automatically expanded in the left-hand pane.	BG
PUSHPIN	True if the display is always on top.	BG
PCBROWSER	Parent class toolbar flag. If true for a file item, the toolbar is on for that file. If you close the parent class toolbar, this field is set to .F. for all open VCXs.	B
VIEWMODE	Indicates whether the Items pane of the Gallery displays large icons, small icons, or a list.	G
FONTINFO	Stores the display font preference.	BG
FORMCOUNT	Used internally by the Browser to track the number of Browser instances where this record's class library is being displayed.	G
UPDATED	The datetime this record was last updated.	BG
COMMENT	A comment field for your use.	BG
USER1,2,3,4	Not used; there for your use.	BG

Additional Component Gallery Data Structures

Here's a brief overview of Gallery-specific structures. The Gallery distributes its metadata in several locations.

Like the Browser, the Gallery keeps some of its metadata in Browser.DBF (described above). That data stores references to the available catalogs, as well as some properties such as whether the catalog is global (auto-open and always in view) or default (in the default view). Delete a Gallery catalog record from Browser.DBF and it won't appear in the Gallery Open dialog. The Gallery catalog records in Browser.DBF contain ".dbf" in their Name field. Since this field is of type memo, you can't easily identify Gallery records in a simple browse of Browser.DBF—what a pain.

The rest of the Gallery metadata is stored in VfpGlry.DBF, which lives in the Gallery subdirectory below the VFP root. VfpGlry.DBF defines the default display and behavior of the Gallery. When you look at the Gallery, you are looking at catalogs whose items are defined in the particular catalog tables, but whose default behavior emanates from definitions in VfpGlry.DBF.

In fact, delete all Gallery records from Browser.DBF and the Gallery will re-initialize the root catalog from data in VfpGlry.DBF.

Many of the records in VfpGlry.DBF point to behavior classes stored in VfpGlry.VCX through fields named ClassLib and ClassName. Thus the records in VfpGlry.DBF are pointers to the behavior classes that, in the case of the native VFP-supplied behaviors, live in VfpGlry.VCX. Of course, any custom gallery behavior you define or modify can live in any VCX you choose. In fact, if you define custom Gallery behavior classes or modify existing ones, we suggest that you keep these in a different class library so that future upgrades of VFP don't clobber your work.

To illustrate some of the functionality of VfpGlry.DBF, Table 5-3 examines some of the fields in a representative record—the one with ID = "fileitem".

Table 5-3: Some of the fields in VfpGlry.DBF for the "fileitem" record.

Field	Value	Meaning
TYPE	"CLASS"	The Type field indicates what type of record this is. You'll surely be stunned to find out that "FOLDER" types are folders. The others aren't quite as obvious. "CLASS" items define the metadata for the various types of things the Gallery can display. "ITEM" types define the native catalogs that ship with VFP. "OBJECT" types are objects attached to the Gallery when it's instanced.
ID	"fileitem"	The unique identifier for this type of item.
TEXT	"File"	The item display text.
TYPEDESC	"ITEM"	This field, used only for records with TYPE = "CLASS", indicates whether record represents a folder object or an item object.
DESC	Text	The text appearing in the Item Description pane.
PROPERTIES	File name:{},cFileName Parameters:{},cParams	Specification for input fields that appear in the Properties dialog for items of this type. Values inside the curly braces are used as the parameter in GETFILE() dialogs.
CLASSLIB	Vfpglry.vcx	The class library where the item's behavior class is stored.
CLASSNAME	_fileitem	The default class that embodies this catalog item.

Field	Value	Meaning
ITEMTPDESC	BMP=_imageitem ICO=_imageitem JPG=_imageitem GIF=_imageitem WAV=_sounditem RMI=_sounditem AVI=_videoitem DBF=_dataitem SCX=_formitem MNX=_menuitem FRX=_reportitem LBX=_reportitem PRG=_programitem APP=_sampleitem OCX=_activexitem HTM=_urlitem HTML=_urlitem PJX=_projectitem TXT=_programitem LOG=_programitem H=_programitem	Alternate classes to use for file items of these particular types.

Other records may use different fields and different values, but this representative record is enough to get you started in hacking the Gallery.

Catalog tables contain records that reference actual catalog items. The main native catalog is called "Visual FoxPro Catalog" and is kept in "VFP Catalog.DBF." All VFP foundation classes, for example, are cataloged there.

The structure of catalog tables is the same as that of VfpGlry.DBF, so much of what we've already seen also applies here. This is a good opportunity to look at a few other metadata fields and how they work. Table 5-4 shows the record with ID = "clireg" in "ActiveX Catalog.DBF." This item allows you to register a custom VFP Automation server remotely using its generated VBR file.

Table 5-4: The "clireg" record in ActiveX Catalog.DBF.

Field	Value	Meaning
TYPE	"ITEM"	This is an item, not a folder.
ID	"clireg"	This item's ID.
PARENT	"actxtools"	ID of the parent catalog record; in this case, it corresponds to a folder named "Tools".
DESC	"This tool allows you to register a custom VFP automation server remotely using the generated VBR file."	The Description window text.
PROPERTIES	cDblClick=<>	You can override the events (KeyPress, Click, DblClick, RightClick) by setting the c[EventName] property. If it's something like cDblClick=DO Foo.PRG, then double-clicking on the item in the Gallery runs that line. If you set cDblClick=<testscript>, then double-clicking runs the code in the Script memo field of the record with ID= "testscript". If you set cDblClick=<>, double-clicking runs the code in the Script memo field of the current record. In this case, DblClick runs the code in the Script field below.

Field	Value	Meaning
FILENAME	(HOME(6) + "CLIREG\CLIREG32.EXE")	The file name to execute when the item is double-clicked. This value is stored in the oThis.cFileName reference, which you can use in scripts. See the Script field below. Note that the whole behavior of this item is defined by the Filename field and, in this case, also the Script field. The ClassName and ClassLib fields are blank in this record.

SCRIPT	<pre>cVBRFile = GETFILE("VBR")
	cCliReg = oThis.cFileName
	
	IF !FILE(m.cCliReg)
	  RETURN .F.
	ENDIF
	
	IF EMPTY(m.cVBRFile) OR ;
	UPPER(JUSTEXT(m.cVBRFile))#;
	"VBR"
	  RETURN .F.
	ENDIF
	oThis.Runcode([RUN /N] + ;
	[&cCliReg. "&cVBRFile."] + ;
	[-NOLOGO])</pre>
		The Script field gives you control over what happens when the user runs the item. Here this scripting code will run when the user double-clicks (see the Property field) items of this type in the Gallery.
		
		Note that, at present, there is no script equivalent of DODEFAULT() so if you script an event, the default behavior for that event will not execute.

Please Sir, I Want Some More

We've just scratched the surface of the Browser and Gallery. If you're interested in finding out more about these powerful and extensible tools, we recommend *Advanced Object Oriented Programming With Visual FoxPro 6.0* by Markus Egger, also available from Hentzenwerke Publishing (www.hentzenwerke.com).

Builders and Wizards (and Bears, Oh My!)

Visual FoxPro comes with things called builders and wizards. Other Microsoft products, like Access for example, are bundled with only wizards. The difference? Mostly parlance. Builders and wizards are very similar. The difference depends on which part of the development process you're working on.

Here's how Microsoft defines wizards:

> Visual FoxPro ships with several wizards. Wizards are interactive programs that help you quickly accomplish common tasks such as creating forms, formatting reports, setting up queries, importing and upsizing data, graphing, creating mail merge output, generating pivot tables, creating crosstab reports, and publishing in HTML format for the Web.

> By answering questions or choosing options on the series of wizard screens, you are telling the wizard to build a file or perform a task based on your responses.

> —VFP Help, under "Wizards, overview"

And builders:

> Builders are tools that aid in setting properties of controls on a form. Unlike wizards, builders are reentrant, so you can reopen a builder on a particular control repeatedly.

> Visual FoxPro includes a number of generic builders for many of the common form controls including grids, list boxes, combo boxes, check boxes, command groups, and option groups.

> —VFP Help, under "Builders, introduction"

The party line at Microsoft is that builders and wizards are dialogs in which the user answers questions or makes selections, and then chooses "OK". This is coincidentally commensurate with the FoxPro skills of most of Microsoft's field sales staff. Builders and wizards make whizzy demos! Nobody reading this book begrudges that, right?

And the hacker's view of all this? The native builders and wizards are automated development mechanisms that exploit Visual FoxPro's open architecture. They are extensible, which means we can supplement or substitute our own builders and wizards. This implies that builders and wizards could be much more than (to paraphrase) "friendly dialogs to help bewildered users set properties." Builders and wizards, emblematic of Visual FoxPro's open architecture, represent a huge opportunity for automated development, be it dialog-based or not.

So here is a wider, more developer-centric definition: A builder is any tool that helps us construct software. This includes native and custom wizards, native and custom builders, and any process that automates building and maintaining software.

So, given all this, what's the distinction between builders and wizards? They are, in fact, incarnations of the same basic mechanisms, and they have much in common. Here are some simple rules of thumb:

- A builder is any mechanism used to construct software.

- A wizard is a builder that starts a construction task.

In other words, a wizard is a special form of builder. If it gets you started on something, you can call it a wizard. Otherwise, it's a builder.

And forget all that nonsense in the help file about the need for dialog boxes and "setting propertics." That's ridiculously myopic. Builders are programs, interactive or not, that audit, beautify, construct, document, edit, format, generate, hide, iterate, join, kludge, look up, measure, name, open, peek and poke, quantify, resize, style, test, undo, verify, warn, x-reference, nothing that begins with "y," zip, and zap.

What's notable is this: Support for custom tools like builders is built into the language, and furthermore, their proliferation is encouraged by the product's developers. Hacking FoxPro has come of age. Moreover, starting with VFP 6, the source code for the wizards and builders is included in the Tools\xSource\VfpSource subdirectory below your root VFP installation (after you unzip xSource.ZIP in Tools\xSource).

Builders

One of the best things about Visual FoxPro is the way the Class and Form designers interact with the development environment. All Visual FoxPro base classes are endowed with both design-time and run-time manifestations, each with distinct programming interfaces.

If you place a control on a form while in design mode, you are actually running an instance of that class—one that has been hobbled to not run events. So unlike prior versions of FoxPro, what you see is the real enchilada, and not just a graphical image (or proxy) of the control. This means that custom programs (builders), written in FoxPro, can manipulate our design-time work.

To convince yourself of this, place any subclass on a form, and then try to modify the subclass definition. It cannot be done—you get error 1948: "Cannot modify a class that is in use." The form instance has a lock on the class even though you're only in design mode.

How Builders are Engineered in VFP

Visual FoxPro gives us access to extend and configure many of its mechanisms, including builders and wizards. In this section, we'll look at how the builder and wizard mechanisms are engineered to allow for our access.

The _BUILDER System Memory Variable

Like _GENMENU, _BROWSER and the others, _BUILDER is a system memory variable used to specify a builder application. You may, as always, substitute your own builder manager for the native Builder.APP. The value of _BUILDER defaults to HOME()+"Wizards\Builder.APP". You can set the default _BUILDER to anything you want in the "File Locations" page of the Tools | Options dialog or by editing your Config.FPW file, or you can change it temporarily in the Command Window or a program.

The Builder.APP Builder Manager Program

The Builder.APP program that comes with Visual FoxPro isn't a builder, but a builder manager. Its function is to take stock of the situation, save the environment, invoke the appropriate builder program, clean up, and return you cleanly back to FoxPro.

Invoking Builders

There are three standard hooks for invoking builders from within FoxPro:

- Builder Lock on the Form Controls toolbar

- On the Forms page of the Options dialog, check the Builder Lock check box

- The "Builder" option on the Form and Class Designer context menus

These mechanisms are readily available whenever the Form Designer or Class Designer is active. Of course, since our definition of "builder" is much wider than Microsoft's, how can we invoke a builder when the Form and Class designers are not active?

Three ways:

- Manual invocation from the Command Window.

- From our own custom toolbars—equivalent to manual invocation, only easier.

- By drag and drop to _SCREEN from the Class Browser or the Component Gallery.

Invoking builders from custom toolbars is a good approach. Calling builders from within click events of toolbar controls is easy to set up. A nice variant: Create a _SCREEN.Timer as a voyeur class that reacts to the activation and deactivation of the Form Designer by showing and hiding the appropriate toolbars, including your builder toolbar.

Browser drag and drop builders are created by placing builder code in the Init method of builder classes stored in VCX or SCX structures, with the Init ultimately returning .F. so no object is created. Presto: To run a builder, drag its class from the Class Browser or Component Gallery to the desktop. The Init code fires (which runs the builder) and returns False. A variant: Several builders can be combined into a container. Here the builder elements execute in Z-order.

The Builder.DBF Registry Table

The builder registration table, Builder.DBF, lives in the HOME()+"Wizards" directory. VFP's Builder.APP checks this table for builders of a particular type. If more than one record of the same type is present, a picklist dialog is presented to you. Otherwise the program specified in the Program field is invoked without fanfare.

Builder.APP does not provide services for registering and unregistering builders. You must maintain registration records interactively.

Tip: Using the Form Wizard, create a Builder.DBF viewer, and then register it as a Type="ALL" builder. You can then use any convenient builder hook to manage the behavior of Builder.APP. For more details, see "Registering Builders" below.

The structure of Builder.DBF is the same as Wizard.DBF, which lets you register wizards.

Field Name	Type	Description
Name	C(45)	Name of the builder. This appears in the picklist displayed by the standard Builder.APP when there's more than one builder for this class of object.
Descript	M	Long description for the builder. This is also displayed by the standard Builder.APP when there is more than one builder for this class of object.
Bitmap	M	Not currently used by builders.
Type	C(20)	Contains a keyword, such as a FoxPro base class name, "ALL", or some other moniker that identifies the type of builder or the context in which it is to be called.
Program	M	The program to invoke.
ClassLib	M	The class library that contains the builder (if in a VCX).
ClassName	M	Name of the class of the builder.
Parms	M	Parameters to pass to the program.

Builder.APP contains a copy of the original Builder.DBF table, so if you accidentally erase this table, it's re-created the next time you run a builder.

Registering Builders

Visual FoxPro's native Builder.APP program relies on the Builder.DBF table that lives in the VFP Wizards directory. To register a builder, add a record to this table. The native Builder.APP offers no help for maintaining Builder.DBF.

The following steps show an easy way to give a registration interface to Builder.APP:

1. Use the Form Wizard to create a form to converse with Builder.DBF. Register this form as a builder. You'll need a wrapper program for this because Builder.APP can't call an SCX directly. Here is the wrapper:

```
* BLDRUTIL.PRG
PARAMETERS X, Y, Z
DO FORM BUILDER.SCX
```

2. Create the following record in Builder.DBF:

Name	Builder.DBF Maintenance
Descript	Edit Builder.DBF
Type	ALL
Program	Bldrutil.PRG

Now you can converse with Builder.DBF just by launching Builder.APP, because the "ALL" builder type is, as you might expect, universal. Whenever you click a Builder button or choose Builder from the right-click menu, Builder.DBF Maintenance appears as one of the choices.

Doug has a neat trick to self-register builders. Use the following code as a template for your main builder program.

```
LPARAMETERS uP1, uP2, uP3, uP4, uP5, uP6, ;
            uP7, uP8, uP9, uP10, uP11, uP12
* Accept parameters passed by the builder system.

#DEFINE ccMAIN "MYGREATBUILDER"   && This is what you've named the
                                  && builder PRG.

LOCAL nOldSelect

* Self-register if called directly.
IF PROGRAM(0) == ccMAIN
    nOldSelect = SELECT()
    SELECT 0
    USE HOME() + "Wizards\Builder" AGAIN
    LOCATE FOR Name = "My Great Builder"
    IF NOT FOUND()
        m.Name = "My Great Builder"
        m.Descript = "<describe My Great Builder>"
        m.Type = "ALL"
        m.Program = SYS(16)
        INSERT INTO Builder FROM MEMVAR
    ENDIF

    USE IN Builder
    SELECT (nOldSelect)
ENDIF
```

```
* Run the actual builder.
DO FORM ADDBS(JUSTPATH(SYS(16))) + "MyGreatBuilder" WITH ;
    uP1, uP2, uP3, uP4, uP5, uP6, ;
    uP7, uP8, uP9, uP10, uP11, uP12

RETURN
```

When you call this builder code directly, it goes through the process to register it. (Do make sure you change the name and description strings in the code to describe what your builder does.) Once registered, it runs the builder. If this program is not called directly, it skips the registration process and runs the builder.

"Builder" Custom Property

If you add a Builder property to your class, Builder.APP recognizes it and invokes the builder specified there. This means you can assign a specific builder to work with the objects you create from classes.

If the builder program specified by the object's Builder property is missing or invalid, Builder.APP generates a friendly warning, and then the usual Builder.APP program executes, which is as graceful a recovery as one could expect.

One disadvantage of using a Builder property: Builder.APP executes this builder without ever presenting a picklist of other registered builders that may apply. The Builder property is interpreted by Builder.APP as an exclusive builder, which is regrettable.

Native Builders

At the time of this writing, Visual FoxPro lists the following builders in Builder.DBF:

Builder	Description
Application Builder	Sets properties specific to an application built by the Application Wizard (see "Wizards in VFP 7" later in this section). These properties include those for splash screens, About dialogs, visual styles, production credits, and files (tables, reports, forms) needed for the application.

Builder	Description
AutoFormat Builder	Applies a style to selected controls on a form. There are two entries for this builder: The entry with type "multiselect" is used when the builder is invoked with multiple objects selected, while the entry with type "autoformat" responds to the AutoFormat button on the Form Designer toolbar.
Combo Box Builder	Sets properties for a combo box control.
Command Group Builder	Sets properties for buttons in a command group.
Edit Box Builder	Sets properties for an edit box control.
Form Builder	Adds controls to a form using fields and a style the user specifies.
Grid Builder	Sets properties for a grid control.
List Box Builder	Sets properties for a list box control.
Option Group Builder	Sets properties for buttons in an option group.
Referential Integrity Builder	Creates triggers and stored procedures that enforce referential integrity between tables in your database.
Text Box Builder	Sets properties for a text box control.

How Builder.APP Handles Multiple Selections

Builders can act on multiple objects as selected in the Form or Class designers. The ASelObj() function can be used to populate an array with object references. The sequence of preselection is irrelevant, and the array is sequenced in object Z-order.

The only native builder with multiple object capability is the AutoFormat Builder, which you see if you invoke FoxPro's standard Builder.APP while many objects are selected.

Parameters Passed to _BUILDER by VFP

VFP passes two parameters to the program designated by _BUILDER. The first parameter is an object reference to the selected object (see ASelObj() in the Reference section), and the second parameter varies according to how the builder was invoked, as in the following table:

Invocation	Second Parameter Passed from VFP to Builder
Builder Lock on the Form Controls toolbar	"TOOLBOX"
Right-click menu	"RTMOUSE"
Form Design Toolbar	"QFORM"
Manual invocation	Whatever you pass upon invocation

Parameters Passed to Builders by Builder.APP

If _BUILDER is set to Builder.APP, then Builder.APP passes three character type parameters to registered builders.

The first parameter is the string "wbReturnValue", which is puzzling unless you know the following: Sometimes Builder.APP or Wizard.APP needs to return a value to the calling routine. Fine, except that someone decided that builders and wizards should not be called as procedures or functions (something we do all the time!). "WbReturnValue" is the name of a memory variable created by Builder.APP and Wizard.APP that can be updated with the return value. In practice you'll probably never need to know this fact.

The second parameter is whatever is contained in the PARMS field of Wizard.DBF or Builder.DBF.

The third parameter is supposed to contain the keyword information that may have been passed into Builder.APP (see the table in the previous section), but actually contains the empty string.

So far, we've never needed to use the parameters passed to builders. ASelObj() can tell us everything we need to know.

Problems with Builder.APP

After working with Builder.APP for some time, we find ourselves working around it more than with it. Here are the things that really bug us about Builder.APP.

You cannot flexibly specify the Type of the builder in the Registry. You are limited to a base class name, "ALL", "MULTISELECT", "RI", or "AUTOFORMAT".

When selecting several items of the same type, say three text boxes, Builder.APP doesn't present a selection of builders for the selected class (in this case, text boxes), but instead invokes the AutoFormat builder. This is somewhat understandable—it's highly unlikely that one would want to set the same data properties for several text boxes on a form. Who's to say, however, that a given builder sets only data properties?

What Custom Builders Can Do

Builders Can Set Properties

According to the help file, setting properties is the primary function of builders. Maybe so for the native Visual FoxPro builders, but that's just the beginning.

Builders Can Add Objects

Builders can add objects to container classes (such as Forms, Pageframes, Containers, and so forth). For example, executing the following code adds a label named lblHello and a command button named cmdQuit to a form in the Form Designer session:

```
*-- You can execute this builder from the
*-- Command Window without touching _BUILDER
*-- or BUILDER.DBF.
*-- Start a Form Designer session.
MODI FORM Junk NOWAIT

*-- Find the parent container, in this case the form.
=ASELOBJ( laObjectArray, 1)

*-- Add a label named lblHello.
laObjectArray[1].AddObject( "lblHello", "Label")

*-- Add a command button named cmdQuit.
laObjectArray[1].AddObject( "cmdQuit", "Commandbutton")
```

```
*-- Set some properties.
WITH laObjectArray[1].lblHello
  .Caption= "Hello"
  .Top= 10
ENDWITH
WITH laObjectArray[1].cmdQuit
  .Caption= "Quit"
  .Top= 100
ENDWITH
```

Builders Can Load Array Members

A weakness in the Form Designer and Class Designer interfaces is that array member properties cannot be changed in the Property Sheet. Builders, on the other hand, can change the contents of array member properties.

Builders Can Add Custom Members

Starting with VFP 6, you can use the AddProperty() method to add new custom properties to any object in the Form Designer or Class Designer. However, until VFP 7, custom methods could only be added to forms in the Form Designer, and to the "outermost" class in the Class Designer. To add a custom method programmatically, you needed to use KEYBOARD commands to open the appropriate menu item and to fill the New Method dialog. It wasn't pretty but it worked. For example, with a form open in the Form Designer, run the following program to add a method named FooFoo3, add a description, and close the New Method dialog.

```
*-- Open the New Method dialog.
KEYBOARD "{f10}cm"
*-- Input the new method name.
KEYBOARD "FooFoo3"
*-- Navigate to, and fill, the description field.
KEYBOARD( "{Tab}{Tab}FooFoo description")
*-- Hit the Add button.
KEYBOARD( "{Tab}{enter}")
*-- Navigate to, and select, the Close button.
KEYBOARD( "{Tab}{Tab}{Tab}{Tab}{Enter}")
```

Thankfully, the guys in Redmond gave us a better way to add custom methods in VFP 7. The WriteMethod method accepts another parameter to optionally create the method if it doesn't exist.

Builders Can Manipulate the Data Environment

You can create a DataEnvironment reference (and access the Cursor and Relation objects therein) by using 2 as the second parameter in ASELOBJ(). For example:

```
*-- Start the Form Designer. This will do.
MODIFY FORM JUNK NOWAIT
*-- Store the DataEnvironment reference in MyArray[1].
=ASELOBJ( MyArray, 2)
? MyArray[1].Baseclass     && "Dataenvironment"
```

Builders Can "Drill Down" to Members Inside Container Classes

Drill-down builders act on an object and, if the object is a container, act on the objects that may be contained therein. Implication: Forget the notion that builders should work only on selected objects.

Visual FoxPro comes with a handy SetAll method for setting properties (see "Globally Set Properties of Many Objects Using SetAll" below), but there are times when you need better control than SetAll can give.

Drill-downs are useful when we need to affect everything, at whatever the level, in a container. For example, a builder that changes the font size on all objects in a form could ignore the selected objects and work directly with the form and all its contents. A builder that enforces standards and guidelines might be expected to audit an entire form, and wouldn't be limited to what controls happened to be selected.

There are a variety of ways to structure a drill-down, all of which employ one or more of the following steps:

1. Find the parent container (if required).

2. Process the container (if required).

3. Process every object in the container.

4. Repeat steps 2 and 3 as required.

In some cases, you'll want to switch steps 2 and 3, so that you drill down to the bottom first, then operate on the containers on the way out. You'd do that when the builder needs information from the contained objects to process the container.

For example, here is a trick-or-treat builder that makes everything in a container a random color. Note the variant: If an object isn't selected (perhaps the builder is invoked from the Command Window), the builder acts on everything.

```
*************************************************************
* Colormix.PRG
* Demonstrates a drill-down builder.
*
* Danger: This will randomly change colors
*         in the Form Designer.
*
* Also an example of using recursion in builders.
*
*
PARAMETERS oSource, cOther
  LOCAL i
  LOCAL ARRAY laSelObj[1]

  * ////////////////////////////////////////////
  * Your recurring builder code goes here in this block.
  *-- If there's a Forecolor property, change it randomly.
  IF TYPE("oSource.ForeColor") <> "U"
    oSource.ForeColor= RAND() * 256^3-1
  ENDIF
  *-- If there's a Backcolor property...
  IF TYPE("oSource.BackColor") <> "U"
    oSource.BackColor= RAND() * 256^3-1
  ENDIF
  * End of your code
  * \\\\\\\\\\\\\\\\\\\\\\\\\\\\\\\\\\\\\\\\\\\\\

  * Are we in a container and, more to the point,
  * are there any objects inside?
  IF ( AMEMBERS( laSelObj, oSource, 2) > 0)
    FOR EACH oObject in oSource

      *-- Recursion hook.
      =colormix( oObject )
    ENDFOR
  ENDIF
RETURN
```

Referential Integrity (RI) Builder ... and Future Wrappers

Unconvinced of the power of builders? Then note that Referential Integrity in Visual FoxPro is enforced by code written by a builder. Not too shabby for power, we'd say. To convince yourself of this, invoke and run the RI Builder from the Database Designer (DD) with a right-mouse click. Then look at the Stored Procedures, also available through a right-mouse click on the DD. All that delineated code was written by the RI Builder (see the "WriteExpression" and "WriteMethod" topics below).

This means that, among other things, if you don't like FoxPro's implementation of Referential Integrity, you can put a wrapper around the current RI Builder, or even create your own. For example, Doug has created a replacement for the RI Builder that doesn't give an error if the database hasn't been packed, doesn't ask if you're sure you want to save your changes (why would you click OK if you didn't want to save?), and fixes a few bugs in the generated code. You can download the source code for his builder from the Technical Papers page at www.stonefield.com.

When multiple copies of a function are found in the same FoxPro source file, the last one gets executed. This means that you can append code to the RI code in the Stored Procedures, and your versions of duplicated functions will execute.

Query Property Expressions with ReadExpression

ReadExpression is a method that returns the expression stored in a property. To write expressions to properties, use WriteExpression.

Example

```
CREATE FORM SYS(3) NOWAIT
=ASELOBJ( aForm, 1)
oForm=aForm[1]

oForm.Caption= "Form Title"
? oForm.Caption                        && "Form Title"
? oForm.ReadExpression("Caption")&& ""--Take Note!

oForm.Caption= CDOW(DATE())
? oForm.Caption                        && "Monday"
? oForm.ReadExpression("Caption")&& ""--Take Note!

oForm.WriteExpression("Caption", "=CDOW( DATE())")
? oForm.Caption                        && "Monday"--Take Note!
? oForm.ReadExpression("Caption")&& "=CDOW( DATE()+1)" ;
  + CHR(0)
```

As shown, it's possible to store an expression to a property and have ReadExpression return blank. This is not a bug. When we say:

```
oForm[1].Caption= CDOW(DATE())
```

we are storing the *value* of CDOW(DATE()) to the Caption property. To store an *expression* to a property, use WriteExpression. Conversely, to determine whether a property is set by value or by an expression, test ReadExpression—if blank, the property was set by value explicitly.

Read Method Code with ReadMethod

ReadMethod is a method that returns method code as text. Use ReadMethod to grab the code (if any) in an object code snippet. All the code in the specified method is returned as a string with embedded character returns, tabs, comments, and whatever else is in the method code.

Reset Events and Methods to Default

When the cursor is on the Properties section of the Property Sheet, the context menu contains, among other things, a "Reset to Default" pad that restores the ParentClass's properties, events, and methods. To reset events and methods to default programmatically, use the ResetToDefault method.

Save a VCX-based Form or FormSet with SaveAs

SaveAs is a design-time and run-time function that saves a VCX-based form or form set as an SCX file. (The form or form set you're saving can be either an SCX or a VCX, but it has to have started out visually, not in code.) You could use the SaveAs method to store all the PEMs associated with an object to another SCX file. Also, you can use CreateObject() to create an object or even a whole form, customize it from the Command Window, and use SaveAs to programmatically save it for future use.

Create New Classes with SaveAsClass

SaveAsClass is a design-time and run-time method that saves any VCX/SCX-based class in a class library.

Here's an interesting thing about SaveAsClass: As long as the class is VCX-based, programmatic class transformations can happen and SaveAsClass will work downstream. This is useful for importing classes developed in code into a VCX. That is, if you subclass a VCX-based class in code, you can still apply SaveAsClass to instances of your subclass.

Example

```
*-- Create a VCX-Based form class called MyForm
Foo= CREATEOBJECT("Form")
Foo.SaveAsClass("MyClasses","MyForm")
*-- MyForm is now VCX-based.

SET CLASSLIB TO MyClasses
*-- A code grandchild of MyForm
Foo= CREATEOBJECT("MyExpandDialogForm")

*-- Create a VCX of the grandchild.
Foo.SaveAsClass("MyClasses","MyExpandedDialogForm")
```

```
*-- SUPPORTING CLASSES
*-- Code transformation, creating a code class
*-- from MyForm VCX class.
DEFINE CLASS MyDialogForm as MyForm
  Width    = 200
  Height   = 200
  Caption  = "Dialog Form"
  BackColor= RGB(192, 192, 192)
ENDDEFINE

*-- Subsequent transformation, creating a code class
*-- from another code class.
DEFINE CLASS MyExpandDialogForm as MyDialogform
  Width    = 400
ENDDEFINE
```

Globally Set Properties of Many Objects with SetAll

The SetAll method sets a property for all, or a certain class of, controls in a Container object.

The following code makes all the current form's pageframe pages use green ink:

```
_SCREEN.ActiveForm.SetAll('ForeColor', RGB(0,255,0), 'Page')
```

Very useful and powerful! See also the "Drilling Down" topic.

A bummer: If you issue SetAll for a user-defined class (that is, not a base class) that isn't instantiated or doesn't otherwise exist, VFP generates error 1733, "Class definition ClassName not found." Curiously, the error doesn't appear if you use SetAll on a base class with no instances. So you'll need to trap the error if you use SetAll for custom classes.

Write Property Expressions with WriteExpression

WriteExpression is a method to write expressions to properties. This function is not as straightforward as is seems because of the special way expressions are stored. VFP expects the expression as a stream of characters preceded by "=". For example, to place the current date expression in a button's Caption, do as follows:

```
*-- WriteExpression() Example
*-- Places a date expression inside a command button.

*-- Start the Form Designer. This will do.
MODI FORM Junk91 NOWAIT

*-- Find the parent container of the selected object.
=ASELOBJ( laObjectArray, 1)
```

```
*-- Add a command button.
laObjectArray[1].ADDOBJECT( "Command1", "CommandButton")

*-- Take Note!  VFP expects "=".
laObjectArray[1].Command1.WriteExpression( "Caption","=DTOC(DATE())")
```

See "Query Property Expressions With ReadExpression" above for more on this.

Write Code to Methods with WriteMethod

WriteMethod is a design-time-only method that writes the specified text to the specified method. Strange as it seems at first, use WriteMethod to concatenate strings to build method code at design time. Use CHR(13) wherever you need a new line; it's good practice to use CHR(13) at the beginning and end of the streams to avoid unexpected line concatenations. VFP 7 adds a new parameter that optionally allows you to create a method if it doesn't exist.

This program appends code to the Form.Click event to bring forth a "Hello World" message:

```
* AppendClick.PRG
* Skeleton builder demonstrating
* adding "Hello World" to Form.Click.
PARAMETERS toPassedObject, tcContextString
LOCAL loForm, lcMessage

*-- Create the Hello World code.
*-- Begin and end with a CR for safety's sake.
lcMessage= CHR(13)+ ;
          "=MESSAGEBOX('Hello World')"+ ;
          CHR(13)
*-- Locate the Form object.
loForm= toPassedObject
DO WHILE loForm.Baseclass <> "Form"
  loForm= loForm.Parent
ENDDO

*-- Append the 'Hello World' code to any existing code
*-- in the Click method.
loForm.WriteMethod( "Click", ;
                   loForm.ReadMethod("Click") + lcMessage)
```

Create a Builder Framework

Ken Levy has created a framework for builders, called BuilderD, that is an excellent demonstration of how a little preparation in the design of your base classes can be leveraged with the builder technology.

What Builders Cannot Do

Just as in interactive Visual FoxPro, there are a number of things you can't do with builders. Here is one of them.

Builders Cannot Modify Certain Properties

Everything you can do interactively from the Command Window is possible with builders. You cannot use builders to modify the following properties.

Class hierarchy properties, including BaseClass, Class, ClassLibrary, OLEClass, and ParentClass, can't be modified using builders. To change an object's class, you need to either substitute a new object with the correct pedigree, or close the Form Designer or Class Designer and then open and change the underlying SCX. There's no way to reconfigure class pointers of in-situ objects because they are full-blown, live objects, even when seemingly just displayed by the design tools.

Properties of collections such as Buttons, Columns, Controls, Forms, Objects and Pages cannot be modified at design time. The collection sequence is a function of the Z-order, and the collection length is determined by the number of instantiated objects.

Collection Count properties, like ControlCount, FormCount and ListCount, are read-only and determined by the number of objects present.

These program-status properties have no tangible meaning at design time and cannot be set by builders: ActiveColumn, ActiveForm, ActiveRow, ActiveControl, Docked, DockPosition, FormIndex, ItemData, ItemIdData, List, ListIndex, ListItem, ListItemId, RelativeColumn, RelativeRow, Selected, SelLength, SelStart, SelText, TopIndex, and TopItemId.

Wizards

In Visual FoxPro, a wizard is a program that begins a task and produces output that serves as a basis for further customization; it helps with a common task you might perform when creating an application. To see some of the wizards provided with Visual FoxPro, select the Wizards option from the Tools menu.

The _WIZARD System Memory Variable

Like the _BUILDER system memory variable, _WIZARD points to the wizard management application. By default, this application is called Wizard.APP and lives in the VFP HOME() directory. You can substitute your own wizard-management program by changing this system memory variable.

The Wizard.APP Wizard Manager Program

Wizard.APP isn't a wizard, it's a wizard invoker. Unlike the native builders, which are completely bound inside Builder.APP, the wizards have many customizable features. The customizable elements are stored in the WizStyle.VCX class library.

Invoking Wizards

There are a number of places in Visual FoxPro where you can easily invoke a wizard. Many of the wizards can be invoked from the File | New dialog in the main menu. Similarly, in the Project Manager, the New button leads to wizards for many types of files.

A wizard can be called programmatically using a call like:

```
DO (_WIZARD) WITH 'FORM'
```

Wizard.APP looks for wizard types that match the parameter passed. If you choose to design your own wizards, you can pass a number of additional parameters, which Wizard.APP will pass along for you.

The Wizard.DBF Metadata Table

The wizard registration table, Wizard.DBF, lives in HOME()+"WIZARDS" directory. This structure is the same as that of Builder.DBF, and the registration workings for Wizard.APP are similar to those of Builder.APP. So to add your own wizard program, simply add a new record to the table. Like Builder.APP, Wizard.APP contains a copy of the original Wizard.DBF table, so if you accidentally erase this table it will be re-created.

Wizards In VFP 7

Here's a list of the wizards that come with VFP 7:

Wizard	Description
Application Wizard	Creates a Visual FoxPro application using the Visual FoxPro application framework and foundation classes.
Cross-Tab	Creates a new cross-tab table based on existing data.

Wizard	Description
Database Wizard	Creates a new database containing the tables and views you specify.
Documenting	Documents and formats FoxPro source files.
Form	Creates a form based on a single table.
Graph	Creates a new graph using MS Graph.
Import	Imports a file in a foreign format to a FoxPro table.
Label	Creates a mailing-label report based on predefined styles.
Local View	Creates a view using local data.
Mail Merge	Creates a Word mail-merge document based on FoxPro data.
One-To-Many Form	Creates a one-to-many form with a grid control for the child table.
One-To-Many Report	Creates a one-to-many report.
Oracle Upsizing Wizard	Creates an Oracle version of a Visual FoxPro database.
Pivot Table	Creates an Excel pivot table based on FoxPro data.
Query	Creates a standard query.
Remote View	Creates a view using remote data.
Report	Creates a report based on a single table.
SQL Server Upsizing Wizard	Creates a SQL Server version of a Visual FoxPro database.

Wizard	Description
Table	Creates a new table.
Web Publishing Wizard	Publishes Visual FoxPro data to the Web.
Web Services Publisher Wizard	Creates and registers Web Services for a VFP COM component.

Wizards are, by their nature, mostly self-explanatory. That's helpful because there is little documentation provided for Visual FoxPro's wizards. However, not only is the source code provided but the class structures are public, which gives us a simpler way to customize and extend certain aspects of wizard behavior than modifying code.

Parameters Passed to _WIZARD by VFP

In most cases, VFP passes a single parameter to _WIZARD: a string to look up in the TYPE field of Wizard.DBF. If the wizard is invoked from the Project Manager, three parameters are passed: a string to look up in the TYPE field of Wizard.DBF, a string of length zero, and the string "NOTASK". The "NOTASK" string is probably used internally by VFP to aid in updating the Project Manager.

Parameters Passed to Wizards by Wizard.APP

Visual FoxPro's native Wizard.APP passes nine parameters to its wizards.

Parameter1: Reference to a variable containing the name of the wizard-generated file. This memory variable gets passed back to VFP when the wizard is finished so other resources, like the Project Manager, can be refreshed upon return from a wizard launched there.

Parameter2: The contents of the Parms field in the wizard registration table.

Parameter3 – Parameter9: Extra parameters passed to Wizard.APP. They're optional parameters that aren't used by the wizards included with VFP, but can be used by your custom wizards.

Implications for wizard writers:

- Your wizards must provide a nine-element PARAMETER statement to handle the call from Wizard.APP.

- The first parameter is useful only if you want to have the wizard output reflected in the Project Manager, and if the wizard emanates from the Wizard button on the New dialog in the Project Manager.

Extending the Form Wizard

The FrmStyle.DBF table and the WizStyle.VCX class library are the hooks we use to extend the Form Wizard. In this section, we'll look at undocumented features of the native Form Wizards.

The FrmStyle.DBF Styles Registry Table

The native Form Wizard offers a number of visual styles with names like "Standard", "Embossed" and "Chiseled". It also gives us the ability to choose between button styles like "Text Buttons" and "Picture Buttons". This style information is stored in FrmStyle.DBF; the actual style classes are stored in the WizStyle.VCX class library.

You can't find FrmStyle.DBF, you say? That's because it isn't there! The Form Wizard has an internal version of this table. The Form Wizard (WZFORM.APP) attempts to locate a FrmStyle.DBF when it is launched. If none is found, it uses its own internal version of the styles table.

Here are the steps to hack your own version of FrmStyle.DBF:

1. Set the default directory to HOME()+"Wizards"

2. Start the Form Wizard with DO WZFORM.APP—this trick won't work otherwise.

3. From the Program menu, choose "Suspend".

4. In the Command Window, execute the following commands:
   ```
   SELECT FormStyles
   COPY TO HOME()+"Wizards\FrmStyle"
   ```

Voila! You now have a copy of FrmStyle.DBF, correctly placed in your Wizards directory, and from here on, the Form Wizard will use this table for its styles. (At this point a real hacker would try other things, like LIST OBJECT, LIST MEMORY, and other commands to reckon how the wizards are engineered.)

The structure of FrmStyle.DBF is:

Field Name	Data Type	Width	Description
StyleName	Char	20	Name of style class (must be Form).
VCXFile	Memo	10	VCX file name where style class exists.
StyleDesc	Char	30	Description for wizard listbox.
StyleType	Char	1	Type of style.
Wizard	Logical	1	Is this used by wizards?
OneMany	Logical	1	Is this used by One-To-Many Wizard?
Builder	Logical	1	Is this used by builders?
BMPFile	Memo	10	BMP file name for wizard visual style.
PreMethod	Char	20	Method to call before style generation.
PostMethod	Char	20	Method to call after style generation.

The StyleType field describes the styles used by the Form Wizard. Visual styles all have a StyleType = 'V' for visual. The StyleType for the three button styles that come with the Form Wizard is '1', '2', or '3'. You can provide your own button-style references using a StyleType = 'B' (for Button). Use the TxtBtns class in WizStyle.VCX as your guide to creating your own button styles.

The Form Wizard automatically consults the WizStyle.VCX class library. Therefore, this is a good place to add your own custom styles. If you decide to use your own VCX, you need to specify that in the VCXFile field. Make sure to include a path so the Form Wizard can locate it.

The WizStyle.VCX Class Library

All the native styles used by the Form Wizard are stored in the WizStyle.VCX library. Feel free to edit these styles or add your own. Better still, subclass those that are already there. Don't forget to back up your work *before* you muck around in here. The open architecture of WizStyle.VCX offers as many pitfalls as benefits, so beware.

A modification we recommend is to interactively change WizStyle.VCX to point the items based directly on base classes to use subclasses instead. This will make forms created with the Form Wizard more maintainable.

Creating Form Wizard Styles

The Form Wizard uses actual forms as visual prototypes to specify layout attributes. The native prototype forms are subclasses of the BaseForm class in WizStyle.VCX.

The process for creating your own form styles is as follows:

1. Create your own custom style by subclassing BaseForm or one of its subclasses (for example, EmbossedForm) in WizStyle.VCX. This new form can be saved to WIZSTYLE or another class library of your choosing. We start with BaseForm or its subclasses because they contain all the custom properties required by WIZARD.APP.

2. Modify the LayoutSty object on the form to provide the configuration you want. The LayoutSty object is a container of shapes that controls the horizontal and vertical spacing of objects as they are laid out on the form. This is the "prototype" referred to earlier. See Figure 5-17 for an interpretation of the layout determinants. This figure shows the default styles, shapes and sizes for most of the objects to be placed upon the generated form. Your custom form title can be based upon the style and positioning of the default label. Three shapes are added to the body of the form to specify the styles and horizontal and vertical placement of objects on the form.

3. Create and register data type classes. Each visual form style specifies a set of classes used for adding fields based on data type. For example, a class containing an edit box is used for Memo fields. Logical fields use check boxes, and so on. Once you have created a set of your data classes, they need to be registered under specific custom properties of the form style.

4. Finally, register this new style in FrmStyle.DBF so the Form Wizard can display a reference to it in its selection dialogs.

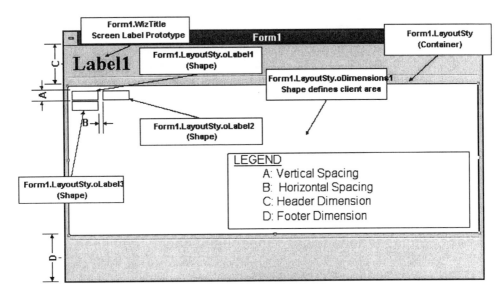

Figure 5-17: Spacing in Wizard forms is determined by the LayoutSty object.

Rules for Creating Form Wizard Styles

Here are guidelines for creating new Form Wizard styles:

- Derive your form style from the BaseForm form class. Why? BaseForm contains the properties needed by the wizard.

- Be aware that your event code (Init, Load, Activate, Deactivate, Destroy) can interfere with code placed there by the Form Wizard, which could cause puzzling errors. Since we don't have the source to the Form Wizard, there isn't much we can do but keep this in mind and hope for the best.

- A form uses an object derived from the LayoutSty class to provide dimensional information for field layout. There are four shapes and custom properties in the LayoutSty container class:

  - The LayoutSty.oLabel1 property contains a reference to the object in LayoutSty, representing the starting position for the field layout.

  - The LayoutSty.oLabel2 property contains an object reference and represents the vertical spacing between fields (difference between oLabel1 and oLabel2).

- The LayoutSty.oCol2 property is used with LayoutSty.oLabel1 to determine the column width. The Form Wizard attempts to lay out fields vertically if it can fit all of the fields on the form; otherwise, it reverts to laying them out horizontally in columns based on the column width derived from this property.

- The LayoutSty.oDimensions property references the shape representing the physical boundary on which fields can be laid out.

BaseForm and its subclasses have a number of custom properties which let you specify the classes to be used for your style and other characteristics of the style:

- The form can stretch to the Maximum Design area setting in your Options dialog if the WizFormStretch property on the form is set (.T.). Only this portion of the form stretches. The header and footer remained fixed in height. The Form Wizard supports only vertical stretching.

- The LayoutSty class included in WizStyle.VCX is referenced by the WizLayout custom property on your form. Your form must have this property set to a valid layout class such as LayoutSty.

- The Form.WizField property contains a reference to a class having a normal text box used for fields with character, number and date data types. Similarly, the Form.WizMemo property points to an edit box class, and so on. The Form.WizLogic property is optional—without this class reference, the Form Wizard defaults to using the Form.WizField class.

- Style objects can come from singular or composite classes. Singular classes (such as Standard and Embossed) consist of a single control like a text box. The label style that accompanies singular style classes is specified by the form's WizLabel property.

- You can place a number of objects inside a container to form a composite style class. Composite style classes are used by styles like Shadow to create special effects. Each container must have a label and a data control (such as a text box). Because the label is stored in the container, the object specified by the form's WizLabel property is ignored.

- You cannot mix singular and composite classes in a visual style.

- When the wizard places an object on the form, its width is based on the underlying table field or caption width.

The WizShape class that is stored in WIZSTYLE should be used for prototyping container objects for composite classes. Put a box based on WizShape around the label/control combination. WizShape has a custom property called WizEffect that controls stretching (see Table 5-5).

Table 5-5: The WizEffect property takes these values to control stretching.

Value	Description
0	Stretch and move with field—commonly used for adding a special effect to just the data-bound control. For example, see the Shadow style.
1	Stretch with label/field—causes stretching for vertically oriented objects as in the Boxed style.
2	Stretch over all—commonly used to place a flexible border shape around both label and field.

The BaseForm class has a number of wizard-related properties that control the behavior of forms based on it (see Table 5-6).

Table 5-6: Custom properties contained in the BaseForm class.

Property	Type	Description
WizBtnLayout	Character	By default, the Form Wizard centers buttons in the footer area. You can place them elsewhere by including an object (such as a shape) on the form style and referencing it through this property. When the Form Wizard places the buttons, it will do so at the object position. Use this in conjunction with WizBtnPos.
WizBtnPos	0	Do not center buttons. By default, buttons are centered in the footer.
	1	Center buttons horizontally.
	2	Center buttons vertically.
	3	Center buttons both vertically and horizontally.

Property	Type	Description
WizBuffering	1	No buffering.
	2	Pessimistic record buffering.
	3	Optimistic record buffering.
	4	Pessimistic table buffering.
	5	Optimistic table buffering.
WizButtons	Character	Name of button class. You can override the button style chosen by the user in the wizard by including a reference to a class containing buttons (or anything else). Use this in conjunction with WizBtnPos for positioning.
WizCaptions	.T.	Automatically use DBC field captions.
	.F.	Do not automatically use DBC field captions.
WizCBoxLbl	Character	Controls which object is used for check box labels. If you are using the WizLogic class, which contains a check box, you can choose to use the check box caption or that of the label object (for example, WizLabel).
WizCodeStyle	.T.	Buttons are automatically added to the form.
	.F.	Buttons are not automatically added to the form.
WizField	Character	Text box class reference for character, numeric and date fields.
WizFormStretch	.T.	Allow the form height to shrink or expand based on the number of fields selected.
	.F.	Do not allow the form to stretch to accommodate more fields.
WizGrid	Character	Name of class for a Grid (1-Many).

Property	Type	Description
WizGridForm	Logical	Use a separate form for Grid.
WizLabel	Character	Name of class for label object.
WizLayout	Character	Name of class for layout object.
WizLblCap	"Proper", "Upper", "Lower"	Label capitalization.
WizLblDefWid	L	Controls whether each label is sized with a fixed width or whether all labels are autosized. For right-aligned labels, set this option .T. so the fields align evenly.
WizLblSpace	Numeric	Space between label and field.
WizLblSuffix	Character	Suffix that can be added to each field label.
WizLogic	Character	Name of class for a logical field (optional—if not used default to WizField).
WizMaxCharFld	Numeric	Maximum width of character type field before converting it to memo (edit box) style.
WizMemo	Character	Name of class for a Memo field.
WizOLE	Character	Name of class for a general field.
WizTitle	Character	Name of class for title (usually a label).
WizUser	Any	For use by user.
WizVerify	Logical	Indicates whether to verify that class objects exist (use for testing but can improve performance if turned off).

If you follow these guidelines of style creation, then you've got all the flexibility you need to make the Form Wizard create forms just as you like them. In the end, it is easiest to just subclass an existing style and modify the subclass to suit.

The builders and wizards supplied by Microsoft do indeed simply set some properties or present a series of dialogs to complete a task. But the underlying technologies these tools demonstrate—an ability to manipulate the design-time environment through the use of flexible, modifiable and extensible programs—give FoxPro developers a rich environment in which to build powerful, complex applications. The Wizard and Builder techniques are ones you should consider for any large development task.

IntelliSense and Sensibility

> We live less and less, and we learn more and more. Sensibility is surrendering to intelligence.
>
> Rémy De Gourmont, *Le Chemin de Velours*

Visual FoxPro developers have long had VB-envy, at least with regard to one particular feature: IntelliSense. Type a statement such as "Dim SomeVariable As" in Visual Basic and a list immediately pops up of all of the types a variable can be defined as—data types as well as objects. Type "SomeObject." and you're presented with a list of the properties, events and methods for that object. This feature is a great productivity booster for several reasons: You can quickly pick the item you want from the list, it avoids spelling mistakes, and it cuts down on trips to the Help file to figure out the syntax for a little-used command.

VFP 7 cures our inferiority complex by adding IntelliSense to our beloved tool, and makes up for the long wait by providing a better version of IntelliSense than Microsoft's other products have (in fact, the VFP team has been showing their cool version to the other product teams). Once you start appreciating how much more productive IntelliSense makes you, you'll wonder how you ever coded without it.

IntelliSense provides VFP developers with several very useful behaviors: automatic keyword completion, command and function syntax tips, and lists of members, values, and most recently used files.

You Complete Me

Xbase descendents have always supported two ways to enter commands and functions: using the full, official keyword (such as BROWSE) or using the first four or more characters (such as BROW). However, veteran developers will tell you that while it's fine to use "REPL" in the Command Window, you really should use the full "REPLACE" in code for clarity.

IntelliSense gives us the best of both worlds: You can now type just enough of a keyword to make it distinct, and then press the spacebar or Enter in the case of a command or "(" in the case of a function, and IntelliSense completes the keyword for you. Type "modi" and press the spacebar, and IntelliSense replaces it with "MODIFY". Because some keywords start with the same set of characters, you have to type enough to distinguish the keyword from similar ones. For example, for MESSAGEBOX(), you can't just type "mess("; that gets expanded to "MESSAGE(".

Some commands, such as ALTER TABLE, REPORT FORM, and OPEN DATABASE, consist of more than one keyword. Since the first keyword must always be followed by the second, VFP automatically adds that keyword as well. Until we got used to it, we found ourselves typing "OPEN DATABASE DATABASE MyData" because we didn't notice that VFP automatically inserted "DATABASE" as soon as we pressed the spacebar after typing "open." Thank goodness, old dogs *can* learn new tricks.

VFP has a long list of SET commands, some of which you don't use very often. IntelliSense helps out when you type "set" and press the spacebar by displaying a list of each of the keywords that can follow it, such as "deleted" and "exact." Some commands include the word "to", such as SET CLASSLIB TO. As you'll see in "I Love IntelliSense, Now Let's Change It" when we discuss the IntelliSense Manager, you can tell IntelliSense whether it should automatically insert the "to" or not (but we suggest you let it insert "to" and get used to it).

By default, VFP uses uppercase when it expands keywords, so even if you type the entire word "modify", VFP replaces it with "MODIFY". Fortunately for those who prefer lowercase (like Doug) or even "camel" case (such as "TableUpdate()"), you can control the case IntelliSense uses through the IntelliSense Manager (which we'll discuss later in the section "I Love IntelliSense, Now Let's Change It").

To prevent IntelliSense from expanding a keyword, you can press Ctrl+Space rather than the spacebar at the end of the keyword. We haven't come across a need to do that yet. To undo an expansion (which we have done), press Ctrl+Z twice. The first Ctrl+Z removes the replacement and the second restores the original keyword, leaving it selected.

You Call That a Tip?

Our favorite IntelliSense feature is Quick Info. This feature is a tip window showing the complete syntax of the command or function you're in the process of typing. What a great productivity booster! How many times do you find yourself bringing up the VFP Help file (or HackFox.CHM) because you can't quite remember the exact syntax for ALTER TABLE or whether the string to search is the first or second parameter in AT()? Figure 5-18 shows the Quick Info tip for the REPLACE command.

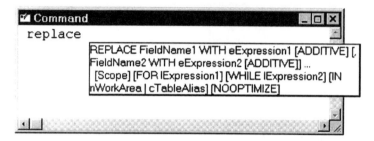

Figure 5-18: Quick Info saves you a trip to the Help file by displaying the complete syntax for commands and functions.

The tip window remains visible as you continue to type the rest of a command or enter the parameters of a function, method, or event, disappearing only when you move the cursor out of the scope of the keyword (for example, completing a function with ")", pressing the spacebar, moving to another line, or moving the cursor with the arrow keys). You can manually hide the tip window by pressing Esc and manually display it with Ctrl+I or the Edit | Quick Info menu item. It's especially useful for functions, methods and events because the parameter you're currently typing appears in bold.

With some functions, the tip window displays information about the values for a specific parameter. For example, the second parameter for MESSAGEBOX() is an additive value for the buttons and an icon for the dialog. IntelliSense makes it easy to figure out which ones to use by showing the complete list of valid values for this parameter (see Figure 5-19). Other functions accept only one of a list of predefined values for some parameters. For instance, the second parameter in DBGETPROP() specifies the type of data object (connection, database, field, table, or view); the list of values for the third parameter, the property, varies with the type of object (for example, DefaultValue is available only for fields). For the type parameter, IntelliSense displays a list of the object types; choose the desired type from the list and IntelliSense inserts it, complete with quotes, in the command line. The list of values displayed for the property parameter includes only those applicable to the selected type; again, you can choose the property from the list to add it to the command line.

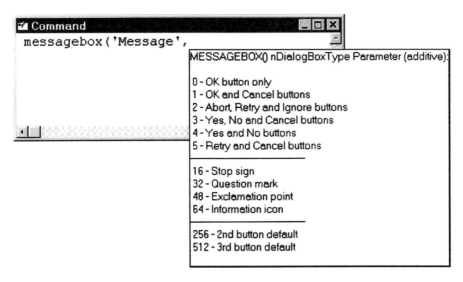

Figure 5-19: The tip window for some functions shows detailed information about the current parameter.

The SYS() function is treated even more specially. Although it's only one keyword, it really consists of a large number of functions, with the specific function determined by the first parameter. IntelliSense displays a list for this parameter showing not only the numeric values but also the meaning for each one. Once you've selected the one you want, the tip window shows the appropriate syntax for the rest of the function call.

Members Only

We're not sure what we were thinking when we said earlier that Quick Info was our favorite IntelliSense feature. Our favorite feature is really List Members, because it does more to save us typing than any other. When you enter the name of an object and press ".", VFP displays a list of all members (properties, methods, events and contained members) of the object. Figure 5-20 shows an example of this feature. As you navigate through the list, a tip window shows the description of each member, once again saving you a trip to the Help file.

To add the selected member's name to the command line, press Tab (the cursor appears right after the member name), Enter (the cursor moves to the next line), or some non-alphabetical character such as Space, ".", "=", or "(" (the character is added at the end of the member name). Press Home, End, Esc, or move the cursor out of the scope of the object to hide the list. You can manually display the list by pressing Ctrl+J or choosing List Members from the Edit menu.

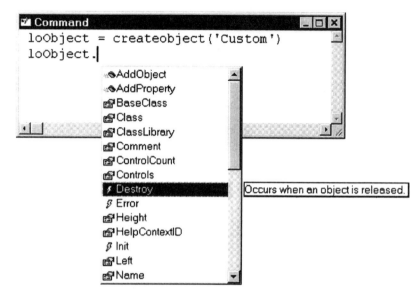

Figure 5-20: IntelliSense's List Members feature displays the members of an object.

If you like List Members so far, you'll love this: It works in object hierarchies, too. Imagine how much you'd have to type to programmatically change the caption of the header in the third column of a grid on page 2 of a page frame in a form:

```
Thisform.PageFrame1.Page2.Grid.Column2.Header.Caption = "some value"
```

Oops, the name of the grid is actually grdCustomers, so when you run this code, it'll bomb. List Members saves you from both making a spelling mistake and having to type all that code; after you type the period following Thisform, you can select PageFrame1 from the member list and press "." to display the member list for the page frame, choose Page2 and press "." to display the member list for that page, and so on, until finally you choose Caption for the header and press "=" to close the list.

List Members doesn't just work with native VFP objects; it works with any instantiated object, such as an ActiveX control you've added to a form or a COM object you've instantiated with CREATEOBJECT(). It even works with objects you haven't instantiated yet but have declared your intention to do so with the new AS clause in the LOCAL and PUBLIC commands. For example, suppose you add this to your code:

```
LOCAL loExcel AS Excel.Application
```

In the rest of the code, when you type loExcel followed by a period, IntelliSense sees that the variable has been "typed" as an Excel.Application class, gets the members for that class by reading its type library, and displays them in the List Members list.

The AS clause doesn't instantiate the object; you still have to do that in code. It just tells IntelliSense how to treat a variable in the editor.

This feature works for any kind of class VFP can instantiate, native or COM. After you type the AS keyword and press the spacebar, a list of types appears. This list includes VFP data types (such as Integer and Numeric), base classes (including Form and Custom), registered type libraries (for example, ADODB and Excel), your own classes, and Web Services. As with many things in VFP, the list of registered types is defined in a table, so you can add type libraries, classes, Web Services, and other types by using the IntelliSense Manager, discussed later.

He's Making a List And Checking It Twice

Some object properties accept only a small range of values. Properties with logical values, such as Form.AutoCenter, can only be set to .T. or .F. Form.BorderStyle is numeric, but can accept only one of a selected list of values (0 to 3). IntelliSense makes it easy to select the correct value for properties like these. When you type "=" after certain property names, IntelliSense displays a list of the valid values for those properties (and their meanings, in the case of numeric values).

For properties with more complex values, IntelliSense displays an appropriate dialog, such as a color picker for properties representing colors (such as BackColor, FillColor, and ForeColor) and an Open Picture dialog for properties containing image file names (such as Icon and Picture, although strangely enough, not for DragIcon, MouseIcon and OLEDragPicture).

As with the List Members feature, List Values supports COM objects as well as native ones. IntelliSense displays a list of values for those properties with enumerations defined in the type library, such an ADO Recordset object's CursorLocation and LockType properties.

IntelliSense extends the values list for the REPLACE, MODIFY MEMO and MODIFY GENERAL commands: If a cursor is open in the current work area, it displays a list of fields in that cursor. A value tip window shows the data type, size, caption and comment for the selected field. In addition, if you type "m." in the Command Window, IntelliSense displays a list of declared variables. The value tip for each variable shows its current value. Unfortunately, these features work only in the Command Window, not in an editor window. Of course, you can always cut and paste from the Command Window into your code, as you find yourself really loving how much work IntelliSense can do for you.

The List Values feature doesn't have its own menu item or hotkey; the List Members item and hotkey (Ctrl+J) serve the same function.

What Have You Done For Me Lately?

Some VFP commands open or process files. Examples include all the MODIFY commands (such as MODIFY PROGRAM), OPEN DATABASE, and REPORT FORM. IntelliSense presents a most recently used (MRU) list for these commands, making it easy to use a file you previously worked with. Figure 5-21 shows this feature with the OPEN DATABASE command. You also get an MRU list of directories with the CD command, which is really handy for those of us who hop back and forth between different projects. The USE command has an MRU list on steroids: In addition to tables you've opened before, it lists the tables and views in the current database, along with a value tip window showing the comment for the selected table or view. The "Auto MRU (Most Recently Used) Files" topic in the VFP Help file has a complete list of commands with MRU lists.

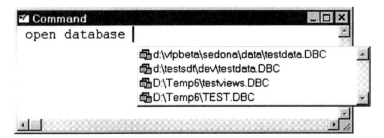

Figure 5-21: The MRU list displayed by IntelliSense makes it easy to select a file you used before.

For reasons that escape us, this feature works only in the Command Window. This is a shame, because when you're working on a particular project, you're likely to use OPEN DATABASE or USE in your code on the same set of files over and over.

You can specify how many items IntelliSense displays by setting the "Most Recently Used list contains" option in the View page of the Tools | Options dialog.

I Love IntelliSense, Now Let's Change It

If you prefer that keywords appear in something other than uppercase, you'll be frustrated typing them in your desired case only to see VFP automatically change them to uppercase when it expands them. Similarly, you might prefer to type the "to" yourself in a command, such as SET CLASSLIB TO rather than inadvertently put in duplicates (SET CLASSLIB TO TO) because you didn't notice that VFP inserted it for you. (In the latter case, we recommend you get over it. It's just another habit you need to break.)

Fortunately, IntelliSense is data-driven. Most of its settings are stored in a table, the name and path of which are stored in the _FoxCode system variable. The default is FoxCode.DBF in your VFP "user" folder (something like C:\Documents and Settings\YourName\Application Data\Microsoft\Visual FoxPro).

The IntelliSense Manager, available in the Tools menu, allows you to configure the behavior of IntelliSense. It has several pages of settings. You can specify how the List Members, Quick Info, and keyword expansion features work (such as what case to use when IntelliSense expands keywords), or even disable IntelliSense altogether (although we can't imagine why you'd want to do that) in the General page. The Types page allows you to define the types listed for the AS clause of a LOCAL, PUBLIC, LPARAMETERS, PARAMETERS, FUNCTION, or PROCEDURE declaration. By default, this list includes VFP data types and base classes, but you can add other things, such as your own classes, registered type libraries (for example, ADODB and Excel), and Web Services.

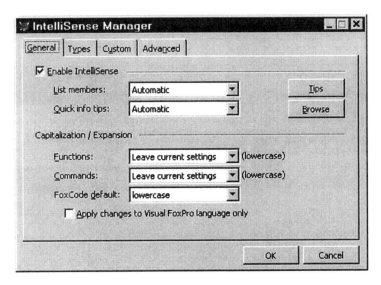

Figure 5-22: You can configure the behavior of IntelliSense using the IntelliSense Manager.

The Custom page allows you to define your own shortcuts. VFP comes with a few custom shortcuts already defined, such as "mc", which expands to MODIFY COMMAND, and "mf", which expands to MODIFY FILE. You can define your own shortcuts by entering the abbreviation to replace and the text to replace it with. For example, you might add "mp" to expand to MODIFY PROJECT, especially if you routinely work in multiple projects. You can even create more complicated shortcuts by entering code that should execute when you type the abbreviation. See the next section, "Please Sir, I Want Some More," for information on scripting shortcuts.

Clicking the Edit Properties button in the Advanced page displays a dialog in which you can fine-tune advanced IntelliSense behaviors, such as whether a second keyword (such as "TO") is included when SET commands are expanded, and whether the capitalization of keywords associated with a command (such as FROM and WHERE in the SQL SELECT command) matches the capitalization chosen for the command. Click the Cleanup button in the Advanced page to display a dialog allowing you to restore the default settings for all records in the FoxCode table (except the custom records you added), pack the table, remove MRU file entries that no longer exist, or remove all MRU entries.

Please Sir, I Want Some More

The IntelliSense Manager application, FoxCode.APP in the VFP home directory, is more than just a fancy way to configure IntelliSense. It's also the driving code for a lot of what IntelliSense does. A good portion of the code is in support of scripting. (In case you're wondering how we knew that, it's because we've actually gone through the code. Yes, the source code for the IntelliSense Manager comes with VFP!)

Scripting allows you to define more complicated shortcuts than simply expanding an abbreviation to some text. For example, "dc", which is one of the predefined shortcuts, expands to the following when it's entered in an editor window:

```
DEFINE CLASS classname AS Session OLEPUBLIC

PROCEDURE Init

ENDPROC

PROCEDURE Destroy

ENDPROC

PROCEDURE Error(nError, cMethod, nLine)

ENDPROC

ENDDEFINE
```

While that simply looks like a block of text, the interesting part is that "classname" is automatically selected so you can type the desired name of the class. That behavior requires some code. If you look at the record for this shortcut in the FoxCode table (look near the end of the table for a record with Abbrev = "dc"), you'll see the following code in the Data memo field:

```
LPARAMETERS oFoxcode

IF oFoxcode.Location #1
   RETURN "DC"
ENDIF

oFoxcode.valuetype = "V"

TEXT TO myvar TEXTMERGE NOSHOW
DEFINE CLASS ~classname~ AS Session OLEPUBLIC

PROCEDURE Init

ENDPROC

PROCEDURE Destroy

ENDPROC

PROCEDURE Error(nError, cMethod, nLine)

ENDPROC

ENDDEFINE

ENDTEXT

RETURN myvar
```

The first line in this code is an LPARAMETERS statement. All FoxCode script is passed a FoxCodeScript object. IntelliSense creates this object, filling its properties with information about the FoxCode record, what you typed, and the current environment (see the "FoxCode Object Reference" topic in the VFP Help file for a description of each property of this object). The "dc" script code checks the value of the Location property and simply returns "DC" if it isn't 1. Location indicates where you were typing when the shortcut was invoked; a value of 1 means the PRG editor. So, if you type this shortcut anywhere but in a PRG, nothing appears to happen, which makes sense, because that's the only logical place for a class definition. The return value, which must be a string, is actually ignored, so a blank string could have been returned with the same results.

Next, the code sets the ValueType property to "V". This property specifies what happens after the script code is done; "V" means IntelliSense replaces the shortcut with the return value of the code (since it wasn't set earlier, IntelliSense ignored the previous "DC" return value). The code then uses the Text command to place several lines of text (in this case, the class definition code) into a variable and returns that variable. Note the "~" characters surrounding "classname" in the text. A single "~" tells IntelliSense where to place the cursor after replacing the shortcut with the text (without a "~", it places the cursor at the end of the text), while two of them specify text to highlight. This makes it easy for you to complete the text by entering more information (such as the class name in this case). If you'd rather use something other than "~", set the CursorLocChar property of the passed object to the desired character.

You can do even more complex things in the script code for a shortcut. One of our favorite shortcuts inserts header comments at the start of a program, including the name of the PRG file and the author's name, email address, and company. None of this is hard-coded in the script, but is instead read dynamically from the editor window title and the Windows Registry.

To create this shortcut, choose IntelliSense Manager from the Tools menu, select the Custom page, type the abbreviation you want to use (such as "header") in the Replace text box, and click on the Add button to add the shortcut to the list. Click on the Script button to bring up an edit window for the shortcut's script code, and enter the following code:

```
LPARAMETERS toFoxCode
LOCAL lcReturn, lcTable
IF toFoxCode.Location <> 0
  toFoxCode.ValueType = 'V'
  lcReturn = GetText()
ENDIF
RETURN lcReturn

FUNCTION GetText
LOCAL loRegistry, lcKey, lcCompany, lnResult, ;
  lcContact, lcAccount, lcEmail, lcText
loRegistry = NEWOBJECT('Registry', ;
  home() + 'FFC\Registry.vcx')
lcKey      = IIF('NT' $ OS() or '5.0' $ OS(), ;
  'Software\Microsoft\Windows NT\CurrentVersion', ;
  'Software\Microsoft\Windows\CurrentVersion')
lnResult   = loRegistry.GetRegKey('RegisteredOrganization', ;
  @lcCompany, lcKey, -2147483646)
IF lnResult <> 0
  lcCompany = ''
ENDIF
lnResult = loRegistry.GetRegKey('RegisteredOwner', ;
  @lcContact, lcKey, -2147483646)
IF lnResult <> 0
  lcContact = ''
ENDIF
```

```
lcKey    = 'Software\Microsoft\Internet Account Manager'
lnResult = loRegistry.GetRegKey('Default Mail Account', ;
  @lcAccount, lcKey, -2147483647)
IF NOT EMPTY(lcAccount)
  lcKey    = lcKey + '\Accounts\' + lcAccount
  lnResult = loRegistry.GetRegKey('SMTP Email Address', ;
    @lcEmail, lcKey, -2147483647)
ENDIF
IF lnResult <> 0 OR EMPTY(lcEmail)
  lcEmail = ''
ELSE
  lcEmail = ', mailto:' + lcEmail
ENDIF
TEXT TO lcText TEXTMERGE NOSHOW
*=================================================================
* Program:        <<WONTOP()>>
* Purpose:        ~
* Author:         <<lcContact>><<lcEmail>>
* Copyright:      (c) <<YEAR(DATE())>> <<lcCompany>>
* Last revision:  <<DATE()>>
* Parameters:
* Returns:
* Environment in:
* Environment out:
*=================================================================

ENDTEXT
RETURN lcText
```

After entering this code, close the edit window and click OK to close the IntelliSense Manager.

Like the "dc" script, this code works only from a code editor, not the Command Window; it uses textmerge to create the text to replace the abbreviation in the command line; and, with the "~" character, it tells IntelliSense to put the cursor in the "Purpose" comment line after the expansion is complete. It has a couple of interesting wrinkles, though. First, it reads your name, company name, and email address from the Registry using the FoxPro Foundation Classes (FFC) Registry class so it can insert them into the header. Second, it uses WONTOP() to insert the name of the file being edited. As you can see, script code can be considerably more complex than simply outputting some text.

For information on how to create your own scripted shortcuts, see the "Using Scripting in FoxCode.dbf" topic in the VFP Help file.

Winding Up

IntelliSense is a wonderful addition to the VFP development environment. It helps you avoid spelling mistakes, boost your productivity, and cut down on trips to the Help file. IntelliSense alone is worth the upgrade cost to VFP 7. If you're like us, you'll find IntelliSense so compelling, you'll even find yourself firing up VFP 7 when you have to maintain VFP 6 applications!

Section 6: Back o' da Book

Great is the art of beginning, but greater the art is of ending;
Many a poem is marred by a superfluous verse.

Henry Wadsworth Longfellow

Here we are at the end of the book. But there are still a couple of things left to do.
"Resource File" is a list of resources: books, periodicals, people and products.
"What's in the Downloads" tells you what's available for download from this book.

Resource File

In this section we list many resources we think may be of benefit to you. These include books worth reading, either for their value as a reference or as food for thought. Following that list is a list of FoxPro 2.x books to aid in your understanding of "legacy" code and techniques. Included at the end is a list of other resources worth checking into. Finally, there are a number of other good book lists out there. A few good lists that include FoxPro books are at www.hentzenwerke.com/thestacks/zthestacks.htm, www.stevenblack.com/SBC%20Bookshelf.asp, and http://fox.wikis.com/wc.dll?Wiki~GoodBooks~softwareEng.

Suggested Reading

Akins, Marcia, Andy Kramek and Rick Schummer, *1001 Things You Wanted to Know About Visual FoxPro*, Hentzenwerke Publishing, 2000, ISBN 0-0655093-3-8. This volume picks up where the *Hacker's Guide* leaves off. It answers all those "How do I" questions, like "How do I create a splash screen?" or "How do I change the grid's display order?" A must-have for serious VFP developers.

Alciere, Rose Mary, *Creating Help for Windows™ Applications*, Wordware Publishing, Inc., 1995, ISBN 1-55622-448-6. A great introductory book on how Windows Help is made. Intended primarily for Windows 3.1, it even includes a chapter specifically aimed at making the Windows API function WinHelp() work with FoxPro for Windows 2.x! The API functions and basics of WinHelp still apply, should you choose WinHelp over HTML Help.

Brentnall, Savannah, *Object Orientation in Visual FoxPro,* Addison-Wesley, 1996, ISBN 0-20147-943-5. An excellent primer on the ideas of object-oriented programming and how they apply to Visual FoxPro. Introduction by Ken Levy—we didn't know he could write comments!

Booch, Grady, *Object Oriented Analysis & Design*, Benjamin Cummings, 1994, ISBN 0-8053-5340-2. One of the heavies of the industry on analysis and design issues. When you're done playing with all the new cool things in VFP and it's time to get back to work, here's one of the tomes to be studying.

Booth, Jim, and Steve Sawyer, *Effective Techniques for Application Developmentwith Visual FoxPro 6.0*, Hentzenwerke Publishing, 1998, ISBN 0-0655093-7-0. We think of this as the third volume in the "VFP How To" set. While the *Hacker's Guide* tells you how the language works, and *1001 Things* shows you how to accomplish specific tasks, *Effective Techniques* focuses on the bigger picture, looking at design issues and good programming practices.

Cooper, Alan, *About Face: The Essentials of User Interface Design*, IDG Books, 1995, ISBN 1-56884-322-4. This must-read book makes you think long and hard about how user interfaces work—not just the ones you write, but the ones you use every day. While you may not agree with everything Cooper suggests, you'll be forced to question your assumptions. Best of all, Cooper is a great writer.

Cooper, Alan, *The Inmates are Running the Asylum*, SAMS, 1999, ISBN 0-672-31649-8. Where *About Face* addresses user interfaces on a granular level, this gem looks at the overall design process and proposes a more rational way to design and implement user interfaces.

Egger, Markus, *Advanced Object Oriented Programming with Visual FoxPro*, Hentzenwerke Publishing, 1999, ISBN 0-0655093-8-9. This book covers so much ground, it's hard to believe it's only about 400 pages. It includes clear explanations of OOP concepts, the best documentation anywhere for the FoxPro Foundation Classes and the Component Gallery, an introduction to the Unified Modeling Language, and much, much more.

Gamma, Erich, Richard Helm, Ralph Johnson and John Vlissides, *Design Patterns: Elements of Reusable Object-Oriented Software,* Addison-Wesley, 1994, ISBN 0-20163-361-2. Often referred to as "The Gang of Four" or "Gamma and Helm" for short, this is *the* book that defined object design patterns and explained how to use them. Our good friend Alan Schwartz advises that, in order to really *get it,* consider reading the core text (about 70 pages) four times. The book contains a catalog of design patterns, explanation of their use, benefits, liabilities and great discussion. Design patterns are not so much "the latest thing" in programming, as much as they are a new vocabulary we can use to express what we have been doing all along.

Granor, Tamar, Doug Hennig and Kevin McNeish, *What's New in Visual FoxPro 7.0*, 2001, ISBN 1-930919-06-9. This is the first book you want to read if you're moving from VFP 6 to VFP 7. It covers all the new IDE, language and COM features in a compact format.

Granor, Tamar and Della Martin, *Microsoft Office Automation with Visual FoxPro*, Hentzenwerke Publishing, 2000, ISBN 0-0655093-0-3. This is the only book out there that addresses automation of Office from a VFP standpoint.

Hentzen, Whil, *The Fundamentals: Building Visual Studio Applications on a Visual FoxPro 6.0 Foundation*, Hentzenwerke Publishing, 1999, ISBN 0-0655093-5-4. The best starter book we know for new VFP developers and for those moving from older Xbase tools to VFP.

Humphrey, Watts, *Managing the Software Process,* Addison-Wesley, 1989, ISBN 0-201-18095-2. From one of the key players in the Software Engineering Institute at Carnegie Mellon University, this book (like most of his books) is worth a read. Watts and the SEI are at the cutting edge of real software engineering.

Jacobson, Ivar, *Object-Oriented Software Engineering*, Addison-Wesley, 1992, ISBN 0-201-54435-0. Some really cool stuff here. In-depth examination of Jacobson's own Objectory system, with good overviews of object-oriented analysis and design, and a comparison of several methodologies out there.

Johnson, Jeff, *GUI Bloopers: Don'ts and Do's for Software Developers and Web Designers*, Morgan Kaufmann Publishers, 2000, ISBN 1-55860-582-7. If Microsoft's user interface guideline documents are too dry for your taste, spend some time with this book. While he doesn't address the tiny details like how many pixels should separate controls, Johnson covers most of the fundamental errors that we all make in creating user interfaces.

Kirtland, Mary, *Designing Component-Based Applications*, Microsoft Press, 1999, ISBN 0-7356-0523-8. While all of the sample code in this book (and there's tons of it!) is either in VB or C++, the author does a great job explaining things like how COM works, what Windows DNA is, and what responsibilities the various layers of an n-tier application have.

KNOWware, *HTML Help in a Hurry™ Course Book,* available from KNOWware, (800) 566-9927 or www.kware.com, 1997. This was the first book available for HTML Help, and the KNOWware team, led by HTML Help MVP Mary Deaton, used the materials to teach Microsoft staff worldwide the basics of HTML Help. The course book is very short (38 pages), but a good basic start.

Maguire, Steve, *Debugging the Development Process: Practical Strategies for Staying Focused, Hitting Ship Dates, and Building Solid Teams,* Microsoft Press, 1994, ISBN 1-55615-650-2. The other "Steve M" from Microsoft has some excellent observations on the development process. Not only is this information applicable to our FoxPro development, but many of the examples give us insight into just what they are thinking at Microsoft.

McCarthy, Jim, and Denis Gilbert, *Dynamics of Software Development,* Microsoft Press, 1995, ISBN 1-55615-823-8. Another view inside Microsoft and another good volume on what is involved in software development.

McConnell, Steve, *Code Complete*, Microsoft Press, 1993, ISBN 1-55615-484-4. Written before the era of Visual FoxPro, this book nonetheless has tremendous relevance for those of us who need to produce long-lasting, reliable and robust code.

Steve explores the art and craft of programming, reflecting on the philosophical implications of many of the designs of coding. An awesome book.

McConnell, Steve, *Rapid Development,* Microsoft Press, 1996, ISBN 1-55615-900-5. Excellent material from a top-notch author on the trials and tribulations of software development. Includes a number of case studies and lists of pitfalls to avoid.

McConnell, Steve, *Software Project Survival Guide,* Microsoft Press, 1997, ISBN 1-57231-621-7. Steve can't stop writing and we can't stop reading! Yet another great book, with excellent supporting materials available on his Web site. A must read.

Microsoft Windows ??? Resource Kit, Microsoft Press—fill in the ??? yourself—"95," "98," "NT," "2000," etc., depending on your (and your clients') particular flavor(s) of Windows. Invaluable books (sometimes in more than one sense), these can be tremendous aids in troubleshooting problems with the underlying Windows system. They typically include manuals and disks with some handy utilities and reference materials. They are also available online in the MSDN library at http://msdn.microsoft.com.

MSDN—The Microsoft Developer's Network—a series of CDs released monthly. What you get depends on your level of participation. (Microsoft changes programs like these so often it makes our heads spin, so we won't even speculate on how many levels there are as you're reading this.) Regardless, you'll find a very large variety of information and software, including all kinds of Software Development Kits (SDKs), documentation for virtually any product you can think of, relevant KnowledgeBase articles, sample code, and tons of software, including versions of Windows, Office, VFP, etc., etc., etc. Having these disks is like carrying around the Microsoft Web site with you—an excellent resource when you need information fast, especially if you can't connect to the Web.

Norman, Donald, *The Design of Everyday Things*, Doubleday, 1988, ISBN 0-385-26774-6. Formerly published as the poorly selling *The Psychology of Everyday Things*, this book is a self-fulfilling example of the fact that books are judged by their covers and user interfaces by their utility. Excellent examples and discussions about why some designs work and others fail. Thought-provoking material for anyone who wants to write a system that others can use.

Plauger, P.J., *Programming on Purpose,* PTR Prentice Hall, 1993, ISBN 0-13-721-374-3. Author of the popular column of the same name in *Computer Language,* Plauger revises and expands some of his best columns into a wonderfully entertaining series of essays on the whys and wherefores of analysis, design and software engineering.

Roche, Ted, *Essential SourceSafe*, Hentzenwerke Publishing, 2001, ISBN 1-930919-05-0. The title says it all here. Ted's book tells you what you need to know to use Visual SourceSafe effectively.

Sessions, Roger, *COM and DCOM: Microsoft's Vision for Distributed Objects,* Wiley Computer Publishing, 1998, ISBN 0-471-19381-X. An excellent book to introduce the concepts of distributed computing using Microsoft's latest technologies. The author doesn't get bogged down in the details of Microsoft Transaction Server or Message Queue, but rather explains the use of these technologies at an understandable level.

Shneiderman, Ben, *Designing the User Interface*, Addison-Wesley, 1998, ISBN 0-201-69497-2. Shneiderman is one of the fathers of the science of Computer-Human Interaction. This book is the third edition of what was originally written as a college text. Like the original, it has plenty of advice, backed up with empirical research, on how to organize user interfaces.

Stahl, Rick, *Internet Applications with Visual FoxPro*, Hentzenwerke Publishing, 1999, ISBN 0-0655093-9-7. This book provides a great introduction to using the Internet with VFP applications, with VFP on both the client and server sides.

Taylor, David, *Object Oriented Technology: A Manager's Guide*, Servio-Addison-Wesley, ISBN 0-201-56358-4. OOP in 128 pages. An excellent overview of why anyone would want to OOPify their code. A good primer, a good start as the first book in your OOP-reading series, and a great book to hand to your boss when asked to justify OOPification.

TechNet—Similar to MSDN above, this is also a CD-based product available from Microsoft. TechNet seems to be more focused on the support professional than the developer, although we have found very good information on these discs as well. Published monthly. If your primary interests include support, the need for new drivers, and workarounds, this disc set can save you several hundred dollars as compared to the cost of MSDN.

Tognazzini, Bruce, *TOG on Interface*, Addison-Wesley, 1992, ISBN 0-201-60842-1. The man who made the Macintosh user interface the shining example it is writes on the many issues surrounding the human-computer interface in a fresh and engaging way. A book that's hard to put down. Very useful knowledge for user interface designers.

Tufte, Edward, *Visual Explanations,* 1998, ISBN 0-961-39212-6, *Envisioning Information*, 1990, ISBN 0-961-39211-8, and *The Visual Display of Quantitative Information*, 1983, ISBN 0-961-39214-2 —all from Graphics Press. Three of the most beautiful books we own. While not specifically aimed at computer graphics, these books can give you some great ideas about what makes a graph worth making, and common mistakes made in graphical presentations and how to avoid them. Applicable both for folks designing graphs and those designing graphical user interfaces.

Urwiler, Chuck, Gary DeWitt, Mike Levy and Leslie Koorhan, *Client-Server Applications with Visual FoxPro and SQL Server*, Hentzenwerke Publishing, 2000, ISBN 1-930919-01-8. A must-read for anyone accessing SQL Server data from VFP applications. It discusses upsizing VFP data to SQL Server, accessing data, distributing database changes, and many other critical topics.

Wexler, Steve, *Official Microsoft HTML Help Authoring Kit,* Microsoft Press, 1998, ISBN 1-57231-603-9. Steve Wexler is a principal in WexTech Systems, Inc., makers of Doc-To-Help, and has been in the help business for quite some time. He writes well and expresses the complexities of HTML Help in an understandable fashion. Written between versions 1.0 and 1.2, there may be some items out of date, but overall, you can pick up a lot from the book.

Winegarden, Cindy, and Evan Delay, *Visual FoxPro Certification Exams Study Guide*, Hentzenwerke Publishing, 2001, ISBN 1-930919-04-2. This book (which Tamar edited) is the only study guide available for the VFP certification exams. It's structured to take you through the various exam goals. While this is not the book for learning VFP, it's a great way to check out your higher-level knowledge.

Yourdan, Edward, *The Decline and Fall of the American Programmer*, Yourdan Press (Prentice Hall), 1993, ISBN 0-13-191958-X. A sweeping survey of the entire software industry, with some very intriguing observations and predictions. Worth the read for anyone considering a career in the industry over the next few decades. Yourdan has a follow-up book, *Rise and Resurrection,* that we haven't gotten around to reading yet, so don't give up hope!

FoxPro 2.x Resources

In a number of places in the book, we refer to the "2.x way of doing things" or the "Xbase way" and refer you here. These are, in our opinions, some of the finest books written on those languages, and serve as a great reference to understanding the many aspects of the product which continue to be supported, unchanged, in the 3.x series, as well as those which have undergone radical transformations.

You'll find that most, if not all, of these books are now out of print. If you need one of them, we suggest you visit one of the forums (listed below) and post a message asking to buy someone's old copy. You can also try Amazon.com and the other online bookstores to see if they have any used copies to offer.

Adams, Pat, and Jordan Powell, *FoxPro Windows Advanced Multi-User Developer's Handbook*, Brady, 1994, ISBN 1-56686-100-4. The authority on multi-user issues, and the tuning and configuration of workstations for optimal performance. Also includes the enormous FPWeror.PRG, a great error-handler for 2.x systems.

Griver, Y. Alan, *The FoxPro 2.6 CodeBook*, Sybex, 1994, ISBN 0-7821-1551-9. We suspect more applications out there are based on this framework than on any other. A simple, straightforward but elegant solution to many of the problems of application development posed by version 2.x.

Hawkins, John, *FoxPro 2.5 Programmer's Reference*, Que, 1993, ISBN 1-56529-210-3. An encyclopedia of FoxPro 2.x commands, this book was (innovatively, we think) organized into more than 40 chapters by separating the commands and functions into logical groups. A great resource when you run into unfamiliar commands or unusual needs.

Slater, Lisa, and Steven Arnott, *Using FoxPro 2.5 for Windows*, Que, 1993, ISBN 1-56529-002-X. When we were asked for the best way to do something, we often found ourselves reaching for this well-worn tome and invoking, "Well, Lisa says...". (Sorry, Steve.) One of the best tutorials around, with remarkable depth as well.

Slater, Lisa, with J. Randolph Brown, Andy Griebel and John R. Livingston, *FoxPro MAChete: Hacking FoxPro*, Hayden Books, 1994, ISBN 1-56830-034-4. This book was our best introduction to the world of the Mac. Three separate chapters introduce FoxPro folk to the Mac, FoxBase/Mac people to FoxPro, and non-Fox, Mac users to FoxPro. The rest of the book focuses on a rapid application development approach that's appropriate for all versions of FoxPro 2.x and the Mac-specific aspects of FoxPro 2.x.

Other Resources

Magazines

All of the magazines below have very good material. The focus of each magazine is a little different, and their editorial style changes over time. We recommend you order a copy or two of each (or get them from the newsstand) and choose the periodical that's right for you. (Just to come clean, Tamar is a technical editor and columnist for *FoxPro Advisor*. Doug is a regular columnist in *FoxTalk*, and our publisher, Whil Hentzen, is the editor.)

CoDe, published by EPS Software Corporation, 13810 Champion Forest Dr., Houston, TX 77069. (281) 866-7444. http://www.code-magazine.com

FoxPro Advisor, published by Advisor Publications, Inc., 4010 Morena Blvd., P.O. Box 17902, San Diego, CA, 92177. (800) 336-6060 in the U.S., (619) 483-6400. http://www.advisor.com

FoxTalk, published by Pinnacle Publishing, 1503 Johnson Ferry Rd. #100, Marietta, GA, 30062. (800) 788-1900, (770) 565-1763. http://www.pinpub.com

Online Resources

CompuServe is far and away our favorite online service for FoxPro technical support. This is no doubt due, at least in part, to the fact that once Fox Software and later, Microsoft, provided their official online presence here. Questions are answered both rapidly and accurately by peer support as well, often in a matter of hours (sometimes even minutes). Hundreds of files containing helpful hints, cool programming tricks, utilities and workarounds are available in the libraries on the forums. Forum messages are archived and available for download. Best of all, forum access is available for free from the Web (though we still prefer our offline readers): http://go.compuserve.com/msdevapps.

The most active FoxPro site is the Universal Thread: http://www.universalthread.com. This Web-based service features many of the forum basics: threading, private messages, and so on. Basic membership is free, and provides access to the basic features. Many people are attracted to the "Premier" memberships for some of the more advanced features, such as enhanced searching, message filtering and forwarding, display options, and more. Premier members also have access to the UT's Web Service, which allows you to read messages programmatically. At the time of this writing, the Web Service is read-only, with no way to post new messages.

The official Microsoft site for VFP is http://msdn.microsoft.com/vfoxpro. Lots of good links and information available nowhere else. Make sure to register your purchase of Visual FoxPro in order to get access to the Owner's Area.

Microsoft also has its hand in http://www.foxcentral.net, created and maintained by Rick Strahl. This site is a clearinghouse for VFP news. It's also available as a Web service, so you can talk to its data programmatically and create your own front end, if you prefer.

Microsoft also operates newsgroups for VFP at microsoft.public.fox.*. Additional newsgroups are found at comp.database.xbase.fox.

If you like listserves, check out the ProFox list. You can sign up at http://www.leafe.com/mailListMaint.html. There's a Web service available for this list, too.

One of the most innovative sites for VFP is the FoxPro Wiki, which is a growing knowledge base: http://fox.wikis.com. It consists of thousands of articles written and edited by the members. If you think something is wrong or could use more information, just edit the document on the fly. Volunteers come along periodically to clean up, so that the site maintains its document (rather than discussion-based) form. The Wiki is yet another VFP Web site that has a corresponding Web service.

A search for "Visual FoxPro" turns up dozens, if not hundreds, more sites, many of them maintained by VFP developers. Since the speed of change on the Web is much faster than the speed of publishing, we won't list any more. Instead, we recommend you spend some time looking for sites that fit your needs.

User Groups, Conferences and Professional Associations

Ted has been involved with user groups for more than 10 years in the positions of founder, president, newsletter editor, bulletin board system operator, master of ceremonies, and flunky, sometimes all at the same time. The rest of us have been saner in our active participation, but all agree that user groups are an excellent opportunity to meet people of similar interests, seek support for vexing problems, share your knowledge, see some of the new innovations, and make contacts that can lead to employment or consulting contracts.

Finding a user group near you could make your life much better. Searching the FoxPro Wiki for "usergroup" (no space) turns up entries for a bunch of them. The Universal Thread has a User Group Meeting Tracker, currently available through the Tools items in its main menu. Microsoft also maintains a list through its Mindshare program (http://www.microsoft.com/mindshare), but this list often gets out of date.

Regardless of the lack of a single, consolidated list of groups, the good news is that after dwindling for a while, the number of FoxPro user groups has increased significantly in the past year, and we continue to hear about new groups forming and old groups being reborn.

Professional conferences are one of our favorite ways to get up to speed quickly. Despite the loss of billable hours as well as the costs of travel, lodging and the conference admission, we are certain that we make money by going to conferences. We meet potential clients, business partners (not to mention co-authors), employee candidates, and resources that advance our careers, at the same time as we learn from some of the most advanced members of our community. Taking an hour-long session from one of the "gurus" can save you weeks of painful trial-and-error research.

Several conferences take place each year. Microsoft has continued the tradition started by Fox Software of an (almost) annual Developer's Conference (we say *almost* because October '93 saw us in Orlando; 15 months later, January '95 found us in San Diego). The September '01 conference was the 12th FoxPro DevCon. Other regional conferences have been very successful the last few years, particularly the Great Lakes Great Database Workshop, hosted by none other than our esteemed publisher (see http://www.hentzenwerke.com for more information on this event—and we do mean event!). These more local events can save a great deal of expense in terms of travel, lodging and admission costs, with a somewhat more limited schedule of events and a smaller speaker list.

ACM, the Association for Computer Machinery (yeah, we're not machinery either, but we're members), is the granddaddy of professional associations for computer folks. With both local chapters and a couple of dozen special interest groups (known as "SIGs"), it has something for everyone who's serious about computers. You can contact them at (800) 342-6626 or acmhelp@acm.org in the U.S. and Canada, 32-2-774-9602 or acm_europe@acm.org in Europe. ACM also has a Web page at http://www.acm.org.

Third-party Products

The FoxPro world has a long history of free and inexpensive tools. Where we once might have included many such items with the book, today it makes much more sense for us to give a list of what's out there and let you download only those items that interest you.

The tools themselves can be divided into a couple of categories: utilities and frameworks. Generally, the utilities take one task and do it very well. (Consider WinZip, for an example from outside the VFP world.)

Frameworks are larger and, for the most part, more expensive products designed to provide all the basics any application could need, leaving you to fill in only the part that makes your application unique. We won't list all the VFP frameworks here, since that's a moving target. The best list we know of is available on the FoxPro Wiki in the documented titled "VFP Commercial Frameworks."

That leaves utilities—and boy, are there a ton of them. This is probably a good place to own up and point out that Doug is the author and co-owner of several widely used VFP utilities: Stonefield Database Toolkit, Stonefield Reports and Stonefield Query. (You think the company's named "Stonefield" or something?) Della works with Red Matrix Technologies on the DataClas/VFP product, and for TakeNote Technologies, which provides the FoxAudit program.

There are literally hundreds of third-party tools. The list that follows is just a small sampling of those we've worked with. See the section "Online Resources" for many places to find the myriad other VFP tools that are available now and for those that have been published since this book went to print.

We've organized the list into loose categories. If no Web site is listed, you should be able to download the tool from the libraries of either the Universal Thread or the CompuServe MSDevApps forum.

Data Management

Stonefield Database Toolkit is a must-have tool that simplifies many of the tasks involved with maintaining databases. The facility for updating databases when their structure changes without losing data is worth the price of the product. http://www.stonefield.com

eView, from Erik Moore, is a tool for maintaining views without using the View Designer. It handles all the properties of the view and its fields, as well as allowing you to edit the actual query on which the view is based.

ViewEdit, from Steve Sawyer, is another tool for view maintenance. This one lets you avoid the View Designer entirely, since you can create new views as well as modify old ones. http://www.stephensawyer.com

FoxAudit, from Jim Duffy, provides complete audit trail support to Visual FoxPro DBC-based applications. It adds complete, automatic, client/server-like, audit trail support to the Visual FoxPro database container. http://www.takenote.com

Client-Server

DataClas/VFP, from Red Matrix Technologies, is a series of Visual FoxPro classes for accessing and maintaining SQL Server data. It makes developing VFP/SQL Server solutions fast and easy. http://www.redmatrix.com

Querying and Reporting

GenRepoX, by Markus Egger, extends the capabilities of the Report Designer by putting a wrapper around it. It lets you do such things as creating multiple detail bands, sorting fields at run time, and much more. http://www.eps-software.com

FoxFire!, from MicroMega Systems, is a report writer (written in VFP) to replace the built-in Report Designer. It's intended for use both by developers and end-users. http://www.micromegasystems.com

FRX2Word, converts VFP reports to Word documents. Originally written by John Koziol, it's now maintained by Fabio Vieira, of Storm Software in Brazil (fabio.storm@uol.com.br).

Web Development

Rick Strahl offers a wide variety of tools, some free and others for sale, that simplify Web development with VFP. His premier product, Web Connection, is a Web development framework. Other tools include wwIPStuff, an interface for working with various Internet protocols, and wwXML, a class for working with XML. http://www.west-wind.com

Active FoxPro Pages, from ProLib Technologies, offers another approach to Web development with VFP. http://www.active-foxpro-pages.com (for information and European distribution), http://www.afpweb.com (for U.S. distribution).

Extending VFP

Struct, from Christof Lange, makes it easier to use API functions that expect structures as parameters. Struct puts an object face on structures and lets you worry only about the data involved.

Other Utilities

HTML Help Builder, also written by Rick Strahl, is the fastest and simplest way to create CHM files. We didn't use it to create HackFox.CHM because we started with Word documents, but it's an indispensable part of our toolboxes for any other help file creation. http://www.west-wind.com

Project Search, by Steven Dingle. This cool utility searches all the files in a project for a text string. It doesn't just search procedures and methods—it checks properties, too. http://www.stevendingle.com

What's in the Downloads

As we said in "How to Use this Book," the reaction to the HTML Help version of the *Hacker's Guide* was tremendous, so much so that we now view it as the primary version of this book. So, the most important thing you can download is the HTML Help version of this book.

That version differs from the printed version in a number of ways. Most importantly, we've chosen to publish the Reference section of the book only in the electronic version. In addition, this section in the HTML Help version contains a complete list of all the files available for download. (That gave us the opportunity to keep adding things until the last possible moment.)

The downloads also include a file called ViewHlp.CHM, which is the help file for HTML Help. (You'll also find some clues to working with HTML Help in "How to Use this Help File.")

Finally, the downloads include an assortment of sample code. For the complete list, see this chapter in the HTML Help version.

Index